THE COMPLETE ENCYCLOPEDIA OF
HOME FREEZING

GENERAL EDITOR
Jeni Wright

THE COMPLETE
ENCYCLOPEDIA OF
HOME
FREEZING

CONTENTS

First published in Great Britain in 1977 by
Octopus Books Limited

This edition published in 1986 by
Treasure Press
59 Grosvenor Street
London W1

© 1977 Octopus Books Limited

ISBN 1 85051 123 3

Printed in Czechoslovakia
50613

Introduction

The tremendous development of home freezing has come about remarkably quickly. The first British book on the subject was prepared in 1958, when the commercial frozen food industry was still in its infancy, and information was drawn from a number of highly technical books issued by the U.S. Department of Agriculture and various American universities. The book was aimed at farmers' wives, and contained only the briefest instructions for freezing raw materials, glossing rather quickly over the invaluable frozen cooked dishes so popular with today's housewife. Ten years later, it was still assumed that only the large country family would ever need a freezer, mainly to preserve farm and garden produce topped up with game and fish, and there was still little reliable information on the subject. In those days there was no notion of the average housewife using a freezer to make the best of seasonal produce, to avoid waste in both garden and kitchen, cope with useful leftovers, and ease the burden of preparing the never-ending stream of family meals.

However, a sudden upsurge of interest in freezing began from 1968 onwards, and every year since then there has been a greater demand for more detailed guidance and more sophisticated recipes, although the same questions are always asked by new freezer owners, and myths are perpetuated like old wives' tales. This encyclopedia has been prepared to coordinate all the expertise which is now available.

The freezer has brought about a revolution in the lives of many families. It has been found that with careful planning a family can save almost one third of its food budget with a home freezer, providing that they garden, bake and buy in bulk. Additionally, the advantages of one-stop shopping trips and preparing meals in advance have given working wives greater freedom (in Britain, about half the married women are now working outside the home), and have encouraged the more creative use of leisure, with more time available for sport or craftwork, adult education or family outings.

Above all, the freezer has given us a new appreciation of food, with increasing pleasure in its preparation. There are those who scoff that they don't want to eat asparagus in December or raspberries in January, but most of us are grateful rather than scornful. We still enjoy fresh seasonal produce when it is cheap and of high quality, but we are also able to preserve these delicious foods with little trouble, and enjoy perhaps a raspberry mousse at Christmas, or freshly made asparagus soup in March, and what can be wrong with that? The use of the freezer has also stimulated an interest in gardening. This has been recognized by the seed merchants who now advise on the best type of seeds to sow if the produce is to be frozen. There is an increasing pride in producing top-class fruit and vegetables at a fraction of shop prices.

The stimulation of interest in good food has extended to shopping trips, with the men of the family often joining bulk-buying shopping trips and taking a part in the choosing of a carcass. The more active ones are proud to bring home their catch from sea and river, or the rewards of a day's shooting, and the growth of interest in these two sports continues to increase. Add to this the growing appreciation of foreign foods, such as pasta and pizza, which freeze very well, and it is easy to see that freezing has considerably broadened the range of foods enjoyed by the average family.

All in all, it may be said that freezing is here to stay, and *The Complete Encyclopedia of Home Freezing* is a timely guide to the enormous range of foodstuffs which can be frozen. Prepared by a team of experts, this informative book has a comprehensive reference section which is arranged in alphabetical order. There are entries for meat, poultry, game and fish, fruit, herbs and vegetables, dairy produce and home baking, with each giving details for preparation, packaging and freezing. Since frozen food can be spoiled by subsequent ill-treatment, there are also details of storage times, with thawing and serving instructions. Many of the entries are for items which have not been covered in previous freezer publications.

We have included a section on the way a freezer works, together with information on freezer maintenance, defrosting, packaging, and general preparations for freezing. For speedy reference, the book also contains an at-a-glance section of charts giving instructions on the freezing of major foods.

One of the most interesting developments in home freezing is the advance preparation of cooked dishes. Many favourite family recipes can be prepared and frozen, but we have also developed a lot of special dishes, and the book features 150 freezer recipes for soups and appetizers, main courses (including lunch, supper and dinner party dishes), vegetables, desserts and puddings, cakes and other bakes, and special treats. Not only do these include full cooking instructions, but also full details for packaging, freezing and thawing.

It has been a considerable editorial task to assemble and present this vast mass of freezing information in an easy-to-read form, but we are confident that nearly twenty years after the first British book on home freezing, we have succeeded in producing a totally comprehensive freezing manual which will be invaluable to every freezer owner.

MARY NORWAK

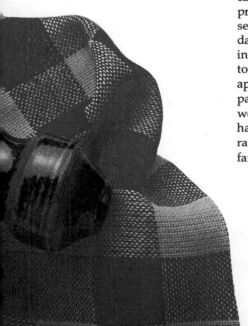

A-Z of Freezing Facts

A

Abalone

The foot of this shellfish is used in cooking, particularly in Chinese dishes. The dark portion should be removed and discarded, and the muscular flesh pounded heavily before it can be used.

TO FREEZE: cut the flesh into slices against the grain, approximately 6 mm/¼ inch thick.

Pound evenly, then pack in freezer bags, interleaving each slice with cling film or freezer tissue. Seal, label and freeze.

TO THAW: unwrap, dip in egg and breadcrumbs and grill (broil) or fry from frozen until golden brown and cooked through. Or poach and use in soup.

STORAGE TIME: 3 months.

Air

The exclusion of air is vital if packages of food are to remain in peak condition while in the freezer. The presence of air dries out food and leads to loss of both flavour and colour (see also **Discoloration, Freezer Burn, Oxidation** and **Rancidity**), so all food must be wrapped as tightly as possible.

There are several ways to remove air before sealing packages for freezing:

1 Squeeze out air by sliding both hands up from the bottom of soft packages to the top, so forcing air upwards and out.

2 Immerse soft packages in a bowl of water so air is forced out under pressure.

3 Draw a knife blade several times through the contents of rigid containers to release trapped air bubbles.

4 Insert a drinking straw* into a soft package, close the top around it, then hold firmly and suck out the air.

5 Use a hand vacuum freezer pump* for soft packages, widely available from freezer packaging suppliers.

*Not recommended for meringues or poultry.

Alcohol

Only freeze alcohol in small quantities because its freezing temperature is lower than that of water. Do not attempt to chill glass bottles of beer, wine, etc., by placing them in the freezer; if left for any length of time the liquid will expand and shatter the bottle. Alcohol can be incorporated in liquids in cooked dishes that are to be frozen.

Almond Paste (Marzipan)

Although almond paste freezes perfectly well, a large piece will take several hours to thaw, and in that amount of time it is possible to make fresh almond paste.

When used as a filling in recipes for Danish pastries, however, or for decorations on festive cakes and yule logs, almond paste and boiled marzipan will freeze successfully. It is well worth preparing such dishes ahead of time and freezing them until the occasion arises when they are needed in a hurry.

Christmas, Wedding, Easter Simnel cakes and others can be baked, coated in almond paste and frozen up to 3 months before they are required.

TO FREEZE: cover with aluminium foil, overwrap in a freezer bag, seal, label and freeze.

TO THAW: leave in wrappings overnight at room temperature, then unwrap and ice in the usual way.

STORAGE TIME: 3 months.

Alumin(i)um Foil

see page 232

Anchovy

Anchovies were once eaten fresh like herrings, but have always been preferred salted. It is best not to freeze salted anchovies, because the combination of fat and salt quickly causes rancidity. Dishes such as pizzas which incorporate anchovies as a garnish are best frozen without the garnish, which can be added just before serving.

Anchovy Butter

see **Butter, Flavoured**

Angelica *(Angelica archangelica)*

A robust herb which can grow to a height of between 2–3 metres/6–10 feet, with a spread of 1 metre/3 feet. Angelica is a native of central and northern Europe, but can be found growing in most countries, frequently on river banks. The plant bears pale to mid-green leaves with large round clusters of tiny green flowers, but it is the thick stems which are mainly used in cooking.

To freeze stems: pick the young, green stems before the flower heads start to open, while they are still too young to have developed 'strings'. Cut into chunks, blanch in boiling water for 1 minute, then drain. Cool rapidly in iced water, drain, then pat dry and pack in freezer bags. Seal, label and freeze.

TO THAW: leave in wrappings to thaw partially at room temperature, then add to salads and soups, as for **Celery.**

To freeze leaves: pack young leaves in bags as for stems.

TO THAW: crumble while still frozen, then sprinkle over salads and soups. Or add frozen leaves to rhubarb before poaching, chopped leaves to marmalade to give it a musky flavour, or make into 'angelica tea' with boiling water. Angelica leaves may also be dried and stems may be candied.

STORAGE TIME: 12 months.

Three methods of removing air from packages of food before freezing.
1 Squeezing out air by sliding hands up from the bottom to the top of a soft package.
2 Closing the top of a polythene bag around a drinking straw before sucking out air.
3 Withdrawing the air with a freezer pump.

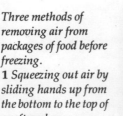

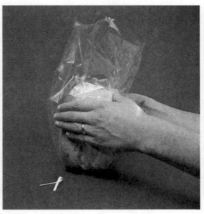
1

2

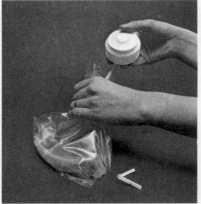
3

Anise/Aniseed (*Pimpinella anisum*)

Originating in Greece, the aniseed plant looks rather like small slender celery, and grows to a height of approximately 46 cm/18 inches with a spread of approximately 30 cm/12 inches. It is an annual herb, which has clusters of flat, loose yellow-white flowers in summer.

TO FREEZE: gather the seeds from the flowers when ripe, then pack dry in small rigid containers, waxed cartons or freezer bags. Cover or seal, label and freeze.

TO THAW: leave in containers or bags to thaw at room temperature, then dry for a few minutes on baking sheets in a cool oven. Use to give a delicate flavour to soups or marinades for fish. Anise can also be used as a flavouring for bread and cakes, and is used commercially in soft drinks and liqueurs.

STORAGE TIME: 9 months.

Anti-oxidant

The name for various additives which help to prevent discoloration or browning in certain fruits when exposed to air while preparing for freezing. Lemon juice is the most common anti-oxidant; see also **Ascorbic Acid** and **Citric Acid.**

Apple

see also **Crab Apple** and **Fruit** for information on packing

As apples are available throughout the year, the only real practical reason for freezing them is that your home-grown produce is unsuitable for storing on racks. Or you may find it more convenient to have a supply of prepared apples (slices, rings or purée) in the freezer ready for use when required.

To freeze dessert apples: peel, core and dice or slice the fruit into a bowl of water with plenty of lemon juice (to keep the apples from browning), then pack in medium syrup. Or dice or slice them directly into the syrup.

TO THAW: leave in unopened container for 1 hour at room temperature. Use in desserts and fresh fruit salads.

To freeze cooking (tart) apples: peel, core and cut into rings or slices 6 mm/¼ inch thick. Keep in water and lemon juice until all are prepared, then blanch in boiling water for 1 minute. Drain, cool under cold run-ning water, then drain, pat dry and pack in rigid containers or freezer bags. Cover or seal, label and freeze.

TO THAW: as for dessert apples above. Use in crumbles, pies, puddings, tarts, etc.

To freeze apple purée: peel, core and slice quickly to prevent browning, then simmer gently in very little water until soft, stirring to prevent sticking and scorching. Remove from the heat and leave to cool, then purée in an electric blender until smooth, if you like. Pack with or without sugar, as for cooking (tart) apples above.

TO THAW: as for dessert apples above, or use from frozen to make hot apple sauce. Serve hot or cold in sauces and with pork dishes, or in numerous desserts and puddings.

See also recipes for *Tarte Française, Blackberry and Apple Pie, Upside-down Toffee Apple Tart* and *Apple Cake.*

STORAGE TIME: 8 to 12 months (rings and slices); 8 months (purées).

Applemint
see **Mint**

Apricot

prepare, freeze and thaw as for **Peach**

Different ways of freezing and using apples can be seen above. From left to right: Dessert apple slices in a medium syrup (see page 53), Tarte Française (see page 194), Apple Cake (see page 214) decorated with cream for serving, thawed apple slices in fruit salad, apple purée and blanched apple rings.

Abalone – Apricot

11

Artichoke

see **Globe Artichoke** and **Jerusalem Artichoke**

Ascorbic Acid

A synthetic form of Vitamin C and an anti-oxidant, ascorbic acid helps to prevent browning in fruits such as apples, apricots, peaches and pears that have a low Vitamin C content. It is usually added to a cold sugar syrup pack for prepared fruit immediately before freezing. Ascorbic acid is available either in powder or tablet form from chemists (pharmacies), and the quantity to use per 600 ml/1 pint/2½ cup syrup pack is 750 mg/¼ teaspoon dissolved in a little cold water.

Below: ascorbic acid is being added to cold sugar syrup.

The top centre photograph shows blanched slices of aubergine being packed into a rigid container in layers interleaved with aluminium foil.

Asparagus

Asparagus must be absolutely fresh if it is to be frozen successfully, and only home-grown asparagus is really worth freezing.

Stalks can be blanched or green, according to taste. For blanched ones, cut off the tips approximately 7.5 cm/3 inches below the surface of the ground when the tips have grown 2.5 cm/1 inch or so above it. For green ones, cut off just below the surface when they are the height you want, and the tips are still tightly closed. Wash and grade the stems according to thickness. Cut or break off the tough end of the stems and use in soups and stocks. Scrape scales from lower part of thick stems if necessary (these can be both unpleasant and difficult to eat).

TO FREEZE: blanch in boiling water — 2 minutes for small thin stems, 3 minutes for medium stems, 4 minutes

for thick stems. Very thin 'sprew' stems freeze particularly well as they contain little water — break into short lengths and blanch for 1 minute. Cool rapidly in iced water, then drain and pat dry. Pack in rigid containers or freezer bags. Cover or seal, label and freeze. There is no need to tie the stems.

TO THAW: remove sprew from containers or bags and leave to thaw in a strainer or on a tea (dish) towel either at room temperature or in the refrigerator, according to time available. Thicker stems are best if cooked almost from frozen: unwrap, leave to thaw until the stems can be separated, then plunge into boiling salted water, bring back to the boil and simmer for 2 to 4 minutes. Drain, toss in melted butter and serve hot with scrambled eggs, dressed crab or as an hors d'oeuvre.

STORAGE TIME: 9 months.

Asparagus Pea*

It is seldom possible to buy this unusual vegetable, but it can be successfully home-grown. Harvest when strangely winged pods are no more than 2.5 cm/1 inch long.

TO FREEZE: wash and pat dry, steam for 1 minute, then cool rapidly in iced water. Drain, pat dry and pack in freezer bags. Seal, label and freeze.

TO THAW: unwrap and place frozen in steamer. Steam for 1 minute (they should be crisp, not soggy). Serve hot with melted butter.

STORAGE TIME: 6 months.

*Not available in Australia.

Aspic

Do not freeze dishes that have been coated in aspic jelly, as this will become cloudy and granular and thus spoil the finished dish. If a recipe — a whole salmon, for example — calls for a coating of aspic, make up to the point of decorating with aspic, freeze until required, then brush with aspic jelly after thawing.

Aubergine (Eggplant/Breadfruit)

Harvest the fruit as soon as they are fully coloured: if left too long on the plant they become dry and hard. When buying, they should always have a 'live', resilient feel when gently pressed.

TO FREEZE: leave unpeeled if young. Wash and cut into rounds approximately 2 cm/¾ inch thick. Blanch in boiling water for 4 minutes, cool rapidly in iced water, then drain and pat dry. Pack in rigid containers, interleaving each layer with aluminium foil, cling film or freezer

tissue. Or pack in freezer bags, leaving 1.25 cm/½ inch headspace.

TO THAW: leave in containers or bags at room temperature or in the refrigerator, according to time available. Pat dry when thawed, and fry in hot oil until brown on both sides. Serve immediately or use in composite dishes.

See also recipes for *Moussaka, Ratatouille, Stuffed Aubergines, Aubergine Galette* and *Mixed Vegetable Medley.*

STORAGE TIME: 12 months.

Avocado

Avocados can be frozen, but they lose their original flavour and texture and are therefore best used in composite dishes once thawed. Choose ripe, but not over-ripe fruit.

TO FREEZE: remove skin, dice or pulp the flesh, allowing 1 × 15 ml spoon/1 tablespoon lemon juice for each avocado to prevent discoloration. Pack immediately into rigid containers, cover, label and freeze. Avocados can also be frozen as part of a dish, with cream cheese, or with grated horseradish and cream, for example.

TO THAW: leave in unopened containers for approximately 2 hours at room temperature. Use immediately after thawing or the avocado will discolour. See also recipe for *Chilled Avocado Soup.*

STORAGE TIME: 2 months.

B

Baba

Babas and savarins, yeast mixtures enriched with eggs, sugar and butter, and sometimes dried fruit, freeze well. Babas are made in individual ring tins or dariole moulds and usually include dried fruit; savarins are made in a large ring mould without dried fruit. Both babas and savarins are soaked in syrup, and sometimes spirit or liqueur, before serving with fresh fruit and cream for dessert. See recipe for *Savarin*.

To freeze babas or savarins: follow one of these three methods:

1   Bake and prick with a fine skewer while hot, then pour over prepared syrup/spirit/liqueur. Allow to soak, then leave to cool. Pack in rigid containers, cover, label and freeze.

TO THAW: unwrap and leave for approximately 3 hours at room temperature. More syrup, etc., may be poured over if wished.

2   Bake and leave to cool. Wrap in aluminium foil, then overwrap in a freezer bag, seal, label and freeze.

TO THAW: unwrap and leave for approximately 2 hours at room temperature, then reheat in a moderate oven (180°C/350°F or Gas Mark 4) for 10 minutes. Prick with a fine skewer and pour over prepared warm syrup/spirit/liqueur.

3   Freeze as for (2) above.

TO THAW: leave wrapped in aluminium foil and bake from frozen in a fairly hot oven (200°C/400°F or Gas Mark 6) for 15 to 20 minutes or until heated through (the length of time will depend on size). Remove from the oven, unwrap and prick with a fine skewer. Pour over warmed syrup/spirit/liqueur.

STORAGE TIME: 3 months.

Baby Food

The freezer makes an ideal storage place for baby foods that are frozen in small quantities. Freezing does not cause loss of nutritive value, and by this method of preservation you can be sure that the food will be as fresh as when it was put in the freezer. Always be sure to observe a high standard of hygiene when preparing and packing any baby food for the freezer. Small rigid containers, yogurt, cream or cottage cheese containers, can be used for freezing individual meals for one baby or toddler, larger containers, foil trays or boil-in-bags can be used when there is more than one child to feed. Sterilize all containers before using. With the use of a freezer it is possible to cook a substantial quantity of a dish — a mixture of meat and vegetables, fish, or fruit purée, for example, then pack into meal-sized portions and freeze individually. This will avoid wastage and will allow the child, or children, to have a more varied diet.

When cooking everyday meals for the adults in the family, reserve one or two portions for the child(ren). Cool quickly and freeze for a later date. For babies not yet on solids, food may be puréed in an electric blender or worked through a Mouli-légumes (foodmill) or sieve before packing and freezing. Most of these dishes can then be cooked straight from frozen by thoroughly reheating in a saucepan (preferably non-stick). This is a great time-saver, and is more economical than commercially prepared baby foods.

Bacon & Cured Pork

It is possible to store both bacon rashers (strips), bacon joints and large cuts of cured pork in the freezer but for *strictly limited* periods only. Unsmoked bacon (pork belly) does not store as well as smoked bacon. Freeze only really fresh bacon which has been mildly cured, such as Danish bacon or sweet-cure bacon; very salt or heavily cured bacon does not freeze well. If fresh, bacon has a pleasant smell, lean, pink meat and firm, white fat. When buying specially for the freezer, check the freshness factor with the retailer or consult the date mark and, if you have any doubts, or if you are freezing leftover rashers (strips) when going away, for example. reduce the recommended storage times given below.

Vacuum-packed bacon is particularly suitable for freezing as the complete exclusion of air and the tight, plastic wrapping helps to extend the storage life. Check that the wrapping is taut and not damaged in any way. If the wrapping is at all loose, simply overwrap in a freezer bag or aluminium foil.

To freeze fresh bacon joints (large cuts of cured pork): set the 'fast freeze' switch according to the instructions in your freezer book, wrap each joint (cut) individually in aluminium foil, shaping and pressing the foil tightly around the joint (cut), excluding as much air as possible. Overwrap in a freezer bag, press out the air again, seal, label and freeze.

To freeze bacon rashers (strips), chops or steaks (ham): follow the packing instructions for bacon joints (cuts) above, dividing rashers (strips) into small, convenient amounts which can be quickly thawed and then eaten promptly. Interleave chops or steaks with cling film before packaging, to facilitate separation for cooking.

TO THAW: slow thawing in a cool place is recommended. The refrigerator is ideal, because the low temperature will continue to preserve the maximum freshness of the bacon while thawing is in progress. The wrapping should be opened immediately on removal from the freezer.

Baby foods such as fruit purées and meat sauce can be prepared in advance and frozen in small quantities.

Small joints (cuts) — thaw 24 hours in the refrigerator or for 8 to 12 hours at room temperature.

Rashers (strips) — thaw small, thin packs for approximately 6 hours in the refrigerator or 2 to 3 hours at room temperature.

TO COOK: cook as soon as possible after thawing. Mild bacon joints (mild cures) usually need no preliminary soaking but, if necessary, soak in cold water in the usual way, then drain and cook as for fresh bacon. Cook thawed bacon rashers (strips), chops and steaks as for fresh. If you think the bacon may be rather salty, simply dip in hot water and pat dry with kitchen paper towels before cooking.

STORAGE TIME: for Bacon and Cured Pork:

Smoked joints (cuts) — up to 8 weeks.

Unsmoked joints (cuts) — up to 5 weeks.

Vacuum-packed joints (cuts), smoked or unsmoked — up to 20 weeks.

Smoked rashers (strips), chops and steaks — up to 8 weeks.

Unsmoked rashers (strips), chops and steaks — 2 to 3 weeks.

Vacuum-packed rashers (strips) and steaks, smoked or unsmoked — up to 20 weeks.

Bag(s)

see page 234

Balm, Lemon *(Melissa officinalis)*

There are several types of balm, but only the common lemon balm is of culinary use. A native of southern Europe, it will grow anywhere throughout the world in a temperate climate, with easy and little attention. The plant grows to a height of 60–120 cm/2–4 feet with a spread of 30–46 cm/12–18 inches in a season, dying down in winter and shooting to life again in spring. The flavour of balm is not as strong as its scent, and it is a herb which is well worth freezing as it cannot be dried successfully.

TO FREEZE: pick the leaves when they are young and tender. Chop them finely, freeze in ice cube trays until solid, then pack cubes in freezer bags, seal, label and return to freezer. Or pick whole sprigs of young growth, blanch for 1 minute in boiling water and drain. Leave to cool, pat dry, then pack in small quantities in freezer bags, seal, label and freeze. Balm sprigs can also be packed straight into bags without blanching, but they will not keep their flavour for so long.

TO THAW: use concentrated cubes straight from the freezer in hot dishes and sauces. Crumble leaves while still frozen, then add to poached fruit, salads and stuffings, or add to root vegetables and toss with melted butter just before serving. The flavour of balm goes well with chicken, fish and veal, and frozen sprigs may be substituted for rosemary when roasting joints of lamb. Torn frozen leaves can be added to China tea to give it a lemon flavour.

STORAGE TIME: 2 months (un-blanched); 6 months (blanched).

Bamboo Shoot

In the Far East, the white interior of young bamboo plants is cut into strips, boiled, packed in water or brine, and exported in jars and cans. Any partially used jars or cans can be stored in the refrigerator with weekly changes of water to keep the bamboo shoots fresh, so there is no need to freeze them in their natural state. In Oriental cooking, however, they can be prepared in a dish and frozen with other ingredients.

Banana (small Canary type)

Bananas lose their texture if frozen whole with their peel.

TO FREEZE: peel and mash with sugar and lemon juice to taste. Pack immediately into small rigid containers, cover, label and freeze. Or peel and slice in half lengthways, coat with chocolate sauce and pack in shallow rigid or aluminium foil containers. Cover, label and freeze.

TO THAW: leave in unopened containers for approximately 5 hours in the refrigerator. Use immediately after thawing or the banana will discolour.

STORAGE TIME: 6 months.

Bap

see **Bread**

Barracouta

This fish from Australia and New Zealand is known as snoek in South Africa.

TO FREEZE: clean the fish and cut into thick steaks or fillets. Pack in freezer bags, interleaving each piece of fish with cling film. Seal, label and freeze.

TO THAW: unwrap and cook thin steaks and fillets from frozen; thaw unwrapped thick steaks for 2 hours in the refrigerator. Cook as for cod or haddock.

STORAGE TIME: 3 months.

Barracuda

This fish from America is a pike-like sea fish.

TO FREEZE: clean, cut into steaks or fillets, then pack in freezer bags, interleaving each piece of fish with cling film. Seal, label and freeze.

TO THAW: unwrap and cook from frozen, using recipes for cod or haddock.

STORAGE TIME: 3 months.

Bars

see **Biscuit**

Basil, Sweet *(Ocimum basilicum. Labiatae)*

A sweetly aromatic herb, basil is a native of southeast Asia, but has been cultivated and grown wild for many centuries in Mediterranean countries. It is one of the most important herbs in cooking, particularly in French, Italian and Greek dishes, and has a particular affinity for tomato-based sauces. The plant reaches a height of approximately 60–90 cm/2–3 feet with a spread of 30 cm/12 inches and has glossy pale green leaves. Do not let it develop small white or purple flowers in summer or these will turn to seed pods and discourage new leaf growth. As the young plants develop in early summer, nip out the centres to encourage them to make bushy growth.

TO FREEZE: pick young leaves early in the morning as soon as they are dry of dew. Chop or cut finely with scissors, freeze in ice cube trays until solid, then pack in freezer bags, seal, label and return to freezer. Or pick fresh leaves or whole sprigs of basil, wash if necessary, pat dry and pack immediately in freezer bags, seal, label and freeze.

TO THAW: leave concentrated cubes to thaw at room temperature, then use as for freshly chopped basil, or add while still frozen to casseroles, sauces, soups, etc., just before serving. Use frozen leaves or sprigs straight from the freezer or they will lose their colour and aroma.

STORAGE TIME: 6 months (cubes); 3 months (whole sprigs).

Bass

A variety of sea fish, bass range from the 9 kg/20 lb American black bass to the more manageable European sea bass or loup de mer.

TO FREEZE: clean the fish, fillet large ones and cut smaller ones into steaks or leave whole. Pack in freezer bags, interleaving each fillet, steak or fish with cling film. Seal, label and freeze.

TO THAW: unwrap and thaw large pieces of fish for 2 hours in the refrigerator. Cook smaller fish from frozen. Salmon recipes are most suitable for cooking bass.

STORAGE TIME: 3 months.

Batch Cooking

When there is time to spare, at weekends, in the evenings or when the children are at school, it is a good idea to cook 'batches' of food for the freezer. This means cooking a large quantity of one particular dish, dividing it into portions to suit your future needs, and freezing it until required. Special batching bags made of different coloured polythene (polyethylene) are now available in the U.K. and U.S. to help with this method of freezing.

Batch cooking saves time: it is far quicker to cook a large quantity of Bolognese sauce, for example, at one time, than to cook small quantities when needed for a particular dish. Batch cooking is economical in the use of fuel because oven and burner space can be used to the full; it is also economical to increase quantities, as fewer ingredients are used: for example, a casserole for four people would need at least 1 onion and 600 ml/1 pint/2½ cups stock. If the recipe is tripled to make three meals for four people it can be made perfectly well with 2 onions and 1½ litres/2½ pints/6 cups stock.

The other great benefit of batch cooking is taking advantage of special offers and bulk buys at supermarkets and butchers. When fruit and vegetables are plentiful in the garden and shops or markets, they can be bought and made into finished dishes for the freezer for use in the future when such items are either expensive or unavailable.

Another good idea for the freezer owner is to 'batch cook' when cooking for family meals or dinner parties. Make up more than the quantity you need (in fact as much as you have time to make) and freeze the quantity you do not use immediately. This builds up a supply of cooked dishes in the freezer which will come in useful at another time. In this way, the freezer can be efficiently organized, with a good proportion of cooked dishes and basic sauces, stocks, etc., to uncooked foodstuffs such as meat, fish, fruit, poultry and vegetables.

Good dishes for batch cooking are biscuits (cookies), bread, cakes, casseroles, flans, lasagne and other pasta dishes, pastries, pâtés, pies, pizzas, purées, quiches, sauces, soups, stews and stock.

Bag(s) – Batch Cooking

A Victoria Sandwich mixture (see page 214) is an ideal candidate for batch cooking. All the cakes and gâteaux below were made from this basic mixture. The cakes can be frozen decorated with butter-cream icing, but jam and fruit fillings are best added before serving.

1

2

Batter
1 *Folding whisked egg white into the fritter batter.*
2 *Dipping an onion ring into the batter.*
3 *Deep frying batter-coated onion rings.*
4 *Draining deep-fried onion rings on kitchen paper towels.*
5 *Placing cold drained onion rings on an interleaving sheet of aluminium foil before packing in layers in a rigid freezer container.*

3

4

Batching Bag(s)
see **Colour Coding**

Batter

Due to the high milk content which separates during freezing, uncooked batters for coating fried foods, for making crêpes and pancakes and for coating fritters, do not freeze success-fully. See also **Fritters** and **Pancakes.** However, fish, cubed meat, onion rings and shellfish that are coated in batter can be frozen *after* deep frying.

TO FREEZE: drain thoroughly on kitchen paper towels, then leave until cold and pack in freezer bags, separat-ing each piece of food with aluminium foil, cling film or freezer tissue. Seal, label and freeze.

TO THAW: leave in wrappings over-night in the refrigerator, then unwrap and reheat on baking sheets in a very hot oven until piping hot.

There are many varieties of com-mercially frozen foods in batter now available — fish is perhaps the most common example — and the quality is usually high. It is a good idea to freeze a selection of items coated in batter, either homemade or commer-cially frozen, as these dishes are time-consuming to make, yet can take as little as 15 minutes to heat through from frozen.

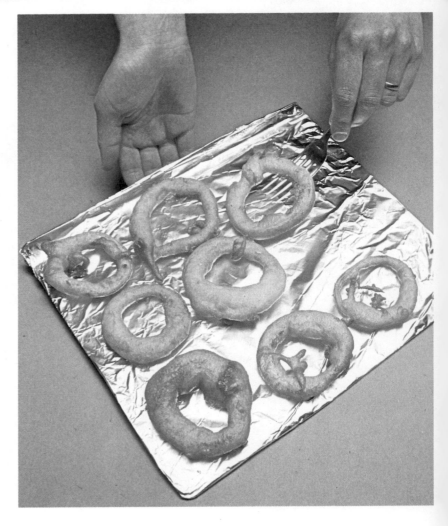

Bay Leaf (*Laurus nobilis*)

Bay leaves keep perfectly well if stored in airtight jars; therefore, there is no need to freeze them. For convenience, however, they can be frozen as part of a **Bouquet Garni.**

Bean

Broad Bean (Fresh Fava) Tips

Break off approximately 7.5 cm/3 inches of the growing tips when the bottom truss flowers begin to turn into embryo pods.

TO FREEZE: wash, then blanch in boiling water for 2 minutes. Cool rapidly in iced water, then squeeze out excess water with hands. Pack in small quantities in rigid containers or freezer bags, cover or seal, label and freeze.

TO THAW: unwrap and put frozen tips in boiling salted water. Bring back to the boil, cover and simmer for 3 to 5 minutes. Drain and serve hot tossed in melted butter or with a savoury white sauce.

Whole Baby Broad Bean (Fava) Pods

Pick before beans are properly formed and before pods have any strings. Blanch, cool, pat dry, freeze and use as for *Tips* above.

Shelled Broad Beans (Fava)

Pick young pods before beans become starchy. Pod, then blanch immediately, cool and pat dry. Freeze and thaw as for *Tips* above.

French (Green) Beans

Pick when very young and stringless.

TO FREEZE: top and tail, wash, then blanch whole in boiling water for 1 to 2 minutes, depending on size. Drain, cool rapidly in iced water, drain and pat dry. Pack in freezer bags, seal, label and freeze.

TO THAW: as for *Broad Bean Tips* above, allowing 5 to 7 minutes simmering time. Drain, toss in melted butter and seasonings and serve hot. See also recipe for *Bean Salad*.

Runner (Snap) Beans

Use small ones.

TO FREEZE: top and tail, string if necessary, then wash. Slice, or for better flavour, cut into 2.5 cm/1 inch pieces. Blanch, freeze and thaw as for *French Beans* above. See also recipe for *Bean Salad*.

Waxed Beans

Pick when young and tender, stringless and bright in colour.

TO FREEZE: top and tail, wash thoroughly, leave whole or cut into 2.5 cm/1 inch pieces. Blanch whole beans in boiling water for 3 minutes,

pieces for 2 minutes. Drain, cool, pack and thaw as for *French Beans* above.

STORAGE TIME: 12 months (for all beans).

Bean Sprout

Bean sprouts lose their crispness if frozen and therefore cannot be used in salads but are perfectly satisfactory in cooked dishes.

TO FREEZE: blanch in boiling water for 1 minute, drain and cool rapidly in iced water. Drain, pat dry and pack in

freezer bags. Seal, label and freeze.

TO THAW: leave in bags in the refrigerator or unwrap and thaw rapidly at room temperature, according to time available. Use in savoury rice dishes, etc.

STORAGE TIME: 2 months.

Bear

see **Game**

Beaver

see **Game**

Various fresh and frozen beans, with two serving suggestions in the foreground — French (green) beans tossed in melted butter and broad beans (favas) in white sauce.

Batching Bag(s) – Beaver

Beef

see also recipe section

Choosing

The quality of beef varies a great deal, and the average consumer finds it difficult, if not impossible, to assess. Even more than when buying other kinds of meat you are dependent upon the judgment and experience of the butcher. If you plan to bulk-buy beef from an unknown supplier it is advisable to test the quality of the meat and try to assess the standards of hygiene by buying several small quantities first. If you explain your family's likes and needs, a good butcher will advise you what to buy and help you to avoid making expensive mistakes.

Ageing

To develop its maximum flavour and tenderness, beef needs to be hung in the butcher's cold room before it is frozen. This process is known as 'ageing', and the average commercial time allowed is 7 to 10 days (2 to 3 days in Australia); however, good beef will taste better if it is hung for 2 to 3 weeks. You may have to pay a little more for it, but if you are bulk-buying this is a point worth discussing with the butcher.

Buying

Ready-frozen beef is available in a wide variety of cuts and pack sizes. These include various kinds of large joints (cuts), steaks, stewing or braising meat, or minced (ground) meat. Although beef is 'in season' all year round, late summer is traditionally a good time to buy — after the cattle have been grazing the summer grass. If the pasture has been lush, the animals should have well-rounded buttocks and enough fat to ensure a good flavour; scrawny, over-lean carcasses do not produce top-quality beef. On the other hand, overfat carcasses are very wasteful and the meat does not keep so well when frozen. Forequarter prices tend to drop in mid-summer when warm weather switches consumer demand away from casseroles and stews.

Bulk-buying

see also **Meat, Fresh**

Because the bones are large and heavy, and take up so much space, beef for the freezer is usually boned completely. If you particularly want joints (cuts) left 'on the bone' remember to say so when you place the order. Up to 30 per cent of the total weight you pay for is wastage in the form of bone and excess fat;

therefore, to reap the full benefit of bulk-buying you need to take and use the bones and fat. For information on dealing with *Beef Bones* and *Beef Fat* see opposite. For more information about the average size of traditional bulk-buys, and the percentage of roasting or stewing meat they contain, see **Meat, Fresh,** *Traditional Bulk-buys* chart.

Freezer Space Needed

Boneless beef packs down closely, so allow 56 litres/2 cu ft for every 9 kg/20 lb of meat. Allow twice as much space for meat on the bone, or bones on their own.

PACKING AND FREEZING: see **Meat, Fresh**

THAWING AND COOKING: see **Meat, Fresh**

STORAGE TIME: joints (large cuts) and medium cuts — up to 8 months. Minced (ground) meat and offal (variety meat/fancy meat) — up to 3 months.

Buying a Forequarter of Beef

As its name suggests, this is a quarter taken from the front, and more muscular, part of the animal. The meat, therefore, consists mostly of braising, stewing and mincing (grinding) cuts. It is a good buy for families who enjoy slow-cooking dishes such as cas-

Cuts From a Forequarter of Beef

Cut	Ways of butchering	Type of meat and cooking

Foreribs	(a) Joints (large cuts)
	   1. On the bone
	   2. Boned and rolled
	(b) Rib steaks
		Cut next to sirloin. Top-quality roasting or grilling (broiling) meat

Back Ribs	Joints (large cuts)	Medium-quality meat for braising, pot roasting, or slow roasting
Top Ribs or Flat Ribs	(a) Joints (large cuts) (b) Minced (ground) meat	Medium-quality meat. Needs moist, slow cooking such as braising or pot roasting
Chuck and Blade (U.S. Rib)	(a) Cubed for casseroles (b) Thick slices for braising (c) Small joints (cuts) for braising	Lean, medium-quality meat, excellent for braising, casseroles or pies
Neck and Clod (U.S. Chuck)	(a) Minced (ground) meat (b) Cubed	Lean, coarse meat with a good flavour for casseroles, sauces and stews
Shin/Hough (U.S. Fore Shank)	(a) Minced (ground) meat for soups (b) Small cubes for slow simmering	Very lean, but muscular meat. Essential to cook very slowly for 4 to 5 hours; excellent flavour for meat soups or stews
Brisket and Flank	Joints (cuts) from boned, defatted and rolled meat	Coarse meat, layered with fat. Excellent flavour if braised very slowly. Good salted (cured) but *do not freeze if salted*

Cuts From a Forequarter of Beef (Aust. & U.K.)*

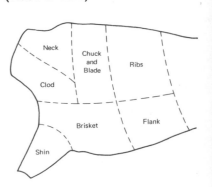

Cuts From a Forequarter of Beef (U.S.)*

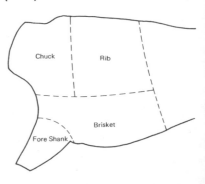

*These are popular ways of cutting a forequarter of beef — there are other variations.

seroles, *daubes* and pies, and ideal for those who like to batch-bake an oven-ful of casseroles for freezing.

If a whole forequarter is too large a purchase for you, consider either sharing it with one or two other families — see **Meat, Fresh**, *Sharing a Bulk-buy* or consider buying, where available, a 'pony', or the rather larger 'crop'. Consult the chart on *Traditional Bulk-buys*, under **Meat, Fresh** for further information on weight and contents of these cuts.

Buying a Hindquarter of Beef

This is the expensive, rear end of the animal, the part that provides the most large joints (cuts) and steaks. It also includes approximately 20 per cent of braising and stewing meat. For average weights and details of contents, consult the chart on *Traditional Bulk-buys*, under **Meat, Fresh**.

If a whole hindquarter is too large a purchase for you, consider either sharing it with one or two other families — see **Meat, Fresh**, *Sharing a Bulk-buy* or consider buying a 'topbit and rump' (round), or the smaller 'sirloin and rump' (loin end) of which 95 per cent is grilling (broiling) and roasting meat. Many butchers will also supply the 'rump' alone.

Cuts From a Hindquarter of Beef (Aust. & U.K.)*

Cuts From a Hindquarter of Beef (U.S.)*

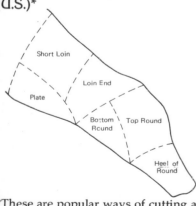

*These are popular ways of cutting a hindquarter of beef — there are other variations.

Beef Bones

Bones turn bad very quickly, so plan to deal with them promptly after delivery, keeping them in the refrigerator meanwhile. Use them for making stock, then freeze the stock, or freeze the bones for converting into stock at a later date. In either case, ask the butcher to saw the bones into small pieces that will fit your sauce-pans and release the marrow.

TO FREEZE: put the bones in a very thick, large freezer bag, seal, label and freeze. Remove bones as required and reseal the bag.

Bone stock: Put the bones, frozen or thawed, into a deep saucepan and add cold water to cover. Bring to the boil slowly, skimming off the scum that rises to the surface. For each 600 ml/1 pint/2½ cups water, add 1 onion, peeled and quartered, 1 carrot, peeled and quartered, 1 bouquet garni and 2 peppercorns. Cover the pan and simmer very slowly for at least 2 hours, skimming thoroughly from time to time. Or pressure cook for 30 minutes. Strain the stock and remove the fat when cold. Use the stock for gravies, sauces and soups. See also **Stock**.

Beef Fat

There are two main types of fat: suet which is very hard and can be chopped or grated (from hindquarters only), and the softer fat from both hind and forequarters which is usually rendered down for dripping.

Suet: the best suet comes from around the kidneys; it should be hard and creamy-white. To use, remove the paper-thin tissues and either chop or finely grate the suet, keeping it well dredged with flour to prevent the pieces from sticking together. Use fresh for mincemeat, suet pastry and steamed puddings, or freeze until required.

Cuts From a Hindquarter of Beef

Cut	Ways of butchering	Type of meat and cooking
Sirloin (including Wing Rib) (U.S. Short Loin)	(a) Roasting joints (cuts) (b) Individual T-bone steaks (c) Porterhouse steaks	Top-quality beef for frying, grilling (broiling) or roasting
Fillet/Undercut	(a) Whole for roasting (b) Individual fillet steaks	Very tender strip of meat from beneath the sirloin. Prime cut for frying, grilling (broiling) or roasting
Rump/Pope's Eye (U.S. Loin End)	(a) Roasting joints (cuts) (b) Slices and steaks	Top-quality meat for frying, grilling (broiling) or roasting
Topside/Buttock/ Round Steak (U.S. Round)	Joints (large cuts) including U.S. standing rump and top round	This inside area of the upper part of the leg is very lean and rather muscular. From top-quality animal, beef can be slow roasted, otherwise braise or pot roast
Silverside/ Buttock/ Round Steak	Joints (large cuts)	This outside area of the thigh and buttock is very lean, but coarse in texture. Needs slow, moist and gentle cooking to tenderize. Traditional cut for boiling and salting (curing), but *do not freeze if salted*
Top Rump/ Thick Flank/ Bed of Beef/ First Cutting (Aust. Round, U.S. Bottom Round)	(a) Joints (large cuts), including U.S. sirloin tip roast (b) Slices for braising, including U.S. bottom round steak	This inside area of the thigh is lean, medium-quality beef with a good flavour. From top-quality animal, good for slow roasting, otherwise better to braise or pot roast
Leg/Hough (U.S. Heel of Round)	Cubed for stewing	Lean coarse-grained meat. Good flavour if casseroled slowly
Hindquarter Flank	(a) Cubed for stewing (b) Minced (ground) meat (c) Made into beefburgers	Coarse-grained meat, needing slow, moist cooking. Best used for casseroles and savoury minced (ground) meat dishes
Goose Skirt	Cubed	Small, thin piece of medium-quality lean meat from below the flank. Good flavour for casseroles and pies

TO FREEZE: put whole, chopped or grated pieces into freezer bags or rigid containers. Seal or cover, label and freeze.

STORAGE TIME: 2 to 3 months.

Fat: ask the butcher to cut the fat into small pieces. Use immediately or freeze it for use at a later date.

TO FREEZE: pack in usable quantities in freezer bags, seal, label and freeze.

STORAGE TIME: 2 to 3 months.

To make dripping: fill a roasting tin (pan) with small pieces of fresh or frozen fat and leave, uncovered, in a *very slow* oven. Leave for several hours or until all the fat has run out and only crisp scraps remain. This process does not have to be continuous: the tin (pan) can be returned to the oven over a period of 2 or 3 days in a cold climate. Strain off the dripping as it accumulates, pouring it through a muslin (cheesecloth)-lined metal strainer to remove all the particles. When cold, refrigerate and use as required. Use for savoury dishes and pastry, or for making dripping cakes.

The photograph below shows good use being made of the bones and fat which go with a bulk purchase of beef. The bones are used for stock, the ordinary fat for dripping and the suet for a steak and kidney pudding.

Beefburger

see also **Beef**

Both homemade and commercially prepared beefburgers can be frozen, although they should not be too highly seasoned or spiced.

TO FREEZE: open (flash) freeze until solid, then pack together in a freezer bag, seal, label and return to freezer.

TO THAW: take burgers out individually, as and when required. Fry from frozen in shallow fat or oil until cooked through. See also recipe for *Swedish Beefburgers.*

STORAGE TIME: 3 months.

Beet, Seakale

see **Chard, Swiss**

Beetroot (Beets)

Use only small 'baby' beetroot.

TO FREEZE: wash, boil for 10 to 20 minutes until just tender, drain and leave to cool (not in iced water). Rub off skin, then leave whole, dice or slice and pack dry in rigid containers,

cover, label and freeze.

TO THAW: leave in containers in the refrigerator or thaw rapidly at room temperature, according to time available. Use cold in salads with French dressing, or hot as a vegetable with a white sauce. See also recipe for *Sweet and Sour Beetroot.*

STORAGE TIME: 6 months.

Beets

see **Beetroot**

Bergamot *(Monarda didyma/Bee Balm)*

A highly scented herb which originated in North America, the bergamot plant reaches a height of 60–90 cm/2–3 feet, and bears bright scarlet flowers in dense clusters from June to September (December to February in Australia).

TO FREEZE: pick young leaves, chop finely, freeze tightly in ice cube trays until solid, then pack in freezer bags, seal, label and return to freezer.

TO THAW: use barely thawed in salads, or cooked with pork dishes. Can also be used thawed or frozen to make tea.

STORAGE TIME: 8 to 10 months.

Berry

see also **Fruit** for information on packing.

When freezing berries it is important to use fruit which is only *just* ripe. Freeze as soon as possible after picking and avoid washing unless absolutely necessary.

Bilberry or Blueberry*

Wash in very cold water, drain and pat dry.

TO FREEZE: open (flash) freeze; pack dry; or pack in heavy syrup.

TO THAW: leave in bags or containers for approximately 2½ hours at room temperature.

STORAGE TIME: 12 months.

*Not grown in Australia.

Blackberry (Bramble)

Freeze only fully ripe blackberries.

TO FREEZE: open (flash) freeze; or pack dry.

TO THAW: leave in bags or containers for approximately 2½ hours at room temperature. Or unwrap, tip into a bowl and thaw rapidly at room temperature.

See also recipe for *Blackberry and Apple Pie.*

STORAGE TIME: 12 months.

Boysenberry

This cross between a raspberry, blackberry and loganberry freezes well. Prepare, freeze and thaw as for *Bilberry* above.

Cape Gooseberry or Goldenberry

Freeze when the outer, papery, lantern-like husk turns yellow or brownish, and the inside berry is golden.

TO FREEZE: open (flash) freeze.

TO THAW: as for *Blackberry* above. Use raw in fresh fruit salads, or cook and use in pies, sauces and tarts.

STORAGE TIME: 12 months.

Cranberry

TO FREEZE: open (flash) freeze; pack dry; or cook with sugar to taste and pack as a sauce in rigid containers, cover, label and freeze.

TO THAW: as for *Blackberry* above, or unwrap and cook from frozen in a little water with sugar to taste. Reheat sauce from frozen in a saucepan, stirring occasionally.

STORAGE TIME: 12 months.

Elderberry

Freeze when the berries are almost black.

TO FREEZE AND THAW: as for *Cranberry* above. Use as for *Cape Gooseberry* above.

STORAGE TIME: 12 months.

Gooseberry

Freeze ripe fruit only.

TO FREEZE: top, tail and wash. Open (flash) freeze; pack dry; or cook and purée with sugar to taste, then pack in rigid containers, cover, label and freeze.

TO THAW: leave in wrappings for approximately 2½ hours at room temperature, or unwrap and tip into a bowl if required to thaw rapidly. Or unwrap and use frozen in pies and tarts, or poach from frozen. Purée thawed gooseberries for use in ices and mousses. See also recipe for *Gooseberry Fool*.

STORAGE TIME: 12 months.

Huckleberry*

Seedier than its kin, the bilberry or blueberry, and considered inferior. Prepare, freeze and thaw as for *Bilberry* above.

*Not available in Australia

Juneberry

Freeze only sweet, juicy berries.

TO FREEZE: open (flash) freeze; or pack dry with sugar.

TO THAW: leave in wrappings for approximately 2½ hours at room temperature.

STORAGE TIME: 12 months.

Loganberry

Harvest when the fruit breaks readily from the parent plant, but before it is in danger of falling off or rotting. Unripe fruit should only be used for making jam.

TO FREEZE: open (flash) freeze; pack dry; or cook and purée with sugar to taste, then pack in rigid containers, cover, label and freeze.

TO THAW: leave in wrappings for approximately 2½ hours at room temperature. Or unwrap and use frozen in pies and tarts, or poach from frozen. Use in fresh fruit salads, ices and mousses, or in summer puddings with red, white and black currants.

STORAGE TIME: 12 months.

Mulberry

Place cloths under tree to catch fruit as it falls of its own accord.

TO FREEZE: open (flash) freeze.

TO THAW: leave in wrappings for 2 hours at room temperature. Use raw in fresh fruit salads and ices. Or unwrap and use frozen in pies and tarts, or poach from frozen.

STORAGE TIME: 12 months.

Raspberry

Pick when fully ripe yet firm: the berry should come away easily from its 'plug'.

TO FREEZE: open (flash) freeze; pack dry; or freeze in small quantities as a sieved purée (raw or cooked with sugar to taste).

TO THAW: leave in wrappings for 2 hours at room temperature: use when they still have a slight 'bite' and have not become mushy. Use raw in fools and fresh fruit salads, and with meringues, sandwich cakes and shortbread. Use puréed fruit in ice creams, mousses, sauces and sorbets. See also recipe for *Iced Raspberry Soufflé*.

STORAGE TIME: 12 months.

Rowanberry*

These are the scarlet or yellow berries of the rowan tree (mountain ash). Pick when fully ripe, wash if necessary and remove stalks. Rowanberries are rather dry and too sour to be eaten raw, but are excellent made into purées and sauces.

TO FREEZE: pack puréed rowanberries in small quantities with or without (brown) sugar in rigid containers, cover, label and freeze.

TO THAW: unwrap and cook from frozen, adding sugar if not already added. Serve with game, ham, pork and other savoury dishes.

STORAGE TIME: 12 months.

*Not available in Australia.

Strawberry

Small, ripe, firm berries are best for freezing, particularly the small dry Alpine varieties. Large berries have too high a water content to freeze without becoming mushy as they thaw.

TO FREEZE: grade for size and hull. Do not wash unless absolutely necessary. Open (flash) freeze; pack dry; or lightly mash fruit that is not firm, sweeten to taste and pack in rigid containers, cover, label and freeze.

TO THAW: leave in wrappings for approximately 1½ hours at room temperature, depending on quantity and size of fruit. Use raw in fools, fresh fruit salads, icecreams, summer puddings and tarts, and with meringues and shortbread. See also recipe for *Strawberry Mousse*.

STORAGE TIME: 12 months.

Tangleberry

Prepare, freeze and thaw as for *Bilberry* or *Blueberry* above.

Beurre Manié

see **Kneaded Butter**

Bilberry/Blueberry

see **Berry**

Bindi

see **Okra**

Birds

see **Game**

A selection of berry fruits with a container of raspberry purée ready for freezing.

Beefburger – Birds

Biscuit (Cookie)

(for U.S. Biscuit, see **Muffin**)

Baked or unbaked biscuits can be frozen successfully. However, as baked biscuits store well in an airtight tin, it is not really worth freezing them, unless you have lots of room in your freezer.

To freeze baked biscuits: the best varieties are those with a high fat content — at least 100 g/4 oz/½ cup butter or margarine to ½ kg/1 lb/4 cups flour. Bake biscuits according to usual recipe, allow to cool on a wire rack, then pack in rigid containers, separating each one with aluminium foil or freezer tissue to prevent breakages. Cover, label and freeze.

TO THAW: leave in wrappings for approximately 30 minutes at room temperature. If the biscuits have become soft during the thawing process, they can be 'refreshed' in a fairly hot oven (190°C/375°F or Gas Mark 5) for 5 minutes or until crisp.

Unbaked biscuit dough: this is a useful item to store in the freezer as it can be made very quickly into crisp, fresh biscuits. One of the easiest ways to freeze it is to roll the unbaked dough into a cylindrical shape — about 5 cm/2 inch diameter — wrap in aluminium foil, label and freeze. When biscuits are required, transfer

roll to the refrigerator and leave for 30 to 45 minutes until dough begins to soften. Slice off as many biscuits as you need and return any remaining dough to the freezer. Bake on baking sheets in a fairly hot oven (190°C/375°F or Gas Mark 5) for approximately 10 minutes or until cooked through.

Another method of freezing unbaked dough is to pipe or shape it onto baking sheets, place in the freezer until solid, then remove with a metal spatula, pack into rigid containers, cover, label and return to the freezer until required. Bake from frozen according to the original recipe, allowing a few extra minutes' baking time. Mixtures that are baked in a tin (pan) and then cut into bars, squares or slices after baking, may be frozen uncooked in the tin (pan), then baked from frozen. See also recipes for *Carolina Cookies*, *Chocolate Chip Cookies* and *Christmas Stars*.

STORAGE TIME: approximately 6 months for both baked and unbaked biscuits.

Blackberry

see **Berry**

Blackcurrant

see **Currant**

Blancher

see page 236

Blanching

To immerse prepared vegetables in fast boiling water for a specific period of time before freezing. Blanching stops the action of enzymes which would otherwise continue to work — and in time cause loss of flavour, colour and nutritive value during storage.

TO BLANCH: fill a large pan with 4 litres/8 pints/10 U.S. pints water and bring to a fast boil. Place vegetables in a blanching basket and plunge carefully into the pan. Blanch no more

than ½ kg/1 lb vegetables at a time for best results, although the blanching water can be used several times over, with topping up only required to maintain the original amount. Timing is important and should start the very instant the water returns to a fast boil, *after* the addition of the vegetables. If blanching is too short or the pan is overloaded with vegetables, so that the water takes longer than 1 minute to return to the boil, enzyme action may not be completely halted. If blanching is too long, then vegetables will be soft and mushy after their final cooking. On completion of blanching, plunge vegetables immediately into ice cold water to stop further cooking, then leave until cool. Drain, pat dry and pack according to type of vegetable.

Some vegetables can be blanched by steam, although this method is not recommended for leafy greens because they can stick together. Steam blanching also takes longer than water blanching.

Blancmange

Blancmange can be frozen, but due to its high milk content, separation may occur if it is kept for more than a few weeks. Frozen individual blancmanges are useful if prepared in advance of children's parties.

1

Blanching
1 *A blanching basket containing not more than ½ kg/1 lb fresh vegetables.*
2 *Plunging vegetables into rapidly boiling water.*
3 *Cooling vegetables in ice cold water.*
4 *Draining and packing.*

2

3

4

2

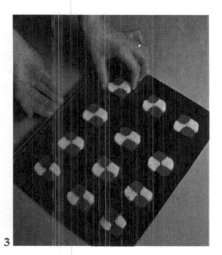

3

4

Bok Choy

see Cabbage, Chinese

Bombe

see Ice(s)/Icecream

Bones for Stock

see Meat, Fresh

Borage *(Borago officinalis)*

A native of the Mediterranean countries, borage was originally cultivated for its medicinal rather than culinary uses. The plant grows from 30–90 cm/1–3 feet, has sky-blue flowers and large, rough leaves which smell of cucumber when bruised.

TO FREEZE: chop young leaves, freeze tightly in ice cube trays until solid, then pack in freezer bags, seal, label and return to freezer. Or pack whole young sprigs in freezer bags, seal, label and freeze.

TO THAW: use partially thawed leaves in salads, crumble frozen sprigs in drinks just before serving.

STORAGE TIME: 6 months.

Bouillon

prepare, freeze and thaw as for **Stock**

Bouquet Garni

The most usual combination of herbs used in a bouquet garni is marjoram, parsley, thyme and a bay leaf. These are tied together with string or cotton, added to long-cooking dishes or marinades, and removed before the dish is served.

TO FREEZE: tie freshly picked herbs together and pack in small quantities in freezer bags, seal, label and freeze. Or blanch in boiling water for 1 minute, then drain and cool. Pat dry and pack in bags. Or chop, freeze in ice cube trays, then pack in bags.

TO THAW: unwrap and use while still frozen as for fresh bouquet garni. Frozen chopped bouquet garni should not be added to dishes that need long slow cooking, but can be added to cooked dishes just before serving.

STORAGE TIME: 2 months (unblanched); 6 months (blanched).

Brains

Freeze brains as soon as possible after purchase.

TO FREEZE: wash thoroughly under cold running water, then pat dry with kitchen paper towels and pack in freezer bags, seal, label and freeze.

TO THAW: leave in wrappings overnight in the refrigerator, then use as soon as possible, as for fresh brains.

STORAGE TIME: 3 months.

Biscuit (Cookie) – Brains

Biscuits
1 A long roll of biscuit (cookie) dough made up of four cylindrical shapes of dough — two plain and two chocolate flavoured — being wrapped in aluminium foil for freezing.
2 The slightly thawed roll being cut into individual biscuits.
3 The biscuits are then placed on a baking sheet and cooked in a fairly hot oven.
4 Serve the cooled biscuits for tea.

Bloater

The bloater is a herring which has been cured without salting while still very fresh. They are best eaten when freshly cured, either grilled (broiled) or fried, or they may be made into paste. Only very fresh bloaters are suitable for freezing.

TO FREEZE: wrap each fish individually in cling film, then pack several fish together in a freezer bag. Seal, label and freeze.

TO THAW: unwrap and cook from frozen.

STORAGE TIME: 3 months.

Blowfish

The small salt-water blowfish, also known as puffers and sea squab, have the ability to puff themselves into balloons when they fear attack. For this reason, their viscera can be highly toxic. Although the fish can be cleaned with great care and the part in the back of the visceral cavity prepared and eaten, it is generally considered too risky.

Blueberry/Bilberry

see **Berry**

Bluefish

A bluefish weighs between 1.35 kg/3 lb and 6.75 kg/15 lb, and the fish is particularly popular along the Atlantic in the U.S.A.

TO FREEZE: clean the fish and remove fins; fillet large ones or cut into steaks, leave smaller fish whole. Pack in freezer bags, interleaving fish with cling film or freezer tissue. Seal, label and freeze.

TO THAW: unwrap and thaw large pieces of fish for 2 hours in the refrigerator; cook smaller fish from frozen. Use salmon or bass recipes for cooking.

STORAGE TIME: 3 months.

Boar

see **Game**

Boil-in-the-bag(s)

see page 233

23

Bramble/Blackberry
see **Berry**

Brandy Butter
see **Butter, Flavoured**

Brawn
see **Pork**

Bread

Bread freezes extremely well, whether baked or unbaked, home-made or baked commercially, although storage times vary depending on the type of bread (see below). It is important that the bread be as fresh as possible when put in the freezer.

TO FREEZE: wrap loaves in freezer bags, seal, label and freeze.

TO THAW: remove from the freezer and leave in wrappings for at least 3 hours at room temperature.

If the bread is likely to be needed in a hurry, or if you prefer to warm the loaves, wrap in aluminium foil before freezing; the bread can then be taken out of the freezer and thawed in the oven in its foil wrapping — this will take approximately 45 minutes in a fairly hot oven (200°C/400°F or Gas Mark 6). The oven method is the best way to thaw French and Italian bread and Viennas, or any loaves which have a crisp crust. Eat straight from the oven because bread becomes stale fairly quickly after thawing this way.

Sliced bread: may be frozen in the wrapping in which it was bought, although it is wise to overwrap in a freezer bag in case the original wrapper is split. It can be useful to keep some sliced bread in the freezer, as slices may be taken out individually and toasted from frozen.

Bread and yeast rolls and baps: may be frozen in quantity in a large freezer bag and you can remove as many as you need. Baps and rolls take approximately 1½ hours to thaw at room temperature, or wrap them in foil and bake from frozen in a fairly hot oven for 15 minutes.

Home-baked bread: particularly well worth making if you have a freezer. There are three ways in which the freezer can make the task of bread-making lighter and more worthwhile:

1 Make and bake as many loaves as possible at one time — this is a good idea as kitchen and utensils will be at the right temperature and the oven can be used to full capacity. Freeze as many of the baked loaves and rolls that are not required for immediate use and thaw as above.

2 Make the dough and knead it, but do not allow to rise. Place in a large greased freezer bag, seal, label and freeze. When the bread is required, remove from the freezer and re-seal at the top of the bag allowing plenty of room for the dough to rise in the bag. Leave to rise for approximately 5 hours at room temperature, or overnight in the refrigerator. Remove from the bag and proceed with original recipe — knock out air, shape into loaves or rolls, place in tins (pans) or on baking sheets, leave to rise and bake. Use this method if time is available to make the dough, but not to wait for the rising stages which normally take several hours. Also remember this method as an emergency measure if you suddenly want to stop in the middle of bread-making.

3 Make the dough and place in a large greased freezer bag. Seal at the top of the bag, leaving plenty of room for the dough to rise. When risen, remove from bag, knock out air and knead according to the original recipe. Return dough to the bag, seal tightly and freeze until required. Thaw and proceed with original recipe as for Method (2) above.

See also recipes for *White Bread, Wholewheat Bread* and *Stolle.*

Partially baked bread: — bought or home-made — can also be stored in the freezer and is useful because it can be ready to eat within 30 minutes or so of coming out of the freezer.

TO FREEZE: wrap bread or rolls in freezer bags, seal, label and freeze.

TO THAW: remove all wrappings and bake from frozen on the oven shelf in a hot oven (225°C/425°F or Gas Mark 7) for approximately 30 minutes for a loaf, 15 minutes for rolls. Check with the baker's instructions if using commercially made partially baked bread.

STORAGE TIMES: vary considerably according to the type of bread. As a general guide commercially baked or homemade white and brown bread will keep up to 6 months, enriched bread (milk, fruit, malt, bridge rolls, etc.) up to 3 months. The maximum storage time for French and Italian breads and loaves with a crisp crust is 1 week only; after this time the crust tends to flake off on thawing. Vienna (crusty) loaves and rolls will freeze successfully for 3 days only. Sliced bread will keep satisfactorily for up to 6 months. Unrisen plain white or brown dough will keep up to 1 month, unrisen enriched dough up to 3 months, risen dough up to 2 weeks. Commercial part-baked bread will keep up to 2 months, homemade part-baked bread will keep up to 4 months.

Bread Sauce

TO FREEZE: make according to your favourite recipe, cool and pack into rigid containers, leaving headspace. Cover, label and freeze until required.

TO THAW: use straight from the freezer — tip into a saucepan (preferably non-stick) and reheat gently with 2 × 15 ml spoons/2 tablespoons each of butter and milk or cream, stirring occasionally. Taste for seasoning before serving.

STORAGE TIME: 1 month.

Breadcrumbs

It is always useful to keep a supply of fresh breadcrumbs in the freezer for coating food such as fish or escalopes, and for use in puddings, sauces and stuffings. Many recipes call for fresh breadcrumbs and it is timeconsuming and not always convenient to prepare them in the midst of cooking a special dish. Fresh breadcrumbs can be made in large quantities in an electric blender.

TO FREEZE: pack breadcrumbs in freezer bags, seal, weigh if you like, label and freeze. As they remain separate once frozen, the exact quantity required can be shaken out of the bag and the remainder returned to the freezer.

TO THAW: there is no need to thaw, unless the breadcrumbs are to be used for coating food, in which case they should be thawed for approximately 30 minutes at room temperature.

STORAGE TIME: 3 months.

Breadfruit

see **Aubergine**

Bream

There is a river bream, but sea bream is the better fish to eat. The fish usually weighs 700–900 g/1½–2 lb.

TO FREEZE: clean and remove head, tail and fins. Pack whole fish in freezer bags, seal, label and freeze. Or skin and fillet before freezing (the scales of sea bream are coarse and there are many spiky bones which make whole fish difficult to cook). Pack in freezer bags, interleaving each fillet with cling film. Seal, label and freeze.

TO THAW: unwrap and thaw whole fish for 2 hours in the refrigerator. Serve stuffed, or bake with onions and garlic. Cook fillets from frozen — they are very good grilled (broiled) with plenty of butter.

STORAGE TIME: 3 months.

Brick Freezing (Preforming)

This is a method of freezing large quantities of food such as casseroles, purées, soups and stews, and of re-packing bulk frozen purchases into usable quantities.

1 Open (flash) freeze until almost solid, then cut into smaller 'bricks' of usable size and quantity and pack individually. 'Bricks' can be stacked in the freezer, thus making economic use of storage space.

2 Line any suitable container, box or carton — called a preformer (forming container) — with a freezer bag or boil-in-the-bag, then fill with the chosen food and cool rapidly. Freeze until solid, remove liner from preformer (forming container), seal, label and return to freezer.

Brill

This rather large flatfish is similar to turbot, although its flavour is not so fine. The flesh is very delicate and needs to be handled carefully.

TO FREEZE: clean, fillet and pack in freezer bags, interleaving each fillet with cling film, seal, label and freeze.

TO THAW: unwrap, poach or fry from frozen, then serve with a sauce. Or unwrap and thaw fillets for 1 hour in the refrigerator, then wrap round a seafood filling and bake.

STORAGE TIME: 3 months.

Brioche

Home or commercially baked brioches — large or small — freeze satisfactorily and can be taken from the freezer a few at a time. After thawing, serve with butter and preserves, or cut off tops and fill centres with a sweet or savoury mixture.

TO FREEZE: cool, then pack in freezer bags, seal, label and freeze.

TO THAW: leave in wrappings for 30 to 45 minutes at room temperature.

Note: if brioches are to be served warm, pack in aluminium foil before freezing, then bake in wrapping from frozen in a very hot oven (250°C/450°F or Gas Mark 8) for 10 minutes or until heated through.

STORAGE TIME: 3 months.

Breadcrumbs

tender, depending on size. Unwrap and use puréed sprouts from frozen in soups, etc. See also recipe for *Purée of Brussels Sprouts*.
STORAGE TIME: 12 months.

Buckling

This is a lightly smoked, unopened herring, which is particularly good made into pâté. Buckling can be frozen, but the flesh is rather soft, and may lose texture in the freezer (compared with the smoked trout which has firmer flesh).
TO FREEZE: wrap each fish individually in cling film, then pack several fish together in a freezer bag. Seal, label and freeze.
TO THAW: leave in wrappings for 3 hours in the refrigerator, then unwrap, remove skins and serve with horseradish sauce and lemon wedges, or use to make pâté.
STORAGE TIME: 3 months.

Bread Sauce – Buckling

Brick Freezing
1 *A large quantity of vegetable soup is open frozen until almost solid, cut into smaller blocks, wrapped in aluminium foil and returned to the freezer.*
2 *A suitable container is lined with a freezer bag, filled with stew and frozen until solid. The bag of food is then removed, sealed, labelled and returned to the freezer.*

Brisling

prepare, freeze and thaw as for **Sprat**

Broccoli (Sprouting)

Cut when shoots are 23–30 cm/9–12 inches long, with bud tips not yet open but just showing their white, green or purple colour. Snap (not cut) off approximately one-third of each shoot where the stem is still tender (more will form later on the lower part of the stem). Stalks should be not more than 2.5 cm/1 inch thick and need no trimming.
TO FREEZE: wash well in salted water, rinse under cold running water, then grade into sizes. Blanch in boiling water: 2 minutes for pencil-thin stems; 3 minutes for medium; 4 minutes for thick stems. Drain, cool rapidly in iced water, then drain and pat dry. Pack in rigid containers or freezer bags, alternating heads and stalks. Cover or seal, label and freeze.
TO THAW: unwrap and put frozen broccoli in boiling salted water. Bring back to the boil, cover and simmer for 3 to 7 minutes or until tender, depending on thickness of stems. See

also recipe for *Broccoli in Cheese Sauce*.
STORAGE TIME: 12 months.

Broken Packaging

see page 232

Broth

prepare, freeze and thaw as for **Soup**

Brussels Sprouts

Freeze small button-tight sprouts only.
TO FREEZE: trim and discard any yellow or damaged leaves, wash sprouts thoroughly and grade into sizes. Blanch in boiling water: 2 minutes for very small sprouts; 3 minutes for small; 4 minutes for medium sprouts. Drain, cool rapidly in iced water, then pat dry. Pack in freezer bags, seal, label and freeze. Large 'blown' sprouts contain too much water to freeze whole: cook them until just tender, then drain and purée in an electric blender or Mouli-légumes (foodmill). Pack in rigid containers or bags, cover or seal, label and freeze.
TO THAW: unwrap and put frozen whole sprouts in boiling salted water. Bring back to the boil, cover and simmer for 4 to 8 minutes or until

Bulk-buying

This most often applies to meat and poultry, ready-prepared frozen and convenience foods and, at the height of the growing season, fruit and vegetables. Buying in bulk saves money and time, and the freezer owner is in the best position to economize by buying food in this way. The cost of the food is lower, and you will need to shop less frequently. Some of the biggest savings are to be made on the bulk purchase of meat — either by purchasing a whole, half or quarter of an animal, or in large quantities of one particular cut. You can also find mixed packs of different cuts at freezer companies, or local butchers and farms specializing in meat for freezers.

When buying in bulk it is wise to remember to look for good quality — there is little point in saving money only to find that the product is inferior. Beware of buys that seem too good to be true and shop at freezer centres, markets and butchers that you trust.

It is also worth considering whether you and your family will benefit from bulk-buys — if you normally do not cook the less expensive cuts of meat such as breast of lamb or flank (rump) of beef, for example, then there is little point in buying these cuts. Think carefully about the type of meat you usually buy, then buy for the freezer accordingly — large quantities (usually a minimum order of 5 kg/10 lb) of one particular cut may be more economical for you than filling your freezer with cuts you will never eat. Also, when buying in large quantities for greater economy, bear in mind the length of time the produce will keep: you may not be able to eat such a large quantity within the recommended storage time. See also **Meat, Fresh.**

Savings can also be made on the purchase of large catering (institution-size) packs available from wholesalers, freezer centres, supermarkets, etc. Most frozen food manufacturers now supply these packs to the general public and the choice is enormous, from basic frozen foods such as icecream and fish to exotic convenience foods and the more expensive vegetables.

Fruit and vegetables can be bought in bulk either fresh or already frozen. Always check for good-quality produce, freshly picked if possible. Good buys are at markets and nurseries, and some farms where you can pick the fruit or vegetable yourself.

Another important point to consider when buying in bulk is the

amount of freezer space available. Use the freezer wisely to store the type of food you would normally buy and eat — there is little point in stocking it full of bulk purchases which do not get eaten, yet take up valuable freezer space for items you would like to buy or cook. To save space in the freezer, re-pack bulk purchases into convenient, usable sizes (see **Brick Freezing**), and wherever possible buy free-flow packs — bulk-buys are usually packed in extremely large containers which are difficult to handle.

Also consider the initial cost of the bulk purchase, as whole carcasses and economy-size catering packs can mean a large capital outlay. Careful budgeting is necessary, bearing in mind the running costs of the freezer viz-à-viz the length of storage time — this will affect the initial cost.

Bulk Cooking
see **Batch Cooking**

Bullace (Golden Damson)*

see also **Fruit** for information on packing.

Freeze when fruit is turning from yellow to gold.

TO FREEZE: wash in iced water, cut in half and remove stones (pits): these tend to flavour fruit during storage and take up valuable freezer space. Pack in medium syrup; or as a purée.

TO THAW: transfer halved fruit and syrup to a heavy saucepan and cook gently from frozen on top of the stove, stirring occasionally. Serve warm with fresh cream. Or thaw in container for 2 hours at room temperature and use halved raw fruit in fresh fruit salads, puréed fruit in pies and tarts.

STORAGE TIME: 12 months.

*Not available in Australia.

Bun(s)
see **Cake(s)**

Burn
see **Freezer Burn**

Burnet *(Sanguisorba minor)*

Salad burnet came originally from Asia and Europe. A perennial herb growing to a height of 30–46 cm/12–18 inches, it has large, round leaves which spread low over the ground and have a flavour similar to borage and cucumber. The leaves are well worth freezing, as they cannot be dried successfully.

TO FREEZE: pick leaves when young. Chop finely, freeze in ice cube trays

until solid, then pack in freezer bags, seal, label and return to freezer. Or wash if necessary, shake dry and put whole into small bags, seal, label and freeze.

TO THAW: leave in wrappings at room temperature until completely thawed, then use in salads and sauces, or sprinkle on meat before grilling (broiling) or roasting. The flavour of burnet marries well with rosemary and tarragon in cooking.

STORAGE TIME: 8 to 10 months.

Butcher Wrap

This is used for sheet wrapping cuts of meat which will be packed together in freezer bags; or for wrapping irregular shapes or large cuts of meat in laminated sheets which will be stored without an overwrap. Set the food on the paper so it sits diagonally across it. Fold both points at the sides over the food, then roll over and over until you reach the end of the paper. Seal the end with freezer tape to hold securely.

Butter

Both salted and unsalted butter freeze well, providing they are fresh when first put in the freezer. Freeze as soon as possible after purchase; do not allow to become soft before freezing.

TO FREEZE: overwrap packs of butter in aluminium foil or freezer bags to prolong storage life, seal, label and freeze.

TO THAW: remove overwrapping and leave for approximately 4 hours in the refrigerator, or for 2 hours at room temperature if the butter is needed in a hurry. Butter that has been frozen may not keep as long as freshly bought butter, so only take as much out of the freezer as you need at one time.

*Butter balls and curls
(see page 30)*

Butter can be flavoured with herbs, garlic, brandy or anchovies before freezing.

To freeze butter balls or curls: shape butter, open (flash) freeze on baking sheets, then quickly transfer to a freezer bag, seal, label and return to freezer.

TO THAW: arrange frozen balls or curls in small serving bowls 1 hour before required.

STORAGE TIME: salted — 3 months; unsalted — 6 months.

Butter, Flavoured

Flavoured butters can be used straight from the freezer for quick accompaniments to steak, chops, grills and fish (anchovy and maître d'hôtel butters), or for stuffing hot French bread (garlic and herb butters). Mint butter is excellent with lamb chops or added to freshly cooked peas or new potatoes just before serving. Brandy butter is traditionally served with plum pudding at Christmas time.

Basic butter recipe: with an electric or rotary beater, or wooden spoon, cream ½ kg/1 lb/2 cups unsalted butter in a large mixing bowl until soft and smooth.

Anchovy butter: drain 2 cans anchovy fillets, then soak fillets in milk to cover for approximately 30 minutes to remove excess salt. Drain and pound to a paste with a mortar and pestle. Beat into the softened butter with freshly ground black pepper to taste and a little anchovy essence. When thoroughly combined, chill in the refrigerator until manageable, then wrap between sheets of greaseproof (waxed) paper and roll into two cylindrical shapes of approximately 2.5 cm/1 inch diameter.

TO FREEZE: wrap each roll in aluminium foil, freeze until solid, then pack in a freezer bag, seal, label and return to freezer.

TO THAW: cut off frozen slices as required, using a knife dipped in hot water.

STORAGE TIME: 3 months.

Brandy butter: beat ½ kg/1 lb/2⅔ cups icing (confectioners') sugar into the softened butter until evenly mixed, then beat in the finely grated rind and juice of 1 orange and 6 × 15 ml spoons/6 tablespoons brandy.

TO FREEZE: transfer to a rigid container, cover, label and freeze.

TO THAW: leave in container for 1 hour in the refrigerator, then beat until quite smooth. Brandy butter should be served chilled — the heat of the pudding will melt it.

STORAGE TIME: 2 months.

Garlic butter: prepare, freeze and thaw as for *Anchovy butter* above, substituting 8 crushed garlic cloves, for the anchovies and seasonings.

STORAGE TIME: 1 month.

Herb butter: prepare, freeze and thaw as for *Anchovy butter* above, substituting 8 × 15 ml spoons/8 tablespoons finely chopped fresh herbs (basil, marjoram, parsley, sage, thyme, etc.) for the anchovies and seasonings. Add salt and freshly ground black pepper to taste.

STORAGE TIME: 3 months.

Maître d'hôtel (parsley) butter: prepare, freeze and thaw as for *Anchovy butter* above, substituting 10 × 15 ml spoons/10 tablespoons freshly chopped parsley and the finely grated rind and juice of 2 lemons for the anchovies and seasonings. Add salt and freshly ground black pepper.

STORAGE TIME: 3 months.

Mint butter: put a good handful of freshly picked mint into a saucepan with a little water and a pinch of sugar, and cook over gentle heat, uncovered, until the water is absorbed by the mint. Purée in an electric blender or work through a sieve. Beat into the softened butter with the finely grated rind and juice of 1 lemon, and salt and freshly ground black pepper to taste. Freeze and thaw as for *Anchovy butter* above.

STORAGE TIME: 3 months.

See also **Chervil**

Buttered Crumbs

These can be kept in the freezer for use as a quick and easy topping for savoury and sweet 'au gratin' dishes such as cauliflower cheese and cannelloni, or desserts such as fruit crumbles or open fruit flans. Melt 50 g/2 oz/¼ cup butter in a frying pan, stir in 100 g/4 oz/2 cups fresh white breadcrumbs and cook gently.

TO FREEZE: when cold pack in freezer bags, seal, label and freeze.

TO THAW: use from frozen: scatter on top of dish and slide under the grill (broiler) to heat through. If for use on a sweet dish, sugar may be added to the frozen crumbs — simply pour sugar to taste into the freezer bag and shake well to combine before use.

STORAGE TIME: 1 month.

Butterfish

These small fish can be found around the Australian coast and along the Atlantic in the U.S.A.

TO FREEZE: clean and wrap individual fish in cling film, then pack several fish together in a freezer bag.

TO THAW: unwrap and pan-fry from frozen in plenty of butter.

STORAGE TIME: 3 months.

Buttermilk

Buttermilk for use in baking (particularly scones) is not always readily available and it is useful to be able to keep some on hand in the freezer.

TO FREEZE: freeze in waxed cartons or rigid containers, leaving headspace. Cover, label and freeze.

TO THAW: leave in containers for approximately 8 hours in the refrigerator. If buttermilk has separated on thawing, whisk briefly.

STORAGE TIME: 6 weeks.

Cabbage

Chinese (Bok Choy)

A salad vegetable like lettuce, Chinese cabbage loses its crisp texture when frozen. However, it can be frozen for use as a last-minute addition to soups and savoury rice dishes, or as a hot vegetable dish tossed in butter and oil after thawing.

TO FREEZE: shred, blanch in boiling water for 1 minute, then drain and cool rapidly in iced water. Drain, pat dry and pack in freezer bags. Seal, label and freeze.

TO THAW: unwrap and leave for a few minutes at room temperature.

STORAGE TIME: 12 months.

Green, Red, White

Freeze young, crisp cabbages only and discard tough outer leaves.

TO FREEZE: shred inner leaves finely, blanch in boiling water for 1 minute, drain, cool rapidly in iced water, then drain and pat dry. Pack in freezer bags, seal, label and freeze.

TO THAW: unwrap and put frozen cabbage in boiling salted water. Bring back to the boil, cover and simmer for 5 to 8 minutes, according to taste. See also recipe for *Austrian Red Cabbage*.

STORAGE TIME: 6 months.

Cake(s)

Both baked and unbaked cakes freeze well, though a fresh mixture can be made in the time it takes to thaw the frozen one.

· Always use the freshest possible ingredients when baking for the freezer; this is particularly important with flour, which quickly goes stale in the freezer. Eggs should also be fresh and well beaten or they will separate and spoil the finished cake. Butter gives the best flavour to a cake, although margarine will give it a lighter texture. Flavourings are important — do not overflavour or include too much spice as this will give the cake a musty flavour once thawed. Avoid using synthetic essences such as almond and vanilla because these can develop strong 'off' tastes in the freezer. It is very important to cool all cakes completely before packaging for the freezer.

Icing: cakes and gâteaux may be iced, decorated and filled before freezing, though a few basic rules should be followed. Glacé, royal, boiled and fondant icings do not freeze satisfactorily. Buttercream icing is the best icing for freezing, due to its high fat content, and whipped cream is also successful.

Sponges, layer and sandwich-type cakes: may be frozen with or without fillings and toppings; if freezing without, separate layers by interleaving with a double layer of greaseproof

(waxed) paper, otherwise sandwich together with chosen filling. (Jam and fruit fillings should not be frozen, but added after thawing, as they make the cake become soggy in the freezer.) Decorate the top of cake and open (flash) freeze until solid, then wrap in aluminium foil or a freezer bag, seal, label and return to freezer. Decorated cakes and gâteaux should be unwrapped before thawing or the decoration will be ruined by the wrapping.

Decorated and filled cakes are easy to cut into slices or portions with a very sharp or freezer knife *before* thawing — a task which is often difficult with creamy fillings once thawed.

Butter, Flavoured — Cake(s)

Fresh cabbages and blanched cabbages packed in freezer bags.

Small iced or uniced cakes and buns and all fragile cakes: can be open (flash) frozen in the same way as large cakes, then packed into cardboard boxes or rigid containers with greaseproof (waxed) paper between individual ones to prevent breakages. Swiss (jelly) rolls (without the jam filling): should be rolled in icing (confectioners') sugar or with greaseproof (waxed) paper before freezing.

Large undecorated cakes: plain, fruit, chocolate, gingerbread, etc. — are best wrapped in aluminium foil, then overwrapped in a freezer bag. When sealing wrappings it is important to extract as much air as possible — see Air. When thawing large cakes, leave them in the wrappings to prevent moisture collecting on the surface of the cakes and making them soft. If you like, cut large cakes into slices before freezing and interleave the slices with foil or greaseproof (waxed) paper. Overwrap in a freezer bag, seal, label and freeze. Individual slices may be taken from the freezer as and when required.

See also recipes for freezing cakes in recipe section.

TO THAW: cakes should be thawed at room temperature. The only exceptions are cakes that are filled or decorated with whipped cream, which should be thawed overnight in the refrigerator. Small cakes will take approximately 1 hour to thaw, large cakes approximately 2 hours. Some very large cakes or those which contain a lot of fruit can take as long as 4 hours to thaw completely.

STORAGE TIMES: large and small plain, fruit and sandwich-type cakes and buns will keep up to 4 months. Sponge cakes made with fat, and most rolled cakes, will keep up to 4 months, fat-free sponges up to 10 months. Decorated and iced cakes and gingerbread will keep up to 2 months.

Calamondin

A small citrus fruit similar to a tangerine. Prepare and freeze as for Tangerine, but thaw and use for making marmalade, as the pulp of calamondin can be very acidic.

Camomile

see Chamomile

Calamondin – Camomile

Cakes can be frozen undecorated with layers or slices separated by interleaving sheets. If decorated before freezing, they should be open frozen before wrapping and unwrapped before thawing. (See recipe section for the cakes in this photograph.)

Canapé

If preparing food for a buffet or cocktail party, it is very helpful to be able to make some items in advance and freeze them until required. Canapés can be frozen successfully if suitable toppings are chosen. Use day-old bread for the base (do not use toast or fried bread) and spread with butter and topping. Avoid toppings that contain mayonnaise, fresh tomatoes or hard-boiled egg whites. Do not coat with aspic before freezing, or this will become cloudy on thawing.

TO FREEZE: open (flash) freeze canapés on trays until solid, then remove from trays and wrap carefully in aluminium foil or freezer bags. Seal, label and return to freezer.

TO THAW: unwrap canapés, place on serving platters and leave for 1 hour at room temperature.

STORAGE TIME: 1 to 2 weeks, depending on topping.

Below: A selection of canapés suitable for freezing. If the canapés are to be stored for longer than two weeks, the anchovies should be added before serving.

Candied Peel

There is little point in freezing candied peel, especially if freezer space is short, as it will keep perfectly well for months in a cool, dry cupboard. Freezing will extend the storage life of candied peel, however, if space in the freezer can be spared.

TO FREEZE: in usable quantities in freezer bags, seal, label and freeze.

TO THAW: leave in wrappings for 3 hours at room temperature.

STORAGE TIME: 12 months.

Right: Caramel can be frozen crushed or in custard desserts or in the form of a sauce for icecream.

Cannelloni

see **Pasta**

Cantaloup

see **Melon**

Capacity

see page 228

Cape Gooseberry

see **Berry**

Caper

Capers keep for months in bottles in the refrigerator, therefore there is no reason to freeze them. If using for decoration on canapés, in vol-au-vents (puff shells), etc., they should be added after thawing. As caper sauce, they can be frozen successfully, see **Sauce(s).** Tartare sauce contains capers, but since it has a mayonnaise base, it should never be frozen as the mayonnaise will not freeze successfully. See also recipe for *Boiled Leg of Lamb in Caper Sauce.*

Capercailzie

see **Game**

Capon

see **Poultry**

Capsicum

see **Pepper(s), Sweet**

Caramel

TO FREEZE: dissolve sugar, or sugar and water, in a pan over low heat, boil until it turns golden then turn into an oiled metal baking tin (pan) and leave until set. Break or crush into pieces. Pack the caramel pieces in small freezer bags, seal, label and freeze.

TO THAW: use straight from the freezer to decorate tops of cakes, gâteaux and fruit desserts.

Caramel used in desserts with egg custards may also be frozen. Make in the usual way, coating the sides and base of the dish with the caramel. Pour in the custard and open (flash) freeze until solid, then wrap in a double thickness of aluminium foil. Seal, label and return to freezer. Bake from frozen according to the original recipe, allowing extra baking time for the custard to set.

Caramel sauce: will freeze successfully for serving with vanilla or coffee icecream.

TO FREEZE: pack in a rigid container, cover, label and freeze.

TO THAW: transfer from container to a heavy saucepan and reheat from frozen.

Caraque

See **Chocolate**

Cardoon*

A relation of the globe artichoke, the cardoon is grown for its edible stems rather than its small prickly flower buds. These stems are blanched in trenches in the same way as celery. Fresh cardoon is used as a salad vegetable, but frozen cardoon loses its crisp texture and should only be used as a hot vegetable (with a white sauce), or in soups and stews. There is no need to freeze home-grown cardoons as they can remain in the ground until required.

TO FREEZE: cut stems into even lengths and peel, or pull, off any outer strings if necessary. Wash thoroughly, then blanch in boiling water for 3 minutes and drain. Cool rapidly in iced water, then drain and pat dry. Pack in rigid containers or freezer bags. Cover or seal, label and freeze.

TO THAW: unwrap and put frozen cardoons in boiling salted water. Bring back to the boil, cover and simmer for 8 minutes. Drain and serve hot. Or thaw in wrappings at room temperature, then unwrap and fry in hot butter and oil until brown.

STORAGE TIME: 12 months.

*Not available in Australia.

Carp

This freshwater fish is found in ponds and sluggish waters, and may grow to 18 kg/40 lb or more. The fish may have a muddy flavour; therefore, it must all be cleaned well.

TO FREEZE: remove the head, taking out the gall stone at the back of the head — this can make the fish taste bitter. Clean and scrape off scales. Leave small fish whole, or fillet larger ones, then put in a colander or sieve under cold running water, or soak for

2 hours in a bowl of salted water, changing the water once during the soaking time. Rinse in a weak solution of vinegar and salted water, then rinse in cold water and pat dry. Pack in freezer bags, seal, label and freeze.

TO THAW: unwrap whole fish, leave to thaw for 4 hours in the refrigerator, then serve stuffed and baked. Or unwrap and cook fillets or small whole fish from frozen. Fry them, or poach gently in red wine. Carp is also good served cold, and can be set in aspic.

STORAGE TIME: 3 months.

Carrot

For best results, freeze sweet early carrots only.

TO FREEZE: leave whole and cut off tops. Wash and scrape only to remove any soil (the outer skin helps retain the flavour). Blanch in boiling water for 3 minutes, drain and cool rapidly in iced water. Drain, then rub off any skin which remains. Pack in rigid containers or freezer bags, cover or seal, label and freeze.

TO THAW: unwrap and put frozen carrots in boiling salted water. Bring back to the boil, cover and simmer for 4 minutes. Drain, toss in melted butter and seasonings and serve hot.

Old Carrots

Large, old carrots are best stored in sand or clamps, although they can be sliced, diced or chopped and frozen for use in soups, stews and other long-cooking dishes.

TO FREEZE: cut off tops, peel and slice, dice, chop or grate. Blanch in boiling salted water for 2 minutes, drain and cool rapidly in iced water. Drain, then pat dry and pack as for whole young carrots above.

TO THAW: do not thaw, but add frozen to casseroles, soups and stews, etc. See also recipe for *Vichy Carrots*.

STORAGE TIME: 9 months.

Carton(s)

see page 234

Cassata

see **Ice(s)/Icecream,** and recipe for *Cassata*

Casserole

Casseroles and stews keep their flavour and texture well in the freezer and can be reheated from frozen within 1 hour. It is a good idea to make double the quantity required for a meal, then you can freeze half. All meat and poultry dishes freeze well, but take care not to use too many herbs or spices as these can become strong once frozen. Barley,

pasta, potatoes and rice are not suitable for freezing in a casserole, but if the recipe calls for one of these it may be added at the time of reheating. There should always be sufficient gravy or sauce to cover completely the meat or poultry before freezing to prevent it from drying out. Vegetables are best if added either towards the end of the cooking time or at the reheating stage, so they do not become overcooked and soft; this is particularly true of root vegetables. Always use lean meat, trimmed of excess fat, and skim off any fat that may form on the surface of a casserole before freezing — fat can cause unpleasant rancidity. Once the casserole is cooked it should be cooled as rapidly as possible — this can easily be done by standing the casserole dish in ice cold water.

There are several ways to package casseroles for freezing:

1 Freeze in foil containers which can be used for reheating directly from the freezer.

2 Line the casserole dish with aluminium foil before cooking, then cool rapidly once cooked and open (flash) freeze until solid. Remove casserole in foil from dish, cover with foil, overwrap in a freezer bag, seal, label and return to freezer.

3 Cook casserole in dish, cool rapid-

ly, then open (flash) freeze until solid. Dip dish in a bowl of very hot water to unmould casserole, then wrap in aluminium foil, overwrap in a freezer bag, seal, label and return to freezer.

4 For neat storage in chest freezers, pour casserole into a freezer bag-lined preformer (forming container), open (flash) freeze until solid, then remove preformer (container), seal, label and return to freezer.

To thaw casseroles:

1 Reheat from frozen in foil container if frozen in this, in a fairly hot oven (190°C/375°F or Gas Mark 5) for 1 hour or until bubbling.

2 Unwrap and return to dish in which casserole was originally cooked, then reheat from frozen in a fairly hot oven (as for 1 above).

3 Unwrap and put into casserole dish, then leave to thaw overnight in the refrigerator. Reheat in a fairly hot oven for approximately 40 minutes or until bubbling.

4 Unwrap and reheat gently from frozen in a heavy saucepan or flameproof casserole dish on top of the stove, stirring occasionally. If necessary, add a little liquid.

5 Unwrap and reheat from frozen in the top of a double boiler.

STORAGE TIME: up to 2 months, according to ingredients used.

See also recipes in recipe section.

Canapé –
Casserole

The four ways of freezing casseroles described on this page are illustrated below.

Catering Pack (Institution-sized Package)

Many commercially frozen foods, such as fish, fruit and fruit juices, icecream, vegetables, etc., can be purchased in economy-size packs for large scale catering, usually at considerably lower prices than normal-sized packs. These catering packs can be split or decanted into more manageable quantities, see **Brick Freezing.**

Some frozen catering packs are made up of small packages contained in one overall large pack for easy carrying out, thus making re-packaging at home unnecessary and storage in the freezer easier, especially if there is only a small space available.

Catfish

The fish known as catfish in the U.S.A. is the same as the English dogfish; Australian catfish are not edible.

TO FREEZE: clean (remove skin if preferred) and cut into steaks or fillets. Pack in freezer bags, interleaving each piece of fish with cling film. Seal, label and freeze.

TO THAW: unwrap and cook from frozen. Catfish lends itself to strong flavours in cooking, such as curry sauce or garlic.

STORAGE TIME: 3 months.

Cauliflower

Freeze only compact, firm white cauliflowers, with tight flower buds which shown no signs of 'feathering' open. Do not freeze whole.

TO FREEZE: break into small sprigs or florets approximately 5 cm/2 inches across. Wash thoroughly and grade into sizes. Blanch in boiling water for 3 minutes, adding a little lemon juice to the water to keep the cauliflower white. Drain, cool rapidly in iced water, then drain and pat dry. Pack in freezer bags, seal, label and freeze.

Blanching cauliflower florets.

TO THAW: unwrap and put frozen cauliflower in boiling salted water. Bring back to the boil, cover and simmer for 4 minutes. Serve with melted butter or a white sauce with cheese or herbs. See also recipes for *Cream of Cauliflower Soup* and *Indian Cauliflower*.

STORAGE TIME: 6 months.

Caviare

The sturgeon's roe, which forms one of the world's greatest delicacies under the name of caviare, is normally purchased in tins (cans) or jars. It is not suitable for freezing because the delicate flavour will spoil, and the texture become soft and wet.

Celeriac (Celery Root)

TO FREEZE: peel and grate, then blanch in boiling water for 1 minute, or dice/slice and blanch in boiling water for 2 minutes. Drain, cool rapidly in iced water, then drain and pat dry. Or cook whole in boiling salted water until tender, then drain, peel and slice. Pack in rigid containers or freezer bags. Cover or seal, label and freeze.

TO THAW: leave in wrappings at room temperature or tip onto a large plate and thaw more rapidly, then use in salads. Or unwrap and cook from frozen in soups, stews and other savoury dishes. See also recipe for *Celeriac Purée.*

STORAGE TIME: 6 months.

Celery

Celery loses its crisp texture as a salad vegetable once frozen, but is worth freezing for its excellent flavour in soups and stews, etc.

TO FREEZE: trim, remove any strings and scrub. Cut into short lengths and blanch in boiling water for 3 minutes. Drain, cool rapidly in iced water, then drain and pat dry. Pack in freezer bags, seal, label and freeze.

TO THAW: unwrap and put frozen celery in boiling salted water. Bring back to the boil, cover and simmer for 10 minutes. Drain and serve with a hot savoury sauce. Or unwrap and cook from frozen in casseroles, soups and stews, etc.

STORAGE TIME: 6 months.

Cepe

prepare, freeze and thaw as for **Mushroom**

C(h)amomile *(Anthemis nobilis)*

The flowers of this herb are dried for use in making tea, and there is little point in freezing them as they are of no other culinary use.

Char

This freshwater fish has flaky flesh and is orange coloured. Potted char, made by cooking the flesh gently with spices in fish stock, then pounding it with butter, is a great delicacy.

TO FREEZE: clean thoroughly, wrap each fish individually in cling film, then pack several fish together in a freezer bag, seal, label and freeze.

TO THAW: unwrap and leave for 1 hour in the refrigerator before cooking. Any recipe for trout would be suitable for char.

STORAGE TIME: 3 months.

Chard, Swiss (Seakale Beet)*

A form of beet grown for its glossy leaves which are prepared in the same way as spinach, and its leaf stems or thick inner ribs which are served like seakale or cooked celery. To keep plants productive, a few of the outer leaves should be twisted regularly from the base; cutting may cause rotting in the remaining pieces.

To freeze leaves: wash, blanch in boiling water for 2 minutes and drain. Cool rapidly in iced water, then drain and squeeze dry. Pack in freezer bags, seal, label and freeze. Use as for spinach.

TO THAW: unwrap and cook from frozen in a little melted butter for 7 minutes.

To freeze inner ribs: cut into 5 cm/2 inch lengths, blanch in boiling water for 3 minutes and drain. Cool rapidly in iced water, then drain and pat dry. Pack in freezer bags, seal, label and freeze.

TO THAW: unwrap and put frozen ribs in boiling salted water. Bring back to the boil, cover and simmer for 7 minutes. Serve with a white sauce, or toss in butter and lemon juice and serve as an accompaniment to roast meats.

STORAGE TIME: 12 months.
*Not available in Australia.

Chayote

Prepare, freeze and thaw this pear-shaped green fruit as for **Marrow/Summer Squash,** after first removing the large stone (seed) in the middle.

Cheese

Hard Cheese

Cheese such as Cheddar, Cheshire, Double Gloucester, Edam, etc., freezes well, although it does tend to become crumbly the longer it remains in the freezer. If stored too long, it can be used for cooking and need not be grated.

TO FREEZE: wrap in blocks of 225 g / ½ lb, in freezer wrap or aluminium foil, then overwrap in a freezer bag to prevent the cheese from drying out and contaminating other foods in the freezer. Seal, label and freeze.

TO THAW: leave in wrappings overnight in the refrigerator. Cheese that has been frozen will become stale more quickly than fresh cheese and it is not possible to re-freeze it once thawed.

Soft Cheese

This can be frozen, but it should be fully matured before doing so. Brie, Camembert, Mozzarella, Port Salut, Roquefort, etc., can be frozen successfully, but a lot depends on the condition of the cheese at the time of freezing. Package and freeze as for *Hard Cheese* above.

TO THAW: allow soft cheese to thaw completely before serving or it will not regain its original full flavour. Thaw for 24 hours in the refrigerator, then for another 24 hours at room temperature.

Cream Cheese

This does not freeze well unless it contains more than 40 per cent butterfat; however, it can be mixed with double (heavy) cream for use in dips for cocktails, etc, and freezes successfully when combined with other ingredients in cooked dishes.

TO FREEZE: pack uncooked cream cheese in cartons or rigid containers, cover, label and freeze.

TO THAW: leave in container overnight in the refrigerator, then stir well with a fork before use.

Cottage and Curd Cheese

Does not freeze satisfactorily as it tends to become watery. It will freeze successfully when combined with other ingredients in cooked dishes such as cheesecake and quiche.

Blue Cheese

Does not freeze successfully as it tends to become too crumbly during freezing, but can be used in cooking.

Grated Cheese

This is very useful if stored in the freezer. Pack in freezer bags, seal, label and freeze. It remains separate once frozen, therefore any amount can be taken from the bag as and when required. Any pieces of left-over cheese can be grated and kept in the freezer for cooking purposes — it can be used straight from the freezer for sauce making.

STORAGE TIME: 3 to 6 months, depending on original freshness and condition of cheese.

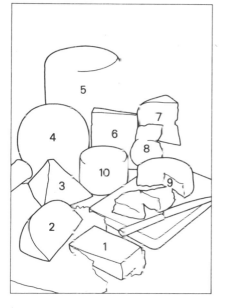

A selection of cheeses suitable for freezing
1 *Leicester*
2 *Edam*
3 *Parmesan*
4 *Edam*
5 *Farmhouse Cheddar*
6 *Emmenthal*
7 *Mature Gouda*
8 *Mozzarella*
9 *Camembert*
10 *Cheshire*

Catering Pack (Institution-sized Package)— Cheese

Cheesecake

Cheesecakes freeze perfectly, whether set by baking, or with gelatin(e) in the refrigerator. They can be made with a base of pastry that is baked in the oven, or with crushed biscuits (cookies) that is set in the refrigerator — both bases freeze well. Cream, curd or cottage cheese, sour(ed) or fresh double (heavy) cream make good fillings.

TO FREEZE: open (flash) freeze cooled or chilled cheesecake in a lightly greased tin (pan) (preferably with removable base) until solid. Remove from tin (pan), wrap in aluminium foil, overwrap in a freezer bag, seal, label and return to freezer.

TO THAW: unwrap and place on serving platter . Leave baked cheesecake overnight at room temperature; refrigerator-type cheesecake overnight in the refrigerator. See also recipes for *Continental Baked Cheesecake* and *Uncooked Cheesecake*.

STORAGE TIME: 1 month.

Chestnuts can be frozen as a purée and then thawed and served as a delicious dessert with whipped cream and grated chocolate.

Cherry

see also **Fruit** for information on packing.

Red and black (Morello) cherries are the most suitable for freezing because they keep their colour once thawed.

TO FREEZE: take off stalks, wash fruit, halve and remove stones (pits), unless you like the almond flavour they gradually impart to the fruit, then pack dry or in medium syrup.

TO THAW: leave in container for 3 hours at room temperature, then use immediately or the fruit will discolour. Use in fruit salads, flans or with syrup as a topping for icecream.

STORAGE TIME: 12 months.

Chervil (*Anthriscus cerefolium*)

A native of southern and eastern Europe, chervil grows to a height of approximately 46 cm/18 inches. It is a sweet-smelling herb, with fern-like green leaves which resemble the flat-leaved variety of parsley and it is often used as a substitute for parsley in cooking. Chervil leaves have a delicate, aniseed-like flavour which is destroyed by long cooking.

TO FREEZE: chop the leaves and tender parts of the stems finely, or cut with scissors. Freeze in ice cube trays until solid, then pack in freezer bags, seal, label and return to freezer. Or pick in bunches, wash and shake dry, then pack in small quantities in freezer bags. Or blanch in boiling water for 1 minute, drain, then cool rapidly under cold running water. Drain, pat dry and pack in bags.

TO THAW: add frozen cubes to hot dishes, or crumble bunches of chervil while still frozen and add just before serving to omelettes and other egg dishes, sauces and soups. Or mix with butter and use to top cooked broad beans (fava), carrots and new potatoes before serving.

To freeze chervil butter: chop freshly picked chervil, blend into butter with salt and pepper to taste, then form into a roll. Wrap in aluminium foil, then overwrap in a freezer bag, seal, label and freeze. Cut slices from the frozen roll and place on grilled (broiled) meat, fish or poultry just before serving.

STORAGE TIME: 2 months (unblanched); 12 months (blanched).

Chest Freezer

see page 228

Chestnut

TO FREEZE: wash and put into a saucepan, then cover with water and bring to the boil. Take out a few nuts at a time with a slotted spoon and peel quickly (the skins stick as the nuts cool). Leave whole or purée in an electric blender, then pack in rigid containers, cover, label and freeze.

TO THAW: leave in containers at room temperature until whole nuts can be separated, purée can be whipped easily with a fork. Use in stuffings for poultry, or as a dessert with whipped cream and grated chocolate. See also recipe for *Chestnut Pancakes*.

STORAGE TIME: 6 months.

Chicken

see **Poultry**

Chicory (Whitloof, French or Large Brussels/ Aust. & U.S. Endive)

Due to its high water content, chicory loses its crisp texture as a salad vegetable once frozen; however, it is worth freezing for use as a cooked vegetable and is particularly good braised with onions and tomatoes.

TO FREEZE: wipe chicory clean (do not soak in water or it will become bitter). Blanch in boiling water for 5 minutes and drain. Cool rapidly in iced water, then drain and pat dry. Pack in freezer bags, seal, label and freeze.

TO THAW: leave in wrappings for approximately 2 hours at room temperature, then gently squeeze out any excess moisture with the hands. See also recipe for *Chicory au Gratin*.

STORAGE TIME: 6 months.

Chilli (Chili or Chile)

Chillis can be stored in the freezer, but as they dry so well there is little point in taking up valuable freezer space with them.

TO FREEZE: remove stalks, seeds and pith. Blanch in boiling water for 1 minute and drain. Cool rapidly in iced water, then drain and pat dry. Pack in freezer bags, seal, label and freeze.

TO THAW: unwrap and leave at room temperature to thaw rapidly. Or use frozen in cooked dishes.

STORAGE TIME: 12 months.

Chinese Cabbage

see **Cabbage**

Chinese Gooseberry (Kiwi Fruit)

see also **Fruit** for information on packing

Chinese gooseberries do not freeze very successfully due to their high water content and delicate flavour and texture. However, you may wish to freeze them if there is a glut.

TO FREEZE: peel off brown furry skin, then pack dry.

TO THAW: use slightly thawed on icecream. Iced Chinese gooseberries also make a refreshing first or last course of a dinner party meal.

STORAGE TIME: 6 months.

Chives (*Allium schoenoprasum*)

A member of the onion family, this herb grows throughout the Northern hemisphere and is immensely useful in cooking as it can be picked fresh throughout the year. Freeze quantities of chives during the summer months when the plant is most prolific. Do not allow to grow to a height of more than 23–30 cm/9–12 inches, or to produce flower heads, or this will cause the mild flavour of the chives to weaken and become useless as a flavouring in cooking.

TO FREEZE: wash and cut into short lengths with scissors. Freeze in ice cube trays until solid, then pack in freezer bags, seal, label and return to freezer. Or cut large handfuls from the plants when they need trimming, wash if necessary, then pat dry and pack in bags as above. Try to keep the strands neatly bunched so that they can be cut easily when required.

TO THAW: put cubes in a small strainer and leave to thaw at room temperature, or use while still frozen. Cut whole strands with scissors while still frozen. Always use chives raw because cooking not only destroys the flavour but makes them useless as an aid to digestion. Use in cream cheese, jacket baked potatoes, omelettes, salads, sauces and savoury pancakes (crêpes), or sprinkle onto chilled or hot soups.

STORAGE TIME: 6 months (cubes); 2 months (whole leaves).

Chocolate

Chocolate retains its flavour well in the freezer, and it can be used with great success in cakes and gâteaux, icecream, icings (frostings), mousses, puddings and sauces, etc. Cakes and gâteaux which have buttercream toppings may be decorated with chocolate before freezing, if you like. It is useful to keep chocolate decorations in the freezer for last-minute decorating of cakes, mousses, soufflés, etc. Pack in rigid containers or boxes to prevent breakages. A slight 'bloom' may appear on the chocolate when it thaws, but the flavour and texture will be unimpaired.

Chocolate squares (thins): grate chocolate (plain or cooking) and place in a bowl over a saucepan of hot water until melted, working it with a palette knife or spoon. Spread it thinly on non-stick silicone paper and leave until almost set. Cut into squares with a sharp knife and leave until completely set. Slide the paper to the edge of a working surface, pull it down and carefully lift off the squares.

Chocolate caraque (scrolls): grate and melt chocolate as for squares above, then spread thinly on a laminated surface or marble slab. When the chocolate is on the point of setting, shave off curls (caraque) with a long, sharp knife: use a sawing motion with the knife held at a slight angle.

Chocolate leaves: grate and melt chocolate as for squares above, then spread over the underneath (vein side) of freshly picked, washed and dried rose leaves, with stems attached. Leave until set on non-stick silicone paper. When set, peel the leaves away from the chocolate very carefully, holding the stem in one hand. See also recipes for *Chocolate Mousse*, *Profiteroles with Chocolate Sauce*, *Chocolate Mocha Bavarian Cream*, *Black Forest Gâteau*, *Brownies*, *Chocolate Chip Cookies* and *Rich Chocolate Cake*.

STORAGE TIME: up to 2 months.

Chop(s)

see individual meats (**Lamb, Pork, Veal**)

Choux Pastry

see *Éclair(s)*, and recipe for *Profiteroles with Chocolate Sauce*

Chowder

prepare, freeze and thaw as for **Soup**

Chocolate
1 *Melt grated chocolate in a bowl over a pan of hot water.*
2 *Spreading the melted chocolate on rose leaves, on a marble slab and silicone paper.*
3 *Making squares and caraque (scrolls).*
4 *Peeling the rose leaves away from the chocolate leaves.*

Christmas fare

Christmas

Your freezer will really come into its own during the months and weeks prior to Christmas, and if you organize it efficiently, you can keep cooking down to a minimum during the actual holiday period. Christmas ham, pork and poultry can be purchased at a reasonable price at peak times during the year and frozen to eat at Christmas time. Most Christmas fare can be prepared beforehand and frozen: brandy butter, breadcrumbs, cheese straws, chestnuts, Christmas cake, cranberry sauce, special party desserts and gâteaux, mince pies and mincemeat, plum pudding, sauces, sausage rolls, stock, stuffings, tangerines, yule logs. A stock of frozen vegetables can gradually be built up over the weeks for use during the festive period.

Christmas leftovers are no problem with a freezer — cold turkey can be sliced and frozen, or made into a variety of cooked dishes which can be put in the freezer for use at a later date.

Chub

A freshwater fish of the carp family, chub can weigh from 1.80 kg/4 lb to 3.60 kg/8 lb, and has many forked bones. It should be prepared very soon after catching, or the flavour will quickly deteriorate.

TO FREEZE: clean, leave whole and pack in freezer bags. Seal, label and freeze.

TO THAW: unwrap and leave for 1 hour in the refrigerator, then stuff and bake. Chub is also available smoked. Freeze as for fresh chub above.

STORAGE TIME: 3 months (fresh); 1 month (smoked).

Chutney

There is very little point in freezing chutney as it keeps perfectly well if correctly covered and stored in a cool, dry place. As most chutneys contain spices, they will not keep for much longer than 1 month in the freezer; after that time the spices will develop a musty flavour.

Citric Acid

An anti-oxidant found in lemon juice, or available in powder form from chemists (pharmacies). Citric acid helps to prevent browning and discoloration in fruits low in Vitamin C such as apples, peaches and pears, when these are exposed to air before freezing. Allow the juice of 1 medium-sized lemon to 900 ml/1½ pints/1 U.S. quart water, or 1 × 5 ml spoon/1 teaspoon citric acid to ½ kg/1 lb dry sugar pack.

Citron

see also **Fruit** for information on packing

Citrons are less acidic than lemons, though they are usually larger and have a much thicker skin. They are worth freezing if difficult to obtain at certain times of year.

TO FREEZE: slice, pack in light syrup and thaw as for **Lemon.** Use in salads or purée in an electric blender, then strain and use as a drink with sugar according to taste.

STORAGE TIME: 12 months.

Citrus Fruit

see individual names (**Calamondin, Citron, Clementine, Grapefruit, Lemon, Mandarin, Orange, Pomelo, Tangelo, Tangerine, Ugli Fruit**)

Clam

Only freeze very fresh clams.

TO FREEZE: wash thoroughly to remove any shell fragments and the sand from the outside of the shells. Open and remove the whole clam. Put into a colander or sieve, letting the juice drain through into a bowl. Wash the fish in salted water, allowing 1 × 15 ml spoon/1 tablespoon salt to 1 litre/2 pints/5 cups water. Pack into rigid containers, then cover with

juice from bowl, leaving headspace. Cover containers, label and freeze.

TO THAW: leave in containers for 2 hours in the refrigerator. Use as for fresh clams.

STORAGE TIME: 3 months.

Cleaning the Freezer

see page 230

Clementine

prepare, freeze and thaw as for **Orange**

Cockle

TO FREEZE: wash cockles very thoroughly, then put in a bowl of cold water and sprinkle on a handful of porridge oats. Leave overnight so that the cockles feed and clean themselves. Pour away dirty water and rinse very thoroughly, then spread cockles out in a heavy pan without liquid. Cover with a lid and heat gently for 1 to 2 minutes until the cockles open. Remove cockles from shells, leave to cool, then pack in rigid containers. Freeze dry, or pour some of the cockle liquid into the containers, leaving headspace. Cover containers, label and freeze.

TO THAW: leave in containers for 2 hours in the refrigerator, then dress with vinegar, salt and pepper. To serve cockles in liquid, reheat gently after thawing and serve with hot melted butter.

STORAGE TIME: 3 months.

Coconut

Fresh unsweetened coconut can be frozen for use in biscuits (cookies), cakes, coconut ice, curries, macaroons, puddings, etc.

TO FREEZE: grate or shred the coconut and pack in rigid containers or freezer bags. Seal, label and freeze.

TO THAW: unwrap and put frozen coconut in a colander to drain. Leave for approximately 2 hours or until completely thawed at room temperature. Use as for fresh coconut.

Sweetened coconut: widely available commercially prepared, and can be frozen as above.

STORAGE TIME: 6 months.

Cod

One of the most important fish in the world, cod flourishes in cold Northern waters.

TO FREEZE: clean thoroughly, then cut into steaks or fillets. Pack in freezer bags, interleaving each piece of fish with cling film. Seal, label and freeze.

TO THAW: unwrap and cook from frozen.

STORAGE TIME: 3 months.

Coffee

The flavour of coffee keeps well in the freezer and it can be used in cakes, gâteaux, icings (frostings), puddings, etc, without any deterioration.

Concentrated liquid coffee: can be made and poured into ice cube trays for use in iced coffee: freeze until solid, then pack cubes in freezer bags, seal, label and return to freezer.

Freshly roasted coffee: in the form of either beans or ground, can be kept in the freezer providing it is absolutely fresh at the time of freezing. Pack in freezer bags in convenient-sized quantities (225 g / ½ lb is probably the largest amount you would use at any one time), extract as much air as possible, seal, label and freeze.

It is also possible to freeze film packs of coffee, either fresh or instant: overwrap in freezer bags before freezing to avoid the possibility of perforation in the freezer, seal, label and freeze.

Instant coffee granules or powder: can also be frozen — large catering (institution-size) packs and jars are less expensive, but would normally lose their freshness by the time you get to the bottom of the pack or jar. Divide large packs into small quantities and pack in bags as for fresh coffee above. See also recipe for *Coffee Cake*.

STORAGE TIME: 3 months (concentrated coffee cubes, fresh ground or instant); 12 months (freshly roasted coffee beans).

Cold Meat(s)
see **Meat, Cooked**

Colour Coding

A system for allocating freezer space and identifying foods or packages by the use of coloured labels or stickers, bags or containers. Colour coding is essential to good freezer management, because it helps to keep track of the freezer's contents — foods of a similar kind can be quickly and easily stored together in the same package, shelf, section or basket, thus avoiding last-minute panics or constant rummaging around in search of a particular item. Coloured plastic sacks or nylon shopping bags can also be used for storing large quantities of the same item.

Commercially Frozen Food

Raw foods such as fish, fruit, meat and vegetables, etc., are frozen on a commercial scale in specially designed factories. Because these foods are prepared when the raw ingredients are in peak condition, with very little time elapsing between, say, harvesting a field of peas or preparing a fish catch and their arrival at the factory for processing, they retain the maximum flavour, colour and nutritive value.

The term also applies to frozen ready-cooked dishes which are prepared on a commercial scale. Such dishes require no preparation other than thawing and/or reheating from frozen to serve.

Christmas – Commercially Frozen Food

Above: A freezer packed with clearly colour-coded food — yellow for baked goods, red for meat and meat dishes, green for vegetables, white for fruit and blue for dishes prepared for a particular occasion.

Left: Coffee keeps well in the freezer, stored in the form of concentrated ice cubes, or as beans or ground coffee packed in freezer bags.

Special compartmented foil trays are available for storing complete meals.

Complete Meals

It is a good idea to freeze a variety of prepared dishes ready for assembly as complete meals that will meet any occasion. It is possible to pack whole menus as one item for short-term use, but not all frozen foods can be stored for the same length of time. For long-term storage and to ensure food is to taste at its best, package together similar courses or dishes ready for easy assembly later as a complete meal. Keep a record of such dishes and menus in the freezer diary for instant recall.

Compressor

This is the motor unit which, together with the condenser and the evaporator, is one of the three main components of a freezer. It is generally housed in a sealed compartment, thus requiring no attention, and consequently most manufacturers will guarantee it for 5 years. During the operating cycle of a freezer, the compressor receives the refrigerant gas from the evaporator, forces it into the condenser where the combined effect of pressure and temperature cause it to condense into a liquid.

Condenser

Rapid cooling of cooked dishes is essential before freezing.

Together with the compressor and the evaporator, the condenser is one of the three main components of a freezer. It is a system of tubes which transfers the heat of food inside the cabinet to the outside. This is done by the changing of the refrigerant gas, received via the compressor, into a liquid; this results in the production of heat which is then given off by the condenser into the room.

There are three main types of condenser:

1 the skin-type which is the most common, and which lies between the inner and outer linings of a freezer cabinet and transfers heat directly through the walls of the cabinet. The outside of a freezer with this type of condenser feels slightly warm and is therefore unlikely to be affected by condensation.

2 the fan-cooled condenser which, as its name implies, uses a fan to force out heat from inside the cabinet through a front grille. The outside of a freezer with this type of condenser remains cold and is susceptible to condensation if kept in a damp atmosphere.

3 the static plate condenser which extracts heat from inside by means of a kind of radiator situated at the back of the cabinet. Air must be allowed to circulate around the freezer at all times.

Conger Eel
see **Eel**

Conservator

A cold cabinet which is capable only of storing ready-frozen foods, a conservator is *not* a freezer, because its temperature cannot be lowered enough to freeze raw materials safely. However, a conservator can be a useful accessory for storing large quantities of food which have been previously frozen in a freezer.

Conserves
see **Preserves**

Consommé

prepare, freeze and thaw as for **Soup**

Container(s)
see pages 232-5

Convenience Foods

It is useful to keep a supply of commercially prepared ready-frozen convenience foods in the freezer, as these can generally be served at a moment's notice. The choice of convenience foods is a purely personal one, but items such as desserts like crêpes and mousses, fish in batter ready for frying, meat pies, and pastry and yeast doughs ready for shaping, are good standbys.

Cooked Dishes

Most cooked dishes prepared at home can be frozen, providing they are prepared hygienically, cooled completely and packaged correctly. The storage life of such foods varies considerably, depending on the ingredients used, but in general it is only 1 to 3 months. As well as correct preparation, it is equally important that cooked dishes be thawed and/or reheated properly, and that a good turnover of such dishes in a freezer is maintained.

Cookie
see **Biscuit**

Cooling

This is a vital process in freezing. Food must be cooled as quickly as possible before sealing and freezing, to help to preserve its prime condition, and to reduce to a minimum the possibility of contamination by harmful bacteria which thrive in warm conditions, or the action of enzymes. Also, less moisture in the form of steam is retained by the rapid cooling of cooked food, so the ice crystals which form during freezing are smaller and therefore less disruptive in food tissues on thawing.

Coquille

see **Scallop**

Coriander *(Coriandrum sativum)*

A slender, sparsely branched herb which grows to a height of 46 cm/18 inches with a spread of 15–23 cm/6–9 inches. A native of the eastern Mediterranean, it grows prolifically throughout southern Europe. The ripe seeds of the coriander plant are used as a spice in cooking, but there is little point in freezing them as they will keep perfectly well if dried and stored in airtight jars. However, the feathery leaves will keep fresher frozen than dried, and are immensely useful as a herb in cooking (see below). Use frozen coriander sparingly, or its flavour can be overpowering.
TO FREEZE: chop the leaves finely once the flowers have dried and the seeds have started to ripen. Freeze in ice cube trays until solid, then pack in freezer bags, seal, label and return to freezer. Or put bunches of freshly picked leaves directly into bags. Or blanch in boiling water for 1 minute, drain, cool rapidly under cold running water, then pat dry and pack in bags.
TO THAW: use frozen cubes in casseroles, chutneys, curries, etc. Crumble leaves while still frozen and use in bread, cakes, cream cheese, milk puddings and poached fruit, or rub into lamb, pork or veal before grilling (broiling) or roasting.
STORAGE TIME: 12 months (cubes); 2 months (whole leaves).

Corn (Sweet)

Freeze young home-grown ears before they have turned starchy; ripening has started when silks at the top of the ears start to dry out and turn brown. To test if ready, make a small gap in the sheath at its fattest part: the kernels should be pale yellow, but fully developed (they will turn golden during cooking). To be at their best, ears *must* be blanched immediately after picking or within 1 hour at the most. Most varieties start to lose their sweetness the moment they are broken from the parent plant.
To freeze corn-on-the-cob: remove leaves, silks and stem and grade into sizes. Blanch in boiling water for 2 to 6 minutes, according to size. Bought ears of unknown freshness will take 4 to 8 minutes to blanch. Drain and cool, then wrap ears individually in aluminium foil or cling film. Open (flash) freeze until solid, then pack in freezer bags, seal, label and return to freezer.

TO THAW: leave in wrappings for approximately 2 hours at room temperature or overnight in the refrigerator. Put thawed corn-on-the-cob into plenty of boiling sugared water, bring back to the boil, cover and simmer for 5 to 10 minutes, according to size. Do not overcook or the kernels will harden. Drain and serve hot, tossed in butter.
To freeze corn off the cob: cut the kernels off blanched cobs with a sharp knife, then pack in usable quantities in freezer bags.
TO THAW: add frozen corn kernels to stews and other composite dishes, a few minutes before the end of cooking. Very fresh young corn may need no further cooking if thawed: leave in wrappings or turn into a strainer and thaw for approximately 30 minutes at room temperature, then toss in melted butter until heated through. Serve with French beans, lightly cooked tomatoes or scrambled eggs.
STORAGE TIME: 12 months.

Cornflour (Cornstarch)

Cornflour is recommended as a thickening agent in some dishes that are cooked especially for storage in the freezer. When thickening with plain white (all-purpose) flour, there can be a tendency for mixtures to separate on reheating, and this is most likely to occur when flour and milk are combined together. Cornflour is used to help avoid this separation. Always keep the quantity of cornflour or flour to a minimum when thickening casseroles, sauces, etc. for the freezer, as the freezing process can cause a mixture to thicken naturally. In most cases, however, this can be rectified by adding more liquid at the reheating stage.

Courgette (Zucchini)

Only freeze small young courgettes. Pick while the large yellow flower is still attached.
TO FREEZE: wash, but do not peel, then blanch in boiling water for 1 minute and drain. Cool rapidly in iced water, then drain and pat dry. Pack in freezer bags, seal, label and freeze.

Cut larger courgettes into chunks or 1.25 cm/½ inch slices, blanch in boiling water for 2 minutes and pack as for whole courgettes above. Or slice unpeeled courgettes thinly and cook gently with a little water until just tender, then purée in an electric blender or work in a Mouli-légumes (foodmill). Pack in usable quantities in rigid containers or freezer bags, cover or seal, label and freeze.
TO THAW: unwrap and put frozen whole courgettes in boiling salted water, bring back to the boil, cover and simmer for 4 minutes. Or thaw slices, chunks and purée in wrappings for approximately 2 hours at room temperature, then use as for fresh courgettes. For the best flavour fry in hot butter and oil rather than

Complete Meals – Courgette (Zucchini)

Corn can be frozen on the cob or as loose kernels, and then served as for fresh.

cook in water. The flavour of courgettes is better if they never touch water again. Use in dishes with cheese, cream, eggs, onions, and tomatoes.

See also recipes for *Ratatouille*, *Mixed Vegetable Medley*, *Courgette and Cheese Casserole* and *Courgette Ragoût*.
STORAGE TIME: 6 months.

Crab

Purchase crab freshly cooked, or cook newly caught crab in boiling water.
TO FREEZE: twist off large and small claws and separate upper from lower shell. Remove intestines and stomach, also 'dead man's fingers' which are small grey-green soft fingers. Pick out meat from body and from claws. Pack white and brown meat separately in rigid containers, cover, label and freeze. Or repack crab meat into scrubbed shells, cover shell with cling film and overwrap in aluminium foil or a freezer bag. Seal, label and freeze.
TO THAW: leave in wrappings for 3 hours in the refrigerator and use immediately after thawing. See also recipe for *Crab Soufflé*.
STORAGE TIME: 1 month.

Crab Apple

Most crab apples are so small that they have no other use than to be made into jelly, which keeps perfectly well stored in jars in a cool, dry place. If you have no time to make jelly when crab apples are being harvested, then freeze the apples to make into jelly at a later date.
To freeze small crab apples: wash thoroughly, pat dry, then pack in freezer bags. Seal, label and freeze. Larger varieties of crab apples can be used to make apple purée, or mixed with cooking (tart) apples. Prepare, freeze and thaw as for **Apple.**
TO THAW: unwrap and use from frozen to make crab apple jelly in the normal way, allowing a little extra cooking time.
STORAGE TIME: 8 months.

Cranberry

see **Berry**

Crawfish

A sea fish similar to lobster, but without large claws. Crawfish has plenty of tender flesh, but the flavour is not as good as lobster.
TO FREEZE: cook live crawfish by steaming or boiling in water, then cool and clean. Remove flesh and pack in rigid containers, leaving headspace. Cover, label and freeze. Scrub the shells thoroughly and freeze separately in freezer bags for serving the fish when thawed.
TO THAW: leave in containers for 3 hours in the refrigerator, then serve hot or cold as for fresh crawfish.
STORAGE TIME: 3 months.

Crayfish (Aust. Lobster)

A small freshwater lobster with a delicious flavour. Clean and boil in a court bouillon with white wine for 10 minutes. Remove central portion of fan-shaped tail to draw out the spinal cord which has a bitter flavour. The fish is best eaten freshly cooked, when the liquid can be sucked out after the tail portion is broken off.
TO FREEZE: leave to cool, then drain and pack in freezer bags. Seal, label and freeze. Pack the cooking liquid separately in rigid containers, cover, label and freeze.
TO THAW: put the frozen cooking liquid in a saucepan and reheat gently until thawed. Unwrap the crayfish and put frozen into the liquid to reheat.
STORAGE TIME: 3 months.

Cream

Only cream that contains at least 40 per cent butterfat can be frozen successfully; cream with a lower butterfat content than this will separate on thawing. The best creams to freeze are, therefore, double (heavy) cream (especially Jersey and Devonshire, Cornish clotted cream and some whipping creams). Dairy cream and non-dairy cream is also available frozen at freezer centres and supermarkets. Always check that the cream is very fresh before freezing.

For best results, cream should be chilled, then whipped lightly before freezing. The addition of a little sugar (1 × 15 ml spoon/1 tablespoon for each 600 ml/1 pint/2½ cups) will help the keeping quality of whipped cream, although this will limit its uses.
TO FREEZE: pack in waxed cartons or rigid containers, leaving headspace. Cover, label and freeze.
TO THAW: leave cream in its container in the refrigerator and thaw for 8 hours per 150 ml/¼ pint/⅔ cup. Whip again before use.
To freeze whipped cream as piped rosettes: whip chilled cream with sugar as above, then pipe onto non-stick silicone paper or aluminium foil placed on a tray. Open (flash) freeze until solid, then remove rosettes carefully and pack in rigid containers, dividing layers with greaseproof (waxed) paper. Cover, label and return to freezer.
TO THAW: place frozen rosettes on desserts, gâteaux, soufflés, trifles, etc. They will take approximately 10 to 15 minutes to thaw at room temperature.
STORAGE TIME: 3 months.

Cream Puff

see **Profiterole**

Crêpe

see **Pancake**

Cress

see **Watercress**

Croissant

Freshly baked croissants, either homemade or baked commercially, freeze very well.
TO FREEZE: leave until completely cold, then pack in a single layer in aluminium foil, rigid containers, or freezer bags. Seal, label and freeze.
TO THAW: leave in wrappings for approximately 2 hours at room temperature, then reheat on a baking sheet, wrapped in aluminium foil, in a hot oven (225°C/425°F or Gas Mark 7) for 5 minutes.

To serve straight from the freezer at breakfast time, croissants can be reheated from frozen instead of allowing to thaw at room temperature: put frozen croissants, wrapped in aluminium foil, on a baking sheet in a moderate oven (180°C/350°F or Gas Mark 4), and bake for 15 minutes. Remove foil and serve warm with butter and preserves.
STORAGE TIME: 3 months.

Croquette

Chicken, fish or potato croquettes, bound with a thick béchamel sauce, can be frozen after they are coated in egg and breadcrumbs and deep fried until golden brown. For freezing, thawing and storage of commercially prepared croquettes, follow package directions.

1

To freeze homemade croquettes:
cook thoroughly, drain and leave until completely cold. Open (flash) freeze until solid, then pack in freezer bags or rigid containers, seal or cover, label and freeze.

TO THAW: leave in wrappings overnight in the refrigerator for chicken or fish croquettes, for 2 hours at room temperature for potato croquettes. (Thawing times will vary according to filling.) Reheat croquettes in a fairly hot oven (190°C/375°F or Gas Mark 5) for 20 minutes or more depending on the filling — croquettes should be hot in the centre when pierced with a skewer. Or thaw the croquettes and deep fry in hot oil for approximately 10 minutes, turning occasionally. This method, however, may cause the breadcrumbs to become too brown. Serve immediately.

STORAGE TIME: 1 months (chicken and fish croquettes); 3 months (potato croquettes).

Cross-flavouring

Cross-flavouring can be a problem in the freezer, particularly if many highly spiced or strong-smelling foods are stored. The best precaution is to overwrap all foods in special heavy-duty freezer bags, sealed securely. Cross-flavouring can spoil delicate items in the freezer in a very short time; insufficiently wrapped food containing strong cheese, smoked fish, garlic and onions, for example, will quickly transfer their flavours to breads or cakes nearby.

Croûte/Croûton

Croûtes or croûtons made from fried (rather than toasted) bread will keep well in the freezer.

TO FREEZE: cut day-old bread, crusts removed, into required shapes approximately 1.25 cm/½ inch thick and deep fry in hot oil until crisp and golden brown. Drain on kitchen paper towels, leave to cool, then pack

1

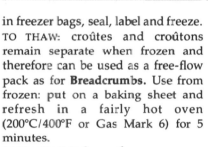

2

2

3

4

in freezer bags, seal, label and freeze.
TO THAW: croûtes and croûtons remain separate when frozen and therefore can be used as a free-flow pack as for **Breadcrumbs.** Use from frozen: put on a baking sheet and refresh in a fairly hot oven (200°C/400°F or Gas Mark 6) for 5 minutes.
STORAGE TIME: 3 months.

Crumble

Fruit crumble (a mixture of flour, butter and sugar baked on a fruit base) freezes very well and you can make several crumbles at a time,

eating one and freezing the remainder. They can be frozen baked or unbaked, and an ideal container would be a foil pudding basin.
TO FREEZE: make up the fruit and crumble topping in the usual way, bake if you like, cover, label and freeze.
TO THAW: bake from frozen, uncovered, in a moderate oven (180°C/350°F or Gas Mark 4) for approximately 30 minutes if previously baked, 45 minutes if unbaked, or until the crumble is heated through.

An alternative method of freezing crumble is to make up the crumble topping and pack this separately in a freezer bag. The crumble can then be used straight from the freezer to top any fresh or frozen fruit mixture.
STORAGE TIME: 2 months.

Crumpet (English Muffin)

TO FREEZE: wrap crumpets, whether homemade or baked commercially, in a single layer in aluminium foil or a freezer bag, seal, label and freeze.
TO THAW: leave in wrappings for approximately 20 minutes at room temperature, then toast on both sides as for fresh crumpets. Serve immediately with butter.
STORAGE TIME: 6 months.

Crab – Crumpet (English Muffin)

Croquette
1 *Preparing croquettes.*
2 *Coating croquettes in egg and breadcrumbs.*
3 *Deep frying croquettes and draining on kitchen paper towels.*
4 *Packing open-frozen croquettes in a freezer bag.*

Cream
1 *Piping rosettes of whipped, sweetened cream onto a baking sheet lined with non-stick silicone paper.*
2 *Transferring open-frozen rosettes to a rigid container.*
3 *Using frozen rosettes to decorate Iced Raspberry Soufflé (see page 189).*

45

Cucumber

Cucumber has too high a water content to be frozen satisfactorily as a salad vegetable; however, it can be frozen raw as a purée for use in hot sauces and iced soups, etc.

TO FREEZE: peel, then chop and purée in an electric blender or work in a Mouli-légumes (foodmill). Pack in rigid containers, cover, label and freeze.

TO THAW: leave in containers at room temperature until thawed before using in cooked dishes as above. See also recipes for *Lebanese Cucumber Soup* and *Baked Cucumber*.

STORAGE TIME: 2 months.

Cucumber should be puréed before freezing for future use in soups and sauces.

Currant (Black/Red/White)

see also **Fruit** for information on packing

TO FREEZE: remove fruit from stems with a wide-pronged fork, wash and dry gently but thoroughly. Discard any unripe or damaged currants. Open (flash) freeze; pack dry with or without sugar; or pack in heavy syrup. Blackcurrants can be crushed and packed dry with sugar, or cooked to a purée with a little water, and brown sugar to taste. Pack in rigid containers, cover, label and freeze.

TO THAW: leave in wrappings for approximately 45 minutes at room temperature.

STORAGE TIME: 12 months.

Curry

Curries successfully freeze.

TO FREEZE: cook in the usual way, cool rapidly, then pack in a foil container. Cover, then overwrap in a freezer bag, seal, label and freeze.

TO THAW: reheat as for **Casserole**.

Curry sauce: useful if kept in the freezer in freezer bags or foil containers. Reheated from frozen in a saucepan it can be added to cooked meat, poultry or vegetables to make a very quick curry.

See also recipes for *Indian Cauliflower* and *Rogan Gosht*.

STORAGE TIME: 2 months.

Custard

Due to its high milk content, cooked custard does not freeze satisfactorily; it tends to separate on thawing. Sometimes it is possible to reconstitute custard by beating briskly while reheating, but this does not always work. Custard used in such dishes as fruit fools can be frozen and stored for a few weeks, but after this time separation may occur.

Uncooked egg custard: crème caramel and custard tart will freeze perfectly well unbaked.

TO FREEZE: heat the milk and pour onto the eggs, sugar and flavourings, stirring well to combine. Strain into mould or pastry case, according to recipe used. Cool rapidly, open (flash) freeze until solid, then wrap in a double thickness of aluminium foil, label and return to freezer.

TO THAW: unwrap and cook from frozen, allow extra baking time for the custard to set.

Custard Marrow (Scallop Squash)*

This is perhaps the most tasty member of the squash family, and the best for freezing.

TO FREEZE: trim small custard marrows and leave whole. Blanch for 1 minute in boiling water, drain, then cool rapidly in iced water. Drain, pat dry and pack in freezer bags, seal, label and freeze. Or trim medium-sized custard marrows but do not peel. Cut into quarters or slices, blanch in boiling water for 2 minutes, then drain, cool, dry and pack in bags.

TO THAW: leave whole custard marrows in wrappings for approximately 1½ hours at room temperature. Unwrap and cook quartered or sliced ones from frozen as for fresh custard marrow, allowing a little extra cooking time until heated through.

STORAGE TIME: 12 months.

*Not available in Australia.

Cutlet

see **Lamb**

Dab

A small flatfish similar to plaice. Prepare, freeze and thaw as for **Plaice**.

Dairy Produce

see individual names (**Butter, Buttermilk, Cheese, Cream, Ice(s)/Icecream, Milk, Yogurt**)

Damson

see also **Fruit** for information on packing

Freeze fully ripe, but unsplit fruit.

TO FREEZE: wash, cut in half and remove stones (pits). Pack dry; in medium syrup; or as a sweetened purée. Pack in rigid containers, cover, label and freeze.

TO THAW: leave in containers for 2 hours at room temperature. Use in fresh fruit salads, or as a sharp contrast to bland-flavoured fools, mousses, pies and puddings.

STORAGE TIME: 12 months.

Danish Open Sandwich

see **Sandwich**

Danish Pastries

see **Almond Paste**

Date

see also **Fruit** for information on packing

There is little point in freezing packaged dates, as they have invariably gone through a preserving process and will keep perfectly well outside a freezer. If you are able to get fresh dates from the palms, then it is certainly worth freezing some.

TO FREEZE: pack whole dates in freezer bags, seal, label and freeze. Or halve dates and remove stones (pits), then pack in light syrup.

TO THAW: leave in wrappings at room temperature until thawed completely. Serve with whipped cream, or use in cakes and stuffings.

STORAGE TIME: 12 months.

Dating

The date of freezing should appear on the label of every package so that the food can be eaten within its recommended storage time, and to enable correct rotation of a freezer's contents. It is essential, therefore, to write the date of freezing clearly on the label of the package before putting into the freezer. As a double check, dates can also be entered in a freezer diary.

In the interest of consumer satisfaction, manufacturers of commercially frozen foods generally show a 'sell by' or 'eat by' date on packs, so that their products are bought and eaten while still at their peak. Such dates do not mean that when the specified period has expired that frozen food product is unsafe, but there can be some loss in flavour, colour and texture.

Decanting

This refers to the redistribution of the contents of a single large pack to several smaller and more convenient packs, which are then less wasteful of freezer space. It particularly applies to bulk-buy packs of fruit and vegetables which are better decanted into separate meal servings. See also *Brick Freezing*.

Deer

see **Game,** *Reindeer, Venison*

Defrosting

see page 230

Dehydration

The loss of moisture and juices from frozen food during storage is called dehydration and it can lead to **Freezer Burn.** Dehydration (also called desiccation) is causd by faulty or inadequate packaging so that food is exposed to air. Meat and poultry are particularly susceptible to dehydration.

Desiccation

see **Dehydration**

Desserts

see under individual names (**Baba (Savarin), Blancmange, Cheesecake, Chocolate, Cream, Custard, Ice(s)/Icecream, Meringue, Mousse, Profiterole, Sorbet, Soufflé**)

Dill *(Peucedanum graveolens)*

This herb closely resembles fennel in appearance, and is a native of the Mediterranean and Black Sea areas. The seeds have a more pungent flavour than the delicate feathery

leaves, and both are used in cooking for their refreshing flavour, which is not unlike caraway.

To freeze leaves: pick fresh young leaves and discard any tough stems. Chop finely and freeze in ice cube trays until solid, then pack in freezer bags, seal, label and return to freezer. Or put freshly picked bunches of leaves into small bags.

To freeze dill seeds: harvest seeds when flower heads are starting to turn brown, but before they are ripe enough to scatter themselves on the ground. Cut down the flower stems, tie in bunches and hang upside-down over a cloth in a sunny place. When quite dry, shake out seeds onto a cloth and pack in freezer bags. Seal, label and freeze.

TO THAW: both leaves and seeds lose their flavour in cooking and should therefore be used while still frozen. Add frozen cubes or crumbled frozen leaves to hot dishes just before serving. Seeds will not freeze together in the pack: shake out as many seeds as required, then re-seal bag and return to freezer. Use in cheese and egg dishes, soups and vegetables, or sprinkle over cabbage, potatoes, salads and sauerkraut. Frozen dill can also be used when pickling cucumber.

STORAGE TIME: 10 months.

Dip(s)

Dips (or dunks as they are sometimes called) can be made well in advance of buffet and cocktail parties and stored in the freezer.

Dips that freeze successfully are made with a base of cream cheese and whipped double (heavy) cream — and should be beaten well after thawing. Add seasonings and sauces according to individual recipes, although it is wise not to use highly spiced recipes for freezing. Diced raw vegetables, particularly salad vegetables such as celery, cucumber, green and red peppers, and tomato, are best added to the dip base after thawing. Do not use mayonnaise and hard-boiled eggs. Classic dips that are most successful are guacamole (avocados, lemon juice, Tabasco sauce), taramasalata* (smoked cod's roe, oil, lemon juice), houmos (chick peas, sesame seed paste, lemon juice), and ceviche (mackerel, lemon juice, onion, green pepper, chili).

TO FREEZE: pack prepared dips in waxed cartons or rigid containers, leaving headspace. Cover, overwrap in a freezer bag, seal, label and freeze.

TO THAW: leave in container overnight in the refrigerator.

*See also recipe for *Taramasalata*.

STORAGE TIME: 1 month.

Guacamole, houmos, ceviche and taramasalata can be frozen in advance to be served as dips at a party.

Cucumber – Dip(s)

Discoloration
see also **Fruit**

Exposure to air causes certain fruits with a low Vitamin C content, such as apples, peaches and pears, to discolour and darken. This is most likely to occur during the preparation and packaging of fruit sections and purées for the freezer. The addition of sugar helps to prevent discoloration, but it can be further counteracted by the addition of an anti-oxidant such as ascorbic acid, citric acid or lemon juice. Quantities to use are 750 mg/¼ teaspoon ascorbic acid dissolved in a little cold water, per 600 ml/1 pint/2½ cup syrup pack; juice of 1 medium-sized lemon to 900 ml/1½ pints/1 U.S. quart water; or 1 × 5 ml spoon/1 teaspoon citric acid to ½ kg/1 lb dry sugar pack. Thaw such packs of fruit in wrappings in the refrigerator and eat as soon as possible after thawing to prevent discoloration taking place.

Dolmades
see **Vine Leaves**

Dough
see **Bread** and **Pastry & Pastry-based Dishes**

Doughnut

Both homemade and commercially baked doughnuts freeze well, although jam-filled doughnuts can become soggy on thawing. Homemade doughnuts should not be tossed in sugar before freezing.

TO FREEZE: wrap in a single layer in aluminium foil or a freezer bag, seal, label and freeze.

TO THAW: unwrap, place on a baking sheet and bake from frozen in a fairly hot oven (200°C/400°F or Gas Mark 6) for 6 to 8 minutes or until heated through.

Toss both homemade and bought doughnuts in plenty of (caster) sugar and serve at once.

See also recipe for *Doughnuts*.

STORAGE TIME: 1 month.

Dove
see **Game**

Dover Sole
see **Sole**

Drink(s)

As the majority of drinks keep perfectly well for months, even years, in bottles and cans, etc., there is absolutely no point in freezing them, and to do so would more often than not spoil the drink. On no account should carbonated drinks — in bottles or cans — be placed in the freezer, as this will cause the container to burst in the freezer. Wines should *not* be placed in the freezer for 'quick' chilling. Fruit juices for making soft drinks can be frozen, however. See **Juice.**

Dripping(s)

Do not freeze dripping(s) — beef or pork — as they will quickly become rancid. They are far better stored in the refrigerator where they will keep for several weeks. When cooking dishes for the freezer, clarified drippings should always be used, otherwise the entire dish may taste rancid after a while.

Drug Store Pack or Fold

This method of wrapping food for the freezer can be done with any suitable sheet wrapping and is used for foods with irregular shapes. To make a drug store fold, place the food (chicken, large cuts of meat, etc.) in the centre of the sheet of paper. Bring two sides of the paper over the food and fold them together over and over until the wrapping is as tight as you can make it. Fold the ends first into points, then under the package to avoid any air pockets and make the wrapping fit closely. Seal with freezer tape only to hold ends securely in place.

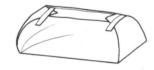

Dry Pack
see **Fruit**

Duck/Duckling
see **Poultry**

Dumpling(s)

Dumplings made from suet, flour and water freeze perfectly well in casseroles and stews. Make and cook in the usual way, adding to the casserole for the last 20 minutes or so of the cooking time.

TO FREEZE: turn the casserole into a rigid container, arranging the dumplings on the top. Cool rapidly, then cover, label and freeze.

TO THAW: reheat from frozen, covered, in a moderate oven (180°C/350°F or Gas Mark 4) for approximately 1 hour or until heated through and bubbling.

STORAGE TIME: 1 month.

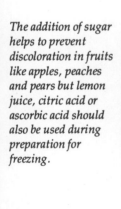

The addition of sugar helps to prevent discoloration in fruits like apples, peaches and pears but lemon juice, citric acid or ascorbic acid should also be used during preparation for freezing.

E

Éclair

Éclairs, made from choux pastry, freeze extremely well; they can be frozen either unbaked or baked.

To freeze unbaked éclairs: make the pastry in the usual way and pipe onto teflon coated baking sheets or trays lined with non-stick silicone paper. Open (flash) freeze until solid, then remove carefully from silicone paper and wrap in freezer bags, rigid containers or aluminium foil. Seal, label and return to freezer.

TO THAW: unwrap and bake from frozen on greased baking sheets in a fairly hot oven (200°C/400°F or Gas Mark 6) for approximately 25 to 30 minutes or until golden brown. Remove from oven, make slits in the sides for steam to escape and leave to cool on a wire rack. When completely cold, fill with whipped cream and dip the tops of éclairs in melted chocolate. Leave to set before serving.

To freeze baked éclairs: make and bake the éclairs in the usual way, make slits in their sides, then leave on a wire rack until completely cold. Open (flash) freeze on trays lined with aluminium foil until solid, remove carefully and pack in freezer bags, rigid containers or aluminium foil. Seal, label and return to freezer.

TO THAW: unwrap frozen éclairs and put on baking sheets. Bake in a moderate oven (180°C/350°F or Gas Mark 4) for 10 minutes, then transfer to a wire rack to cool. Fill and ice as for unbaked éclairs above. Or thaw the éclairs in their wrappings for 1 hour at room temperature, unwrap and 'refresh' in a moderate oven for 5 minutes. Cool, fill and ice as above. STORAGE TIME: 3 months.

Eel

Both conger and freshwater eels can be frozen. Conger eels are a seafish, with a flavour similar to scallops.

TO FREEZE: skin, clean and remove head. Cut into 7.5 cm/3 inch lengths, wash well, then leave to soak in lightly salted water. Drain, pat dry

and pack in freezer bags. Seal, label and freeze. Elvers (tiny young eels) only need thorough washing before packing in ½ kg/1 lb bags for freezing.

TO THAW: unwrap and cook from frozen. Eels can be baked or poached or used in pies and soups. Or coat elvers in flour and deep fry from frozen in hot oil or fat as for whitebait. STORAGE TIME: 3 months.

Egg(s)

Owning a freezer gives you the opportunity to buy eggs in large quantities when prices are low at certain times of year. It is also useful to be able to freeze leftover whites when making mayonnaise, or yolks when making meringues, for example. Eggs freeze satisfactorily, either raw or cooked, in numerous different dishes such as bread, cakes, custard, icecream, mousses, pastry, quiches, soufflés, etc., providing they are really fresh at the time of freezing. They cannot be frozen in their shells, however, which expand and burst at such a low temperature. Hard-boiled eggs should not be frozen as the whites become leathery. There are several ways to freeze raw eggs:

To freeze whole eggs: whisk yolks and whites lightly together, but do not allow to become frothy. Stir in 1 × 2.5 ml spoon/½ teaspoon salt for every 3 eggs if for use in savoury dishes, 1 × 5 ml spoon/1 teaspoon (caster) sugar for every 3 eggs if for sweet dishes. Pour into waxed cartons or rigid containers, cover, label and freeze. Remember to state clearly on the label the quantity of eggs frozen and whether salt or sugar has been added.

Approximate quantity: 1 whole egg = 55 ml/2 fl oz/¼ cup.

To freeze egg yolks: mix 3 egg yolks with 1 × 1.25 ml spoon/¼ teaspoon salt or 1 × 2.5 ml spoon/½ teaspoon (caster) sugar. Egg yolks may be frozen together in quantities suitable for making up dishes at a later date, in which case, pour into containers, label and freeze as for whole eggs above. Or freeze egg yolks individually: pour into ice cube trays or individual sections of plastic egg cartons, open (flash) freeze until solid, then pack in freezer bags, seal, label and return to freezer. State clearly on the label whether salt or sugar has been added.

To freeze egg whites: these can be frozen without whisking or additives. Pour into waxed cartons or rigid containers, cover and label — stating the quantity of whites frozen — and freeze until required. Or freeze egg

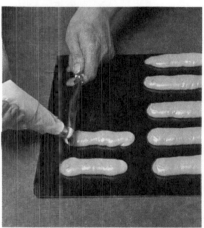

Éclair
1 Preparing choux pastry.
2 Piping the pastry onto baking sheets.
3 Packing open-frozen, unbaked éclairs into rigid containers for freezing.
4 Filling and icing the baked éclairs.

whites individually, without additives, as for freezing egg yolks above. Approximate quantity: 1 egg white = 40 ml/approximately 1½ fl oz/3 tablespoons.

To thaw whole eggs, egg yolks and egg whites: transfer from containers to a bowl and thaw for at least 1 hour at room temperature: the length of thawing time will depend on the number of eggs to be thawed. Use as soon as possible after thawing.
STORAGE TIME: 6 months.

Egg yolks and whites can be frozen together or separately.

Eggplant
see **Aubergine**

Elderberry
see **Berry**

Elk
Elk, the largest of the round-horned deer, has a flavour similar to beef. Prepare, freeze and thaw as for **Game**, *Venison*, but take care that the elk is skinned as soon as possible, so this large animal can cool quickly.

Emergency
see page 231

Endive (Curly Endive/ Aust. & U.S. Chicory)
Available in autumn and winter only, endive cannot be frozen successfully as a salad vegetable because it loses its crisp texture. The small-leaved varieties are not suitable for freezing at all, but Batavian broad-leaved and

Excess fat should be removed from all dishes before freezing, either by skimming or draining.

other large-leaved varieties are excellent frozen for use as a cooked vegetable.
TO FREEZE: discard any greenish leaves, cut endive into halves or quarters lengthways and wash thoroughly. Blanch in boiling water for 1 minute and drain. Cool rapidly in iced water, then drain and pat dry. Pack in freezer bags, seal, label and freeze.
TO THAW: unwrap and put frozen endive in boiling salted water, bring back to the boil, cover and simmer for 2 minutes or until tender. Drain and serve hot tossed in butter, French dressing, or a white sauce with freshly chopped herbs.
STORAGE TIME: 6 months.

Enzyme
Enzymes are a kind of natural protein present in all food and they affect the rate at which food deteriorates and eventually spoils. They are not poisonous, but if food ages to the point where it is rotten, then it becomes unsafe to eat. Enzyme action will cause discoloration, 'off' flavours, loss of nutritive value and eventually cause food to go bad. Whereas extreme heat can stop enzymes from working completely (see **Blanching**), freezing merely puts them into a state of suspended animation. On thawing, the enzymes resume their work rapidly, which is why it is necessary to cook or eat frozen foods immediately, and not to leave them sitting around in warm temperatures for long periods.

Equipment
see page 236

Escalope
see **Veal**

Escargot
see **Snail**

Escarole
prepare, freeze and thaw as for **Endive/Aust. & U.S. Chicory**

Evaporator
Together with the compressor and the condenser, the evaporator is one of the three main components of a freezer. Like the condenser, it is a system of tubes whose function is to absorb heat from food being frozen. During the operating cycle of a freezer, liquid refrigerant from the condenser is converted into a gas in the evaporator: heat is then absorbed from the food storage cabinet and, therefore, from the food itself.

Fancy Meat
see **Meat, Fresh**

Fast Freeze
see page 229

Fat, Animal
Animal fats can be something of a problem in a freezer, as they do not keep well. After a short while they begin to turn rancid and, if in contact with other foods, will turn these rancid as well. When cooking dishes for the freezer, use the minimum amount of fat possible and skim well after cooling, to remove excess fat. Kitchen paper towels can also be used for skimming fat off casseroles, etc., and for draining fatty foods which are to be frozen. Try not to use dripping(s) unless clarified, when frying food for freezing. Remove as much fat as possible from meat and poultry before cooking and avoid dishes that contain a lot of bacon as this does not keep well in the freezer. Due to its high fat content, pork will not keep as long in the freezer as other meats. See **Pork** for storage times.

Fava

see **Bean**, *Broad*

Fennel *(Foeniculum vulgare)*

A native of the Mediterranean, fennel grows in most temperate countries, usually in coastal areas. The plant grows to a height of 150–240 cm/5–8 feet, and the seeds have a robust aniseed scent, although it is the leaves and stems that are more generally used in cooking.

To freeze leaves and stems: pick when young. Chop or finely cut with scissors and freeze in ice cube trays until solid, then pack in freezer bags, seal, label and return to freezer. Or put bunches of leaves into bags.

TO THAW: add frozen cubes to sauces and soups just before serving. Crumble leaves while still frozen, or use whole immediately after taking from freezer. Use in stuffings for fish, particularly oily varieties, or to flavour liver, pork, poultry and veal. Or sprinkle onto salads, or freshly cooked beans, cauliflower, peas and potatoes just before serving.

To freeze fennel seeds: cut off the flower stems when they start to die and turn brown, before the ripe seeds fall. Hang over a cloth in a warm place until the seeds can be shaken out, then put into small freezer bags or waxed cartons, seal or cover, label and freeze.

TO THAW: unwrap and pound in a mortar and pestle while still frozen, then add to apple pies, biscuits (cookies) and bread, or sprinkle over baked or poached fish.

STORAGE TIME: 6 months (leaves and stems); 10 months (seeds).

Fennel Root (Finocchio)

Fennel root is not suitable as a salad vegetable after freezing because it loses its crispness, but it can be cooked.

TO FREEZE: scrub the root and cut into quarters. Blanch in boiling water for 3–5 minutes. Drain, cool rapidly in iced water, then drain and pat dry. Pack in freezer bags, seal, label and freeze.

TO THAW: unwrap and boil or sauté from frozen.

STORAGE TIME: 6 months.

Feta Cheese

see recipe for *Greek Spinach Puffs*

Fettucine

see **Pasta**

Fig

see also **Fruit** for information on packing

Freeze only freshly picked, ripe fruit.

TO FREEZE: wipe if necessary (do not wash). Snip stems off carefully and do not peel. Open (flash) freeze; pack dry without sugar; or pack in light syrup.

TO THAW: leave in wrappings for approximately 1½ hours at room temperature. Serve raw or gently cooked in syrup.

STORAGE TIME: 12 months.

Finnan Haddie

This is a smoked haddock from Finnan, near Aberdeen, Scotland.

TO FREEZE: wrap each fish individually in cling film, then pack several fish together in a freezer bag. Seal, label and freeze.

TO THAW: unwrap and poach from frozen. Or thaw in wrappings for 2 hours in the refrigerator, remove skin, rub with butter and grill (broil). Serve hot with more butter.

STORAGE TIME: 3 months.

Fish

see individual names

Flan

see **Pastry & Pastry-based Dishes**

Flapjack

see **Biscuit**

Flash Freezing

see **Open Freezing**

Flathead

A round, white fish found around the whole coast of Australia.

TO FREEZE: clean and fillet, then pack in freezer bags, interleaving each fillet with cling film. Seal, label and freeze.

TO THAW: cook from frozen.

STORAGE TIME: 3 months.

Flavour

In general, the freezer does not alter the flavour of food, providing the recommended storage times are followed. It is not advisable, however, to freeze highly spiced foods or those which contain many herbs, as the flavour of herbs and spices often becomes more pungent in the freezer. For this reason, always decrease the amount of herbs and spices given in ordinary recipes — extra may be added on reheating if the dish then seems too bland. Try to use fresh herbs wherever possible, as there is less likelihood of these becoming strong or musty.

Synthetic flavourings for cakes, etc., such as almond, rum and vanilla, should be avoided, because they can develop very strong flavours in the freezer; ideally, use ground almonds, real alcohol if possible and vanilla pods or sugar.

To ensure that the flavour of one food in the freezer does not contaminate another, always use overwrapping. See **Cross Flavouring.**

Flounder

A flat sea fish which is best frozen as fillets. Prepare, freeze and thaw as for **Plaice.**

Foil

see page 232

Fondant

see **Icing**

Forcemeat

see **Stuffing.**

Frankfurter

TO FREEZE: pack in freezer bags, seal, label and freeze. Commercial vacuum packs of frankfurters can be put straight into the freezer.

TO THAW: leave in wrappings overnight in the refrigerator, then cook as for freshly bought frankfurters and serve with a salad or sauerkraut.

STORAGE TIME: 3 months.

Free Flow Pack (Flash Freezing)

This is the term used to describe a pack (usually of fruit or vegetables) that has been open (flash) frozen and is therefore 'free flowing'. See **Open (Flash) Freezing.**

For foods to be stored in the freezer, fresh herbs should be used in preference to dried, and vanilla pods, ground almonds and liquers rather than artificial essences.

51

Freezer (Capacity, Types of, etc.)
see page 228

Freezer Bag
see page 234

Freezer Burn

This term describes the greyish-white patches found on the surface of food, particularly on meat and poultry, caused by dehydration during storage. The patches are not harmful and can be cut off when the food is thawed. Freezer burn is prevented by careful wrapping so that all air is excluded.

A piece of meat affected by freezer burn

Freezer Tissue
see page 234

Freezer Wrap
see page 233

French (Green) Bean
see **Bean**

Fried Food

For best results when freezing fried food, always drain well on kitchen paper towels, then open (flash) freeze on trays before wrapping for the freezer.

TO THAW: reheat in the oven with or without thawing, although the finished dish may not be quite as crisp as it was before freezing.

See also **Batter, Doughnuts** and **Fritters.**

STORAGE TIME: 1 month.

Fritters

Fritters can be frozen, although the success of freezing them depends on how well they have been drained before freezing. Make your favourite recipe and coat in fritter batter.

TO FREEZE: deep fry in very hot oil until crisp and golden brown, then remove from the oil with a slotted spoon and drain well on kitchen paper towels. Open (flash) freeze on trays, then pack in freezer bags, seal, label and return to freezer.

Fruit
1 Open (flash) freezing (free flow pack)
2 Dry sugar pack
3 Syrup pack

TO THAW: unwrap and bake from frozen on baking sheets in a hot oven (220°C/425°F or Gas Mark 7) for 10 to 15 minutes, depending on the fritter filling. Serve immediately.

Commercially frozen fritters are now widely available: store in the freezer and reheat according to package directions.

Frosting
see **Icing**

Fruit

see also under individual names
There are three basic methods of freezing fruit:
1 open (flash) freezing or free-flow pack;
2 in dry sugar (dry sugar pack);
3 in cold syrup (syrup pack).

Open (Flash) Freezing (Free Flow Pack)

Use for soft fruit — berries, cherries and currants — which you want to serve whole and uncooked, either in salads or as a decoration. Put very dry fruit with a low water content directly into freezer bags or rigid containers. Remove air and leave 1.25 cm/½ inch headspace. Seal or cover, label and freeze.

Put more juicy fruit (blackberries, raspberries, strawberries) on open trays and freeze until solid, then remove from freezer and transfer to freezer bags. Seal, label and return to freezer.

The great advantage of this method is that the fruits keep their shape and character and that a handful or more can be taken from the bag or container while still frozen. Do not use this method for fruit which discolours quickly while being prepared for the freezer (see *Syrup Pack* below).

Dry Sugar Pack

This is the most suitable method for freezing soft, juicy fruit and the purpose of this method is to draw out the oxygen from the fruit cells. Pricking the fruit helps the process and improves the result. The quantity of sugar necessary varies with the sharpness of the particular fruit, but is usually 100–175 g/4–6 oz/½–¾ cup sugar to ½ kg/1 lb fruit, unless otherwise stated. It is important to coat the fruit thoroughly in sugar: either roll the fruit gently in the sugar, turn the fruit and sugar over gently in a bowl, or put the fruit directly into a rigid container with layers of sugar between. Leave 2 cm/¾ inch headspace. Cover, label and freeze. Use just before fruit has completely thawed.

Syrup Pack

This is the best method for freezing hard, non-juicy fruit which discolours quickly while being prepared. Because juice does not flow from these fruits readily, the syrup should be as concentrated as possible, then it will not detract from the flavour of the fruit. The amount of sugar needed for the syrup will depend on the type of fruit to be frozen, and your own personal taste in sugar (see *Syrup Strength* below).

If you are going to freeze a quantity of fruit by this method, make plenty of syrup in advance, preferably the day before. As a general guide, you will need 300 ml/½ pint/1¼ cups to ½ kg/1 lb fruit. Dissolve the sugar slowly in the water, then bring to the boil, stirring to prevent sugar sticking. Remove from the heat, strain if necessary, cover and leave to cool. Chill in the refrigerator overnight or until required. (It is better to have too much syrup rather than too little as the fruit may discolour if you have to

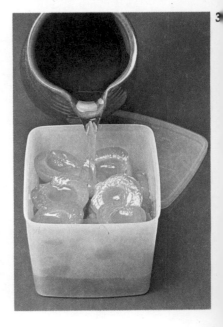

mix and cool more.) Put prepared fruit in rigid containers, pour over the chilled syrup to cover completely, leaving 2 cm/¾ inch headspace. To prevent fruit bobbing above surface, put crumpled greaseproof (waxed) paper on top, cover, label and freeze. To prevent fruits such as apples, peaches and pears discolouring as soon as they are peeled, slice the fruit directly into the container which has already been partly filled with syrup. Push new slices under the syrup as they are added so they will be coated. With large quantities, peel, slice or dice the fruit into a solution of 900 ml/1½ pints/3¾ cups water to the juice of 1 lemon. Transfer fruit quickly to containers with a slotted spoon and cover with the prepared syrup.

Syrup

Coarse, white sugar gives the best general results. Honey can be used but it will penetrate the flavour of the fruit, and brown sugar will colour it.

Syrup Strength

2 cups sugar to 4 cups water makes a 30 per cent light syrup.
3 cups sugar to 4 cups water makes a 40 per cent medium syrup.
4 cups sugar to 4 cups water makes a 50 per cent heavy syrup.

For most palates a 40 per cent syrup is the most suitable, but a weaker one should be used for the more delicately flavoured fruits, or you will taste more sugar than fruit. A heavy syrup makes the fruit flabby, but the sweetness is a matter of taste and depends on the ultimate use of the fruit.

TO THAW: defrost in unopened container.

Serve soft fruits while still slightly chilled, to retain their shape and texture when to be used whole. Fruit purées take twice as long to defrost as whole fruit.

Fruits which are to be used in sponge cakes, shortbread, etc., must be only partly defrosted or the sponge, shortbread, etc., will become soggy. Serve immediately.

Galantine

Galantines, usually made from boned chicken, turkey or veal, are spread with a stuffing and rolled, sewn and baked, or simmered in stock. Take care that the stuffing does not contain too many herbs or spices. Freeze whole or sliced.

To freeze whole: bake or simmer according to recipe used, then leave until completely cold. Wrap in aluminium foil, then overwrap in a freezer bag, seal, label and freeze.

TO THAW: leave in wrappings for 24 to 48 hours in the refrigerator (depending on size).

To freeze sliced galantine: cook and leave until completely cold, then slice. Wrap individual slices in aluminium foil — if you like, the galantine can be reshaped again —

A chicken galantine during preparation and after cooking. Freeze whole or in slices.

and pack in a freezer bag. Seal, label and freeze.

TO THAW: leave in wrappings for 4 to 5 hours in the refrigerator. By this method of freezing it is possible to take out as few or as many slices as are needed at any one time — for packed lunches, picnics, or impromptu supper meals, etc.; and slices thaw more quickly than a whole galantine.

STORAGE TIME: 6 months.

2

Game

Freezing has greatly increased the popularity of most types of game, as they are now available throughout the year rather than on a seasonal basis. However, the respective 'close seasons' restrict availability quite considerably, and advance planning is essential if a constant supply is required in the freezer.

August to March is the major British game season.

When choosing game for freezing, select young, plump animals and birds, and avoid those which have been badly shot. Birds should have .soft, limp feet; if they are hard and scaly it is an indication that the bird is old. The breastbone will be soft and pliable if it is a young bird.

The hanging of game requires a little expertise because the time may vary according to the type of game, weather, individual taste and age of the game. Hang game birds undrawn by the neck. A good test of a well-hung bird is the ease with which the feathers can be extracted, and a greenish tinge should begin to develop on the thin abdomen skin. Pluck only when ready for freezing. After plucking, draw and truss the birds ready for the freezer. Some game birds such as snipe and woodcock are occasionally served undrawn, but as a general rule it is advisable to draw birds which are to be stored in the freezer.

N.B. Prepare and freeze water birds as soon as possible to prevent a fishy flavour developing in the intestine.

Packaging

As with poultry, the correct packaging of game for freezing is essential if the flavour is to be retained and freezer burn prevented. Game often has a strong smell; therefore, take extra care to avoid contaminating other products in the freezer. Cover any extremities of a game bird with a double layer of aluminium foil or cling film. Closely wrap the whole bird in foil, then overwrap in a freezer bag. Seal, label and freeze. If the bird smells very 'high', use several bags and seal each one very tightly, labelling the outermost one.

Joints of game should be wrapped individually and packed as for whole birds.

Pack and freeze giblets and offal (variety meats/fancy meats) separately. See **Poultry.**

Thawing and Cooking

All game must be thawed thoroughly before cooking. See individual game below and **Poultry** thawing instructions.

Cook game immediately after thawing, because the maturing process will recommence once the game reaches room temperature. If left for longer than 24 hours after thawing, the game could become too 'high' for average tastes.

If you like, you can marinate game before cooking; this will ensure a moist result and also lessen the 'game-like' flavour. Prepare the marinade, put the unwrapped frozen game into it, then cover and leave to thaw in the refrigerator. Baste or turn the meat frequently.

The recommended storage time for most game birds is 6 months. After this time, game will begin to 'age' and become stronger in flavour as it would if it were hung. The longer the game is left in the freezer, the more it will 'age'. How long you leave game in your freezer is really a matter of personal taste, but in general it is best not to leave it for longer than 12 months.

Availability of British game throughout the year*

	Aug	Sept	Oct	Nov	Dec	Jan	Feb	Mar	Apr	May	June	July
Capercail		████████████████										
Grouse		████████████████										
Hare			██████████████████████									
Leveret						█████████████						
Partridge		███████████████████										
Pheasant			████████████									
Pigeon	████████████████████████████											
Plover			███████████									
Ptarmigan	██████████████											
Quail	███████████████											
Rabbit			████████████████████████									
Snipe	████████████████											
Squab										████████		
Venison (buck)	███████											█████
Venison (doe)			█████████									
Wigeon				███████████								
Wild Duck		██████████████████████████████										
Woodcock	███████████████████											

*Not applicable in Australia and U.S.A.

Bear (U.S.)

All kinds of bear, except black bear, are edible. Remove all fat immediately after killing, or it will turn rancid very quickly and affect the flavour of the meat. Bear meat is very tough and needs marinating in oil, vinegar, wine or cider for at least 48 hours before cooking. Like pork, it can carry trichinosis; therefore, it must be cooked thoroughly after marinating. Young bear needs approximately 2½ hours cooking if stewed, while older animals need up to 4 hours. Bear may also be roasted or fried and the saddle or loin are the most popular cuts.

TO FREEZE: prepare joints (large cuts), steaks or stewing meat, pack in freezer bags (interleaving steaks with cling film). Seal, label and freeze quickly.

TO THAW: leave in wrappings overnight in the refrigerator, then marinate for 48 hours before using any beef recipe.

STORAGE TIME: 8 months.

Beaver (U.S.)

Freeze only young animals. Skin and remove all fat or it will turn rancid quickly — beaver has a strong taste even when fresh. Carefully remove the glands in the small of the back and under the forelegs, between rib and shoulder.

TO FREEZE: hang in a cold place for 5 days. Leave the meat in large pieces for roasting, or cut into cubes for stewing, then pack in freezer bags, seal, label and freeze quickly.

TO THAW: leave both large and cubed pieces of meat in wrappings overnight in the refrigerator, then roast with plenty of fat, or stew. Any recipe

for beef is suitable for beaver.

STORAGE TIME: 8 months.

Boar (U.S.)

Wild boar is a great delicacy and may be grilled (broiled), braised, roasted or smoked like ham. Cook young animals in the same way as pork, but marinate older animals for 24 hours before cooking, using recipes for pork. Prepare joints (cuts) as for **Pork,** including the saddle for a special occasion. Boar pâté is a great delicacy: make it with fresh boar meat, then freeze it as for **Pâté.**

TO FREEZE: prepare joints and cuts, then pack in freezer bags. Seal, label and freeze quickly.

TO THAW: leave in wrappings overnight in the refrigerator, then marinate older meat for 24 hours before cooking.

STORAGE TIME: 8 months.

Capercailzie*

This is the largest bird in the grouse family. Prepare, freeze and thaw as for *Grouse.*

*Not available in Australia.

Dove (U.S.)

Prepare, freeze and thaw as for *Pigeon* allowing one dove for each person. When roasting dove, tie a piece of pork fat over the breast of each bird, or the meat will become dry.

STORAGE TIME: 12 months.

Grouse*

A British game bird with feathered feet, grouse is brownish-red in colour. Choose young birds with plump breasts and soft, full feathers. If purchasing from a market or poulterer, check if the bird has been hung;

normal hanging time is approximately one week in warm weather — longer in the winter.

WEIGHT RANGE: 1–2 kg/2–4 lb.

IDEAL SIZE: 1.5 kg/3 lb.

SERVINGS: 1–2 persons.

TO FREEZE: draw, truss and freeze whole or halved (split), depending on the size of bird.

TO THAW: leave for 24 hours in the refrigerator (whole, half or split birds).

STORAGE TIME: 6 months.

*Not available in Australia.

Hare*

There are two kinds of hare, the Blue Hare and the English Brown Hare; the latter is bigger and more flavoursome. When choosing, look for sharp claws, tender ears and a short neck.

Hang by the feet (with head down) for 7 to 10 days, then skin and 'paunch', taking care to collect the blood for use in cooking later. Do not wash the hare but wipe down with a damp cloth. Trussing a hare is a rather difficult task and, as there is very little meat on the legs, it is more sensible to cut these off, reserving the body carcass intact for roasting or jugging. Use the legs in casseroles, game pie or stews. See also recipe for *Hare Casserole.*

WEIGHT RANGE: 3–5.5 kg/7–12 lb.

IDEAL SIZE: the larger the hare the better the flavour.

SERVINGS: a large hare 5.5 kg/12 lb will serve 9–10 persons.

TO FREEZE: freeze whole or jointed (cut up).

TO THAW: Whole — 24 hours in refrigerator (under 3.5 kg/8 lb); 48 hours in refrigerator (over 3.5 kg/8 lb). Joints (cut up) — 12–15

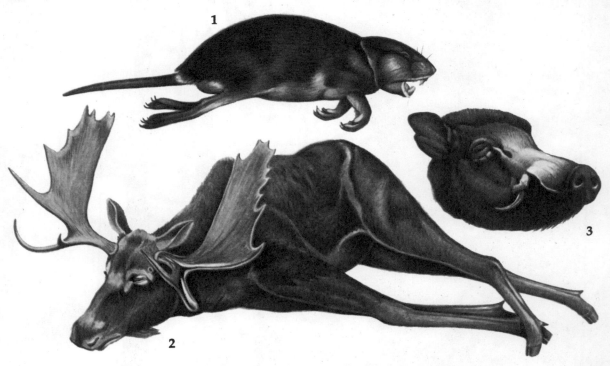

1

2

3

hours in the refrigerator. Thaw in a marinade for best results.
STORAGE TIME: 8 months
*Rarely available in Australia and U.S.A.

Hazel Hen (U.S.)

Since this bird lives in pine forests, the flesh can taste resinous, and if eaten fresh should be poached in milk for 15 minutes before proceeding with recipe.
TO FREEZE: it is best to cook hazel hen in a casserole or pâté, then freeze the cooked dish. Use any recipe for guinea fowl or pheasant.
TO THAW: as for **Casserole** or **Pâté**.
STORAGE TIME: 2 months.

Kid (U.S.)

This young goat often replaces spring lamb in Spanish-speaking countries, because it is less expensive to raise and will not yield wool, one of the reasons to preserve the young lambs. The meat can be tasteless, so add enough flavourings to enhance it. Prepare, freeze and thaw whole kid as for **Lamb** and cooked kid dishes as for **Casseroles.**

Leveret*

A young hare which serves 6 to 8 persons. Prepare, freeze and thaw as for *Hare.*
*Rarely available in Australia and U.S.A.

Moose (U.S.)

This largest member of the deer family can weigh as much as 800 kg/1800 lb, as the Alaskan moose do. Unlike the other deer, they are instantly recognizable by the flat, fan-shaped horns, which are often called palms. Skin as soon as possible

after shooting to allow animal to cool quickly, then prepare, freeze and thaw as for *Venison.*

Muskrat (U.S.)

The best part of the muskrat for eating is the upper leg or 'ham', but the animal may be prepared and cooked as for *Rabbit.* It has many small bones and is sometimes boned before cooking so that one can appreciate the dark 'gamey' flesh without difficulty.
TO FREEZE: joint (cut up) the animal like a rabbit, then soak for 24 hours in salted water. Drain thoroughly, rinse and pat dry, then pack in a freezer bag, seal, label and freeze.
TO THAW: as for *Rabbit.*
STORAGE TIME: 8 months.

Ortolan*

Ortolan is a small garden bird similar to a finch and it is not hung or drawn, simply plucked and trussed. It is best to roast these birds and serve whole. Can be difficult to obtain.
WEIGHT RANGE: 225–450 g/½–1 lb.
SERVINGS: 1 person.
TO FREEZE: freeze whole.
TO THAW: leave for 12 to 15 hours in the refrigerator.
STORAGE TIME: 3 to 4 months.
*Not available in Australia.

Partridge*

Choose young birds with plump breasts and pliable legs for roasting. Older birds are only suitable for casseroles and stews. Hang for 7 to 10 days, then pluck, draw and truss.
WEIGHT RANGE: 675 g–1 kg/1½–2 lb.
IDEAL SIZE 675 g/1½ lb.
SERVINGS: 1 person.
TO FREEZE: freeze whole for roasting, quarters for casseroles and stews.
TO THAW: leave for 24 hours in

refrigerator (whole or quarters).
STORAGE TIME: 6 months.
*Not available in Australia.

Pheasant

Hen birds are more suitable for freezing than cock birds because they usually have more flavour and are less dry. However, pheasants are often sold in a brace (1 cock and 1 hen bird together). Hang for 7 to 10 days, then pluck, draw and truss. See also recipe for *Pheasant in Cream and Brandy Sauce.*
WEIGHT RANGE 1.5–2 kg/3–4 lb.
IDEAL SIZE: 2 kg/4 lb.
SERVINGS: 3–4 persons.
TO FREEZE: freeze whole for roasting, jointed (cut up) for casseroles and stews.
TO THAW: leave for 24 hours in refrigerator (whole, jointed or cut up).
STORAGE TIME: 6 months.

Pigeon*

Select carefully because quality varies considerably. Look for a fat breast, flexible beak, thick neck and supple breastbone.

Only young birds are suitable for roasting, use older birds in casseroles. Pluck, draw and truss, but do not hang. See also recipe for *Pigeons with Grapes.*
WEIGHT RANGE 675 g–1.5 kg/1½–3 lb.
IDEAL SIZE: 1.25 kg/2½ lb.
SERVINGS: 2 persons.
TO FREEZE: freeze whole for roasting, quarters for casseroles.
TO THAW: leave for 24 hours in refrigerator (whole or quarters).
STORAGE TIME: 6 months.
*Not available in Australia.

1 *Muskrat*
2 *Moose*
3 *Boar*
4 *Pigeon*
5 *Pheasant*
6 *Partridge*
7 *Grouse*

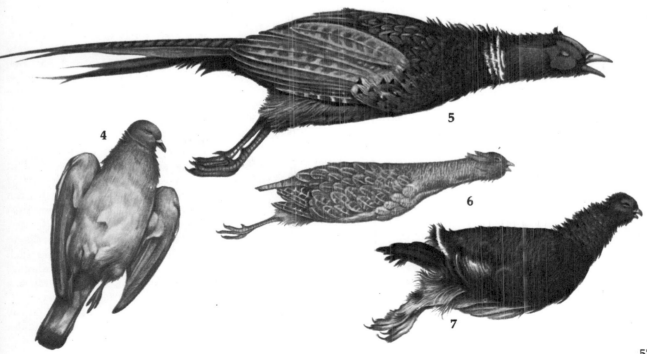

1 *Hare*
2 *Rabbit*
3 *Woodcock*
4 *Mallard*
5 *Squirrel*

Plover*

Plover is a kind of wading bird. Prepare, freeze and thaw as for *Ortolan*.
*Not available in Australia.

Ptarmigan*

A member of the grouse family with black or grey plumage in summer, white in winter. Prepare, freeze and thaw as for *Grouse*.
*Not available in Australia.

Quail*

A migratory bird similar to partridge. Prepare, freeze and thaw as for *Ortolan*.
*Not available in Australia.

Rabbit

Choose young, plump animals with sharp claws, tender ears and a short, stumpy neck. Gut or 'paunch' wild rabbits immediately after killing, hang for 4 to 5 days, then skin and prepare for the freezer. Truss for roasting by drawing the back legs forward, front legs back, and running a skewer through the head into the neck. Joint (cut up) for casseroles: cut off the legs and divide the back into three or four pieces, depending on size.
WEIGHT RANGE: 1.25–1.5 kg/2½–3 lb (wild); 2.75–4 kg/6–9 lb (tame).
IDEAL SIZE: 1.5 kg/3 lb (wild); 3.5 kg/8 lb (tame).
SERVINGS: Allow 225–350 g/½–¾ lb per person.
TO FREEZE: freeze whole or jointed (cut up).
TO THAW: leave for 24 hours in refrigerator (under 3.5 kg/8 lb); 48 hours in refrigerator (over 3.5 kg/8 lb).
STORAGE TIME: 8 months.

Raccoon (U.S.)

TO FREEZE: skin the animal, clean and soak overnight in salted water. Scrape away all fat, both inside and out, then leave whole or joint (cut up) as for *Rabbit*. Wrap in greaseproof (waxed) paper and chill in the refrigerator for 7 days, then pack in freezer bags. Seal, label and freeze.
TO THAW: leave in wrappings overnight in the refrigerator, then blanch in boiling water for 50 minutes. Drain well, wash in warm water, then put into fresh cold water, bring to the boil and simmer for 15 minutes. Drain well, then roast with stuffing. Older raccoon is best used for stewing, using any recipe for beef.
STORAGE TIME: 6 months.

Reindeer (U.S.)

The name reindeer refers to a large variety of deer, but the type in America is called caribou — recognizable by the burst of semi-circular antlers on both sexes. Reindeer is a delicate meat and can be hung or not, according to taste. Prepare, freeze and thaw as for *Venison*.

Snipe*

A game bird with a straight bill, snipe frequents marshland and is generally considered to be a water bird. Prepare, freeze and thaw as for *Ortolan*.
*Not available in Australia.

Squab*

A young pigeon which has enough meat for one serving only. Prepare, freeze and thaw as for *Pigeon*.
*Not available in Australia.

Squirrel (U.S.)

The grey squirrel is the preferred one for eating; the red variety is slightly more 'gamey'. The flesh may be fried or grilled (broiled), roasted with stuffing, or stewed.
TO FREEZE: skin the squirrel and remove head, feet and internal organs. Also be sure to remove two small glands from the small of the back and under each foreleg between ribs and shoulders. Joint (cut up) as for *Rabbit*, wrap individual pieces in cling film, then pack in freezer bags, seal, label and freeze.
TO THAW: leave in wrappings overnight in the refrigerator, then cook as for *Pigeon* or *Rabbit*.
STORAGE TIME: 6 months.

Venison (Deer)*

When choosing, look for animals that are aged between 1½ and 2 years. The flesh of the buck is considered better than that of the doe, and the lean meat should be dark with plenty of white fat — this shows good condition. Venison tends to be a little tough; therefore, hang it in a cool, airy place for 10 to 14 days, depending on weather conditions. It is ready for freezing as soon as the 'high' smell is noticeable. To avoid wastage and to have well-cut joints, it is best to have deer butchered professionally. It should be butchered in a similar way to a beef carcass. The loin and haunch are the best cuts for roasting — other joints and cuts should be used in casseroles. Trim off as much fat as possible before freezing, or this can develop a strong flavour during storage.
TO FREEZE: Pack well in order to prevent loss of flavour: wrap each joint or cut individually in aluminium foil or cling film, then overwrap in a freezer bag, seal, label and freeze.
TO THAW: leave for 24 hours in the refrigerator (joints or cuts under

5

3.5 kg/8 lb); 48 hours in the refrigerator (joints or cuts over 3.5 kg/8 lb). Thaw in a marinade.
STORAGE TIME: 12 months (large cuts and steaks); 4 months (minced/ground meat).
*Not available in Australia, but available in New Zealand.

Wigeon*

This is a type of wild duck.
For size and servings, see *Wild Duck;* prepare, freeze and thaw as for **Poultry,** *Duck.*
*Not available in Australia.

Wild Duck

Hang for 2 to 3 days before preparing for the freezer.
SIZE: 1–1.5 kg/2–3 lb.
SERVINGS: 2 persons.
Prepare, freeze and thaw as for **Poultry,** *Duck.*

Woodchuck (U.S.)

TO FREEZE: prepare this animal like *Rabbit,* and carefully remove some eight or nine small glands in the small of the back and under the forearm. Cut in joints and soak overnight in salted water. Drain and pat dry, then pack in freezer bags, seal, label and freeze.
TO THAW: leave in wrappings overnight in the refrigerator, then cook as for *Rabbit.*
STORAGE TIME: 6 months.

Woodcock*

A game bird related to the snipe. Hang woodcock for approximately 2 days, then truss, but do not draw before freezing. They are usually roasted and served whole.
Prepare, freeze and thaw as for *Plover.*
*Not available in Australia.

Gammon

see **Bacon**

Garfish

Prepare, freeze and thaw as for **Pike**

Garlic

It is not really necessary to freeze garlic as it stores perfectly well in a 'rope' in a cool, airy place. However, if there is danger of them not keeping well by this method, they can be stored in the freezer.
TO FREEZE: wrap the whole bulb (not individual cloves) well in aluminium foil or freezer film, overwrap in a freezer bag, seal tightly, label and freeze. Remove garlic at once if there is a trace of its pungent scent when you open the freezer.
TO THAW: remove individual cloves from frozen garlic bulb as required. Leave at room temperature for 2 to 3 minutes until thawed, then use as for fresh garlic.
STORAGE TIME: approximately 3 months.

Garlic Bread

Frozen garlic bread can be taken out of the freezer and served within 30 minutes.
TO FREEZE: make cuts in a long French loaf approximately 2.5 cm/1 inch apart. Peel and crush 2 garlic cloves and work into 225 g/½ lb/1 cup softened butter. Season to taste. Spread garlic butter between the slices, wrap in aluminium foil, then overwrap in a freezer bag, seal, label and freeze.
TO THAW: remove bag, place loaf on oven shelf and bake from frozen in a moderate oven (180°C/350°F or Gas Mark 4) for 15 minutes. Open the foil wrapping, increase the heat to very hot (230°C/450°F or Gas Mark 8) and bake for another 10 minutes until crisp. Serve hot with cheese, pâté, soup, etc.
STORAGE TIME: 1 week.

Garlic Butter

see **Butter, Flavoured**

Garnish(es)

The freezer makes an excellent storage place for garnishes which can be prepared in advance of parties, special occasions, etc. See individual entries: **Breadcrumbs, Buttered Crumbs, Butters, Cheese, Chocolate, Cream, Croûte/Croûtons, Herb(s), Meringue, Praline, Soup Garnishes.**

Gâteau

see **Cake(s)**

Gelatin(e)

Gelatin(e) can be used as a setting agent for mousses, soufflés, etc., to be stored in the freezer. Always follow the instructions on the pack for exact quantity, and ensure that the gelatin(e) powder is thoroughly dissolved before adding to fruit purées, liquids, etc. Gelatin(e) should not be used to set clear or moulded jellies that rely solely on the gelatin(e) as a setting agent — they are likely to become granular and cloudy on thawing. However, gelatin(e) can be used successfully as a setting agent for icecream. See **Ice(s)/Icecream.**

Gherkin

Gherkins are a type of small outdoor cucumber which are raised specially for pickling. If frozen, they would lose their crispness and therefore their appeal.

Giblet

see **Poultry**

Garlic bulbs can be frozen wrapped in foil or freezer film and overwrapped in a freezer bag.

Glacé Fruit

These have already been preserved in sugar and gain nothing from being frozen.

Glass Containers for Freezing

see page 233

Globe Artichoke

Cut off the large central heads while the leaves are still closely folded, and before the base starts to swell.

To freeze whole artichokes: pull off outer and coarse lower leaves. Trim off spiky leaf tops, according to variety, and remove stem. Wash well under cold running water or by soaking for 30 minutes in cold water, to remove any insects. Blanch in boiling water for 7 to 10 minutes, according to size, adding a little lemon juice to the blanching water. Drain, cool rapidly in iced water, then drain well upside-down. Squeeze dry, pack into freezer bags and seal, label and freeze.

TO THAW: leave in wrappings for approximately 4 hours at room temperature until thawed completely, then unwrap and boil rapidly until a skewer goes easily through the base. Serve hot or cold with melted butter or vinaigrette sauce.

To freeze artichoke hearts: boil whole artichokes until tender in salted water. Drain, cool slightly, then pull off the leaves and discard. Scoop out the choke with a spoon and discard. Leave the heart to cool (not in water), then pack in rigid containers, interleaving layers with aluminium foil or freezer tissue. Cover, label and freeze.

TO THAW: leave in containers for approximately 4 hours at room temperature. Serve cold with a vinaigrette sauce or in mixed green salads; serve hot in casseroles, or sauté gently in butter, fill with grated cheese, chopped mushrooms and grill (broil).

STORAGE TIME: 6 months.

Goldenberry

see **Berry**

Golden Damson

see **Bullace**

Goose

see **Poultry**

Gooseberry

see **Berry**

Gooseberry, Chinese

see **Chinese Gooseberry**

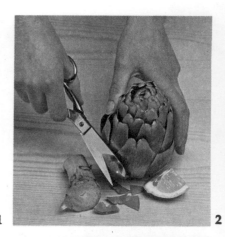

Globe Artichoke
1 *Pulling off outer and coarse lower leaves.*
2 *Removing stem and spiky leaf tops.*
3 *Washing thoroughly.*
4 *Blanching in boiling water for 7 to 10 minutes.*
5 *Cooling and draining.*
6 *Serving with vinaigrette sauce.*

Goulash

This Hungarian dish of beef, lamb or veal cooked in a casserole with onions, paprika and tomatoes, freezes well. Freeze and reheat as for **Casserole.** Sour(ed) cream is always added to goulash at the reheating stage. See also recipes for *Goulash Soup* and *Beef Goulash.*
STORAGE TIME: 2 months.

Granadilla

see **Passion Fruit**

Grape

see also **Fruit** for information on packing
TO FREEZE: open (flash) freeze seedless grapes in the bunch. Peel, halve and seed large grapes, then pack in light syrup.
TO THAW: leave in wrappings for approximately 2 hours at room temperature. Use raw in fresh fruit salads, or cooked in sauces for fish and game, etc. See also recipes for *Pigeons with Grapes, Grape Jelly* and *Peach and Grape Crème Brûlée.*
STORAGE TIME: 12 months.

Grapefruit

see also **Fruit** for information on packing
TO FREEZE: peel and divide into whole segments without a trace of skin or pith. Open (flash) freeze; pack dry with sugar; or pack in light syrup.
TO THAW: leave in wrappings for approximately 2½ hours at room temperature. Use in shellfish cocktails, green salads to accompany a rich main course, as a breakfast refresher or dessert.
STORAGE TIME: 12 months.

Gravy

Gravy can be kept in the freezer providing it is not too thick — for best results it should be thickened with cornflour (cornstarch).
TO FREEZE: pack cold gravy in usable quantities in waxed cartons or rigid containers, leaving headspace. Cover, label and freeze. Or pour leftover gravy into ice cube trays, open (flash) freeze until solid, then pack in freezer bags, seal, label and freeze.
TO THAW: unwrap and reheat from frozen in a heavy saucepan, adding extra thickening at this stage if necessary. Or add to sauces, soups, stocks, etc.
    Sliced cooked meat and poultry can be packed with gravy to make useful quick meals when required. Ensure that both meat or poultry and gravy are completely cold, place meat or poultry in bottom of an aluminium foil dish, pour gravy over to cover, then cover with a foil lid, overwrap in a freezer bag, seal, label and freeze. Reheat from frozen in foil dish in a moderate oven (180°C/350°F or Gas Mark 4) until thoroughly reheated and bubbling — the length of time will depend on the quantity of meat and gravy.

Grayling

A freshwater fish similar to trout, but as it spawns later, it is at its best in the autumn and early winter. Fresh grayling has the delicate flavour of water thyme, but this may fade during freezing.
TO FREEZE: clean well, pat dry and wrap each fish in cling film, then pack several fish together in a freezer bag. Seal, label and freeze.
TO THAW: unwrap and cook from frozen. Use any recipe for trout.
STORAGE TIME: 3 months.

Green Bean

see **Bean**

Greengage (Greengage Plum)*

see also **Fruit** for information on packing
Use ripe, but unsplit, fruit.
TO FREEZE: cut in half and remove stones (pits) but do not skin. Open (flash) freeze; pack in light syrup; or purée with sugar to taste. Pack in rigid containers, cover, label and freeze.
TO THAW: leave in wrappings for approximately 2½ hours at room temperature. Use raw in salads, cooked in pies, puréed in fools.
STORAGE TIME: 12 months.
*Not available in Australia.

Greens

see individual names (**Broccoli, Brussels Sprouts, Green Cabbage, Cauliflower, Kale, Spring Greens**)

Grey Mullet

see **Mullet**

Grilse

This is a young salmon which has just left the sea to move upstream. Prepare, freeze and thaw as for **Salmon.**

Ground Beef

see **Beef**

Grouse

see **Game**

Guacamole

see **Dips**

Guava

Freeze while firm and yellow. Guavas must be cooked, as they are too sour to eat raw.
TO FREEZE: wash thoroughly, remove stem and blossom, peel, halve and scoop out seeds. Leave as halves or slice and pack dry with sugar; or pack in light syrup.
STORAGE TIME: 12 months.
Guava Sauce: prepare the fruit for freezing as above, slicing halves directly into a light syrup. Cook until tender, then cool. Work through a sieve and pack in rigid containers. Cover, label and freeze. Reheat from frozen in a heavy saucepan on top of the stove, stirring occasionally.
STORAGE TIME: 12 months.

Gudgeon

A tiny freshwater fish of the carp family.
TO FREEZE: wash thoroughly, pat dry and pack in ½ kg/1 lb freezer bags. Seal, label and freeze.
TO THAW: coat with flour and deep fry from frozen in hot oil or fat as for whitebait. Or use any recipe for smelt.
STORAGE TIME: 3 months.

Guinea Fowl

see **Game**

Gumbo

see **Okra**

Gurnet

An ugly sea fish with a very large head, which means that a 275–350 g/10–12 oz fish is needed for each person. The red and grey gurnet are the ones normally eaten, and they are similar to mullet.
TO FREEZE: remove the head and clean the fish thoroughly. Leave small fish whole, fillet large ones. Pack in freezer bags, interleaving each fish or fillet with cling film. Seal, label and freeze.
TO THAW: unwrap and poach or grill (broil) from frozen. Serve hot with butter. Gurnet is also good served cold with mayonnaise.
STORAGE TIME: 3 months.

Haddock

Haddock may be eaten fresh or smoked.

TO FREEZE: clean thoroughly, fillet large haddock, leave small ones whole. Smoked haddock needs no preparation before freezing. Pack in freezer bags, interleaving with cling film, seal, label and freeze.

TO THAW: unwrap and poach or fry fillets from frozen. Or unwrap and thaw whole fish for 4 hours in the refrigerator, then stuff and bake. Unwrap and poach smoked haddock from frozen in water or milk, or a mixture of both. See also recipe for *Smoked Haddock Mousse*.

STORAGE TIME: 3 months.

Hake

This is a close relation of cod, and a useful fish because it has few bones.

TO FREEZE: fillet, then pack in freezer bags, interleaving each fillet with cling film. Seal, label and freeze.

TO THAW: unwrap and cook from frozen, as for cod or haddock.

STORAGE TIME: 3 months.

Halibut

This large flatfish can reach a weight of 90 kg/200 lb. It has a delicate flavour which can be lost in freezing, so it is best to serve it with a good, well-seasoned sauce if it has been frozen. Very young halibut, approximately 2.25 kg/5 lb in weight and called chicken halibut, are the best ones for freezing.

TO FREEZE: clean thoroughly, then leave whole or cut in slices. Pack in freezer bags, interleaving each piece with cling film. Seal, label and freeze.

TO THAW: unwrap and cook from frozen. Sole and turbot recipes may be used for cooking halibut.

STORAGE TIME: 3 months.

The two containers on the left of the photograph on this page show correct headspace before and after freezing. The two on the right illustrate what happens if no headspace is allowed.

Ham

see also **Bacon & Cured Pork**

Due to its high salt content, ham does not keep well in the freezer; freeze only for the maximum recommended storage time (below).

To freeze raw ham: leave in the piece, wrap in cling film, then overwrap in a freezer bag, seal, label and freeze.

To freeze cooked ham: pack joints and large cuts as for raw ham. Pack sliced boiled ham in freezer bags, interleaving each slice with cling film or freezer tissue, seal, label and freeze.

TO THAW: leave joints and large cuts (raw or cooked) in wrappings overnight in the refrigerator; thawing time will vary according to the size of the ham. Thaw slices in wrappings for approximately 3 hours in the refrigerator.

STORAGE TIME: 2 months (raw); 1 month (cooked).

Hamburger

prepare, freeze and thaw as for **Beefburger**

Hare

see **Game**

Hash

The best varieties for freezing are beef and corned beef, chicken, potato, turkey and veal.

TO FREEZE: prepare completely except for the addition of any egg yolks or cream at the end. Pack into rigid containers, cover, label and freeze.

TO THAW: leave in container for 3 hours at room temperature, then tip into a saucepan with cream and stir gently until it comes to the boil. Taste for seasoning and serve.

STORAGE TIME: 2 months.

Hazel Hen

see **Game**

Headspace

This is the space left between the lid of a rigid container and the food and/or liquid, to allow for expansion when frozen. If headspace is not left, the lid of the container will be forced off and the contents can suffer from dehydration. 1.25–2.5 cm/½–1 inch

is sufficient headspace to allow, erring on the generous side for narrow-topped containers.

Heat Sealing

A method of sealing freezer bags by applying heat. Use either a special sealing iron or a domestic iron. In the case of the latter, first exclude as much air as possible from the bag, then place a thin strip of brown paper across the mouth of the bag. Run a warm iron along the paper — the heat transferred to the bag will seal the open ends.

Heavy Duty Bags

see page 234

Herb(s)

see individual names

Herb Bread

Prepare, freeze and thaw as for **Garlic Bread** substituting 4 × 15 ml spoons/4 tablespoons freshly chopped herbs for the garlic. Use any fresh herbs that are available — basil, chives, marjoram, parsley, sage, thyme, etc. Crushed garlic can also be added.

Herb Butter

see **Butter, Flavoured**

Herring

The herring has an excellent flavour and high food value, but its oiliness and the number of bones it contains can be unpopular. Only freeze really fresh herrings.

TO FREEZE: clean carefully and remove the backbone together with a number of the smaller bones. Open herrings out and pack in pairs in freezer bags, interleaving each herring with cling film. Seal, label and freeze.

TO THAW: unwrap and grill (broil) or fry from frozen. Or stuff and bake.

STORAGE TIME: 3 months.

Horseradish

If freezer space is short, horseradish will keep perfectly well refrigerated in jars. Grate fresh horseradish and add sugar and wine vinegar to taste.

TO FREEZE: grate or mince young roots, sprinkle with white wine vinegar to prevent discoloration, then pack in small rigid containers. Cover, label and freeze.

TO THAW: leave in containers in the refrigerator or, to thaw rapidly, remove from container and leave at room temperature. Mix with sugar, seasonings and cream and use as a cold sauce with beef, freshwater fish or shellfish.

STORAGE TIME: 6 months.

Herb Bread

1 *Making cuts in a French loaf approximately 2.5 cm/1 inch apart.*

2 *Chopping herbs to mix with softened butter.*

3 *Spreading herb butter between the slices before wrapping the loaf in foil and freezing.*

4 *Serve with pâté or cheese after thawing and heating through in the oven.*

Hyssop *(Hyssopus officinalis)*

A highly aromatic herb which grows from the Mediterranean to central Asia. The hyssop bush grows to a height of 46–60 cm/18–24 inches, with a spread of 23–30 cm/9–12 inches. Both the dark green highly fragrant leaves, and the flowers which bloom from July to September (Aust. January to March), are used as a flavouring in cooking. Hyssop is often compared to sage and winter savory, combining a sweet scent with a spicy piquancy which is slightly bitter.

TO FREEZE: pick the young leaves and tips of the shoots throughout the summer. Wash if necessary under cold running water, shake dry, then put directly into freezer bags, seal, label and freeze. Or pick shoots, with or without flowers, blanch in boiling water for 1 minute, cool at once under cold running water, pat dry and pack in bags.

TO THAW: use while still frozen: chop or crumble into cottage cheese, salads, stews and stuffings, or toss with butter and freshly cooked beans just before serving. The distinctive flavour of hyssop goes particularly well with cranberries, white sauces and thick soups and adds a subtle taste to fresh fruit salads or fruit baked in pies.

STORAGE TIME: 2 months (unblanched); 8 months (blanched).

Ice(s)/Icecream

No freezer should be without a stock of icecream, homemade and/or commercially prepared. With a supply of icecream in the freezer, desserts can be made in moments by serving with different toppings and sauces, and in hot weather there is nothing so cooling and refreshing as a mouth-watering ice — without a trip to the shops.

Commercially Frozen Icecream

Many different flavours are available, in different sized packs, from individual varieties to the more unusual bombes*, sorbets and water ices, and large catering (institution-size) packs containing 4 litres/1 gallon and more. When buying large packs, it is wise to consider how long they will last and whether the family will tire of eating one flavour for such a long time. If the icecream is taken in and out of the freezer too often, its quality and flavour will deteriorate. Never allow icecream to thaw while it is out of the freezer; the best ways to avoid this are to use a good quality, efficient scoop, this will enable you to remove icecream from its container while it is still quite hard; or to buy 'soft scoop' icecream that does not need to stand at room temperature before it can be scooped. Dip the spoon in a jug of warm water between each scoop. Always return the icecream carton to the freezer immediately after use and cover the top with aluminium foil before replacing the carton cover. Do not re-freeze icecream if it is inadvertently left to thaw while out of the freezer: ice crystals will form in it during the re-freezing process, causing the texture to become coarse, grainy and unpleasant to eat.

STORAGE TIME: 4–6 weeks.

*Not available in Australia.

Homemade Icecream

This is quite simple to make in the freezer. There are numerous recipes for icecream, but basically they are made with a base of either egg

63

A wonderful selection of homemade and commercially frozen icecreams can be stored at home when you own a freezer.

custard or egg yolks and sugar syrup (mousse), to which cream is added. Some icecreams are set with gelatin(e).

Different colourings, flavourings, fruit and other ingredients are then added to the basic mixture. The amount of sugar used in making icecream at home is very important; too little sugar will make the icecream watery and tasteless, too much sugar will make the icecream hard. It is,

therefore, worth experimenting with the amount of sugar and to keep using a good recipe once you have found one. This is particularly important when making water ices.

TO FREEZE: make icecream according to your favourite recipe, pack into icecream or freezer trays and freeze for approximately 3 hours. Remove the icecream from the freezer every hour, turn into a mixing bowl and beat well with an electric beater or

wire whisk. Return to icecream or freezer trays. Before serving the icecream will need to soften a little and the length of 'softening' time will depend very much on the original recipe used. In general, the icecream should soften to the right texture if taken from the freezer and kept in the refrigerator for approximately 1 hour. If the icecream is not required for immediate use it should be taken from icecream trays and packed in

usable quantities in rigid containers (used icecream cartons are ideal). It is best to use up homemade icecream once it has been taken out of the freezer, as it does not respond as well as commercial icecream to constant transferring from freezer to air.

STORAGE TIME: up to 3 months.

Sorbets (Sherbets) and Water Ices

These are made with sugar syrup and fruit juice or purée. This mixture is put into the freezer until slushy, then whipped egg white, and sometimes gelatin(e), is added to hold the mixture together and give it a light texture. Freeze and pack as for icecreams above. At the times of year when soft fruit is plentiful, it is a good idea to make some of these into fruit juices and purées which can be made into sorbets or water ices when required (if they are made into ices immediately and stored in that form they will only keep their flavour and texture for 2 to 3 weeks). Fruit-flavoured ices and sorbets should be thawed for 10 to 15 minutes at room temperature before serving. Sorbets and water ices such as lemon and orange look very attractive if frozen in the hollowed shells of the fruit (see recipe for Orange Sherbet).

STORAGE TIME: 2 to 3 months (homemade); 4 to 6 weeks (commercially frozen).

Ice Glazing
1 An open-frozen fish being dipped into cold water for its first coating of ice.
2 The same fish, now well coated with a thick layer of ice, being dipped into cold water for the last time.

Bombes/Moulds

Spectacular-looking desserts for dinner parties, these can either be commercially prepared or homemade. Special moulds are available for homemade bombes, although metal jelly (gelatin) moulds can be used with equal success.

TO FREEZE: press layers of different-flavoured and coloured icecream into the mould, freezing each layer until solid before adding the next layer. Or press some icecream around the insides of the mould and freeze other icecream or fruit in the middle. Cover the mould with aluminium foil, label and freeze until required.

TO THAW: hold a hot cloth around the base of the mould for half a minute or so, place a chilled serving platter over the top of the mould and invert the bombe onto the platter.

See also recipes for *Orange Sherbet, Baked Alaska, Brown Bread Icecream* and *Cassata*.

STORAGE TIME: 2 to 3 months (homemade); 4 to 6 weeks (commercially frozen).

Ice Crystals

Freezing forms ice crystals on the surface of food and also converts the water content of food cells into crystals. The size of these ice crystals depends on how quickly the food is frozen, and the faster this is done, the smaller they will be. Because water expands when frozen, the smaller the crystals are the less damage will occur in the structure of food; therefore, there will be less natural juice and flavour to escape during thawing. This is particularly important to bear in mind when freezing meat. Fluctuations of temperature within a freezer can also cause extra ice crystals or frost to form inside frozen packages.

Buttercream icing and melted chocolate are particularly suitable for use on cakes which are to be decorated before freezing.

1

2

Ice Cubes

Ice cubes can be frozen in quantity in the freezer for use in drinks, or for quick cooling of fruit and vegetables after blanching.

TO FREEZE: make the cubes in ice cube trays in the usual way, then transfer to trays and open (flash) freeze for approximately 2 hours. Pack in freezer bags, seal, label and return to freezer. The ice cubes can be taken out individually if they have been open (flash) frozen in this way.

Ice cubes can be flavoured — with coffee, fruit juices, tea, etc., and can then be added to drinks and punches without diluting their flavour.

It is quite simple to make decorated ice cubes for use in drinks at cocktail parties — put a strip of lemon, lime or orange rind, a sprig of mint or a maraschino cherry into each section of the ice cube tray, cover with water, freeze, open (flash) freeze and pack as for ordinary ice cubes.

Ice Glazing

A method of freezing a whole fish by encasing it in several layers of ice. Ice glazing is particularly suitable for large fish such as salmon, because it can be difficult to find suitable wrappings. Fish frozen in this way requires very careful handling, owing to the brittleness of the ice, and is best stored only for a short period.

TO ICE GLAZE: clean the fish, then open (flash) freeze on 'fast freeze' control until solid. Remove fish from freezer, dip it in fresh cold water when a thin film of ice will form all over. Return the fish at once to the freezer and open (flash) freeze again until that layer of ice is solid. Repeat this process several times until the coating of ice is at least 6 mm/¼ inch thick. Store immediately, wrapped in a freezer bag or tissue if you like.

Icing (Frosting)

Buttercream icing, and other icings with a high proportion of fat, keep very well in the freezer and can be put directly onto cakes to be frozen, or frozen separately.

TO FREEZE: pack in rigid containers, cover, label and freeze.

TO THAW: leave in container for approximately 2 hours at room temperature; use as for fresh icing.

Melted chocolate can be used to ice the tops of cakes for freezing with satisfactory results. Other icings such as boiled, fondant and royal icing tend to crack and crumble on thawing and are therefore not satisfactory for freezing. Glacé icing is likely to soften on thawing and unless used for icing very small cakes before freezing, would be difficult to handle. For icing cakes, see **Cake(s)**.

STORAGE TIME: 4 months (buttercream icing).

Ink Fish

prepare, freeze and thaw as for **Octopus**

Installation

see page 229

Institution-sized Package

see **Catering Pack**

Insurance

see page 230

Interleaving Sheets

see page 234

J

Jam

Commercially prepared jam or jam made at home by the boiling method keeps perfectly well for months in a cool, dry store cupboard, but the freezer can be of use in jam-making because you can store fresh fruit in it at the height of the soft fruit season. This fruit can then be used for jam-making at a later date.

TO FREEZE: wash fresh fruit, hull if necessary, and pack in usable quantities in freezer bags without sugar. Seal, label and freeze.

TO THAW: fruit may be used from frozen to make jam in the usual way: put fruit in a saucepan and thaw over gentle heat before adding sugar. Jam made with fruit in this way will taste just as good and fresh as if it were made with fresh fruit, although the pectin content of the fruit may be lowered. If this is so, use slightly more fruit than the recipe recommends, or add a little liquid pectin.

Uncooked freezer jams: are excellent in both colour and flavour, though less solid than boiled jams. They are made from crushed fresh fruit, sugar, lemon juice and liquid pectin, and are left at room temperature until set.

TO FREEZE: pack in small quantities in waxed cartons or rigid containers, seal, label and freeze.

TO THAW: leave in container for approximately 1 hour at room temperature. Stir well before serving, then eat as soon as possible as uncooked jams do not keep long after thawing. Do not use jam as a filling for cakes, pastries, sandwiches, etc. for the freezer, as it can cause sogginess on thawing.

STORAGE TIME: for fresh fruit for jam-making, see individual fruit entries; for uncooked jams — 6 months.

Japonica (Quince)

Small-fruited, ornamental japonicas are best used in jam and jelly-making only. Pick the true, large-fruited quince when fully ripe.

TO FREEZE: peel, core and slice, then simmer in syrup until barely tender. Leave to cool, pack in the cooking syrup in rigid containers, cover, label and freeze.

TO THAW: leave in containers at room temperature until they are thawed sufficiently to let a fork go through them. Use in desserts as for fresh quince.

STORAGE TIME: 12 months.

Jars

see page 233

Jelly

Jellies (moulded clear gelatins) are not suitable for the freezer: although they remain set on thawing, they become cloudy and therefore lose their appeal.

Jerusalem Artichoke

TO FREEZE: peel the tubers, slice or cut into cubes and put at once into cold water with a little lemon juice to prevent discoloration. Drain and blanch in boiling water for 1 to 2 minutes. Drain, cool rapidly in iced water, then drain and pat dry. Pack in freezer containers, seal, label and freeze. Or scrub and boil whole for approximately 15 minutes or until the skins can be pulled off easily (this method is much easier than peeling them raw). Sieve or purée in an electric blender or work in a Mouli-légumes (foodmill), then pack in rigid containers, cover, label and freeze.

TO THAW: put frozen artichoke slices or cubes in boiling salted water. Bring back to the boil, cover and simmer for approximately 3 minutes, according to quantity and thickness of artichoke slices (cubes). They should be slightly underdone, otherwise they will disintegrate. Or thaw sliced artichokes in

---

Jam
1 *The ingredients for strawberry freezer jam.*
2 *Crushing the fruit to mix with the sugar, lemon juice and liquid pectin.*
3 *Packing the jam in rigid containers for freezing.*
4 *Serve thawed freezer jam as for ordinary jam.*

Jerusalem artichokes can be frozen sliced, diced, puréed or in soups.

containers at room temperature until they feel only slightly crisp when tested with a fork. Add to salads with French dressing, use in casseroles and stews, sauté them in butter, or cook 'au gratin'. Thaw puréed artichokes completely in containers at room temperature, or use frozen to make soups.

See also recipes for *Scallop and Artichoke Soup* and *Braised Jerusalem Artichokes*.
STORAGE TIME: 3 months.

John Dory

This rather ugly fish, with large jaws and an oval body, is very popular in Australia. It has firm white flesh with a good flavour and is at its best in autumn and winter. It may be cooked using recipes for sole fillets.
TO FREEZE: remove head and fins and cut into fillets. Pack in freezer bags, interleaving each fillet with cling film. Seal, label and freeze.
TO THAW: unwrap and fry or grill (broil) from frozen, or thaw for 2 hours in the refrigerator and coat in batter for deep-frying.
STORAGE TIME: 3 months.

Joint (Cut)

see individual meats (**Beef, Lamb, Pork, Veal**)

Juice

Juice made from fresh fruit keeps well in the freezer, with or without added sugar.
TO FREEZE: pour into rigid containers or canning jars, leaving headspace, cover, label and freeze. Or freeze in ice cube trays.
TO THAW: leave in containers overnight in the refrigerator or for several hours at room temperature.

Commercially frozen fruit juices in concentrated form can be used from frozen as for fresh fruit juice: in concentrated form they are particularly useful in cooking as they make exceptionally flavourful sauces, etc. Fruit juices sold in cans and cartons may be decanted into rigid containers or canning jars in usable quantities, frozen and thawed as for fresh fruit juice.
STORAGE TIME: 4 months.

Juneberry

see **Berry**

K

Kale

Freeze only tender young shoots, picking them at the point where the stem breaks easily.
TO FREEZE: wash, blanch in boiling water for 1 minute and drain. Cool rapidly in iced water, then drain and pat dry. Pack in freezer bags. Seal, label and freeze.
TO THAW: unwrap and put frozen kale in boiling salted water. Bring back to the boil, then cover and simmer for 8 minutes. Drain and serve as for greens.
STORAGE TIME: 12 months.

Kid

see **Game**

Kidney

see **Meat, Fresh**

Kipper

A split, salted and smoked herring which is most popular grilled (broiled), poached or made into pâté.
TO FREEZE: pack whole fish or fillets in freezer bags, interleaving each piece of fish with cling film. Seal, label and freeze.
TO THAW: unwrap and cook from frozen as above. See also recipe for *Kipper Pâté*
STORAGE TIME: 3 months.

Kiwi Fruit

see **Chinese Gooseberry**

Kneaded Butter/Beurre Manié

A mixture of butter and plain white (all-purpose) flour that is used for thickening sauces, soups, stews, etc., kneaded butter is one of the invaluable aids to the freezer cook. As it is advisable to freeze sauces, etc. *before* thickening, a quantity of ready-made kneaded butter is indispensable for thickening at the reheating stage.
TO FREEZE: blend together butter and flour in the ratio of equal weights of butter and flour. Open (flash) freeze

in small quantities (1 × 15 ml spoon/1 tablespoon is a useful measure) on trays until solid, then pack in freezer bags. Seal, label and return to freezer. Use spoonsful of the thickener when required by mixing with a little hot liquid in a small bowl, then stirring this mixture into the bulk of the liquid or by adding directly to the hot liquid. Heat gently, until the liquid thickens, stirring constantly.
STORAGE TIME: as for butter (salted — 3 months; unsalted — 6 months).

Kohlrabi

Very young and tender kohlrabi, no more than 5 cm/2 inches diameter, is the most successful for freezing.
To freeze young kohlrabi: cut off tops and trim. Wash, blanch whole in boiling water for 3 minutes and drain. Cool rapidly in iced water, then drain and pat dry. Pack in freezer bags, seal, label and freeze.
To freeze older kohlrabi: peel and dice or slice, blanch for 2 minutes and drain. Cool and pack as above.
TO THAW: leave in wrappings at room temperature until the root feels

slightly crisp when tested with a fork, then put in boiling salted water. Bring back to the boil, cover and simmer for 10 minutes, or according to size. Drain and serve hot.

Or unwrap and slice, dry and use as bases for cocktail savouries; if already diced or sliced, thaw, pat dry and deep-fry as fritters.
STORAGE TIME: 12 months.

Kumquat

see also **Fruit** for information on packing
This tiny member of the citrus family can be frozen for use as a dessert, or for preserving at a later date.
TO FREEZE: wrap whole fruit in aluminium foil and open (flash) freeze; or pack in medium syrup. If for preserving, chop coarsely or slice, then pack dry with sugar.
TO THAW: leave in wrapping for approximately 2 hours at room temperature. Serve raw as a dessert on its own, or with fresh cream, icecream or liqueur; or make into a preserve.
STORAGE TIME: 12 months.

Kneaded Butter
1 Blending together the butter and flour.
2 Arranging small quantities of kneaded butter on baking sheets before open freezing.
3 Packing open-frozen pieces of kneaded butter in a freezer bag.
4 Stirring the kneaded butter into a hot sauce. If preferred, the kneaded butter can be mixed with a little of the hot liquid in a small bowl, before being added to the bulk of the liquid.

Lamb

see also recipe section

Choosing Home-produced Lamb

Look for fine-grained, pink meat and plump, well-rounded legs and shoulders. The covering of fat should be thin, firm and white, and the outer layer of skin pliable, thin and smooth. A reasonable amount of fat is necessary for good flavour and quality, but avoid an excessively fatty carcass. As lamb ages, the colour of the meat deepens and the fat takes on a yellowish hue. To develop the maximum flavour and tenderness, ask for the lamb to be hung in the butcher's cold room for 1 week after slaughter and *before* freezing.

Choosing New Zealand or Other Imported Lamb

Lamb that is imported frozen should not be allowed to thaw before being re-frozen in a home-freezer. Ask for lamb that has not been thawed and which will therefore retain all its original quality. It can still be cut to suit your needs, but naturally it is not possible for joints (cuts) to be boned entirely. Order the lamb, and arrange delivery so that it can be transferred to your freezer with an absolute minimum of delay. For a large quantity, have the 'fast freeze' switch in operation ready to receive it.

When buying lamb in the frozen state it is impossible to judge the quality by appearances, but all New Zealand lamb is graded (by weight plus the proportion of meat to fat and bone) before it is frozen and shipped. Any of the PL, the PM or YM grades are very suitable for a bulk buy for the home freezer.

Buying

Lamb is at its choicest when young in spring and early summer. The New Zealand seasons are the reverse of ours, so imported spring lambs usually begin to arrive in January and remain in good supply until the summer. Home-killed spring lambs are usually expensive but prices drop as the supply increases — the peak season is normally from August to October.

Available as joints (large cuts), single portion cuts, as a side (one of each cut) or a whole lamb (two of each cut), lamb is usually supplied 'on the bone' unless you ask for specific cuts to be boned. Offal (variety meats/fancy meats) may or may not be included in a bulk buy (except the kidneys in the case of English lamb), so specify what you want.

Freezer Space Needed

Allow 56 litres/2 cu ft for every 9 kg/20 lb of lamb on the bone.

Weight Range of Whole Carcass

Home-killed lamb: 12–20 kg/26–45 lb; New Zealand and Australian: 8–16 kg/17.5–35 lb.

PACKING AND FREEZING: see **Meat, Fresh.**

THAWING AND COOKING: see **Meat, Fresh.**

STORAGE TIME: joints (large cuts) — up to 6 months.

Chops or small cuts — up to 6 months. Offal (variety meats/fancy meats) — up to 3 months.

Cut	Approximate weight range*		Ways of butchering	Type of meat and cooking
	kg	lb		
Shoulder (Foreshank)	1.25-2.5	2½-5½	(a) Whole if small (b) Halved if large, providing two small joints (cuts) (c) Boned for stuffing (d) Boned and cubed for kebabs and casseroles (e) Minced (ground) meat	Fattier, but cheaper than leg or loin. Sweet, succulent meat, excellent for roasting. If carving is considered a problem, use (c) (d) or (e)
Breast	675 g-1	1½-2	(a) Whole (b) Cut into 2.5 cm/1 inch wide riblets	Needs slow, moist cooking to tenderize. If wide enough to be boned, stuff and slow roast, otherwise cut into riblets and cook in a savoury barbecue sauce
Leg (Sirloin and Hind shank)	1.25-2.25	2½-5	(a) Whole if small (b) Halved if large, providing two small joints (cuts) (c) 2.5 cm/1 inch thick steak(s) cut from fillet end for kebabs; rest of leg for slow roasting joint (cut) (d) 1.25 cm/½ inch thick fillet steaks for frying or grilling (broiling)	Very lean, top-quality roasting cut. Fillet end excellent for grilling (broiling) steaks, or for kebabs. Mature lamb or knuckles are good for braising

Loin	1.5-2.25	3-5	(a) Whole if small
			(b) Boned for stuffing
			(c) Halved if large, providing two joints (cuts):
			  1. best loin
			  2. chump end
			(d) Chops:
			  1. loin
			  2. chump
				Top-quality roasting meat with a thin covering of fat. To facilitate carving, ask butcher to chine it. The chump (sirloin) end adjoins the leg and is bonier than the neck end. Chops can be fried, grilled (broiled) or sautéed

Saddle	3.5-5	7¾-11	Both loins joined by backbone	Roasting joint (cut)
Best End of Neck (Hotel Rack)	675 g-1	1½-2	(a) Whole (b) Boned for stuffing or, if large, making noisettes (c) Cutlets (d) Two best ends (racks) butchered to make 'Crown Roast' or 'Guard of Honour'	Very versatile cut. Useful small roast. Allow two cutlets or noisettes per portion. Cutlets are an ingredient of traditional mixed grill (broil)
Middle Neck and Scrag (Chuck)	1.25-2.25	2½-5	Chopped into pieces for casseroles and hotpots	Very bony cut, but with excellent flavour when cooked by slow, moist heat. Meat and stock can be used for pies

* **Weight range:** Cuts from young, spring lamb are considerably smaller than those from more mature animals; therefore, the chart gives these weight variations and alternative ways of butchering

Cuts From a Side of Lamb (U.K.)*

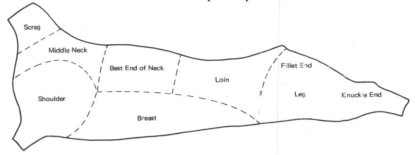

Cuts From a Side of Lamb (Australia)

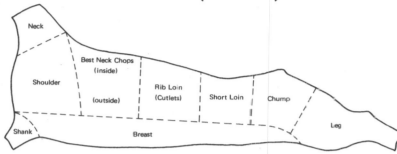

Cuts From a Side of Lamb (U.S.)*

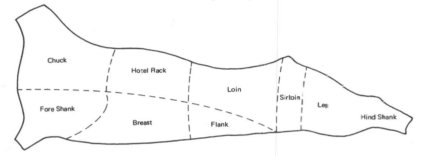

*These are popular ways of cutting a side of lamb — there are other variations. If you want lamb for the freezer cut in a special way, remember to give the butcher clear written instructions when you place the order.

Lamprey

An eel-like fish which caused the death of Henry the First of England, who died of a surfeit of them. This was possibly because the two poisonous filaments in the back were not removed.

TO FREEZE: wash lampreys thoroughly and remove filaments. Pack in freezer bags, seal, label and freeze.

TO THAW: unwrap and leave small fish to thaw for 2 hours in the refrigerator, large fish for 4 hours. Poach small lamprey in red wine, stuff and bake large ones or use any recipe for eel.
STORAGE TIME: 3 months.

Lard

Lard can be stored in the freezer if wished, although it will also keep very well for several weeks in the refrigerator.

TO FREEZE: lard bought in bulk should be left in its original wrapping (preferably in 225 g/½ lb packs). Overwrap in aluminium foil, label and freeze.

TO THAW: leave in wrappings for 4 hours in the refrigerator or for 2 hours at room temperature.

Lard may be used when cooking dishes for the freezer, to fry foods and to make pastry, etc. Always remember to use sparingly, however, as too much fat can cause food to become rancid in the freezer (see **Fat**).
STORAGE TIME: 5 months.

Lasagne

see **Pasta**

Leek

TO FREEZE: cut off roots and green tops (these can be used in soups). Wash thoroughly: slit leaves from the top down the outer sides for a few cm/inches, then stand them upside-down in water almost to cover, for 30 minutes. Drain. Blanch small ones whole, larger ones sliced, in boiling water for 3 minutes. Drain, cool rapidly in iced water, then drain and pat dry. Pack in freezer bags, seal, label and freeze.

TO THAW: unwrap and put frozen leeks in boiling salted water. Bring back to the boil, cover and simmer for 6 to 8 minutes. Drain and serve hot as a vegetable dish with a savoury white sauce, in flans, soufflés and soups, etc. See also recipes for *Vichyssoise, Cock-a-Leekie, Leek Pie* and *Leek Salad.*
STORAGE TIME: 6 months.

Leftovers

Leftovers from a meal that has been freshly prepared should be cooled quickly, packaged according to the type of food, labelled and frozen. Remains of a joint, provided it has been freshly cooked, can be sliced, wrapped in aluminium foil and frozen. *Never* re-freeze cooked food that has been taken out of the freezer and reheated, although it is quite safe to take raw foods (meat, poultry, vegetables, etc.) from the freezer, thaw, then make up into cooked dishes and re-freeze. When reheating dishes from the freezer always be sure to reheat thoroughly.
STORAGE TIME: 6 to 8 weeks (sliced cooked meat).

Lemon

see also **Fruit** for information on packing
To freeze whole lemons: wrap individually in cling film or aluminium foil.
To freeze slices: peel fruit if you like, then slice thinly or divide into segments, pack dry with or without sugar; or pack in light syrup.

After thorough washing, leeks can be frozen whole, sliced or in soups (see Vichyssoise page 134).

Lemons can be frozen whole, as grated zest or as slices which are ideal for adding, still frozen, to drinks.

To freeze lemon 'zest': grate or slice the zest finely from the peel (this can be done very easily using frozen lemons), then wrap in aluminium foil or pack in freezer bags, seal, label and freeze.

TO THAW: unwrap and thaw for 1 to 1½ hours at room temperature, or until required texture for recipe to be used.

See also recipes for *Lemon Soufflé, Lemon Mille-Feuille Gâteau, Lemonade* and *Lemon Cream Gâteau.*

STORAGE TIME: 12 months.

Lemon Curd (Cheese)

Homemade lemon curd is well worth freezing as it does not keep for more than a few weeks in the store cupboard.

TO FREEZE: in the usual way, leave until cold, then pack in small containers as it will not keep long once thawed. Special freezerproof glass jars, cottage cheese, cream or yogurt cartons make ideal containers or the rigid plastic-type can be used. Cover, seal, label and freeze.

TO THAW: leave for approximately 3 to 4 hours at room temperature.

See also recipe for *Lemon Curd.*

STORAGE TIME: 3 months.

Lemon Sole

see **Sole**

Lemon Thyme *(Thymus x citriodorus)*

Right: Lollipops (Popsicles)

prepare, freeze and thaw as for **Thyme**

Lettuce

As with all salad vegetables with a high water content, freezing causes loss of crisp texture and is therefore not recommended. If there is a surplus of tender hearts, however, these are worth freezing for use in soups.

TO FREEZE: blanch in boiling water for 2 minutes, then drain and squeeze out water. Pack in freezer bags, seal, label and freeze.

TO THAW: unwrap and use frozen.

STORAGE TIME: 6 months.

Leveret

see **Game**

Lime

prepare, freeze and thaw as for **Lemon**

Ling

The largest member of the cod family, often salted and dried. Prepare, freeze and thaw as for **Cod.**

Liquids

All liquids expand when frozen and it is, therefore, essential to leave headspace in rigid containers to allow for this. If headspace is not left, the lid will be forced off in the freezer and the contents can be affected by dehydration or oxidation. Allow 1.25–2.5 cm/½–1 inch headspace, depending on the container; narrow-topped containers need more headspace than wide-topped ones.

Liver

see **Meat, Fresh**

Lobster (Aust. Crayfish or Lobster)

Lobster must be absolutely fresh and freshly boiled for freezing. The best lobsters are medium-sized but heavy, and the male has the firmest flesh.

TO FREEZE: put live lobsters in a court bouillon, cook for approximately 25 minutes, then cool in the cooking liquid. Remove from cooking liquid, pack closely in freezer bags or aluminium foil, then seal, label and freeze quickly. Or, split shell in half lengthways, remove tail and claw meat, cut into neat pieces and pack in freezer bags or rigid containers. Seal, or cover, label and freeze.

TO THAW: leave in wrappings for approximately 6 hours in the refrigerator before serving cold, or preparing as a hot dish.

STORAGE TIME: 1 month.

Loganberry

see **Berry**

Lollipops (Popsicles)

Commercially made iced lollipops can be bought in numerous different shapes, sizes and flavours, and it is nice to be able to keep a choice of these, especially during the summer months. These, and ice pops and freezer drinks for children, can be bought in bulk at supermarkets and freezer centres, and it is well worth taking advantage of special offers.

Kits are now available for making ices on a stick at home; they are usually made from rigid plastic and come complete with stand for easy storage in the freezer, with either wooden or plastic sticks. Special syrup for flavouring can be bought for use with these kits, but homemade fruit juices may be used with good results.

Loose Pack

A method of freezing foods before they are wrapped so that individual items stay separate in the pack instead of freezing together as a solid mass. This makes it easy to take out however much is needed, the rest going back into the freezer before thawing takes place. The loose pack method is ideally suited to fruit and vegetables, and is also called **Free Flow Pack (Flash Freezing).**

Lovage *(Levisticum officinale)*

A stately herb, lovage grows to a height of 120–180 cm/4–6 feet, and will thrive anywhere. The succulent light green leaves of the plant are not unlike those of celery and there is also a similarity in taste, although lovage is sharper and more peppery, and must be used very sparingly. Both the leaves and the oval brown seeds of

the flower heads are used in cooking, and may be frozen successfully.

To freeze leaves: only pick perfect, young leaves. Chop them coarsely or cut with scissors, freeze in ice cube trays until solid, then pack in freezer bags, seal, label and return to freezer. Or pick whole bunches, wash if necessary under cold running water, shake dry and put directly into bags.

TO THAW: use frozen cubes in casseroles and fish soups, crumble leaves into salads or bland fish and vegetable dishes, or rub into meat before roasting. Always use frozen lovage sparingly as soon as you have taken it out of the freezer; the flavour is quite strong and can easily dominate all other flavours in a dish.

To freeze seeds: tie dead flower heads into bunches and hang in a dry place over a cloth until the seeds can be shaken out. Put into small waxed cartons or freezer bags, cover or seal, label and freeze.

TO THAW: use frozen or thawed whichever is more convenient, and leave them whole or crush in a mortar and pestle. Lovage seeds keep their distinctive flavour in long-cooking dishes and in spiced biscuits (cookies), bread and cakes.

STORAGE TIME: 6 months (cubes); 2 months (bunches); 10 months (seeds).

Lychee

see also **Fruit** for information on packing

TO FREEZE: shell off jackets and pack in heavy syrup.

TO THAW: leave in container in refrigerator and serve while still frosted in fresh fruit salads and with icecream.

STORAGE TIME: 12 months.

Macaroni

see **Pasta**

Mackerel

Mackerel is a fish similar in size to herring, and it has a beautiful flavour whether served hot or cold. It must be eaten very fresh, when it is stiff and opalescent, with bright protruding eyes; when it is limp, the fish is indigestible and can be poisonous. It should be frozen within 1 hour of catching to retain the best flavour. Smoked mackerel is becoming increasingly popular served as a first course, or made into pâté, and it freezes well.

TO FREEZE: clean fresh fish and pack in freezer bags. Seal, label and freeze. Wrap smoked mackerel individually in cling film, then pack several fish in a freezer bag. Seal, label and freeze.

TO THAW: unwrap and cook both fresh and smoked mackerel from frozen. If smoked mackerel is to be served cold, leave to thaw in wrappings for 3 hours in the refrigerator.

See also recipe for *Baked Smokies*.

STORAGE TIME: 3 months.

Mandarin

prepare, freeze and thaw as for **Orange**

Mandarin (Aust.)

see **Satsuma**

Mange Tout

see **Pea**

Mango

see also **Fruit** for information on packing

Freeze only fully ripe fruit.

TO FREEZE: peel, cut out large stone (pit), slice and pack in medium syrup, adding 1 × 15 ml spoon/1 tablespoon lemon juice to every 1 litre/2 pints/5 cups syrup.

TO THAW: leave in container for 1½ hours at room temperature; use raw in fresh fruit salads, etc.

STORAGE TIME: 12 months.

Margarine

TO FREEZE: leave in original wrappings (preferably 225 g/½ lb packs) and overwrap in aluminium foil or freezer tissue. This applies to both hard and soft tub margarines which should be frozen as soon as possible after purchase.

TO THAW: remove overwrapping and leave for 4 hours in the refrigerator. Or thaw for approximately 2 hours at room temperature.

STORAGE TIME: 5 months.

Marjoram

Knotted or Sweet (*Origanum marjorana*)

The most fragrant and versatile of the three main kinds of culinary marjoram, which owes its common name to the fact that its flower heads are produced in pairs of green clusters looking like knots. Sweet marjoram is grown widely in many parts of the world and is an invaluable herb in cooking. It grows to a bushy plant, 30–46 cm/12–18 inches high and wide. Due to the fact that the plant usually dies in winter (particularly in colder climates), it is well worth freezing quantities of it during the summer months when the sweetly spiced leaves and flower buds grow in abundance. Sweet marjoram has a milder and more subtle flavour than wild marjoram (oregano), and can therefore be used liberally without overwhelming other flavours in a dish.

Wild Marjoram or Oregano (*Origanum vulgare*)

This variety grows to a height of 60–90 cm/2–3 feet and can be found widely throughout Europe. It has a

Lemon Curd (Cheese) – Marjoram

Freeze ripe mangoes in medium syrup (see page 53) and lemon juice.

Marmalade

There is no point in freezing ready-prepared marmalade as it will keep perfectly well if stored correctly in jars in a cool, dry place. If you are making marmalade, however, and are short of time during the one season when Seville oranges are available, the freezer can be useful. Oranges can be frozen whole, or cooked to a pulp (without sugar) before freezing. When making marmalade with frozen fruit or pulp it is advisable to add either a little commercial pectin or extra oranges, as some of the natural pectin is lost during the freezing process and the resulting marmalade may not have a good 'set'.

To freeze whole oranges: wash and dry them, then put in freezer bags, seal, label and freeze until required. When ready to make marmalade, thaw oranges first.

TO THAW: leave oranges in wrappings overnight in the refrigerator, then use as for fresh oranges.

To freeze cooked pulp: cool rapidly, then pack in rigid containers, cover, label and freeze.

TO THAW: leave pulp in containers overnight in the refrigerator, then transfer to a heavy saucepan, add sugar and boil until thick according to recipe used.

STORAGE TIME: 6 months (both whole oranges and pulp).

Marrow (Large Summer Squash)

Due to their high water content, most marrows do not freeze successfully, and become mushy on thawing, although very young ones are worth the effort.

TO FREEZE: peel, cut into chunks and remove seeds. Blanch in boiling water for 2 minutes. Drain, cool rapidly in iced water, then drain and pat dry. Pack in rigid containers, leaving 1.25 cm/½ inch headspace. Cover, label and freeze.

TO THAW: unwrap and reheat from frozen in an uncovered steamer for 1 to 2 minutes. Serve hot with melted butter or a white sauce.

STORAGE TIME: 6 months.

Marzipan

see **Almond Paste**

Mayonnaise

Do not freeze mayonnaise, or dips, sandwich filling, sauces and other dishes that contain mayonnaise. These will separate during the freezing process and not resemble their original state.

Seville oranges can be wrapped in freezer bags and frozen, to be made into marmalade at a later date.

more powerful, biting taste than sweet marjoram and if grown in a warm climate is more aromatic than in cooler regions. Use sparingly at first to gauge its pungency.

Pot Marjoram (Origanum onites)

A variety with less flavour than the other marjorams, but worth growing and freezing for bouquets garnis to use in long-cooking dishes. It grows to a bushy 60 cm/2 feet, and has small, dark green leaves throughout the year.

TO FREEZE: always cut marjoram for freezing before the knotted flower buds start to open. Cut the stems down quite close to the ground so that more growth will form. Wash sprigs if necessary under cold running water, shake dry, then pack in small bunches in freezer bags, seal, label and freeze. Or strip off the leaves and buds, freeze in ice cube trays until solid, then pack in bags.

TO THAW: chop bunches finely while still frozen and add to hot vegetables with butter just before serving, or sprinkle over egg and cheese dishes, sauces and soups. Use cubes frozen or thawed in casseroles, pizza and tomato dishes, or with minced (ground) meats, pork and veal.

STORAGE TIME: 2 months (whole sprigs); 8 months (cubes).

Meat, Cooked

see also **Casserole, Curry, Galantine, Meat, Fresh, Pâté** and **Terrine**

Cooked meat and most composite meat dishes can be frozen, but it is important to observe the following points:

1. All cooked meat should be handled with the utmost regard for hygiene. Hands, packaging materials, utensils, work surfaces, etc., must be scrupulously clean.

2. Meat should be frozen as soon as possible after cooking. This means cooling it rapidly and chilling it in the refrigerator before freezing, in as short a time as possible.

3. Careful packaging is essential to protect the meat from the drying effect of the cold air in the freezer.

4. Pack in small, shallow units of preferably not more than four portions. This makes freezing, thawing and/or reheating speedier.

TO THAW: when thawing is necessary, slow thawing in the refrigerator is preferable to faster thawing at room temperature.

TO REHEAT: whether reheating from frozen or thawed, it is very important that the food is thoroughly heated right through and served really hot. Many dishes, such as casseroles, sliced meat in gravy and pies can be reheated from frozen, either in the oven or on top of the stove. Reheating from frozen in the oven is a lengthy process and not an economical use of fuel; therefore, it is worth remembering to thaw dishes overnight in the refrigerator if possible, so that they can be reheated quickly.

Prime meat, on the bone, can be roasted from frozen with the aid of a meat thermometer (see page 78).

STORAGE TIME: the life of cooked meat dishes in the freezer varies according to the ingredients. When using your own recipes, always label with the date frozen and build up your own records. As a guide, 1 month is safe for all dishes, up to 2 months is fine for most, and some show little signs of deterioration after 3 months. There are no hard and fast rules, but err on the cautious side when trying new dishes.

Meat, Fresh

see also **Bacon, Beef, Lamb, Meat, Cooked, Mutton, Pork, Veal**

Meat freezes and stores very satisfactorily, but for the best results you should freeze only top-quality meat from animals that have been expertly reared, slaughtered, conditioned and butchered. In most cases it is impossible for consumers to know the history of the meat they are buying, so it is always advisable to deal only with suppliers whose standards of quality and hygiene you know to be completely reliable. This is particularly important if you buy bulk quantities and meat on special offer or on sale, as few things could be more disappointing than a freezer full of poor-quality meat.

Freezer Space Needed

Boneless meat needs roughly half as much storage space as meat on the bone. So if space is at a premium, or you have a small upright freezer, it may help to have most, if not all, the meat boned. As a general guide, allow 56 litres/2 cu ft of space for every 9 kg/20 lb of *boneless* meat, but allow twice this space for meat on the bone, or for bones on their own.

Storage Time

Meats stored at −18°C/0°F or below, have a reasonably long storage life, but don't buy more than you can use within the recommended storage period. Meat kept beyond this time does not become harmful in any way, but it suffers a gradual deterioration in flavour and quality. Use the following chart as a guide for storage times:

Joints (cuts) of beef — use within 8 months.

Joints (cuts) of lamb, pork or veal — use within 6 months.

Mince and offal (ground meat and variety meat/fancy meat) — use within 3 months.

For further details on storage life, see individual meat entries (**Bacon, Beef, Lamb, Pork, Veal**).

Packaging meat
1 Freezing mince as patties and in usable quantities in freezer bags.
2 Laying steaks and chops in rigid containers.
3 Padding sharp bones with foil before wrapping joints and large cuts in freezer bags.
4 Wrapping kidneys in foil and layering slices of liver in shallow foil trays.

Seasonal Availability

Some meat is seasonal in quality, and in the quantity coming on the market at different times of the year. Demand from consumers is also seasonal and variable. During periods of peak supply, or when the demand is low, buying prices may be advantageous for bulk buying. For further details on buying, see individual meat entries (**Bacon, Beef, Lamb, Pork, Veal**).

Deliveries*

Some suppliers deliver to your door, but others are cash and carry. If you are without transport, check this carefully before ordering.
*Not applicable in Australia and U.S.A.

Buying

Meat for the freezer is offered in several ways and different suppliers offer different services. For instance, some will butcher and package the meat but have no freezing facilities; others will butcher, wrap, freeze and deliver. Consider your own facilities for freezing before deciding to order fresh meat to freeze at home. In Australia, meat for the freezer may be purchased in the piece or butchered; transportation, packing and freezing are the responsibility of the consumer.

Ready-frozen Meat

Freezer centres, specialist frozen meat suppliers and some cash and carries and markets offer various single cuts, their own selection packs, whole lambs or cut up sides of pork. This is a convenient way of buying meat provided you like the quality and type of cuts offered. After buying, immediately insulate the meat in a special insulated container or several layers of newspaper and transfer it to your own freezer as quickly as possible, so that it does not have time to thaw or lose quality.

Fresh Meat

Most butchers specializing in freezer trade will supply meat for the freezer at competitive or discount prices. These can be single cuts, or a selection of mixed cuts and meats to suit your own personal requirements. You choose the meat and specify how you want it butchered.

Salted or Cured (Smoked) Meat

Never risk freezing salted or cured (smoked) meats as their storage life is unpredictably short. (In Australia, salt or cured meats can be stored at −18°C/0°F for a maximum of 2 months.)

Buying in Bulk

The bigger the purchase the greater the cash saving is likely to be. But savings quickly evaporate if the family becomes bored with too much of one kind of meat, or if unfamiliar cuts remain unused until they are finally thrown out or given away. One solution is to get together with another family — see *Sharing a Bulk-buy* below. Another solution is to buy a small bulk-buy — see chart *Traditional Bulk-buys* page 80. Butchers' traditional bulk-buys include all the cuts, which means, depending on the animal, varying proportions of braising, mincing (grinding) and stewing meat as well as chops, roasting joints (cuts) and steaks. To bulk-buy successfully you need to decide what kind of meat suits your particular family and way of life. For instance, families who like only grills (broiled meat) and roasts, would not appreciate the mainly braising and stewing cuts from a beef forequarter. The following chart is a guide to the approximate weight range and the percentage of the different types of meat you can expect from the traditional bulk-buys.

Sharing a Bulk-buy

The larger the bulk-buy the lower the price per kg/lb and, theoretically, the greater the cash saving. Many butchers specializing in freezer trade will divide big buys between two or three purchasers, enabling them to take advantage of the lower price. For example, two families could share a pig, having one side each. Sharing a side of beef, or a hindquarter is a little more complex. It helps if all the families concerned agree upon the butchering (i.e. settle for having all the meat boned, joints (cuts) of a similar size such as approximately 1.5 kg/3 lb each, and packs of mince (ground) meat and stewing steak weighing ½ kg/1 lb. When fillet or rump steak is involved it can be cut into steaks and shared equally, or the families could agree to alternate taking these cuts. When sharing bulk-buys, always give the butcher clear, preferably written, instructions.

See *Traditional Bulk-buys* chart on page 80.

3

4

Ordering

Various problems and disappointments can be avoided by careful advance planning.

1. Check that you have enough room in the freezer to accommodate the meat. See *Freezer Space Needed* page 75.

2. Order well in advance so the meat can be supplied in the best condition for freezing. See also individual meat entries (**Beef, Lamb, Pork, Veal**).

3. Give the butcher clear, preferably written, instructions about how you would like the meat butchered. That is to say, the weight of the individual joints (cuts), whether braising meat is to be cubed or sliced, the number of chops or steaks in a pack, and so on. Specify any joints (cuts) you want boned, or in the case of beef, which joints (cuts) you want left on the bone. For further details of cuts, see individual meat entries (**Beef, Lamb, Pork, Veal**).

4. Check whether the meat is packed and labelled, and how this is done.

5. Ask for beef bones to be sawed into manageable sizes, and fat to be cut in small pieces. Suet should be kept separately.

6. Arrange a definite time for delivery so the 'fast freeze' switch on your freezer can be turned on in advance.

7. If the butcher does not package the meat, check that you have enough packaging materials in stock to do the job at home.

Packaging

It is particularly important to protect meat from dehydration in the freezer by close wrapping it in tough moisture- and vapour-proof material. See that sharp bones are padded to prevent them puncturing the wrapping. If a butcher has packaged the meat and the wrapping material appears thin, overwrap or group similar packages together in a large freezer bag.* Similarly, if the butcher's packaging is loose rather than clinging tightly to the meat (indicating that air has not been expelled), quickly re-package it.

*Not applicable in Australia.

Useful packaging materials for meat are:

1 heavy-duty aluminium foil or cling film — for joints and large cuts.

2 heavy-gauge freezer bags or rigid containers — for mince (ground meat) and cut up stewing meat.

3 cling film, freezer tissue, double greaseproof (waxed) paper, interleaving sheets or plastic wrap for separating chops and steaks.

4 labels, freezer tape and ties.

5 large freezer bags for bones and fat.

Preparation

1 Make sure all utensils and work surfaces are scrupulously clean.

2 Deal with minced (ground) meats and offal (variety meats/fancy meats) first, then small cuts. Keep the rest of the meat refrigerated meanwhile.

Mince (ground) and cut up stewing meat: weigh straight into freezer bags in amounts convenient for your size of family, for example ½ kg/1 lb, etc. Press into a neat shape, expelling as much air as possible (see **Air**). Or pack closely in small rigid containers. If you like, form mince (ground) meat into patties and wrap individually in aluminium foil. Seal, label and freeze.

Chops and steaks: trim away surplus fat and skin. Wrap individually in cling film, then pack in freezer bags. Or pack, not more than two deep, in rigid containers, interleaving layers with cling film, greaseproof (waxed) paper or plastic wrap. Seal with a lid or overwrap with aluminium foil. Label and freeze.

Joints and large cuts: remove any surplus fat. Pad any sharp bones or skewers with cling film or foil to prevent them piercing the wrappings. If necessary, tie the meat in a neat shape ready for cooking. Wrap in freezer bags or cling film, pressing the wrappings closely to the meat and expelling as much air as possible (see **Air**). Label with name, weight and date, and freeze.

Offal (variety meat/fancy meat): must be very fresh. Prepare as if for cooking. Wrap individual items such as small hearts or kidneys closely in cling film or aluminium foil, then group them in convenient numbers in freezer bags. Lay slices of heart, liver (lamb's fry), or pieces of tripe, in shallow foil trays, then overwrap in aluminium foil or cling film. Treat oxtail as stewing meat, fresh ox tongue as a joint (large cut), and lambs' tongues as small hearts or kidneys. Label and freeze.

Stuffing: never freeze stuffing in meat; wrap and freeze separately.

Freezing

Consult the instruction book or manufacturer's recommendations for your particular freezer, but generally you can freeze only one-tenth of the capacity of your freezer in every 24 hours.* So freezing a bulk-buy such as a side of pork could take 2 days. It is very important to keep the meat in the refrigerator in the meantime. Never overload the freezer as this can reduce the rate of freezing and lead to loss of meat quality. Excessive 'drip' is one result of slow freezing.

1 Switch to 'fast freeze' or the coldest setting at least 2 hours before starting to freeze. Clear the freezing compartment, or the special shelf in an upright freezer, and separate frozen foods from those being frozen.

2 Freeze minced (ground) meat, offal (variety meat/fancy meat) and cut-up meat first.

3 Place each package so it is in contact with the base and/or sides in a chest freezer or with the freezing shelf in an upright model. As soon as these packages are frozen solid, transfer to the storage area and introduce new packs for freezing.

4 When all the meat is frozen, group similar kinds of pack together. In the case of a chest freezer, large plastic shopping bags keep the freezer tidy and make it easier and quicker to find what you want.

5 Attach a list of the frozen meat to the freezer door, or make entries in a freezer diary if you have one. This way you can keep a track of what is in stock and how much is left.

6 Remember to switch the control back to 'normal' approximately 12 hours after the last batch of meat goes into the freezer.

*In Australia it is safe to freeze larger quantities than this in 24 hours — consult manufacturer's recommendations for exact amounts. When freezing larger quantities, the 'fast freeze' switch should be on for 48 hours.

Thawing

Frozen meat can be thawed before cooking or cooked from the frozen state. For example, if the meat is to be deep-fried, minced (ground) or stuffed, thawing is obviously essential, and joints (cuts) over 1.5 kg/3 lb in weight or boneless joints (cuts) should also be thawed before cooking. If cooking frozen joints or cuts, use a meat thermometer. Leave meat to thaw in the original wrapper and, if possible, in the refrigerator. This slow thawing takes much longer than thawing at room temperature, but the meat will retain more natural quality because there is less loss of juice. After thawing, keep the meat in the refrigerator and cook as soon as possible.

Meat before and after freezing is illustrated opposite. If it is thawed after freezing, meat should be cooked in exactly the same ways as for fresh.

Thawing Times

*Chops, slices, steaks approx. 2.5 cm/1 inch thick:	2–3 hours at room temperature; 8–12 hours in the refrigerator.
Small joints (cuts) 1.5 kg/3 lb and under:	1½–2 hours per ½ kg/1 lb at room temperature; 4–5 hours per ½ kg/1 lb in the refrigerator.
Large joints (cuts):	2–3 hours per ½ kg/1 lb at room temperature; 5–7 hours per ½ kg/1 lb in the refrigerator.

*Not applicable in Australia.

Cooking Thawed Meat

Providing the meat is fully thawed, cook in exactly the same way and for the same time as fresh meat. In the case of beef, some of the juices may 'drip' out of the meat during thawing. These juices contain valuable nutrients and should therefore be used in the dish you are cooking if possible.

In the case of a joint (cut) cooked very slowly in the oven, pour the 'drip' over the meat during cooking when it will form a soft 'mat' in the base of the cooking dish. After transferring the meat to a serving platter and pouring off the excess fat, this 'mat' can be whisked to form a richly flavoured gravy. Don't allow the gravy to boil if the 'drip' has been added, or overheating will cause it to coagulate.

Cooking Meat from Frozen

Roasting: Suitable for top-quality roasting joints (cuts) of up to 1.5 kg/3 lb in weight, preferably 'on the bone', as the bone is a good conductor of heat. Cooking from frozen is not recommended for boned and rolled joints (cuts). Because of the risk of food-poisoning micro-organisms surviving in inadequately cooked meat, especially pork, it is essential to use a meat thermometer to determine when the meat is cooked. Cook the meat slowly in a moderate oven (180°C/350°F or Gas Mark 4) using the following times as a guide:

Braising: seal all cut surfaces in hot fat to prevent loss of juices, then add liquid and flavourings and cook in a very slow oven for one and one-half to two times as long as the normal time.

Frying: place chops or steaks in a lightly oiled pan and cook over low heat, turning frequently until thawed. Raise the heat for the last few minutes to brown. Allow about half as long again as when cooking thawed meat.

Grilling (broiling): brush chops or steaks with a little oil or melted butter, place 2.5–5 cm/1–2 inches further from the heat than usual and cook gently until the meat has thawed. Turn frequently, and put close to the element for quick browning towards the end of cooking. Time as for *Frying* above.

Stewing: diced stewing meat, or pieces of lamb, can be covered with liquid and cooked from the frozen state, taking care never to allow the liquid to rise above simmering point. Good-quality stewing meat which is normally first coated with flour and sealed in hot fat needs to be thawed enough to separate the pieces before coating and frying.

Cooking Meat from Frozen

Meat	Temperature	Time per ½ kg/lb	Reading on meat thermometer
Lamb Whole legs	160°C/325°F or Gas Mark 3	45 minutes	82°C/180°F
Shoulders, best end, half legs	180°C/350°F or Gas Mark 4	45 minutes	
Beef Thick joints (cuts)	180°C/350°F or Gas Mark 4	50 minutes	76°C/170°F (well done); 71°C/160°F (medium)
Thin joints (cuts)	180°C/350°F or Gas Mark 4	45 minutes	
Pork Thick joints (cuts)	180°C/350°F or Gas Mark 4	60 minutes	87°C/190°F
Thin joints (cuts)	180°C/350°F or Gas Mark 4	55 minutes	
Veal	180°C/350°F or Gas Mark 4	50 minutes	76°C/170°F (well done)

Traditional Bulk-buys (Aust. & U.K.)

Bulk-Buy	Average weight range in kg/lb		Average % loss of bone & fat	Average % of grilling and roasting meat	Average % of braising and pot roasting meat	Average % of mincing and stewing meat	General Comments
	kg	lb					
Whole Lamb, English*	12-20	28-45	None	85%		15%	In bulk buying, lamb, pork and veal are usually jointed and supplied 'on the bone' unless you request otherwise
Whole Lamb, New Zealand Side of Lamb, Australian	9-16	20-35	None	85%		15%	
Side of Pork	18-27	40-60	None	100%			
Fore end of Pork	9-13	20-30	None	100%			
Whole medium Calf* (Veal)	18-36	40-80	None	70%		30%	
Beef Hindquarter	63-72	140-160	28%-30%	80%	5%	15%	Beef is usually completely boned, but you pay for the whole purchase — meat, bones and fat. You can use the bones for making *Stock*, the fat for rendering down for *Dripping(s)* and the *Suet* (hindquarter beef only) for making mincemeat, pastry and puddings
Topbit (Aust. butt) & rump	45-54	100-120	28%-30%	85%	5%	10%	
Sirloin & rump	20-30	45-65	28%-30%	95%	5%	None	
Rump (boneless)	7-9	15-20	None	100%	None	None	
Forequarter	63-72	140-160	30%-32%	15%	55%	30%	
Pony (chuck, blade back & short ribs)	34-43	75-95	20%-21%		85%	15%	
Crop (pony & neck & fore ribs)	43-50	95-115	20%-21%	20%	65%	15%	

Offal (Fancy Meat): Except the kidneys with English lamb, offal are not generally included in a bulk-buy. However, you can often make a special arrangement with the supplier. Fancy meats are occasionally supplied with hindquarters of beef in Australia.
* Not applicable in Australia.

Traditional Bulk-buys (U.S.)

Bulk-Buy	Average weight range in lb	Average % loss of bone and fat	Average % of broiling and roasting meat	Average % of braising and pot roasting meat	Average % of ground and stewing meat	General Comments
Whole Lamb	28-35	None	85%		15%	See Australian & U.K. chart for general comments
Side of Pork	40-60	None	100%			
Whole Calf (Veal)	25-40	None	70%		30%	
Beef Hindquarter	140-160	28%-30%	80%	5%	15%	
Forequarter	140-160	30%-32%	15%	75%	10%	

Variety Meats: You may have to make special arrangements to request the variety meats from lamb.

It is worth keeping a supply of mince in the freezer at all times as it can be made into a wide variety of quick dishes like the hamburgers, spaghetti bolognese and stuffed peppers illustrated below.

Meat Loaf

see **Pâté & Terrine**

Melon

see also **Fruit** for information on packing

Firm melons such as cantaloup, honeydew and rockmelon freeze very well, although they are not as crisp as fresh melons when thawed. Watermelons cannot be frozen. Choose fruit ripe enough to have a full flavour, but not over-ripe.

TO FREEZE: cut in half and remove seeds. Peel and cut the fruit into cubes or slices, then pack immediately in a light syrup; or pack dry with sugar.

TO THAW: leave in container in the refrigerator and serve while still frosted, sprinkled with a little lemon juice.

STORAGE TIME: 12 months.

Meringue

Meringues are a very useful way of using up leftover egg whites and they can be frozen with or without cream fillings.

Make and bake as usual and cool on a wire rack.

To freeze unfilled shells: open (flash) freeze on trays until solid, then carefully pack in rigid containers or freezer bags, seal, label and return to freezer.

If using bags, do not suck air out with a straw or draw it out with a pump before freezing as this will cause the meringues to collapse.

TO THAW: use straight from the freezer for decorative purposes, but if they are to be sandwiched together with cream, unwrap and leave to thaw for approximately 2 hours at room temperature.

To freeze meringues with cream: make, bake and cool, then sandwich together with stiffly whipped cream, adding a little sugar, if you like. Open (flash) freeze on trays until solid, then pack in rigid containers, separating each meringue with cardboard or aluminium foil to prevent breakages. Cover, label and return to freezer.

TO THAW: remove from containers and leave for 3 to 4 hours at room temperature.

It is not advisable to freeze puddings and desserts with soft meringue toppings as these will not hold their shape once thawed. This type of dish is best frozen without the meringue topping, which can be added when the dish is reheated for serving.

See also recipe for *Meringue Chantilly*.

STORAGE TIME: 3 months.

Meat Loaf – Meringue

Meringue
1 *Piping large and small meringues onto baking sheets before baking in the usual way.*
2 *Sandwiching the large meringues together with crème chantilly (see page 222).*
3 *Sealing freezer bag of small unfilled meringues, without having withdrawn air.*
4 *Packing open-frozen, filled meringues into rigid containers, separating them with foil.*
5 *Small meringues are ideal for decorating desserts like Rhubarb Suédoise (see page 190) and Meringues Chantilly (see page 222) are delicious served alone.*

5

Micro-organisms

The generic name for countless bacteria, moulds and other minute organisms, both harmful and beneficial, which are present everywhere. Any kind of food preparation should be carried out as quickly and hygienically as possible to prevent these micro-organisms from being active and causing food spoilage and food poisoning. It is therefore important not to keep prepared or partially prepared foods for any length of time at temperatures that encourage their growth, i.e. between 10°C/50°F and 63°C/145°F. It is for this reason that cooked foods must be cooled rapidly before freezing, and if food cannot go into the freezer immediately, it should be stored temporarily in a refrigerator.

Freezing does not destroy all micro-organisms, whether they are harmful or not. Some remain dormant and spring back to life with renewed zest as soon as the temperature rises to their individual needs. However, as long as food remains frozen at −18°C/0°F or below, and there are no great temperature fluctuations, there is no danger of micro-organisms multiplying and affecting food. On the other hand, when frozen food is thawed and partially warmed up, any food-poisoning organisms present can quickly start work. This is why thawing in a refrigerator rather than at room temperature is recommended for certain foods, and why reheating must be thorough.

Mint sauce frozen as ice cubes is illustrated on this page.

Milk

TO FREEZE: freeze only homogenized milk in waxed cartons; do not freeze in bottles which will crack at such a low temperature — if necessary, transfer to rigid containers. Allow 2.5 cm/1 inch headspace, cover, label and freeze.
TO THAW: leave in container overnight in the refrigerator. Use quickly once thawed. If the milk separates on thawing, tip it into a saucepan, bring to the boil, leave to cool, and it will be reconstituted.

Milk can be used in dishes and sauces, etc., that are to be frozen, but wherever possible add the milk on reheating — in the case of soups, for example, which are made of a combination of stock and milk, the soup should be frozen without the milk, which is then added on reheating.
STORAGE TIME: 1 month.

Mince (Minced Beef)

see **Beef**

Mincemeat (Fruit Mince)

Homemade mincemeat freezes very well, either on its own or made into flans or pies.
To freeze mincemeat: make according to your favourite recipe. If mincemeat is the cooked variety, then cool quickly. Pack in waxed cartons or rigid containers. Cover, label and freeze until required.
TO THAW: leave in carton for 3 to 4 hours at room temperature.
To freeze mince pies: make as usual in large flan or small patty tins (pans), but do not bake. Open (flash) freeze until solid, then remove from tins (pans), transfer to freezer bags or rigid containers, seal or cover, label and return to freezer.
TO THAW: take pies out individually, as and when required. Return to tins (pans), brush with beaten egg and bake from frozen in a fairly hot oven (200°C/400°F or Gas Mark 6) for approximately 20 minutes or until cooked through.

See also recipe for *Mince Pies*.
STORAGE TIME: 1 month (for both mincemeat and mince pies).

Mint, Spearmint *(Mentha spicata)* / Applemint *(Mentha rotundifolia)*

Of the great variety of mints which have been grown for 2,000 years for their culinary and medicinal properties, there are two outstanding ones of value to the cook. Spearmint is the one most often grown commercially for sale fresh; the plant grows and spreads to approximately 90 cm/3 feet and is a vigorous herb with narrow leaves and a strong aroma of spearmint. Applemint is even more robust, with round slightly hairy leaves; it is the best variety to use for making mint sauce.
TO FREEZE: pick young sprigs or take individual leaves from tougher stems. Wash if necessary under cold running water, then shake dry. Chop finely or cut with scissors, freeze in ice cube trays until solid, then pack in freezer bags, seal, label and return to freezer. Or put whole sprigs and leaves directly into bags. For large quantities to be used in sauces at a later date, purée whole bunches in an electric blender with a little water, pour into small rigid containers, cover, label and freeze, or freeze in ice cube trays as above.
TO THAW: use cubes frozen or thawed in casseroles and stews. Chop or crumble whole frozen sprigs or leaves while still frozen, or cut them with scissors directly onto freshly cooked young vegetables just before serving.

Frozen sprigs can be added whole to peas or new potatoes as they cook. Use puréed mint straight from the freezer in white and vinegar-based sauces.
To freeze mint sauce: purée approximately 225 g/½ lb freshly picked mint leaves in an electric blender, then moisten with a little wine or cider vinegar and stir in 25–50 g/1–2 oz/2–4 tablespoons (caster) sugar, according to taste. Freeze in ice cube trays until solid, then pack in freezer bags, seal, label and return to freezer.
TO THAW: unwrap and put cubes into a jug or bowl. Add a little vinegar or water and vinegar and leave to thaw for approximately 10 minutes in a warm place. Once thawed, mint sauce will keep for several days in the refrigerator. See also **Butter, Flavoured** for *Mint Butter* recipe.
STORAGE TIME: 3 months (whole sprigs); 8 months (cubes).

Mirabelle

prepare, freeze and thaw as for **Plum**

Moisture/Vapour-proof Wrapping

Describes various non-porous wrapping materials specially designed for freezing to protect food from dehydration or freezer burn. Pages 232-4.

Mold/Mould

see **Jelly**

Moose

see **Game**

Morello Cherry

prepare, freeze and thaw as for **Cherry**

Pie, *Mixed Vegetable Medley, Individual Mushroom Quiches, Kidney and Mushroom Casserole* and *Mushrooms in Sour(ed) Cream*.
STORAGE TIME: 3 months.

Muskrat
see **Game**

Far left: Sweet and savoury mousses can be frozen in freezerproof dishes or moulds. Garnish or decorate before serving.

Mushroom
1 Transferring open-frozen mushroom tops from a baking sheet to a rigid container before returning them to the freezer.
2 Frying frozen mushroom tops in butter.
3 Serve mushroom tops as for fresh and use thawed frozen stalks for soup.

Mousse(s)

Both sweet and savoury mousses freeze extremely well, whether made with cream, eggs or gelatin(e), or a mixture of these.

TO FREEZE: make mousse according to your favourite recipe and, if possible, freeze in the serving dish (providing it will withstand the low temperature of the freezer). Cover well with aluminium foil, label and freeze until required.

TO THAW: transfer mousse to refrigerator and leave for at least 2 hours for a mousse set with cream or eggs, 6 hours for a mousse set with gelatin(e). If a chilled mousse is liked, serve straight from the refrigerator; if a softer texture is preferred, leave to stand for 1 hour at room temperature before serving. Always decorate mousses just before serving, not before freezing.

STORAGE TIME: 1 month; if containing gelatin(e) — 2 months.

Mozzarella
see **Cheese**

Muffins (U.S. Biscuits)

Both homemade and commercially baked muffins freeze well.

TO FREEZE: cool, if necessary, pack in freezer bags, seal, label and freeze until required.

TO THAW: leave in wrappings for approximately 20 minutes at room temperature then refresh as follows: for muffins, split and toast on both sides and spread with butter. For biscuits: reheat wrapped in foil in a moderate oven (180°C/350°F or Gas

Mark 4) for 10 minutes or until hot to the touch. Split, butter and serve.

For English muffins, see **Crumpets**.
STORAGE TIME: 6 months.

Mulberry
see **Berry**

Mullet

Red mullet is the fish found in the English Channel and the Mediterranean, while grey mullet is a coarser fish found on Australian, European and North American coasts. Some cooks prefer to cook red mullet without cleaning, but for freezing purposes it is better cleaned and drawn.

TO FREEZE: pack in freezer bags, seal, label and freeze.

TO THAW: unwrap and grill (broil), fry or bake from frozen, or use frozen in soups.

STORAGE TIME: 3 months.

Mushroom

TO FREEZE: wipe, but do not peel. Trim off stems, open (flash) freeze whole until solid, then pack in rigid containers or freezer bags. Cover or seal, label and freeze. Freeze stems in separate bags for use in sauces, soups, stews and stock.

TO THAW: toss frozen mushrooms in melted butter or put under grill (broiler) until heated through. Or, if using in composite dishes, thaw in wrappings in the refrigerator until mushrooms begin to soften.

Mushrooms also freeze well in prepared dishes and purées. See *Duxelles of mushrooms* under **Soup Garnishes**, and recipes for *Mushroom and Onion Soup, Country Chicken and Mushroom*

Mussel

Mussels freeze well, but they must be very thoroughly cleaned. Scrub the shells with a stiff brush and remove any fibrous pieces (beards) sticking out from the shell.

Put them in a large heavy saucepan, cover with a damp cloth and put over a medium heat until they open — this will take approximately 3 minutes. Discard any shells which have not opened, or which are broken or have holes in them. Leave to cool in the saucepan.

TO FREEZE: pack with or without shells, in their juices, in rigid containers. Cover, label and freeze.

TO THAW: leave in containers for 3 hours in the refrigerator, then prepare as required.

STORAGE TIME: 1 month.

Freeze mussels in rigid containers with or without their shells.

Mutton

Although there are various technical definitions, in general terms, a lamb over 12 months old is classed as mutton.

The carcass weight range is from 18–33 kg/40–75 lb, averaging 22–27 kg/50–60 lb. Young mutton of top quality makes very good eating, but it coarsens as age increases. Prepare, freeze and thaw as for **Lamb.**

The cuts are similar to lamb cuts, but naturally larger. When choosing, look for thick shoulders and plump stocky legs. A thin covering of fat is desirable, and the flesh, although much deeper in colour than lamb, should not be really dark.

Avoid buying very lean and scrawny carcasses.

Nasturtium Seed

These are usually pickled when fresh, but they can be frozen if wished. Pick the seeds on a dry day.

TO FREEZE: open (flash) freeze until solid, then pack in freezer bags. Or put directly into bags, seal, label and freeze.

TO THAW: remove from bags and leave for 30 minutes at room temperature. Use to add 'tang' to green salads.

Nectarine

see also **Fruit** for information on packing

TO FREEZE: wipe fruit and leave on skin or remove it as you wish. To do so, cover with boiling water and leave for 20 to 30 seconds until the skins come off easily but the fruit has not started to cook. Plunge into cold water for 2 minutes, then rub or peel off the skins. Cut in half to remove stones (pits), slice if wished, then pack immediately in a heavy syrup.

TO THAW: leave in unopened container for approximately 3 hours in the refrigerator, then use immediately to avoid discoloration.

STORAGE TIME: 12 months.

Nettle*

Only young nettle tops are edible in early spring and summer and, as they have a limited use, it is hardly worth freezing them. Use them fresh to add flavour to soups.

*Not applicable in Australia.

Nutritive Value

The nutritive value of food is not altered by the freezing process: its quality will remain exactly as it was at the time of freezing. For the best results, therefore, it is advisable only to preserve food by freezing it when it is in peak condition. There are certain factors that will cause nutrient losses in frozen food, however, and these are: bad handling during preparation; faulty or inadequate packaging; slow freezing; fluctuations in storage temperature which speed up the rate of deterioration; careless thawing.

Nuts

Except for the salted varieties, most nuts will keep fresher in the freezer than they would if kept in a store cupboard and it is certainly well worthwhile buying and freezing them in large quantities.

TO FREEZE: leave nuts whole or ready-cut, or chop or split them according to future use; they may also be buttered or toasted before freezing. Pack in usable quantities in rigid containers or freezer bags, seal, label and freeze.

TO THAW: leave in wrappings for approximately 3 hours at room temperature.

STORAGE TIME: 12 months; buttered or toasted nuts — 4 months.

Freeze nuts whole, split or chopped.

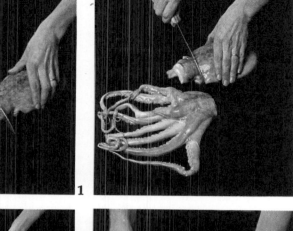

O

Octopus

The best octopus are approximately 1 kg/2 lb in weight, otherwise the fish may be tough. Cut off the tentacles then the eyes and beak-like mouth. Clean out the body. Do not pierce the ink sac. Cut out the anus. Discard the ends of the tentacles. Beat the meat to tenderize it, then cut tentacles crossways in 2.5 cm/1 inch slices. Cut body meat into diamond shapes.

TO FREEZE: blanch flesh in boiling water for 2 minutes, plunge into cold water, then strip off skin. Cool thoroughly, then pack in freezer bags, seal, label and freeze.

TO THAW: leave in wrappings for 3 hours in the refrigerator, then cut into small pieces and fry until crisp in hot oil, or grill (broil) over charcoal. Or poach in red wine with garlic, herbs, onions and tomatoes.

STORAGE TIME: 3 months.

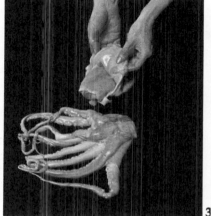

Odour

Occasionally an unpleasant odour is noticeable on opening a freezer. This is most likely caused by inadequate or damaged wrapping around packs of strong-smelling foods. It is also possible that those same 'smelly' items have cross-flavoured other more delicate foods in the cabinet, so it is always advisable to overwrap items which have a strong odour.

If a freezer has been out of use for some time owing to repairs or moving house, for example, it can have a stale, musty smell—it may even have been used for storing various non-frozen items while inoperative. If this is the case, then wash out the inside of the cabinet with warm water to which a little bicarbonate of soda (baking soda) has been added. Dry well, then leave the lid or door open for at least 24 hours to let fresh air circulate all around. If any mildew or other mould should appear in the cabinet, wash as above, then wipe over with a solution of sterilizing agent. Dry and air as above.

Octopus
1 Cutting off the tentacles.
2 Removing the eyes and beak-like mouth.
3 Cleaning out the body.
4 Cutting out the anus.
5 Cutting the tentacles into pieces.
6 Stripping off the skin after blanching.
7 Serve poached in a sauce of red wine, onions, tomatoes, garlic and herbs.

Offal

see under individual meat names and **Meat, Fresh**

Okra (Bindi)

Also called gumbo and lady's fingers, these small green pods should be prepared for freezing when they are only a few inches long.

TO FREEZE: cut off the stems without breaking into the pod itself, blanch in boiling water for 3 minutes, then drain and cool rapidly in iced water. Drain thoroughly, pat dry and pack in rigid containers or freezer bags. Cover or seal, label and freeze.

TO THAW: put frozen okra into boiling water, bring back to the boil and simmer for 6 to 8 minutes, drain and toss in butter. Or add frozen to soups and stews, or fry in butter.

STORAGE TIME: 12 months.

The two photographs in the centre show fruit spread out on a lined baking sheet to be open frozen, and open-frozen fruit being packed into bags to be returned to the freezer.

Olive

There is little point in freezing olives as they can be obtained throughout the year and keep perfectly well in the refrigerator. However, if you buy olives cheaply in bulk or have left-overs from an opened can, they will keep much longer in the freezer.

TO FREEZE: pack them in usable quantities in their oil or brine in freezer bags or rigid containers. Seal or cover, label and freeze.

TO THAW: leave in wrappings at room temperature until required texture for use.

STORAGE TIME: 3 months.

Freeze oranges in slices, segments, as juice or grated zest, or freeze Seville oranges whole.

Onion

Onions are available throughout the year and keep very well on racks or in ropes; therefore, there is little point in using valuable freezer space by freezing them whole. Very small (pickling) onions are worth freezing as they are not always easily obtainable and yet are often called for in special recipes. It is a good idea to freeze a small quantity of sliced or chopped onions for emergency use.

To freeze small onions: peel, blanch in boiling water for 2 minutes, then drain. Cool, drain and pat dry. Pack in freezer bags or rigid containers, seal or cover, then overwrap in freezer bags, label and freeze.

TO THAW: unwrap and add frozen onions to casseroles, etc., or add frozen to a stiff white sauce, so that their juices will thin the sauce and add to the flavour.

To freeze large onions: peel and chop or slice. Blanch in boiling water for 1 minute, drain and cool rapidly in iced water. Drain and pat dry, then pack in small quantities as for whole small onions above. Can be frozen chopped unblanched.

TO THAW: leave raw onions in wrappings for 15 minutes at room temperature, then use slightly frozen in salads. Unwrap and add blanched frozen onions to any cooked dish.

See also recipes for *French Onion Soup, Mushroom and Onion Soup, Onions à la Grecque, Tarte aux Oignons* and *Onions Braised in Cider.*

STORAGE TIME: 3 months.

Open (Flash) Freezing

This is a method of freezing certain foods before they are wrapped and packed so that they remain separate or 'free flowing' in the pack instead of freezing together in a solid mass. It is an ideal way of freezing large quantities of vegetables like mushrooms, peas and peppers (capsicums), and delicate juicy fruit such as raspberries and strawberries. It can also be used for freezing rosettes of whipped cream, portions of gâteau or piped duchesse potatoes, etc. Prepare vegetables or fruit for freezing, line a tray

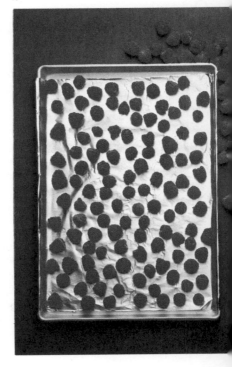

with aluminium foil or greaseproof (waxed) paper, spread out the fruit or vegetables so they are not touching, then place the tray in the freezer and freeze until the food is solid. Remove from the freezer, pack in freezer bags, seal, label and return to freezer. Delicate items like gâteaux should be open (flash) frozen until solid before wrapping to prevent the packaging from doing any damage to the gâteaux.

Orange

see also **Fruit** for information on packing

TO FREEZE: peel and slice or divide into segments. Pack dry with sugar; or pack in medium syrup. Or squeeze and freeze the juice in small rigid containers or ice cube trays. See **Juice.** Grate orange peel, mix with sugar to taste, then pack in small freezer bags. Seal, label and freeze. Use with pancakes (crêpes).

TO THAW: leave in wrappings for approximately 2 hours at room temperature.

To freeze Seville oranges: wash and pat dry, then wrap individually in cling film or aluminium foil, or pack in freezer bags. Seal, label and freeze. Or freeze as for ordinary oranges.

TO THAW: thaw unwrapped for 1½ hours for use in marmalade or sauces and savoury dishes.

See also recipes for *Crêpes Suzette, Orange Sherbet, Orange Salad* and *Orange Marmalade Cake.*

STORAGE TIME: 12 months.

Oregano
see **Marjoram,** *Wild*

Ormer
A shellfish found in Jersey and Guernsey. Prepare, freeze and thaw as for **Scallop.**

Ortolan
see **Game**

Overwrapping
Overwrapping in the form of aluminium foil, polythene (polyethylene), stockinette, etc., is used to prevent cross odours from being transferred from one food to another, and to give extra protection from low temperatures, or to pad protruding bones on meat and poultry. Pack the food in the normal way, then overwrap using one of the wrappings mentioned above — even ordinary brown paper can be used, providing the initial wrappings are suitable for freezer storage. It is sometimes a good idea to overwrap simply to cushion packs against heavy handling and possible puncturing in the freezer.

Oxidation
This is the absorption of oxygen from the air into the fat cells of food, mainly fatty foods and meat. Oxidation turns fat rancid and foods develop an 'off' flavour; it is not harmful, but it makes food unpleasant to eat. Correct wrapping and the removal of air from packages prevents oxidation occurring during storage.

Oxtail
TO FREEZE: pack raw oxtail in a freezer bag, seal, label and freeze. Or cook in casseroles and soups and freeze when cold.

TO THAW: leave raw oxtail in wrappings overnight in the refrigerator, then unwrap and use as for fresh oxtail. Thaw or reheat casseroles and soups from frozen, whichever is most convenient.

STORAGE TIME: 3 months (raw); 2 months (in casseroles and soups).

Oyster
These highly regarded molluscs can be frozen but it must be done on the day they are taken from the water.

TO FREEZE: wash thoroughly and scrub the shell. Open over a muslin (cheesecloth)-lined strainer to catch the juice in a bowl beneath, then wash in salted water, allowing 1 × 15 ml spoon/1 tablespoon salt to 600 ml/1 pint/2½ cups cold water. Pack in rigid containers, cover with strained juice, then cover containers, label and freeze.

TO THAW: leave in containers for 6 hours in the refrigerator, then serve raw. Or add while still frozen to hot soup or sauce and cook without boiling for approximately 4 minutes. (Be careful not to overcook oysters or they will be spoilt — they are ready when the edges curl.)

Or add frozen oysters and their juice to meat pies and puddings for a delicious extra touch.

STORAGE TIME: 1 month.

Oyster Plant
see **Salsify**

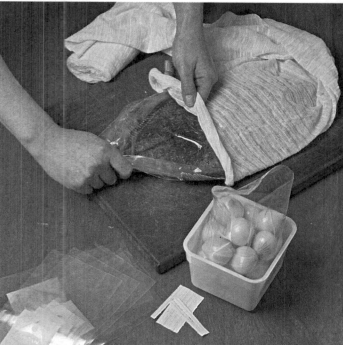

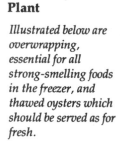

Offal – Oyster Plant
Illustrated below are overwrapping, essential for all strong-smelling foods in the freezer, and thawed oysters which should be served as for fresh.

Packaging
see page 232

Pancake (Crêpe)

Pancakes keep very well in the freezer, either filled or unfilled, although with filled pancakes it is essential to choose fillings that are suitable for freezing — hard-boiled eggs and tomatoes, for example, should be avoided.

To freeze unfilled pancakes: make in the usual way, adding 1 × 15 ml spoon/1 tablespoon vegetable oil to each 100 g/¼ lb/1 cup quantity. Cool quickly on a wire rack. Stack the pancakes one on top of the other, interleaving each one with grease-proof (waxed) paper. Wrap the pancake stack with aluminium foil or place in a freezer bag, seal, label and freeze.

TO THAW: leave in wrappings overnight in the refrigerator or for 2 to 3 hours at room temperature. Or remove the pancakes individually from the stack while frozen and spread out to thaw for 15 to 20 minutes at room temperature. To reheat thawed pancakes, place stack in a fairly hot oven (190°C/375°F or Gas Mark 5) and reheat for 20 to 30 minutes; individual pancakes may be reheated in a lightly greased hot pancake or frying pan for approximately ½ minute on each side.

To freeze filled pancakes: make and cool both pancakes and fillings and either roll up pancakes with fillings inside, or stack them with filling between each one. Put into a greased freezerproof baking or aluminium foil dish, cover well with foil, label and freeze.

TO THAW: reheat from frozen in dish covered with foil in a fairly hot oven (200°C/400°F or Gas Mark 6) for approximately 30 minutes or until heated through. Remove foil covering and sprinkle with grated cheese and/or breadcrumbs if you prefer a golden topping. Or freeze pancakes

and filling separately and make up after thawing, if that is more convenient. See also recipes for *Crêpes Suzette* and *Chestnut Pancakes*.

STORAGE TIME: 4 months for unfilled pancakes; approximately 2 months for filled pancakes, according to type of filling.

Papaya

This fruit, also called pawpaw, resembles a melon with a yellowish colour and orange flesh. The juicy flesh is used for drinks, pies and sherbets, and is sometimes combined with meat in West Indian dishes. They are a high source of Vitamins A and C, and of an enzyme called papain, which is used in meat tenderizers.

TO PREPARE: wash the fruit, peel, remove seeds and cut into slices. Freeze and thaw as for **Mango.**

Parsley *(Petroselinum crispum)*

There are two main varieties of this well-known and widely used herb, which is cultivated for its leaves and stems. Curled parsley, with rich green leaves, has little flavour and is best used as a garnish; French or Italian parsley has straight, flat leaves and has far more flavour in both leaf and stem. Parsley leaves are at their best fresh as both the flavour and vitamin content are lost in cooking; the stems are best used as flavouring in casseroles, stuffings and other savoury dishes. Both leaves and stems freeze successfully and are worthwhile storing in the freezer for their wide variety of culinary uses.

TO FREEZE: pick large bunches when the plant is full of vigour and not running to seed. Wash only if absolutely necessary and shake dry. Break leaves from stems, pack separately in freezer bags, seal, label and freeze. For large quantities to be used in sauces at a later date, purée whole bunches in an electric blender with a little water, press into small rigid

containers, cover, label and freeze. Or freeze in ice cube trays. Or chop leaves and stems and freeze separately in ice cube trays until solid, then pack in bags.

TO THAW: use while still frozen in omelettes, salads, sauces and soups, but never let it come to boiling point in any dish or sauce, or the flavour will be spoilt. Chop or crumble frozen sprigs within seconds of removing from the freezer and sprinkle generously onto any hot or cold dish just before serving.

To freeze parsley sauce: purée whole

2

bunches of washed parsley leaves and tender stems in an electric blender with a little water, then stir into a cooled white sauce. Pour into a rigid container, cover, label and freeze.

TO THAW: unwrap and put into a heavy saucepan, then reheat gently from frozen on top of the stove, adding more liquid if the mixture is too thick. Do not boil. See also recipe for *Maître d'hôtel butter* under **Butter, Flavoured**.

STORAGE TIME: 3 months (sprigs); 6 months (sauce); 8 to 10 months (cubes).

Above: Freeze parsley sprigs in freezer bags, or chop and freeze in ice cubes, or purée and freeze in rigid polythene containers or ice cubes.

Left: Pancake (crêpe)
1 *Turning pancake out of pan onto wire rack to cool.*
2 *Stacking and rolling cold pancakes with cold fruit filling.*
3 *Packing filled pancakes in aluminium foil dishes for freezing.*

Parsnip

Freeze only young parsnips which have had some frost or snow (they are at their best if left in the ground during winter and harvested fresh as and when they are required).

TO FREEZE: trim and peel or scrub, then dice or cut into rings or strips. Blanch in boiling water for 2 minutes and drain. Cool rapidly in iced water, then drain and pat dry. Pack in freezer bags, seal, label and freeze.

TO THAW: unwrap and put frozen parsnips in boiling salted water. Bring back to the boil, cover and simmer for 10 to 15 minutes, depend-

ing on size. Or thaw completely at room temperature and add to juices and fat of roast joints 30 minutes before the end of cooking, add to stews, or use as a plain vegetable mashed with butter and plenty of freshly ground pepper and served piping hot.

STORAGE TIME: 6 months.

Partridge

see **Game**

Passion Fruit

Named for Christ's crown of thorns, also called granadilla, passion fruit is easily recognizable because of its prickly base. The sweet and acidic flesh is used for making drinks, ice-cream toppings and sherbets. Varieties include the giant granadilla and the purple passion fruit.

As the fruit is highly perishable, it should be frozen as soon as possible after harvesting.

Prepare, freeze and thaw as for **Mango**.

Pasta

Most kinds of pasta — fettucine, lasagne, macaroni, noodles, ravioli, spaghetti, tagliatelle, etc., will freeze successfully. Cook in boiling salted water until slightly undercooked and just chewy. Drain in a colander and cool under cold running water. Shake off as much moisture as possible, then pack in freezer bags, seal, label and freeze. There is no need to thaw pasta when required, simply add to boiling salted water and cook until tender; the cooking time will depend on the length of time the pasta was cooked before freezing. It is sensible to freeze pasta in quantities suitable for future use.

Perhaps the most useful way to freeze pasta is in composite dishes — cannelloni, lasagne, macaroni cheese, etc.* Make in aluminium foil or other freezerproof dishes, over-wrap in a freezer bag, seal, label and freeze. Unwrap and bake from frozen in a fairly hot oven (200°C/400°F or Gas Mark 6) for approximately 1 hour or until heated through and bubbling. If you like a crisp, golden-brown topping, sprinkle the top with grated cheese.

Do not freeze pasta in casseroles, soups and stews, etc., or it will become 'slushy' and unpleasant — pasta can easily be added at the reheating stage.

*See also recipes for *Spaghetti alla Bolognese, Cannelloni* and *Macaroni Cheese Casserole*.

STORAGE TIME: 1 month (boiled pasta); 3 months (composite dishes).

**Packaging –
Pasta**

The most useful way of freezing pasta is in cooked dishes like lasagne, cannelloni and macaroni cheese.

Illustrated above are some of the many ways in which pastry can be frozen — as slabs of a usable size, as pie shells or lids interleaved with freezer film, as unbaked double crust pies or as baked vol-au-vent cases.

Pastry & Pastry-based Dishes

see also recipe section

Most types of pastry freeze well, flaky, puff and shortcrust (pie) pastries in particular. Pastry may be baked or unbaked, frozen in the piece or made into éclairs, flans, pastries, pies, profiteroles, quiches, tarts, vol-au-vents, etc. For choux pastry, see **Éclair** and recipe for *Profiteroles with Chocolate Sauce*. For suet crust pastry, see **Pudding.**

When freezing pastry, thought must be given to its future use. If it is frozen unbaked in the piece, a 225 g / ½ lb / 2 cup quantity (based on the amount of flour used) will take 2 to 3 hours to thaw, in which time it is possible to make up a fresh batch. Freeze in pieces if large quantities are needed for a special occasion, or if you are making up a large batch of pastry at one time and freezing it in small quantities to be used at times when it is convenient.

To freeze unbaked shortcrust (pie) pastry in the piece: roll into oblong shapes of usable size, wrap in aluminium foil, then overwrap in a freezer bag. (Several blocks can be placed in one bag providing they are individually wrapped in foil.)

TO THAW: leave in wrappings for 2 to 3 hours at room temperature or overnight in the refrigerator. Unwrap and use as for fresh pastry.

Perhaps a more useful way to freeze unbaked pastry is in the form of pie, flan or tart shells and pie lids.

To freeze unbaked shells: freeze in aluminium foil pie dishes or ovenproof flan dishes if possible; if the dish cannot be spared, open (flash) freeze until the pastry case is solid, then remove from dish and wrap in foil or a freezer bag. Seal, label and return to freezer. The pastry can be left in the dish, if you like, in which case open (flash) freeze, then wrap.

TO THAW: simply return frozen shell to original container if not frozen in this and bake from frozen as for fresh pastry, increasing the baking time by 5 to 10 minutes. Shells can be filled with fresh or frozen fillings before baking.

To freeze unbaked pie lids: make these to fit pie dishes, then pack in freezer bags, interleaving each lid with aluminium foil or freezer film. Seal, label and freeze.

TO THAW: take individual pie lids out of package as required, leave to thaw at room temperature until manageable, then place over fillings and bake as for fresh pastry.

To freeze double crust pies, open tarts and tartlets: these are best frozen unbaked with uncooked fillings. Make according to usual recipe as if for baking — in aluminium foil containers where possible. Open (flash) freeze until solid, then remove from container, wrap in foil or a freezer bag, seal, label and return to freezer.

TO THAW: unwrap and return to original container if it has been removed for storage in the freezer, then bake from frozen as for fresh pastry, allowing 5 to 10 minutes extra baking time. Make a slit in the centre of top crust once the pastry has thawed.

To freeze unbaked flaky and puff pastry: prepare up to the last rolling before freezing. Roll the pastry into an oblong shape, then wrap in aluminium foil, overwrap in a freezer bag, seal, label and freeze.

TO THAW: leave in wrappings overnight in the refrigerator for best results, but for speed the pastry can be thawed for 3 to 4 hours at room temperature. It is a good idea to make a quantity of this kind of pastry at one time, as it is time-consuming to make, yet very useful to keep in the freezer. (Commercially prepared frozen flaky and puff pastries are also excellent, and it is well worth keeping a few packs in the freezer for emergencies.)

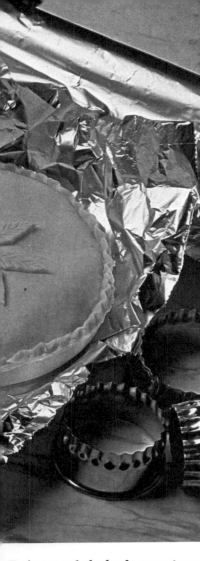

To freeze unbaked vol-au-vent cases or patty shells: shape them on trays, open (flash) freeze until solid, then pack carefully in freezer bags, seal, label and return to freezer.

TO THAW: unwrap and bake from frozen with or without filling, depending on whether to be served hot or cold.

Baked pastry: never as crisp and fresh-tasting after freezing as unbaked pastry, but it has the advantage of keeping longer in the freezer.

TO FREEZE: make flan cases, pasties, pies, quiches, tarts, tartlets, vol-au-vents, etc., according to usual recipe, using aluminium foil dishes where possible. Brush inside pastry base with egg white if a sweet or fruit filling is to be used, with melted butter if the filling is a meat, vegetable or other savoury mixture. Bake as usual, cool rapidly, then wrap in aluminium foil or freezer bags. Seal, label and freeze. If the dish cannot be spared, open (flash) freeze until solid, then remove the dish and return the pastry to the freezer, wrapped in aluminium foil or a freezer bag. Frozen baked pastry is very fragile and can crumble easily; therefore, handle, wrap and thaw with great care and, if possible, store in the freezer in the dish in which it was baked.

TO THAW: leave in wrappings for approximately 3 hours at room temperature, depending on size. If to be served hot, unwrap and 'refresh' in the oven until heated through.
STORAGE TIME: 3 months (unbaked); 6 months (baked), 3 months (baked pastry containing meat).

Pâté & Terrine

All pâtés, meat loaves and terrines made from fish, game, liver, meats, poultry, etc., can be frozen.

To freeze unbaked pâtés and terrines: pack required quantity into small containers and cool rapidly if the ingredients have been cooked. Cover with cling film, then overwrap in aluminium foil or a freezer bag to prevent cross-flavouring if garlic, herbs, or onion have been included in the ingredients. Seal, label and freeze.

TO THAW: remove wrappings, place in baking tin (pan) and bake according to original recipe, allowing extra cooking time.

To freeze baked pâtés and meat loaves: cool rapidly after baking, then ease carefully out of the baking tin (pan). Remove as much jelly and cooking fat as possible, then wrap in cling film and overwrap as above. If you like, pâté can be sliced before freezing: interleave each slice with cling film, then reshape the pâté and place in a freezer bag — slices can then be taken out of the package individually and used for packed lunches, picnics or snacks, etc.

TO THAW: leave in wrappings overnight in the refrigerator. Unwrap and leave to stand at room temperature for 1 to 2 hours before serving cold. If a meat loaf is to be served hot, unwrap, cover with foil and bake from frozen in a fairly hot oven (190°C/375°F or Gas Mark 5) for approximately 50 to 60 minutes or until centre of meat loaf is hot when tested with a skewer.

See also recipes for *Kipper Pâté*, *Country-Style Pâté*, *Pork Terrine*, *Smoked Trout Pâté* and *Polish Meat Loaf*.
STORAGE TIME: 1 month.

Pawpaw

Another name for **Papaya**. Pawpaw is also the name of a completely different fruit which is a member of the custard apple family and native to North America. The fruit looks like a shorter, browned version of the banana when it is about to become too soft to eat. The flesh is creamy, yellow and sweet with many seeds. Do not pick until after the first frost, peel like a banana and do not freeze.

Pea
Podded Peas

Freeze only young pods *immediately* after picking to preserve their sweetness.

TO FREEZE: shell, blanch in boiling water for 1 minute, shaking the basket to distribute the heat evenly. Drain, cool rapidly in iced water, then drain and open (flash) freeze on trays until solid. Pack in freezer bags, seal, label and return to freezer. Or pack directly into bags or rigid containers, seal or cover, label and freeze.

TO THAW: unwrap and put frozen peas in boiling salted water. Bring back to the boil, cover and simmer for 4 minutes. Drain and serve as for fresh peas.

See also recipes for *Petits Pois Française* and *Peas in Sauce*.
STORAGE TIME: 12 months.

Mange Tout (Snow/Sugar Pea)

Freeze edible pods before peas start to swell and strings form.

TO FREEZE: top and tail, then blanch in boiling water for ½ to 1 minute, depending on size of pods. Drain, cool rapidly in iced water, then drain, pat dry and pack in freezer bags. Seal, label and freeze.

TO THAW: unwrap and put frozen mange tout in boiling salted water. Bring back to the boil, cover and simmer for 3 minutes, then drain and serve hot with melted butter.
STORAGE TIME: 12 months.

Mange tout fresh, blanched for the freezer and cooked ready for serving.

Peach

see also **Fruit** for information on packing

Work quickly when preparing peaches for the freezer so that the fruit does not have time to discolour.

TO FREEZE: scald firm peaches for 10 to 15 seconds, drain and cool, then rub off skins, halve and stone (remove pits). Skin and stone (pit) fully ripe peaches under cold running water (scalding will soften and discolour flesh). Leave in halves or slice, then brush with lemon juice. Pack immediately in medium syrup.

TO THAW: leave in unopened containers for approximately 3 hours in the refrigerator. Use in flans, fresh fruit salads, and icecreams, or in peach Melba.

See also recipe for *Peach and Grape Crème Brûlée*.

STORAGE TIME: 12 months.

Pear

see also **Fruit** for information on packing

Pears lose a little texture and flavour in freezing, and are only worthwhile if you have a large crop from your own garden. They are notoriously difficult to store as they seem to become over-ripe the moment you turn your back, so they are certainly safer in the freezer. Freeze ripe, firm pears.

To freeze eating pears: peel, core and cut in halves or quarters. Pack immediately in medium syrup. For softer pears: sprinkle prepared fruit with lemon juice, then poach for 1½ minutes in a light syrup with a few cloves or a little cinnamon, if you like. Drain, leave to cool, then cover with a fresh light syrup and pack as above.

To freeze hard cooking pears: peel, leave whole or halve, put in a saucepan and barely cover with water. Add sugar and spices to taste and poach gently until pears are just tender. Remove from the heat, leave to cool, then pack pears and cooking syrup in rigid containers, cover, label and freeze.

TO THAW: leave in unopened containers for approximately 3 hours at room temperature. Use eating pears as a dessert in fresh fruit salads or with icecream and chocolate sauce. Use cooking pears cold as a dessert with sponge cake, or reheat and serve with cream.

See also recipe for *Pears in Red Wine*.

STORAGE TIME: 12 months.

Peel, Candied

see **Candied Peel**

Red and green peppers (capsicums).

Pepper, Sweet (Capsicum), Green and Red

Freeze green and red peppers separately (green peppers usually stay firmer than red ones).

TO FREEZE: wash well and remove stems, then cut in half and remove seeds and membranes. Leave in halves or slice into strips. Open (flash) freeze until solid, then pack in freezer bags, seal, label and return to freezer. Or pack directly into bags. Or blanch in boiling water, halves for 3 minutes, slices for 2 minutes. Drain, cool rapidly in iced water, then drain and pat dry. Pack as for unblanched peppers.

TO THAW: leave in wrappings for 1 to 2 hours at room temperature. Use raw unblanched peppers in salads, blanched peppers for rice dishes, stews and stuffings, etc.

See also recipes for *Spanish Summer Soup, Ratatouille, Peperonata, Stuffed Peppers* and *Mixed Vegetable Medley*.

STORAGE TIME: 12 months.

Peppermint *(Mentha piperita)*

This herb is cultivated in the same way as other mints, but is mainly used commercially in confectionary and liqueurs, and as an infusion. Home-grown peppermint can be frozen for use in making peppermint tea.

TO FREEZE: pick young sprigs, wash if necessary under cold running water, shake dry, then put immediately into freezer bags, seal, label and freeze.

TO THAW: use straight from the freezer to make tea by pouring over boiling water. Drink either hot or cold.

STORAGE TIME: 4 months.

Perch

A freshwater fish with a delicate flavour, perch may be cooked like grayling or trout.

TO FREEZE: clean thoroughly, wrap in cling film, then overwrap in freezer bags, seal, label and freeze.

TO THAW: unwrap and cook from frozen.

STORAGE TIME: 3 months.

Periwinkle

Commonly known as winkle, this tiny fish is similar to a snail.

TO FREEZE: wash thoroughly, then boil for 20 minutes in salted water. Drain and leave to cool, then remove from their shells with a pin, first taking off the thin protective cap. Pack in small rigid containers, cover, label and freeze.

TO THAW: leave in containers for 2 hours in the refrigerator, then serve cold.

STORAGE TIME: 1 month.

Persimmon

see also **Fruit** for information on packing

Freeze only very ripe fruit.

TO FREEZE: peel whole fruit, then wrap individually in aluminium foil. Or cut into chunks or slices — there are no pips (seeds) or stones (pits) — and pack in heavy syrup, adding 2 × 5 ml spoons/2 teaspoons lemon juice to each 1 litre/2 pints/5 cups syrup.

TO THAW: leave in wrappings for 3 hours at room temperature. Use immediately after thawing or the fruit will lose flavour and darken.

STORAGE TIME: 2 months (whole fruit); 12 months (syrup pack).

Petits Pois

prepare, freeze and thaw as for **Pea**

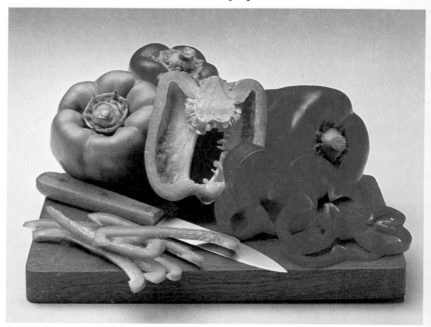

Pheasant

see **Game**

Pickerel

This is a young pike. Prepare, freeze and thaw as for **Pike.**

Pickle(s)

see **Chutney**

Picnic

The freezer can be immensely useful for storing picnic food, as whole picnic meals can be prepared in advance and packaged ready for taking out. With careful planning you can guarantee that everything will taste freshly made — something which is often hard to achieve with picnic fare. Good ideas for 'freezer picnics' are filled bread rolls (buns) or sandwiches, sliced cooked roast beef, chicken and pork, cheese, meat loaves and pâtés, savoury and sweet pies, quiches, sausage rolls, soup (this can be reheated from frozen and poured into a thermos flask to keep hot until required), cakes and pastries and individual fruit tarts. Raw salad vegetables will not freeze satisfactorily as they will become limp; salads should be made fresh on the day of the picnic, with dressings carried separately.

Pie

see **Pastry & Pastry-based Dishes**

Pigeon

see **Game**

Pig's Foot

see **Pork**

Pig's Head

see **Pork**, *Brawn*

Pig's Trotter

see **Pork**

Pike

A freshwater fish, pike is rather dry, coarse and bony. Although not particularly popular for eating in Britain, it is a delicacy in France and Germany. Pike can grow to 13.5 kg/30 lb, but the best size for eating is 2.25–3 kg/5–7 lb. To make pike more tender, and to help dissolve some of the smallest bones, hang the fish by the jaw and push salt as far as possible down its throat. Hang for 12 hours.
TO FREEZE: remove head and scales, then pack in freezer bags. Seal, label and freeze.
TO THAW: unwrap and leave to thaw for 4 hours in the refrigerator, then

bake, boil or poach, either whole or cut into pieces.
STORAGE TIME: 3 months.

Pilchard

This fish is a member of the herring family and is particularly abundant in the English counties of Devon and Cornwall. Freeze only very fresh pilchards.
TO FREEZE: clean thoroughly, wrap each fish individually in cling film, then pack several fish together in a freezer bag. Seal, label and freeze.
TO THAW: unwrap and cook from frozen. Pilchards are particularly good grilled (broiled), or use any herring or sardine recipe.
STORAGE TIME: 3 months.

Pimiento

see **Pepper, Sweet**

Pineapple

see also **Fruit** for information on packing
Freeze only fully ripe fruit.
TO FREEZE: peel and core, then cut into chunks or slices. Pack dry without sugar in rigid containers, interleaving each layer with aluminium foil. Cover, label and freeze. Or pack dry with sugar. Or in light syrup. Crush any leftover pieces of pineapple with sugar to taste, pack in rigid containers, cover, label and freeze.
TO THAW: leave in containers (or remove for faster thawing) for approximately 3 hours at room temperature. Use in icecreams, salads, etc., or caramelize slices in butter and brown sugar and serve hot.
STORAGE TIME: 12 months.

Pita/Pitta

Pita, the flat Arab or Greek bread, keeps beautifully in the freezer. Although traditionally served with houmos (chick pea and sesame seed dip), kebabs and taramasalata (smoked cod's roe pâté), it is also very useful for quick sandwiches and snacks. Available from most Middle Eastern grocery stores, pita is usually sold in polythene (polyethylene) bags.
TO FREEZE: overwrap in freezer bags, seal, label and freeze.
TO THAW: pita does not need to be thawed, in fact it is better *not* to thaw: simply take individual pitas out of bag as required, place on oven shelf and 'refresh' in a fairly hot oven (200°C /400°F or Gas Mark 6) for approximately 10 minutes. Leave to stand for 1 to 2 minutes until cool enough to handle, then split and stuff with cheese, kebabs, cooked meats, salad, etc., or use to dip into houmos or *Taramasalata* (see recipe in soups and appetizers chapter).
STORAGE TIME: 4 months.

Cheese, quiche, pâté, sausage rolls, French bread and orange slices in syrup, can all be kept in the freezer and taken out for a picnic when the sun shines.

Peach – Pita/Pitta

Pita wrapped ready for the freezer, and thawed and filled ready for serving.

The left-hand pizza above is ready to be frozen unbaked. The right-hand pizza has been frozen unbaked, topped with anchovies when removed from the freezer, baked, and is now ready to serve.

Centre left: Plums can be frozen cooked in tarts (see Plum Tart page 197) or uncooked in syrup. They must be used immediately after thawing to prevent discoloration.

Pizza

Both commercially baked and homemade pizzas freeze well either whole or sliced. Freeze with traditional toppings — cheese, ham, mushroom, tomato sauces, etc. Anchovies can become strong and should therefore be used sparingly, or added at the reheating stage. For the best flavour, always use fresh herbs. Homemade pizzas can be frozen baked or unbaked.

To freeze unbaked pizza: prepare dough in the usual way, arrange topping on dough, then place on a sheet of aluminium foil large enough to enclose the whole pizza. Open (flash) freeze until solid, then wrap pizza in the foil, label and return to freezer. (If more than one pizza is being frozen, open (flash) freeze each individually, then store several together in a freezer bag, seal, label and return to freezer.)

TO THAW: unwrap, place on a preheated baking sheet and bake from frozen in a very hot oven (230°C/450°F or Gas Mark 8) for approximately 30 to 35 minutes or until heated through and bubbling.

To freeze baked pizza: cool rapidly after baking, then place on foil and open (flash) freeze as for unbaked pizza.

TO THAW: unwrap, place on a preheated baking sheet and bake from frozen in a fairly hot oven (200°C/400°F or Gas Mark 6) for approximately 20 minutes or until heated through and bubbling.

See also recipe for *Pizza*.
STORAGE TIME: 1 month.

Plaice

A flat fish which can grow to 4.5 kg/10 lb, plaice is recognizable by its white underside, and dark upper side with bright orange spots. When choosing, look for firm, thick flesh, and bright eyes and spots.

TO FREEZE: clean the fish and fillet it, then pack in freezer bags, interleaving each fillet with cling film. Seal, label and freeze.

TO THAW: unwrap and fry or grill (broil) from frozen, or poach from frozen and serve with a savoury sauce.
STORAGE TIME: 3 months.

Plantain

This member of the banana family is widely used in Latin American cooking and always eaten cooked. It can be frozen successfully as part of a cooked dish.

Plastic Container

see page 234

Plate Meal

This is an individual meal and made up of cooked foods, packaged and ready for reheating. It is an ideal way to freeze food for latecomers to family meals, if mealtimes have to be staggered, or for single meals at irregular times. A simple plate meal to make up is to take part of the weekly roast, slice it and pack with vegetables and gravy to stop the meat from becoming dry.

Plover

see **Game**

Plum

see also **Fruit** for information on packing.

TO FREEZE: wash (but do not remove skin), halve and remove stones (pits). Pat dry, then pack in medium syrup.

TO THAW: leave in unopened containers for approximately 2 hours at room temperature. Use immediately after thawing or the fruit will discolour. Use in fools, pies, etc., or poached in its own syrup.

See also recipe for *Plum Tart*.
STORAGE TIME: 12 months.

Pollack

A fish similar to cod, found off Newfoundland and on the European coasts of the Atlantic. Prepare, freeze and thaw as for **Cod**.

Polythene (Polyethylene Wrapping)

see page 234

Pomegranate

see also **Fruit** for information on packing

Freeze fine, ripe fruit, particularly at times of glut as pomegranates are not always available. Do not freeze whole or they will burst.

TO FREEZE: cut in half, scoop out juicy pips (seeds), leaving behind every particle of membrane, then pack in heavy syrup.

TO THAW: leave in container for 3 hours at room temperature. Serve on their own sprinkled with a little lemon juice, or with fresh fruit salads and icecream.
STORAGE TIME: 12 months.

Pomelo

prepare, freeze and thaw as for **Grapefruit**

Pompano

A fish which comes from the South Atlantic and Gulf coasts of North America, pompano reaches a length of 46 cm/18 inches, and is covered with small scales of blue, gold and silver.

TO FREEZE: clean and leave whole, or skin the fish and cut into fillets. Pack in freezer bags, interleaving each fish or fillet with cling film, seal, label and freeze.

TO THAW: unwrap and cook from frozen. Pompano is good baked in aluminium foil, or poached in white wine.

STORAGE TIME: 3 months.

Pork

see also recipe section

Choosing

Look for young, lean pork with fine-grained, pale pink meat. The rind should be thin and supple and the fat creamy-white, firm and not excessive in quantity. Avoid buying pork with soft, oily fat, or coarse, dark-coloured meat, especially if the latter is sticky or flabby. Pork for the freezer should be freshly killed but thoroughly chilled in the butcher's cold room before freezing. It does not require ageing like beef.

Buying

With modern refrigeration it is safe to buy pork at any time of the year, and you can forget the old advice about only when there is an 'R' in the month. Ready-frozen pork is available as individual joints (cuts) — legs, loins, etc., single portion cuts — chops, etc., or as a whole side of pork which includes all the cuts. Pork is usually jointed (cut) 'on the bone' with the skin left on, so if you require any special butchering remember to

Cuts From a Side of Pork (U.K.)

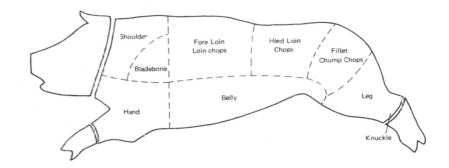

Cuts From a Side of Pork (Australia)

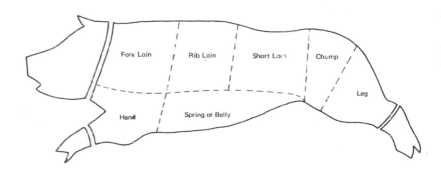

Cuts From a Side of Pork (U.S.)

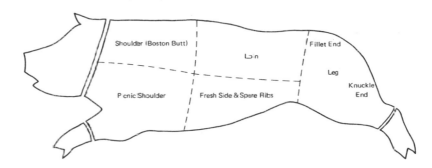

give written instructions when you order the meat.

Bulk-buying

Offal (variety meat/fancy meat), ears and tail are not normally included in a bulk-buy, but a side of pork usually includes two trotters (feet) and half the head. You need to check exactly what is included in a bulk-buy to arrive at a fair estimate of the price. With modern methods of rearing the quality of meat is not seasonal, but as consumer demand for pork usually falls in hot weather, mid-summer can be a favourable time for a bulk-buy (not applicable in Australia).

Freezer Space Needed

Allow 56 litres/2 cu ft for every 9 kg/20 lb of pork on the bone.

Weight Range of Carcasses

From 36–54 kg/80–120 lb for a whole pig, or 18–27 kg/40–60 lb for a side.

PACKAGING AND FREEZING: see **Meat, Fresh.**

THAWING AND COOKING: see **Meat, Fresh.**

STORAGE TIME: Joints (large cuts) and chops — up to 6 months.

Offal (variety meat/fancy meat), cubed meat, unseasoned minced (ground) meat — up to 3 months.

Sausages or sausagemeat — up to 1 month.

Brawn

This has a tendency to 'weep' when thawed, although this can be overcome to some extent by freezing in rigid containers not more than

Centre right: Brawn should be made in shallow containers for freezing.

Pizza – Pork

3.75 cm/1½ inches deep, and thawing slowly in the refrigerator. Serve surrounded with salad to hide any drops of moisture. The following recipe for brawn usually freezes successfully and is a good way to use the pig's head if this is supplied with a bulk-buy of pork.

Pig's head brawn: ask the butcher to clean half a lightly salted pig's head and to brine it lightly for 2 to 3 days. (If longer than this you will need to soak it overnight in cold water before cooking.) Wash the head thoroughly and put into a large saucepan with ½ kg/1 lb cubed shin of beef, 1 onion, 8 peppercorns, 1 bay leaf, a sprig each of marjoram, parsley and thyme and enough cold water just to cover. Bring slowly to the boil, then skim off the scum that rises to the surface.

Cover the pan with a lid and simmer very gently for 3 to 4 hours or until the meat is very tender and the bones slip out easily. Lift the head and all the shin of beef out of the pan and let the stock continue to bubble, uncovered, until reduced. Meanwhile, remove all the bones from the head, and skin the tongue. Chop the meats into small pieces and pack in shallow rigid containers, allowing 1.25 cm/½ inch headspace.

Season the stock well and strain enough into each container just to cover the meat. Leave until cold and firmly set, then remove any fat from the surface. Cover the container, label and freeze.

Crackling

Freezing does not impair crackling. Ask the butcher to score the rind very closely and thoroughly. Before cooking, rub it with oil and sprinkle with salt and pepper.

Rind

If you have any joints butchered in the French manner, i.e. boned and skinned, ask the butcher to cut the rind in pieces and to include it with the meat. Freeze the rind and use in slow-cooking beef casseroles to add richness and body.

Fat

In French butchering the fat covering the back of a pig is highly esteemed. Any excess fat is cut in thin sheets and used for barding, i.e. wrapping around lean cuts of beef or placing over the breasts of chicken. It is also cut into fine strips and used for larding, i.e. threading through lean cuts of coarse-textured beef to keep them moist during cooking.

TO FREEZE: for easy separation, pack the fat in freezer bags, interleaving each sheet with cling film. Seal, label and freeze.

STORAGE TIME: up to 3 months.

To make lard: cut any excess pork fat into pieces and extract the fat in exactly the same way as for **Beef**, *Beef Dripping(s)*. Keep the oven temperature very low and pour the liquid fat off at frequent intervals, otherwise the fat may tend to darken in colour.

STORAGE TIME: 2 to 3 months.

Portions

Many foods can be frozen in ready-to-serve portions, but it is for you to decide what suits you best — what type of meal and for how many. Sometimes mixed portion packs are useful, i.e. single portions and multi-portions for the family.

Potato

For best results, potatoes should be frozen in cooked form.

Cut	Average weight range		Ways of butchering	Type of meat and cooking
	kg	lb		
Leg	4-6	9-13	(a) Whole if small (b) Large legs cut into two or three joints providing a fillet end, knuckle end and perhaps a centre leg cut (c) Fillet can be cut in thin slices for cooking like escalope of veal	Top-quality roasting meat with good crackling. Can be boned and stuffed. Knuckle end can be braised or slow roasted

Loin	4.5-7	10-15	(a) Joints (large cuts) on the bone
			(b) Boned and rolled, then cut in joints
			(c) Chops
			  1. Chump (sirloin end) chops from leg end
			  2. Middle (centre) loin chops
			  3. Loin cutlets (rib end chops) from neck end
				Fine-grained, top-quality roasting meat with good crackling. Chops can be baked, grilled (broiled) or sautéed.
				Note: The tenderloin strip from under the loin comes from large pigs only, and is usually not large enough to separate in small pigs recommended for freezing

Belly (Fresh Side and Spare ribs)	2.25-4.25	5-9	(a) Boned for stuffing and rolling
			(b) Joints
			  1. Thick end
			  2. Streaky end
			(c) Streaky end cut in thin slices
			(d) From large pigs only, belly can be boned to provide spare ribs
				Thick end joint (cut) is fairly lean, and can be stuffed. Streaky end is layered with fat and needs very slow roasting. May also be pickled (cured) and boiled but *do not freeze pickled (cured) pork.* Slices can be baked, fried or grilled (broiled). Spare ribs can be barbecued

Shoulder (Boston Butt)	2.5-4	5½-9	(a) Boned and rolled, then cut into joints (roasts) (b) Blade joint (cut) for roasting, rest for spare rib cutlets or butterfly chops (c) Boned and cubed for pies (d) Minced (ground) for pâtés, sausages, etc.	A versatile cut of sweet, tender meat which can be used for many different purposes as indicated
Hand, with shank attached (Picnic Shoulder)	2-4	4-9	(a) Joint (large cut) (b) Boned for stuffing	Rather coarse, but lean meat lacking flavour of top-quality cuts. Hand can be slow roasted, or boned and stuffed, then roasted. Shank is best detached and cooked by moist heat
Head			(a) Half head for making Brawn see above (b) Chap (lower portion), detached with tongue attached	Chap can be scored and slow roasted, or pickled (smoked) and boiled. *Do not freeze if pickled*
Trotters, split in half (Pig's Feet)				Usually simmered until tender and then served with a piquant sauce, or grilled (broiled). Also used for enriching French-type beef casseroles

New Potatoes

Choose small, newly dug ones, from which the skins can be brushed or scraped easily.

TO FREEZE: if skins are hard to scrape, wash and blanch in their jackets, then peel skins off while they are still warm. This method adds to the flavour of those potatoes that are sold as 'new', but may have been in store all winter and resurrected for the spring market. Boil until just barely tender, drain, cool rapidly in iced water, then drain and pat dry. Pack in freezer bags, seal, label and freeze.

TO THAW: unwrap and reheat from frozen in butter, or steam.

See also recipes for *Vichyssoise, Swiss-style Potato Cake, Mixed Vegetable Medley* and *Potato and Cheese Casserole.*
STORAGE TIME: 12 months.

Poultry

Poultry is the name given to birds which are bred specifically for human consumption. Both fresh and frozen poultry are available throughout the year, but it is important to remember when buying fresh poultry for home-freezing that there are 'seasons' for the different kinds of poultry. It is during these 'seasons' that the best poultry can be bought, both from the point of view of quality and of price.

Before buying fresh poultry for freezing at home, compare prices carefully with those of frozen poultry which is available throughout the year, often cheaper than that available fresh. Quality is another factor to

To the left can be seen two good ways of freezing potatoes — as chips and duchess(e) potatoes.

Chipped (French-fried) Potatoes

Use old or waxy potatoes.

TO FREEZE: deep fry in hot oil or fat for 2 to 3 minutes (do not let potatoes brown). Drain and cool quickly, pack in freezer bags, then seal, label and freeze.

TO THAW: unwrap and thaw at room temperature until you can pat them dry. Re-fry in hot deep oil or fat for 3 to 4 minutes until golden. Drain.
STORAGE TIME: 3 months.

Croquette or Duchess(e) Potatoes

To freeze uncooked: form mashed potatoes into required shapes on trays, using butter and egg but no milk. Open (flash) freeze until solid, then slide into an aluminium foil container and seal with cling film or cover with foil.

TO THAW: put frozen potato shapes onto greased baking sheets, brush lightly with beaten egg and cook from frozen in a fairly hot oven (200°C/400°F or Gas Mark 6) for 20 to 30 minutes, until heated through and slightly brown.

To freeze cooked: cook in the usual way, cool quickly, then open (flash) freeze on trays until solid. Pack in rigid containers, cover, label and freeze.

TO THAW: leave in containers for 2 hours at room temperature, then reheat on baking sheets in a moderate oven (180°C/350°F or Gas Mark 4) for 20 minutes.
STORAGE TIME: 3 months.

Mashed Potatoes

TO FREEZE: boil, drain and mash while hot with milk and butter. Cool quickly and pack in freezer bags or rigid containers. Seal or cover, label and freeze.

TO THAW: unwrap and reheat gently from frozen in a double boiler or in a heavy saucepan with a little warmed milk and butter.
STORAGE TIME: 3 months

Jointing poultry (see page 100)

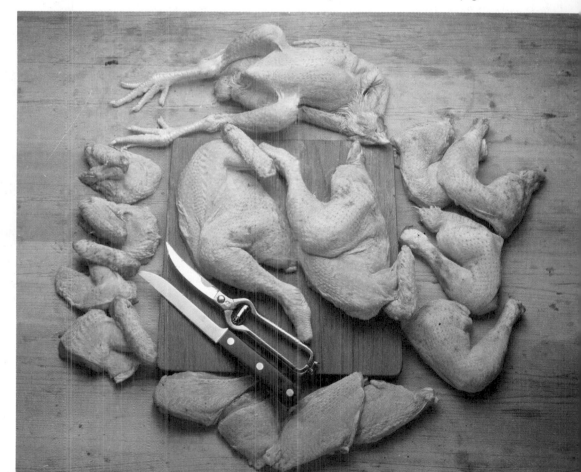

Poultry which has been frozen can be cooked as for fresh, but must always be completely thawed. Illustrated here are poussins (cooked), chicken (in casserole), guinea fowl, duck (plucked and unplucked), goose and turkey.

consider — it may be worthwhile buying fresh if the quality seems to be superior to that available frozen. On the whole, frozen poultry maintains an exceedingly high quality and constitutes good value for money throughout the year, but the final choice between fresh and frozen is purely a personal one.

Halved, split and cut up birds and joints are also available frozen in various pack sizes.

Points to Look for When Buying Fresh Poultry for Home Freezing

1 Young, plump birds have the best eating quality.

2 The legs should be smooth and pliable, with very fine scales which overlap slightly.

3 The beak and breastbone should be slightly pliable.

4 The skin over the breast should be white and unwrinkled and the breast itself must be plump and well-rounded.

5 The feathers should be soft and full. The wing quills should extract quite easily, and there should be no hairs on the skin.

6 The eyes should be clear and bright.

7 It is advisable to smell the bird quite closely before selection. A fresh bird should not have any unpleasant smell.

Preparation for Freezing

Plucking and hanging: pluck immediately after killing, preferably while the bird is still warm. If purchase is made from a market, establish the age of the bird and buy only if killed within the last 24 hours. Lay the bird flat and begin plucking at the top of the breast — pulling the feathers out in the opposite direction to which they lie. Pull out any broken quills with tweezers. To make plucking easier, it is common practice to immerse the bird in boiling water to loosen the feathers. This is not recommended when the bird is being prepared for freezing.

Singe the bird to remove the last traces of feather and down, being careful not to discolour the skin as this may incur an unpleasant flavour after cooking. Hang the bird by the feet (head down) in a cool place — an outhouse or well-ventilated pantry — for 2 to 4 days, according to the weather and age of bird. Warm, humid weather speeds up the hanging process considerably, and older birds are hung for a longer period than young ones.

In Australia, hang the bird by the feet and chill quickly at a temperature of approximately 0°C/32°F.

Drawing: you will need a very sharp knife and several bowls of cold water. Cut off and discard the head, leaving approximately 7.5 cm/3 inches of neck. Lay the bird on its breast and make a slit at the base of the neck up to the end. Pull away the loose skin and cut off the neck close to the top of the spine. (Reserve the loose skin — it will be used later for trussing.) Save the neck as part of the giblets. Turn the bird over onto its back and make a cut at the opposite end, between the tail and vent.

Place your fingers inside the bird and, holding firmly with the other hand, draw out the gall bladder, gizzard, heart, intestines and liver. Discard the gall bladder and intestines, but retain the gizzard, heart,

liver and neck, as these are the giblets. Turn the gizzard inside out by making a small cut on one side; discard sac.

Because the bird is to be frozen, and probably stored for a considerable period, it is necessary to ensure that the inside is thoroughly clean. Place the bird under the cold water tap, allow the water to run through, then pat dry with kitchen paper towels. Cut the skin round the knee joint at the base of the drumstick, twist, then pull sharply. If it is an older bird the sinews may not extract so easily, in which case place a skewer under each individual sinew and jerk it quickly. The sinews must be removed or the drumsticks could be quite tough. Finally, wipe the outside of the bird.

Trussing

It is not a good idea to stuff a bird before freezing as the storage life of the bird exceeds that of the stuffing in most cases and, when thawing, the stuffing usually takes much longer to thaw than the chicken. It is therefore recommended to freeze the poultry separate from the stuffing. Trussing ensures a good shape for cooking as

Poultry

well as carving purposes. A poorly trussed bird is very difficult to carve well, therefore it is important not to ignore this stage in the preparation of poultry for the freezer.

Fold the neck skin under the body and fold the tips of the wings back towards the backbone so that they secure the neck skin in place. Set the bird on its back and press the legs well into the sides beneath the breast. Pass the tail ('parsons's nose') through the slit in the skin previously made. Thread the trussing needle with thin twine. Insert the needle close to the second joint of the right wing, push it right through the bird, then secure the left wing as the needle comes out at the opposite side. Insert the needle again in the first joint of the left wing, pass it through the flesh at the back of the body, catching the tips of the wings and the neck skin, and pass it out through the first joint of the wing on the right side. Tie the ends of the string in a bow. Re-thread the needle to truss the legs. Pass it through the back of the bird under the drumsticks, then over one leg, through the skin flaps on either side of the breast tip, over the other leg, and tie a bow.

If the tail ('parson's nose') will not stay in the slit, you can bend it right up and into the small opening in the cavity.

Jointing (Cutting Up)

If preparing several birds at a time it is wise to joint (cut up) one or two so that a selection of cuts is available for future use. Whole birds can be jointed (cut up) after freezing, but it is easier and more convenient to joint them before they are frozen.

Half (split) birds: using poulterer's shears or a sharp knife, cut along either side of the backbone. Open out the bird and cut along the breastbone. Make long, firm cuts.

Joints, cut-up birds or portions: cut through the skin between each leg and the carcass, then break the thigh joint by pulling the leg down and away from the body. If the legs are large as with a turkey, separate again at the knee joint. Cut off each wing together with a good slice of breast to which it is attached. Cut out the wishbone and attached neck by cutting at right angles to the breastbone and cutting towards the neck end. Cut off the breast meat in two sections, getting the knife as close to the rib cage as possible.

Packing for the Freezer

Good packaging is essential when freezing poultry — to preserve flavour, to prevent the skin from becoming dry, and to avoid **Freezer**

Burn which occurs when the food is directly exposed to freezer temperatures and causes the moisture to evaporate from the flesh, leaving it discoloured and flaky. Freezer burn in the extreme would leave the food inedible, but if the food is affected only slightly, the results will be negligible.

Whole birds: wrap several thicknesses of aluminium foil or cling film around the extremities of the bird, i.e. wing tips and drumstick ends, to prevent them from piercing wrappings during storage. Wrap the whole carcass tightly in one large piece of foil, taking care to keep smaller pieces of foil or film in place. Secure the ends of the foil by folding several times. Overwrap in a freezer bag, seal, label and freeze. It is a wise precaution to check poultry wrappings in the freezer from time to time, to ensure that they are still intact, and that the wing tips and/or drumstick ends have not pierced through the freezer bag.

Halved and cut-up birds, joints and portions: treat halved birds in the same way as whole ones. Wrap each half individually in aluminium foil, then put the halves in one freezer bag. Seal, label and freeze. Wrap joints or portions individually in aluminium foil, then label each one and put several in one freezer bag, seal, label and freeze. If a lot of birds have been jointed (cut up) at the same time, divide into drumsticks, wings, etc., and pack in freezer bags — this obviates the necessity for individual labelling.

Carcass

Use the carcass to make stock, either for immediate use or for storing in the freezer. If there is no time to make stock, then store the carcass in the freezer. Flatten it with a rolling pin, wrap in aluminium foil, then overwrap in a freezer bag, seal, label and freeze.

To make stock: put the carcass in a large pan with water to cover, and herbs, seasonings and vegetables to taste. Bring to the boil, skim with a slotted spoon, then lower the heat, half cover with a lid and simmer very gently for approximately 1½ to 2 hours. Strain the contents and return the stock to the pan. Taste for seasoning.

TO FREEZE: leave to cool, then chill until firm, skim off fat and pour into rigid containers. Cover, label and freeze.

TO THAW: put frozen stock in a saucepan, cover and heat gently until bubbling, stirring occasionally to pre-

vent sticking. Use as for freshly made stock in casseroles, sauces, soups, etc.

STORAGE TIME: 3 to 4 months.

To freeze concentrated stock cubes, see **Stock.**

Giblets

The giblets comprise selected interior parts of the bird, i.e. gizzard, heart, liver and neck. The gizzard should be split and cleaned carefully and the sac discarded. Giblets can be frozen raw (with the liver frozen separately) and stored in the freezer until required, or prepared and cooked first.

TO FREEZE: prepare and cook in the normal way. Leave to cool, then put in a freezer bag, seal, label and freeze.

TO THAW: leave in wrappings for approximately 12 hours in the refrigerator.

STORAGE TIME: 2 to 3 months.

Thawing Poultry

Whole birds: it is essential that all whole birds are completely thawed before cooking, otherwise it is extremely difficult to estimate whether the bird is cooked thoroughly or not. The flesh may be cooked to perfection, but the interior carcass still frozen. Always thaw poultry in the refrigerator if possible. Fast thawing at room temperature or in cold water produces excessive drip, which reduces the flavour of the bird. Put the bird in its wrappings in a large, shallow dish, then put in a central position in the refrigerator.

All domestic refrigerators register different temperatures; therefore, thawing times can only be approximate. Check carefully in the cavity to ensure that there are no traces of ice crystals. If thawing at room temperature, the length of time allocated

Thawing Times

Weight		Thawing time
kg	lb	Hours
Under 3½	Under 8	24
3½	8	36
4	9	36
	10	36
5	11	42
	12	42
6	13	48
	14	48
	15	48
7	16	56
	17	56
8	18	60
	19	60
9	20	60
Over 9	Over 20	72

should be halved — but this is of course dependent on the ambient temperature. Once thawed, use as for fresh poultry.

Halved and cut-up birds, joints and portions: it is not vital to thaw these completely before cooking because there is no hollow carcass to cause concern, but it is a wise precaution. Allow 12 to 15 hours in the refrigerator. Once thawed, use as for fresh poultry.

Boiling Fowl (Stewing Chicken)

These should be no more than 18 months old. Choose carefully: boiling fowl can only be used for boiling, casseroling or stewing, so do not pay too high a price.

See also recipe for *Cock-a-Leekie*.
WEIGHT RANGE: 2–3 kg/4–7 lb.
IDEAL SIZE: 2 kg/4 lb.
SERVINGS: 5–8 persons.
TO FREEZE: it is best to freeze whole for boiling, jointed (cut up) for casseroling and stewing. Time permitting, it is often better to freeze joints and portions in a prepared dish, because this will ensure a more tender result.
TO THAW: leave for 24 hours in the refrigerator (whole); 12 to 15 hours in the refrigerator (joints and cut up). Prepared dishes can be reheated from frozen.
STORAGE TIME: 10 to 12 months (whole); 3 to 4 months for joints or cut up in a prepared dish.

Capon

A young cockerel (approximately 9 months old) that has been neutered at an early age to produce a large, plump bird in a short time. The flesh should be white and the breast plump. Capons are good value for the money — the small carcass contains a lot of flesh and is very tender when cooked.
WEIGHT RANGE: 2.25–3.5 kg/5–8 lb.
IDEAL SIZE: 2.75 kg/6 lb.
SERVINGS: 6–10 persons.
TO FREEZE: freeze whole, jointed or cut up.
TO THAW: leave for 24 hours in the refrigerator (whole); 12 to 15 hours in the refrigerator (joints and cut up).
STORAGE TIME: 10 to 12 months.

Chicken

There are two types of chicken: 1-year-old cocks and hens for roasting, and fowl which are older hen birds that need long boiling, casseroling or stewing (see above).

See also recipes for *Chicken Vol-au-vents, Country Chicken and Mushroom Pie, Chicken with Tarragon* and *Coq au Vin*.

Roasting chickens: choose only young, plump birds.
WEIGHT RANGE: 1.5–2.25 kg/3–5 lb.
IDEAL SIZE: 1.75 kg/3½ lb.
SERVINGS: 4–6 persons.
TO FREEZE: freeze whole for roasting, jointed (cut up) for grilling (broiling) or frying.
TO THAW: leave for 24 hours in the refrigerator (whole); 12 to 15 hours in the refrigerator (joints and cut up).
STORAGE TIME: 10 to 12 months.

Duck

A duckling is aged from 6 weeks to 3 months old, a duck from 3 to 12 months. Use older ducks for casseroles and pâtés only — they will not roast successfully. When buying a fresh duck, look for a young bird with soft pliable feet. The bill and feet should be yellow.
WEIGHT RANGE: 2–2.75 kg/4–6 lbs.
IDEAL SIZE: 2 kg/4 lb.
SERVINGS: Allow ½ kg/1 lb (dressed weight) per person. 2 kg/4 lb will serve 4 persons.
TO FREEZE: freeze whole, jointed or cut up.
TO THAW: leave for 24 hours in the refrigerator (whole); 12 to 15 hours in the refrigerator (joints and cut up).
STORAGE TIME: 4 to 6 months.

Goose

Look for a fresh young bird with yellow bill and feet. The flesh should be a pale pink colour, the fat a creamy yellow. Geese require hanging for 5 to 7 days.
WEIGHT RANGE: 2.75–5.5 kg/6–12 lb.
IDEAL SIZE: 4.5 kg/10 lb.
SERVING A 4.5 kg/10 lb bird will serve 7–8 persons.
TO FREEZE: freeze whole, jointed or cut up.
TO THAW: see poultry thawing chart.
STORAGE TIME: 4 to 6 months.

Guinea Fowl*

Look for a bird with a plump breast and smooth-skinned feet. Guinea fowl require hanging for several days; they should then be plucked before freezing.
WEIGHT RANGE: 1.5–3 kg/3–7 lb.
IDEAL SIZE: 2 kg/4 lb.
SERVINGS: A 2 kg/4 lb bird will serve 4–5 persons.
TO FREEZE: freeze whole, jointed or cut up. Guinea fowl tends to be rather dry and is therefore best if used in casseroles which can be prepared for the freezer.
TO THAW: leave for 24 hours in the refrigerator (whole); 12 to 15 hours in the refrigerator (joints and cut up).
STORAGE TIME: 4 to 6 months.
*Not available in Australia.

Poussin (Broilers and Fryers)

A poussin is a 4- to 8-week-old chicken which becomes tender quickly during cooking, whether whole, split in half or cut into pieces.
WEIGHT RANGE: ½ kg–1.5 kg/1–3 lb.
IDEAL SIZE: 1 kg/2 lb.
SERVINGS: 1–3 persons.
TO FREEZE: freeze whole, split in half, or cut up (raw or in a prepared dish).
TO THAW: leave for 12 to 15 hours in the refrigerator (whole or split in half); 12 hours in the refrigerator (cut up).
STORAGE TIME: 10 to 12 months (whole or split in half); 4 months (cut up raw or cooked).

Turkey

Turkeys are available throughout the year in a whole range of sizes from 2.75–13.5 kg/6–30 lb. The smaller birds are obviously not as economical as the larger ones as there is less flesh. Preparing large birds at home is difficult; it is therefore worthwhile buying ready-dressed birds. The flesh should be white and the breast-bone pliable. A freshly killed bird will have bright, prominent eyes.
WEIGHT RANGE: 2.75–13.5 kg/6–30 lb.
IDEAL SIZE: 4.5–6.75 kg/10–15 lb.
SERVINGS:
2.75 kg/6 lb — 6– 8 persons.
3.5 kg/8 lb — 8–10 persons.
4.5 kg/10 lb — 12–14 persons.
5.5 kg/12 lb — 14–16 persons.
6.25 kg/14 lb — 18–20 persons.
7.25 kg/16 lb — 22–24 persons.
8.25 kg/18 lb — 26–28 persons.
9 kg/20 lb — 28–30 persons.
TO FREEZE: freeze whole or joint (cut up) small turkeys. Cooked leftovers can be made into prepared dishes and stored in the freezer for future use.
TO THAW: see poultry thawing chart.
STORAGE TIME: 10–12 months.

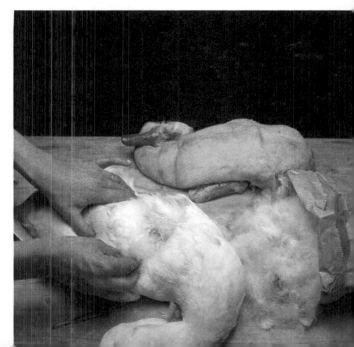

Plucking a duck (see page 98)

Power Failure

see page 231

Praline

Praline (a crushed mixture of burnt sugar and almonds) can be kept in the freezer to use for decorating gâteaux, icecream, mousses, soufflés, etc.

TO FREEZE: make in the usual way, crush when cold, then pack in usable quantities in freezer bags, seal, label and freeze.

TO THAW: unwrap and use frozen.

Prawn (U.S. Shrimp)*

These crustacea are best frozen when very fresh.

TO FREEZE: wash thoroughly in fresh cold water, then plunge into lightly salted water and cook until just pink, which will take approximately 3 minutes. Remove from the heat, cool in the cooking liquid, then drain well. Pack in freezer bags in their shells, seal, label and freeze. Or remove shells, pack in small rigid containers, cover, label and freeze.

TO THAW: unwrap and leave for 2 hours in the refrigerator, then serve chilled. Or use frozen in dishes that are to be cooked.

See also recipes for *Devilled Prawns (Shrimp), Salmon and Prawn (Shrimp) Quiches* and *Fish Pie*.

*For Australian prawn, see *Scampi* and *Shrimp*.

Preformer/Preforming

see **Brick Freezing**

Preserves

There is no point in freezing conserves and preserves of fruit as these keep perfectly well if stored correctly in clean, dry jars — and space in the freezer is best kept for other items that will not keep by any other method than freezing. Certain jams are worth making for the freezer, however. See **Jam**. See also recipes for *Lemon Curd* and *Marmalade*.

Prickly Pear

As its name suggests, this pear-shaped fruit from the cacti family is covered with prickles, which have usually been removed before it arrives in the markets. The fruit grows mainly in the southwestern U.S. and is also called Indian fig, Barbary fig and tuna.

TO PREPARE: If prickles have not been removed, work with gloves and rub them off with straw or singe them. Peel the fruit, halve and remove seeds. Freeze and thaw as for **Mango**. Use in Mexican dishes.

Profiterole (Cream Puff)

Prepare, freeze and thaw as for **Éclair**. See also recipe for *Profiteroles with Chocolate Sauce*.

Prunelle

Prepare, freeze and thaw as for **Plum**

Ptarmigan

see **Game**

Pudding

Most puddings freeze extremely well. The only real exception is custard-based and milk puddings which may separate on thawing. Traditionally, puddings are baked or steamed mixtures and can be either savoury or sweet.

Suet crust pastry puddings: can be frozen cooked or uncooked, although uncooked puddings will take a long time to cook after freezing (meat puddings are always best frozen with a cooked filling). Avoid putting jam or syrup in the base of these puddings as this can cause the mixture to become soggy in the freezer — chocolate and coffee flavourings, dried fruit and nuts give the best results.

TO FREEZE: make and bake or steam pudding in the usual way, using an aluminium foil basin if possible. Cool rapidly, cover with foil, label and freeze.

TO THAW: place in a steamer, cover and steam from frozen for approximately 2 hours for a fruit pudding, 3 hours for a meat pudding (600 ml/1 pint/2½ cup size). If more convenient, thaw the pudding for 4 hours at room temperature, then steam for approximately 45 minutes until heated through.

Sponge puddings: a combination of fruit and cake mixture, can be frozen before or after cooking.

TO FREEZE: make in the usual way and, if freezing before cooking, put mixture into an aluminium foil basin. Cover with foil, label and freeze. To freeze after cooking make and cook in the usual way, in an aluminium foil basin if possible. Cool quickly then seal basin with foil, label and freeze.

TO THAW: if frozen uncooked, grease the inside of foil covering, replace on top of basin and steam from frozen for approximately 2 hours for an uncooked pudding (600 ml/1 pint/2½ cup size). If frozen cooked, reheat from frozen in steamer for 45 minutes to 1 hour.

Bread and butter pudding: best frozen uncooked.

TO FREEZE: make in a buttered foil or pie dish, cover with foil, label and freeze.

TO THAW: uncover and bake from frozen in a warm oven (160°C/325°F or Gas Mark 3) for 1¾ hours or until set. Or thaw overnight at room temperature, then bake according to original recipe.

Fruit charlotte: best frozen uncooked.

TO FREEZE: make in the usual way in a buttered foil or pie dish, cover with foil, label and freeze.

TO THAW: uncover and bake from frozen in a fairly hot oven (190°C/375°F or Gas Mark 5) for approximately 1 hour or until golden brown and heated through. Or thaw overnight in the refrigerator, then bake as for uncooked charlotte, allowing approximately 45 minutes.

For other puddings and desserts, see recipe section and also under individual names (**Baba, Blancmange, Cheesecake, Crumble, Custard, Ice(s)/Icecream, Jelly, Meringue, Mousse(s), Pancake, Pastry & Pastry-based Dishes, Profiterole, Rice, Soufflé, Waffle**).

STORAGE TIME: up to 3 months for meat puddings, sponge, bread and butter puddings and charlottes; up to 4 months for fruit puddings made with suet crust pastry.

Pumpkin

Pumpkins store well in a cool, airy place which is free from damp and frost.

Freezing is only worthwhile if ready-prepared pumpkin is likely to be required at short notice.

TO FREEZE: peel and remove seeds, then cut into pieces and bake, boil or steam in a little water until soft. Drain and leave in pieces, or mash. Leave to cool, then pack in rigid containers, cover, label and freeze.

TO THAW: remove from containers and reheat frozen pumpkin in a double boiler with plenty of butter and seasoning. Or thaw for approximately 2 hours in containers and use in pies, etc.

STORAGE TIME: 12 months.

Purée

Both fruit and vegetable purées take up less space in the freezer than the whole fruit or vegetable. Fruit purées can be frozen with or without sugar, according to taste and future use, and can be used for making baby foods and numerous desserts and puddings including mousses, soufflés, fools, icecreams and sherbets. Vegetables can be puréed for use in baby foods and soups.

To freeze fruit purée: pour into rigid containers, leaving headspace, cover, label and freeze.

TO THAW: leave in containers for 2 to 4 hours at room temperature, depending on quantity.

To freeze vegetable purée: cook vegetables until tender, then drain, cool rapidly, purée and freeze in rigid containers as for fruit purée. Or freeze in ice cube trays until solid, pack in freezer bags, seal, label and return to freezer. Use frozen to add flavouring to casseroles, stews and stocks. Add seasoning at the reheating stage for vegetable purées.

STORAGE TIME: up to 6 months, according to type of fruit or vegetable (see individual entries).

Quail
see **Game**

Quelite
prepare, freeze and thaw as for **Spinach**

Quiche
see **Pastry & Pastry-based Dishes** and recipe section

Quick Freezing
see **Fast Freezing**

Quince
see **Japonica**

Steamed fruit puddings freeze very well. The one illustrated above was frozen cooked in an aluminium foil basin and then reheated from frozen in a steamer.

Power Failure – Quince

The photographs in the centre illustrate refreshing after blanching.

Rabbit

see **Game**

Raccoon

see **Game**

Radish

It is not possible to freeze summer salad radishes because they lose their crispness and flavour in the process. Winter radishes can be used in recipes instead of turnips, although they have a milder flavour. They are hardy and make huge roots which can be left standing in the ground and pulled as required during the winter months. Freeze them for convenience, or if it is likely that weather conditions will make it difficult to get them out of the ground just when you wish.

TO FREEZE: peel, grate and pack in freezer bags. Seal, label and freeze. Or peel, dice, blanch in boiling water for 2 minutes, then drain. Cool rapidly in iced water, drain, pat dry and pack in freezer bags. Seal, label and freeze.

TO THAW: leave grated radish in wrappings for at least 2 hours at room temperature, then use in salads, or mix with mayonnaise and serve as an accompaniment to cold meat. Unwrap and put frozen diced radishes in boiling salted water. Bring back to the boil, cover and simmer for 5 to 10 minutes until just tender, according to size. Drain and serve as for turnips, tossed in butter and plenty of seasoning.

STORAGE TIME: 6 months.

Rancidity

Rancidity is caused when oxygen has been absorbed by the fat cells in food. It can occur only if wrappings are faulty or inadequate. It is not harmful, but fatty foods (particularly bacon and meat) develop an 'off' taste which makes them unpleasant to eat.

Raspberry

see **Berry**

Raspings

Raspings, or dried breadcrumbs, will keep for 1 month in an airtight screw-top jar if stored in a cool, dry place. They may also be packed in freezer bags and frozen as for fresh **Breadcrumbs.**

STORAGE TIME: 3 months.

Ravioli

see **Pasta**.

Red Cabbage

see **Cabbage**

Redcurrant

see **Currant**

Red Mullet

see **Mullet**

Red Pepper

see **Peppers, Sweet**

Red Snapper (Schnapper)

A fish which flourishes along the east coast of North and South America, and along the coasts of Australia.

TO FREEZE: clean thoroughly and leave whole, or fillet. Wrap fish or fillets individually in cling film, then pack several together in a freezer bag.

TO THAW: unwrap and cook fillets from frozen. Or unwrap whole fish and leave to thaw for 4 hours in the refrigerator before cooking. Red snapper is particularly good cooked in a highly spiced sauce.

STORAGE TIME: 3 months.

Re-freezing

Most thawed frozen food can be re-frozen if it is first cooked or reheated. Bread, plain cakes, fruit and unfilled pastries, can be re-frozen safely without necessarily cooking or reheating. The only thing likely to happen to such food that is re-frozen is that it will lose some of its colour, flavour and texture. However, raw foods such as fish, meat, poultry and vegetables *must be cooked* before re-freezing, and only then if you are absolutely certain that they have been in a thawed state for no longer than they normally would have been before cooking.

Refresh

To plunge cooked vegetables, particularly green ones, into cold water to stop the cooking process and preserve the colour; they are then reheated to serve. Green vegetables are plunged into ice cold water after blanching and before freezing.

Refrigerator-freezer

see page 228

Reheating

Many frozen foods can be reheated without thawing, either on top of the stove or in the oven, according to how they were prepared before freezing. Items packed in boil-in-the-bags can be transferred directly from the freezer to a large pan of boiling water. Preformed foods such as casseroles, purées, sauces, soups and stews, can be unwrapped and transferred directly from the freezer to a saucepan or casserole, for reheating either on top of the stove or in the oven. Baked items or cooked foods packed in foil containers can be transferred directly to a preheated oven for best results (remove cardboard lids from foil dishes before reheating). Slight thawing is sometimes necessary to remove wrappings prior to reheating.

Reindeer

see **Game**

Rhubarb

see also **Fruit** for information on packing

Freeze only stems which have not become stringy.

TO FREEZE: wash, dry and cut into 2.5 cm/1 inch lengths. Pack dry with sugar. Or blanch in boiling water for 1 minute, drain, then cool rapidly in iced water. Drain and pack in heavy syrup.

TO THAW: leave in containers (or remove for faster thawing) for 3 hours at room temperature. Raw fruit can be cooked from frozen. Use poached with spices to taste, or in desserts.

STORAGE TIME: 12 months.

Rice

Boiled rice: can be frozen successfully, providing it is undercooked and frozen 'dry'.

TO FREEZE: boil in salted water until barely tender and still 'nutty', then drain and rinse thoroughly under cold running water until rice is cold. Shake in a colander until as dry as possible. Pack loosely in freezer bags, seal, label and freeze.

TO THAW: use from frozen: put into boiling salted water and simmer until tender (cooking time will depend on length of previous boiling), or reheat in melted butter until tender. Use as for freshly boiled rice, also in paella, risottos, soups and stuffings, etc.

Rice in cooked dishes: it is not advisable to freeze rice in cooked dishes which contain a lot of liquid such as casseroles and soups, as the rice tends to go 'mushy' during freezing. If such a recipe calls for rice, add it after freezing, at the reheating stage. Rice can be successfully frozen in such dishes as *Stuffed Peppers* and courgettes, however, and leftover rice is useful for these. Freeze cooled leftover rice in freezer bags as described above.

To freeze pudding rice: cook the pudding in the usual way, then cool, pack in a rigid container or freezer bag, cover or seal, label and freeze.

TO THAW: transfer to a heavy saucepan and reheat from frozen over gentle heat with a little fresh milk, stirring occasionally to prevent the pudding from sticking to the pan.
STORAGE TIME: 2 months.

Rissole

prepare, freeze and thaw as for **Croquette**

Roach

A river fish of the carp family.
TO FREEZE: clean thoroughly, then pack in freezer bags, seal, label and freeze.
TO THAW: unwrap and cook from frozen: dip in seasoned flour, fry in butter, then serve with lemon.
STORAGE TIME: 3 months.

Rockmelon

see **Melon**

Rock Salmon

A fish similar to cod and pollack, sometimes known as coalfish or saithe.
TO FREEZE: clean thoroughly, then fillet or cut into thick slices. Pack in freezer bags, interleaving each piece of fish with cling film. Seal, label and freeze.
TO THAW: unwrap and cook from frozen. Or unwrap and leave to thaw for 2 hours in the refrigerator, then dip in batter and deep fry in hot oil.
STORAGE TIME: 3 months.

Roe

Both the hard and soft roes of herring may be frozen. Do not freeze roes purchased from the fishmonger or fish market because these are usually frozen and thawed before selling and should not be re-frozen.
TO FREEZE: remove the roes from the fish, wash thoroughly and remove any dark pieces. Pack in small, rigid containers, cover, label and freeze.
TO THAW: unwrap and leave for 2 hours in the refrigerator, then poach to serve on toast, or coat in flour and fry.
STORAGE TIME: 2 months.

Roll

see **Bread**

Rollmop

This is a bloater or herring fillet that is preserved in vinegar. There is no point in further preservation by freezing.

Root Vegetables

see individual names (**Beetroot (Beet), Carrot, Celeriac, Garlic, Horseradish, Jerusalem Artichoke, Kohlrabi, Leek, Onion, Parsnip, Potato, Radish, Salsify (Scorzonera), Swede (Rutabaga), Turnip**)

Rosehip Syrup

There is no point in freezing homemade rosehip syrup because it is already preserved and will keep perfectly well on a shelf.

Above: Boil rice until almost cooked before freezing, then reheat to thaw and use as for freshly boiled rice.

Left: Freeze herring roes when very fresh, then cook and serve as usual after thawing.

**Rabbit –
Rosehip Syrup**

Rosemary *(Rosmarinus officinalis)*

A native of the Mediterranean region, the rosemary bush is usually small and dense with dark green leaves, but can grow to a height of 2 metres/6 feet. It is one of the most useful and fragrant of all herbs in cooking and is well worth freezing for times when fresh rosemary is not available; if dried, rosemary loses some of its pungency and is not so successful.

TO FREEZE: break off whole young sprigs before they start to flower and put directly into freezer bags. Seal, label and freeze.

TO THAW: crumble while still frozen, then chop finely or cut with scissors immediately and use in stuffings, etc. The leaves are usually removed from dishes such as casseroles and sauces before serving as they do not soften during cooking. Use whole frozen shoots to scatter around lamb, pork or veal before roasting, or on poached fish.

STORAGE TIME: 10 months.

Rotation of Stock

The regular turnover of a freezer's contents is essential so that old stock is used first and within its recommended storage period.

Rowanberry

see **Berry**

Rue *(Ruta graveolens)*

A herb which is most commonly used in making infusions. Rue has little culinary use, therefore there is no reason to freeze it.

Runner Bean

see **Bean**

Running Costs

see page 230

Rutabaga

see **Swede**

Blanch salsify without peeling, then cut up and remove skin.

Safety

see page 229

Sage *(Salvia officinalis)*

There are several varieties of this evergreen herb which is a native of the Mediterranean area, but it is the broad-leaved garden type which has the best flavour in cooking.

TO FREEZE: pick young end shoots early in the year and take the lower leaves from the woody stems before flower buds appear. Put bunches directly into freezer bags, seal, label and freeze. Or blanch in boiling water for 1 minute, cool at once under cold running water, shake dry, then put into bags.

TO THAW: crumble while still frozen or leave whole and use frozen or thaw at room temperature. Use in rich dishes with duck, goose and pork, also in liver pâté and stuffings. Use frozen sage sparingly as its flavour is strong and can impart a bitter flavour to dishes if used to excess.

STORAGE TIME: 4 months (unblanched); 10 months (blanched).

Salad Dressing

Salad dressings should not be frozen, either on their own or as part of a dish. This applies both to oil and vinegar or mayonnaise-based dressings, and salad creams.

Salad Vegetables

see individual names

Salmon

Fine river salmon should be frozen quickly after catching, and medium-sized fish are the best ones to freeze. Keen fishermen insist that to preserve the fine flavour of salmon it should not be gutted before freezing.

TO FREEZE: remove scales, and as much blood as possible, but wash the fish as little as possible. Either clean them out completely before freezing or leave ungutted (see above). Leave salmon whole or cut into slices. Pack in freezer bags, interleaving slices with cling film. Seal, label and freeze.

TO THAW: unwrap whole fish and leave to thaw for 6 hours in the refrigerator before cooking. Or grill (broil) or poach thin slices from frozen. See also recipe for *Koulibiac*.

STORAGE TIME: 3 months.

Salmon Trout

This sea fish is about the size of a large trout, with pinkish flesh.

TO FREEZE: clean thoroughly, leave whole and pack in freezer bags. Seal, label and freeze.

TO THAW: unwrap, leave for 4 hours in the refrigerator, then cook as for salmon or trout.

STORAGE TIME: 3 months.

Salsify (Scorzonera/Oyster Plant/Vegetable Oyster)

Scorzonera is the black-rooted variety of salsify, and considered to have a finer flavour. Leave the roots in the ground until just before freezing because they bleed badly if damaged when lifted — and so lose flavour.

TO FREEZE: scrub roots, but do not peel. Blanch in boiling water for 2 minutes, then drain and cut into 5 cm/2 inch lengths. Remove skin while still warm, then leave to cool. Pack in freezer bags, seal, label and freeze. Or boil until almost tender, then peel, cool and pack in bags.

TO THAW: leave in bags for approximately 2 hours at room temperature, or unwrap and cook from frozen according to recipe. Toss in butter and lemon juice, or cook in a cream sauce made with cider or wine vinegar. Serve as a first course or vegetable accompaniment.

STORAGE TIME: 12 months.

Salt Beef

see **Meat, Fresh**

Salt Pork

see **Meat, Fresh**

Sandwich

Sandwiches freeze well, providing you use suitable fillings. Avoid hard-boiled egg whites, jam, mayonnaise and salad cream, raw salad vegetables such as celery, cucumber, lettuce, tomato and watercress, and season lightly. Sandwiches can be made for the freezer with most breads — white, brown, rye — rolls, cut and uncut loaves and pita bread.

TO FREEZE: make in the usual way, leaving the crusts on the bread and spreading butter or margarine and

filling evenly to facilitate even thawing. Pack individually, wrapped in aluminium foil, or stack four to six sandwiches together, interleaving each one with foil and keeping the same filling in each stack. Wrap stacks in a freezer bag, seal, label and freeze away from the wall of the freezer.

TO THAW: leave in wrappings overnight in the refrigerator or for 4 hours at room temperature. (Individual sandwiches take approximately 2 hours to thaw at room temperature.) For quick thawing if sandwiches are needed in a hurry, they may be toasted from frozen. Unwrap and toast lightly on both sides.

To freeze fancy pinwheel, rolled, club and ribbon sandwiches: wrap securely in aluminium foil and freeze before cutting.

TO THAW: leave in wrappings over-

night in the refrigerator, cutting them after they have thawed for 4 hours.

To freeze open sandwiches and canapés: open (flash) freeze on trays until solid, then wrap in cling film and overwrap in foil.

TO THAW: unwrap and leave for 1 hour at room temperature.

Sandwich fillings: can be frozen separately. See above for types of filling to avoid.

TO FREEZE: pack filling in a rigid container, cover, label and freeze.

TO THAW: leave in container overnight in the refrigerator or for 2 to 3 hours at room temperature.

STORAGE TIME: 2 months for sandwiches; 1 month for open sandwiches and canapés; 1 to 2 months for fillings.

Sardine

The young pilchard is a sardine, most usually preserved in oil in tins (cans).

To freeze fresh sardines: clean thoroughly, then pack in freezer bags or rigid containers. Seal or cover, label and freeze.

TO THAW: unwrap and grill (broil) from frozen.

STORAGE TIME: 3 months.

Satsuma (Mandarin)

see also **Fruit** for information on packing

A small citrus fruit with a loose outer orange-like skin.

TO FREEZE: peel, then leave whole, slice, or divide into segments without breaking outer membrane. Open (flash) freeze; or pack dry with sugar.

TO THAW: leave in bags (or remove for faster thawing) for approximately 1 hour at room temperature. Use slightly frosted as for other citrus fruit.

STORAGE TIME: 12 months.

Sandwiches no longer have to be made at the last moment to avoid the bread becoming stale. Make them in advance (avoiding unfreezable fillings) and bring them out when required for picnics, packed lunches, snacks or cocktail parties.

Rosemary – Satsuma (Mandarin)

Sauce

Parsley, tomato and chocolate sauces are ideal candidates for the freezer, as are other sauces suggested by their ingredients above — mushroom, bread, apple, cheese, and caper.

Most sauces may be frozen, whether savoury or sweet. Avoid freezing cream- and egg-based sauces, which tend to separate on thawing, and keep seasoning to a minimum — this can be adjusted at the reheating stage. Suitable, and useful, sauces to freeze are apple, barbecue, béchamel, Bolognese, bread, caper, cheese (Mornay), chocolate, cranberry, curry, fruit and hard sauces, Melba, mushroom, mustard, tomato and white sauce.

TO FREEZE: make sauce in bulk, cool rapidly and freeze in usable quantities (150 ml/¼ pint/⅔ cup, 300 ml/½ pint/1¼ cups or 600 ml/1 pint/2½ cups). Pour into rigid containers, leaving headspace, cover, label and freeze. Or freeze small quantities of sauce in ice cube trays, open (flash) freeze until solid, then pack in freezer bags, seal, label and freeze.

TO THAW: leave in containers for 2 to 3 hours at room temperature for cold sauces; unwrap and reheat from frozen in a heavy saucepan for hot sauces, adding a little liquid if necessary and stirring occasionally. Adjust seasoning before use. Frozen cubes of sauce can be added to casseroles, soups, etc., when reheating.

See also recipe section.

STORAGE TIME: approximately 3 months, depending on type of sauce.

Sauerkraut

To freeze in a cooked dish, see recipe for *Hungarian Pork with Sauerkraut*.

Sausage, Sausagemeat & Sausage Rolls

To freeze sausages: only freeze freshly made sausages, as soon as possible after making or purchase. If making sausages at home for freezing, do not overseason. Pack in usable quantities in freezer bags, seal, label and freeze.

TO THAW: unwrap, cover loosely, and thaw at room temperature until sausages can be separated. Or leave in wrappings overnight in the refrigerator and thaw completely. Use as for fresh sausages, allowing a little extra cooking time for partially thawed sausages.

To freeze sausagemeat: as for *Sausages* above.

TO THAW: leave in wrappings overnight in the refrigerator, then unwrap and use as for fresh sausagemeat.

To freeze sausage rolls: these are best frozen unbaked, whether made with flaky, puff or shortcrust (pie) pastry. Make in the usual way, but do not brush with glaze or bake. Open (flash) freeze until solid, then pack in freezer bags, seal, label and return to freezer.

TO THAW: take sausage rolls out individually, as and when required. Place on a baking sheet, brush with beaten egg and bake from frozen in a fairly hot oven (200°C/400°F or Gas Mark 6) for approximately 20 minutes or until cooked through.

STORAGE TIME: 3 months (sausages, sausagemeat and sausage rolls).

Savarin

see **Baba** and recipe for *Savarin*

Thaw frozen scones in the oven and serve as for freshly made scones.

Savory (Summer — *Satureja hortensis*/Winter — *Satureja montana*)

Two varieties of this herb are mainly used in cooking, the annual summer savory and the winter perennial savory. Both plants grow to a height of approximately 30 cm/12 inches and are similar in appearance, bearing pale mauve and white flowers during the summer months. Savory is known in some parts of Europe as the 'bean plant' because of its affinity with bean, lentil and pea dishes. Summer savory has a lighter, more refined flavour than winter savory, which has a stronger flavour and is more commonly used in cooking, particularly in bean dishes and terrines.

TO FREEZE: the bitter-tasting leaves should be picked while young, preferably before flowers appear. Pick whole sprigs and put directly into freezer bags. Seal, label and freeze. Or pick leaves individually, chop finely and freeze in ice cube trays until solid, then pack in bags.

TO THAW: leave sprigs whole or crumble while still frozen. Add fresh or dried sprigs to the water in which beans are cooking, discard before serving, then sprinkle crumbled or chopped frozen leaves on top and toss in butter.

Use savory sparingly in egg and fish dishes, salads, sauces, soups, stews and stuffings.

Or sprinkle onto pork, mushrooms, tomatoes or veal before grilling (broiling).

STORAGE TIME: 10 months.

Scallion

see **Spring Onion**

Scallop (Coquille)

These shellfish should be frozen on the day they are caught, but in any case they tend to develop an oily taste in freezer conditions.

TO FREEZE: scrub the shells thoroughly, open them and remove the black fringe from around the scallop. Wash the fish thoroughly in salted water, then cut the fish and its orange roe away from the shell. Rinse well, drain, then pat dry and pack in freezer bags or rigid containers. Seal or cover, label and freeze.

TO THAW: leave in wrappings for 2 hours in the refrigerator. Cook as for fresh scallops.

See also recipe for *Scallop and Artichoke Soup*.

STORAGE TIME: 1 month.

Scallop Squash

see **Custard Marrow**

Scampi (Aust. Prawn)

This is not the true name of a fish, but is the name under which Dublin Bay or Gulf prawns or Norway lobsters are commonly served. They must be very fresh and are best frozen raw in unshelled tails.

TO FREEZE: soon after catching, twist off the head and carapace with legs and claws attached. Wash the tails and pack in freezer bags or rigid containers. Seal or cover, label and freeze.

TO THAW: unwrap and cook small quantities of frozen tails in boiling salted water for approximately 6 minutes. Cool in the liquid and serve, or prepare in batter, breadcrumbs or sauce.

STORAGE TIME: 1 month.

Schnapper

see **Red Snapper**

Scone

Both homemade and commercially baked scones freeze well, whether savoury or sweet, drop or girdle (griddle) scones.

TO FREEZE: leave until completely cold, wrap in aluminium foil, then overwrap in a freezer bag, seal, label and freeze.

TO THAW: remove freezer bag and place foil-wrapped scones on a baking sheet. Reheat from frozen in a moderate oven (180°C/350°F or Gas Mark 4) for approximately 10 minutes or until heated through. Cool for 1 to 2 minutes on a wire rack, then serve immediately. Scones may also be split and toasted from frozen if they are needed in a hurry.

See also recipe for *Scones*.

STORAGE TIME: up to 6 months.

Scorzonera

see **Salsify**

Scrod

The baby cod, called scrod, is usually filleted after cleaning.

TO FREEZE: pack in freezer bags, interleaving each fillet with cling film.

TO THAW: cook from frozen as for **Cod.**

STORAGE TIME: 3 months.

Sea Bass

see **Bass**

Seafood

see individual names

Seakale

A luxury vegetable which needs good soil and a great deal of attention and skill to grow: the tender growths have to develop in total darkness to blanch. It is not advisable to freeze seakale, because this would ruin its delicate structure and flavour.

Seakale Beet

see **Chard, Swiss**

Sealing

see also **Air**

Correct sealing is essential to exclude air from packages. There are various ways of doing this: by heat, using a special heat-sealing unit or a domestic iron, the latter being suitable only for sealing polythene (polyethylene) wrappings; with wire, paper or plastic-coated ties or string; with freezer or masking tape; by means of clip-on or screw-top lids; or by moulding aluminium foil around or over food without the need for any further type of closure.

Seasoning

Seasoning, in the form of salt and pepper, herbs and spices, should be kept to a minimum when preparing dishes for the freezer. Freezing tends to bring out the flavour of seasonings and if care is not taken, seasoning can become overpowering. Always use fresh herbs and spices wherever possible, as these tend not to become as strong as their dried counterparts during the freezing process. When thawing and reheating a dish, taste for seasoning before serving and adjust accordingly.

Seville Orange

see **Marmalade** and **Orange**

Shad

An extremely bony fish, shad migrates from the sea to the rivers. It is similar to herring, but with a deeper body. The roe is a delicacy which may be fried and served with bacon.
TO FREEZE: clean thoroughly and remove backbone. Leave whole and pack in freezer bags. Seal, label and freeze.
TO THAW: unwrap and leave for 3 hours in the refrigerator, then stuff before baking.
STORAGE TIME: 3 months.

Shaddock

Named for the skipper who brought this fruit from the East Indies across to the West Indies, this gigantic member of the citrus family can be as large as a melon. The rind is very thick and the reddish interior can be slightly bitter; the shape varies from round to pear-shaped. Prepare, freeze and thaw as for **Grapefruit**.

Shallot

prepare, freeze and thaw as for small **Onion**

Shark

The best pieces of shark flesh to use are along the backbone. Prepare, freeze and thaw as for any white fish fillets. Belly sections need long simmering to break down the flesh.
STORAGE TIME: 3 months.

Shellfish

see individual names

Sherbet

see **Ices)/Icecream** and recipe for *Orange Sherbet*

Shortbread

TO FREEZE: make and bake this rich butter mixture in the usual way, cut into triangles or fingers while soft, then leave to cool on a wire rack. Wrap in aluminium foil or pack in a rigid container, seal, label and freeze.
TO THAW: unwrap and leave for 2 to 3 hours at room temperature.
STORAGE TIME: 3 months.

Shortening

freeze and thaw as for **Lard**

Shrimp (Aust. Prawn)

Both brown and pink shrimps must be very fresh for freezing and should be frozen on the day they are caught.
TO FREEZE: wash in fresh cold water, then plunge in lightly salted water and cook until just brown or pink, which will take approximately 2 minutes according to type. Cool in the liquid, drain, pat dry, then pack with or without shells in rigid containers. Cover, label and freeze.

Or stir shelled shrimps in melted butter and seasonings to taste, pack in small pots, then leave to cool. Wrap in freezer bags, seal, label and freeze.
TO THAW: leave in containers or remove bags from pots of shrimps, leave for 2 hours in the refrigerator, then serve chilled.
STORAGE TIME: 1 month.

Silverbeet

see **Spinach**

Silver Dory

prepare, freeze and thaw as for **John Dory**

Silver Foil

see page 232 (*Aluminium Foil*)

Shellfish —see Scallop (Coquille), Scampi (Aust. Prawn) and Shrimp (Aust. Prawn) fresh, frozen and ready to be served.

Sauerkraut – Silver Foil

Skate

This is one of the few fish which is better left for a day after catching so that the flesh becomes tender before cooking.

TO FREEZE: clean and leave small ones whole, cut larger ones into pieces. Pack in freezer bags, seal, label and freeze.

TO THAW: unwrap and cook on the bone from frozen. Or unwrap and leave to thaw for 3 hours in the refrigerator, then skin and cut into fillets. Skate is traditionally served with black butter, made by melting butter until very dark brown, then adding capers, finely chopped parsley and wine vinegar.

STORAGE TIME: 3 months.

Freeze freshly smoked fish whole, in fillets or as pâté (see Smoked Trout Pâté page 140).

Sloe

This plum-like fruit is too bitter for use in desserts, but it can be made into chutney or jelly, or used to flavour gin. Freeze them if you cannot deal with them at the time of harvesting, but do not want to waste them.

TO FREEZE: wash, dry thoroughly and pack in freezer bags. Seal, label and freeze. There is no need to thaw them before use: simply increase the cooking time in recipes that call for fresh sloes.

Smell

see **Odour**

Smelt(s)

A very small fish with a delicate flavour, smelt live near coasts and ascend to the rivers to spawn.

TO FREEZE: clean carefully, removing the gills and entrails. Do not wash, but wipe and pat dry gently. Pack in

freezer bags, seal, label and freeze.

TO THAW: unwrap and cook from frozen by coating in flour and frying, or by poaching in water, wine and herbs to taste. Or unwrap and leave to thaw for 2 hours in the refrigerator, then thread on skewers with a little bacon, and grill (broil) or deep fry in hot oil or fat.

STORAGE TIME: 3 months.

Smoked Fish

Freshly smoked fish of good quality (haddock, kippers, mackerel, salmon, trout) may be frozen. Do not buy smoked fish for freezing from a fishmonger or fish market unless you know for sure that it is fresh, as quite often fish is frozen and thawed before selling and should not be re-frozen.

TO FREEZE: wrap individual fish or pieces of fish in cling film, then overwrap in a freezer bag. Seal, label and freeze.

TO THAW: leave in wrappings for 3 hours in the refrigerator. Serve cold, or cook as for fresh smoked fish.

See also recipes for *Smoked Haddock Mousse, Kipper Pâté* and *Smoked Trout Pâté*.

STORAGE TIME: 3 months.

Snail (Escargot)*

Snails are best if left to fast for 10 days to get rid of any vegetable poisons; they may then be fattened before cooking. Scrub them, and remove the membrane which closes them. Put in water to cover and add a handful of salt to the water for every 50 snails. Leave to soak for 4 hours, changing the water frequently. Rinse in several waters to clear slime, then blanch in boiling water for 8 minutes. Drain and remove from shells, then cut off and discard the black end. Dry the snails and shells. Put a little snail butter (butter mixed with crushed garlic, minced parsley, chopped shallot and salt and pepper) into each shell. Put back snails and top with more snail butter.

TO FREEZE: open (flash) freeze until solid, then pack in freezer bags or rigid containers. Seal or cover, label and return to freezer.

TO THAW: leave in wrappings for 2 hours in the refrigerator, then unwrap and bake just long enough to make the snails very hot.

STORAGE TIME: 1 month.

*Not available in Australia.

Snap Bean

see **Bean**

Snapper

see **Red Snapper**

Snipe

see **Game**

Snow Pea

see **Pea,** *Mange Tout*

Sole

A European flatfish with a fine, delicate flavour, the Dover sole is the best variety, with lemon sole, Torbay sole and witch being inferior types. The best fish for eating should be without roes.

TO FREEZE: skin the fish and leave whole, then pack in freezer bags. Seal, label and freeze.

TO THAW: unwrap and grill (broil) or fry from frozen. Or unwrap and leave to thaw for 2 hours in the refrigerator, then cut into fillets and poach or bake in a sauce.

STORAGE TIME: 3 months.

Sorbet

see **Ice(s)/Icecream**

Sorrel, French *(Rumex scutatus)*

French sorrel is the only variety of this herb which is worth growing domestically, although there are many other types. The plants usually grow to a height of 30–46 cm/12–18 inches, and have clusters of tiny yellow-green, red-tinted flowers which start to appear in early summer. These must be removed to encourage the production of more succulent young leaves. Since sorrel dies down in winter, it is well worth freezing if a constant supply is required. Fresh sorrel may be used as a salad ingredient, but once frozen it loses its crispness and is therefore best treated and cooked as for **Spinach.**

TO FREEZE: pick the leaves, remove stems and middle rib vein if tough. Wash under cold running water and pat dry. Chop coarsely, freeze in ice cube trays until solid, then pack in freezer bags, seal, label and freeze. Or put whole bunches of washed and dried leaves into bags. Or cook freshly picked sorrel leaves until tender, purée in an electric blender or work in a Mouli-légumes (foodmill), then cool rapidly and pack in rigid containers, cover, label and freeze.

TO THAW: add frozen cubes to sauces and soups, or make into a sauce and serve with duck.

Or wrap frozen whole leaves around fish, pork or veal before cooking. Reheat puréed sorrel from frozen in a heavy saucepan on top of the stove, or in the top of a double boiler as for **Spinach.**

STORAGE TIME: 2 months (bunches); 6 months (cubes); 8 months (purée).

Soufflé
1 *Adding stiffly beaten egg whites to the basic white sauce and egg yolk mixture.*
2 *Folding-in the egg whites.*
3 *Gently pouring the soufflé mixture into a freezerproof soufflé dish.*
4 *Wrapping the dish in a freezer bag.*
5 *The soufflé ready to serve.*

Soufflé

Sweet and savoury uncooked soufflés that are set with gelatin(e) can be frozen ready to serve, but cooked varieties can only be frozen before baking.

TO FREEZE: make in the usual way in soufflé dish(es) that will withstand the cold temperature of the freezer, using aluminium foil collars rather than greaseproof (waxed) paper ones. Leave any decoration, piping, etc., until serving time. Open (flash) freeze until solid, then wrap each soufflé (with its foil collar) in a freezer bag seal, label and return to freezer.

TO THAW: unwrap, remove collar carefully, then leave overnight in the refrigerator or for approximately 4 hours at room temperature. Decorate after thawing and serve chilled.

To freeze soufflés for baking later: make in the usual way, pour mixture into a freezerproof soufflé dish, then wrap in a freezer bag, seal, label and return to freezer.

TO THAW: leave in wrappings for approximately 30 minutes at room temperature, then unwrap and bake in a fairly hot oven (190°C/375°F or Gas Mark 5) for approximately double the length of time stated in soufflé recipe used, until well risen and golden.

See also recipes for *Crab Soufflé*, *Lemon Soufflé*, *Iced Raspberry Soufflé* and *Spinach Soufflé*.

STORAGE TIME: 3 months.

Soup

Most soups freeze extremely well: try to keep a stock of soups in the freezer with a good variety of flavours and textures. They will stand you in good stead.

TO FREEZE: make soup in the usual way, avoiding recipes that call for barley, pasta, patoes or rice which will make the soup become mushy (these can be added at the reheating stage). Use herbs and spices sparingly at this stage — more can always be added after reheating. If soup is to be puréed, this should be done before freezing, while the soup is still warm: the soup is then frozen in concentrated form.

Do not include cream, eggs or milk before freezing as these can cause separation and curdling: add them to the soup at the reheating stage. One advantage of freezing soups in this way is that they will not take up too much room in the freezer. Cool the soup rapidly, skim off any surplus fat which may cause rancidity, then pour soup into a rigid container, leaving 1.25 cm/½ inch headspace for wide-topped containers, 2.5 cm/1 inch headspace for narrow-topped containers. Cover, label and freeze. Or pour the soup into a freezer bag-lined preformer (forming container), freeze until solid, then remove preformer (container), seal, label and return to freezer.

Always be sure to freeze in usable quantities that suit your own requirements; if too large a quantity is frozen in a block and some is left over after reheating, it must not be re-frozen once thawed. The most useful quantities are either 300 ml/½ pint/1¼ cups or 600 ml/1 pint/2½ cups, but bear in mind whether extra liquid is to be added at the reheating stage.

TO THAW: hold sealed container or bag under warm running water for a moment or two to release soup, then tip into a heavy saucepan and heat gently from frozen, stirring occasionally. A little liquid may be added if the soup tends to stick and any cream, eggs or milk should be added at this stage. If soup appears to be separating, whisk briskly until smooth, or blend at high speed for a few seconds. Soups that are to be served cold should be thawed in container overnight in the refrigerator. Always taste soups for seasoning before serving and adjust accordingly.

See also Soups and Appetizers Chapter in recipe section.

STORAGE TIME: 3 months, according to ingredients used.

113

stored in the freezer, then always use tried and tested recipes.

STORAGE TIME: 1 month (for spiced biscuits (cookies) and cakes).

Spinach (Silverbeet)

Freeze the small thinnings of summer spinach before this quick-growing annual gets into its stride and before dry weather when it rapidly goes to seed. As the plants get bigger, pinch out the central growing stem to stop them flowering and pick the outer leaves regularly.

To freeze thinnings: wash thoroughly under cold running water. There is no need to cut off their tiny roots as these add to the flavour. Blanch in boiling water for 30 seconds, drain, then cool rapidly in iced water. Squeeze out excess moisture gently, then pack in freezer bags, leaving headspace. Seal, label and freeze.

TO THAW: unwrap and transfer to a colander or strainer. Leave for 30 minutes at room temperature, then toss quickly in hot melted butter and seasonings to taste. Serve immediately.

To freeze thicker leaves and stems: wash thoroughly under cold running water, then blanch in boiling water for 2 minutes, shaking the basket so that the leaves separate. Drain and cool rapidly in iced water, then gently squeeze out excess moisture. Pack in bags as for *Thinnings* above.

TO THAW: unwrap and put frozen spinach in boiling salted water. Bring back to the boil, cover and simmer for 5 to 7 minutes, then drain. Or put frozen spinach in hot melted butter and seasonings to taste, and cook gently until heated through. Serve immediately. Use also in composite dishes.

See also recipes for *Greek Spinach Puffs, Spinach Quiche* and *Spinach Soufflé*.

STORAGE TIME: 12 months.

Watercress, Cream of Cauliflower and Mushroom and Onion Soup (see recipe section) are ready to be frozen. Tomato Soup has been reheated and garnished ready to serve. The croûtons will be frozen and used to garnish the cauliflower soup when required. The remaining ingredients photographed will be made into soup using the frozen stock cubes.

Soup Garnishes

These can be frozen alongside the soups in your freezer, and will add the finishing 'just made' touch.

Freshly chopped or sprigs of herbs: can be packed in freezer bags, then sprinkled or crumbled onto hot or cold soups just before serving.

Croûtes and croûtons: can also be frozen then floated on top of soups after reheating.

Duxelles of mushrooms: is another useful garnish which can be added to most soups, particularly those made with vegetables: chop mushrooms and stalks very finely and cook gently in a little butter with herbs and seasoning to taste. Cook until quite dry, then remove from heat and leave to cool. Pack in usable quantities in small rigid containers, cover, label and freeze. Add to soups at reheating stage — there is no need to thaw beforehand.

STORAGE TIME: 3 months (duxelles).

Spaghetti

see **Pasta** and recipe for *Spaghetti Bolognese*

Spearmint

see **Mint**

Spice(s)

There is no point in freezing spices (as one would fresh herbs) as they have a long shelf life if kept correctly in airtight containers. Certain spices can also develop strong 'off' flavours in the freezer, and it is wise to add spices sparingly to dishes that are being cooked for the freezer; this applies to biscuits (cookies) and cakes in particular. Always buy spices from a reliable source — a health food store or supermarket with a quick turnover, for example. Buy in small quantities and use within 3 months to be sure that they are absolutely fresh. Experiment with amounts of spices and the length of time they can be

1

Spoilage

Food in the freezer may deteriorate or lose quality due to a number of factors: the action of enzymes or food-spoilage organisms; inadequate or faulty packaging which can lead to oxidation, dehydration and freezer burn; or careless thawing.

Sponge

see **Cake**

Sprat

The sprat is a small herring-like fish which is best grilled (broiled) or fried in batter. Smoked sprats are an unusual delicacy.
TO FREEZE: clean, then pack in ½ kg/1 lb freezer bags, seal, label and freeze.
TO THAW: unwrap and leave for 2 hours in the refrigerator, then cook as for fresh sprats.
STORAGE TIME: 3 months.

Spread

see **Dip**

Spring Greens (Collards)

The early shoots of brassicas.
TO FREEZE: wash thoroughly, peel or discard any hard stems, chop or leave whole. Blanch in plenty of boiling water for 2 minutes, drain, then cool rapidly in iced water. Drain, pat dry and pack in freezer bags. Seal, label and freeze.
TO THAW: unwrap and put frozen spring greens in boiling salted water. Bring back to the boil, cover and simmer for approximately 5 minutes until stems are just tender. Drain and serve hot with butter and seasoning to taste, or in a savoury sauce.
STORAGE TIME: 12 months.

Spring Onion (Scallion) or Green Onion

In common with all salad vegetables, spring onions lose their crispness during the freezing process; however, they do not become so limp that they cannot be used in salads.
TO FREEZE: remove roots and most of the green top, then wipe and peel off the very fine outer skin if necessary. Leave whole or chop and pack in small quantities in freezer bags. Seal, overwrap to avoid cross-flavouring, seal, label and freeze.
TO THAW: leave in wrappings (or remove for faster thawing) for approximately 30 minutes at room temperature. Use slightly chilled in salads.
STORAGE TIME: 2 months.

Squab

see **Game**

Squash

see **Custard Marrow** and **Marrow**

Squid

Prepare, freeze and thaw small squid as for **Octopus.** See also recipe for *Calamares Salad.*

Squirrel

see **Game**

Star Symbols*

A system of marking frozen food compartments of refrigerators with star symbols to indicate the recommended storage periods for commercially frozen foods only.
One black star (*) equals −6°C/21°F and can store ready-frozen food for up to 1 week.
Two black stars (**) equal −12°C/10°F and can store ready-frozen food for up to 1 month.
Three black stars (***) equal −18°C/0°F and can store ready-frozen food for up to 3 months.
However, a 6-pointed white star in front of the three-star refrigerator symbol ✩*** indicates a food freezer capable of freezing fresh food as well as storing ready-frozen food. This four-star symbol distinguishes a food freezer from a conservator, which can only store ready-frozen food.
*Not applicable in U.S.A. Australia — check for approval by Standards Association.

Steak

see **Beef**

Sterilization

In order to re-use freezer containers and wrappings, they should be immersed in a chemical sterilizing solution to rid them of any harmful food-spoilage organisms that might be present.

Stew

prepare, freeze and thaw as for **Casserole**

Stock

If you have a freezer you should never need to rely on commercially made stock cubes, which tend to make foods salty and give them all a similar flavour. Stock can be made from the bones and trimmings of fish, meat or poultry (if you buy meat and poultry in bulk you will have an endless supply of these), vegetables, herbs and other seasonings.
TO FREEZE: make in large quantities in the usual way, using a pressure cooker if possible to economize on fuel and time. Strain and leave to cool. Skim off any surplus fat, then pour into rigid containers, leaving 1.25 cm/½ inch headspace for wide-necked containers, 2.5 cm/1 inch for narrow-necked containers. Cover, label and freeze.
TO THAW: stock can be used from frozen: hold the container under warm running water for a moment or two to release the stock, then tip into a heavy saucepan and reheat gently, stirring occasionally.
To freeze concentrated stock: if freezer space is short, strained stock can be boiled before freezing to reduce it by as much as one-third. Leave to cool, then pour into ice cube trays and freeze until solid. Transfer cubes to trays, open (flash) freeze for approximately 2 hours, then pack in a freezer bag, seal, label and return to freezer. Cubes can then be used individually to add flavour to casseroles, sauces, soups and stews, etc. Simply add them in their frozen state and dilute to taste if necessary.
If there is no time to make stock, uncooked bones may be stored in the freezer in bags until required. See **Beef,** *Beef Bones.* See also recipes for stock under **Beef** and **Poultry.**
STORAGE TIME: 3 months.

1 Blanch fresh spinach, cool rapidly, squeeze out and pack in freezer bags.
2 Thaw and cook in boiling water or butter.
3 Frozen spinach can be used in composite dishes like Greek Spinach Puffs (see page 137) and Spinach Quiche (see page 184), but they should not then be refrozen.

Storage Times

see individual entries and charts

Straw, Drinking

see **Air**

Strawberry

see **Berry**

Stuffing

Stuffings and forcemeat for fish, meat and poultry may be frozen successfully, but they should be frozen separately in their own bag or container.

TO FREEZE: make in the usual way and leave to cool if the stuffing has been cooked. Pack in usable quantities in freezer bags or rigid containers. Seal or cover, label and freeze.

TO THAW: leave overnight in the refrigerator or for approximately 3 hours at room temperature, then use as for fresh stuffing. If stuffing is to be served separately and not stuffed into fish, meat or poultry, it can be frozen in an aluminium foil container and baked from frozen, allowing a little extra cooking time than for fresh stuffing.

Dry stuffing ingredients: can also be frozen and are useful in that they remain free flowing and can be used instantly as for **Breadcrumbs.** Mix breadcrumbs with herbs and seasonings, then pack in freezer bags, seal, label and freeze. Use frozen with eggs and suet to make traditional stuffings.

STORAGE TIME: 3 months (freshly made stuffing); 6 months (dry stuffing).

Sturgeon

A fish similar to shark found in the Northern Hemisphere, the roe of which is used as **Caviare.** The sturgeon flesh is hard and white, and the fish is commonly hung for 2 to 3 days, then marinated in white wine

Stuffing can be frozen in usable quantities in aluminium foil containers, but if preferred it can be formed into forcemeat balls, open frozen and then packed into freezer bags before returning to the freezer.

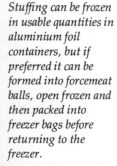

for 24 hours before cooking.

TO FREEZE: hang the fish, then cut into pieces, wrap in a freezer bag, seal, label and freeze.

TO THAW: unwrap, cover in a white wine marinade, then leave in the refrigerator for 24 hours. Drain, then grill (broil) or fry in butter.

To freeze smoked sturgeon: wrap individual fish in cling film, then pack several fish together in a freezer bag. Seal, label and freeze. Thaw in wrappings overnight in the refrigerator, and use as for fresh smoked sturgeon.

STORAGE TIME: 3 months (fresh and smoked).

Suet

see **Pudding**

Sugar Pack

see **Fruit**

Sugar Pea

see **Pea,** *Mange Tout*

Swede (Rutabaga)

Freeze only young roots.

TO FREEZE: wash, peel and cook in boiling salted water for approximately 15 minutes. Drain, cool slightly, then purée in an electric blender or work in a Mouli-légumes (foodmill). Leave until completely cold, then pack in rigid containers, cover, label and freeze.

TO THAW: put frozen swede in a double boiler with butter and salt to taste, reheat gently, then sprinkle with freshly grated nutmeg or seasonings to taste and serve hot with any meat dish.

STORAGE TIME: 6 months.

Sweetbread

see **Meat, Fresh**

Sweetcorn

see **Corn**

Sweet Potato (Yam)

Like ordinary potatoes, these are best if cooked before freezing.

TO FREEZE: peel and cut into 1.25 cm/½ inch slices or 6 mm/¼ inch rounds. Parboil, drain, then leave to cool. Or peel, halve and boil until barely tender. Drain, then cool rapidly in iced water, drain and pat dry. Pack in freezer bags, seal, label and freeze.

TO THAW: leave in wrappings at room temperature until soft when tested with a fork, then pat dry and fry in hot butter until evenly browned. Thawed sweet potatoes can also be fried in hot butter and sugar until caramelized. Or unwrap and deep fry from frozen in hot oil or fat. Drain and serve hot.

To freeze sweet potato purée: peel, cut into chunks, boil until completely tender, then cool slightly. Purée in an electric blender or work in a Mouli-légumes (foodmill) or through a sieve. Leave until completely cold, then pack in rigid containers, cover, label and freeze.

TO THAW: unwrap and reheat from frozen in a double boiler with butter, sugar and salt and pepper to taste.

STORAGE TIME: 6 months.

Swordfish

A large fish which can weigh up to 270 kg/600 lb, swordfish tend to be very dry when cooked.

TO FREEZE: pack large, thick steaks (weighing approximately 1.5 kg/3 lb each) in freezer bags. Or freeze a 1–2 kg/2–4 lb centre cut whole for baking. Seal, label and freeze.

TO THAW: unwrap and leave for 6 hours in the refrigerator, then bake with plenty of butter. Salmon recipes can be used for swordfish.

STORAGE TIME: 3 months.

Syrup

see also **Fruit, Syrup Pack,** etc.

Fruit syrups may be frozen and will often keep better by this method of preservation than by the bottling (canning) method which can be tricky if you are not accustomed to it.

TO FREEZE: make syrup in the usual way, leave to cool, then pour into ice cube trays and freeze until solid. Transfer cubes to trays, open (flash) freeze for approximately 2 hours, then pack in a freezer bag, seal, label and return to freezer. Cubes can then be used individually (diluted to taste) for desserts, drinks, etc.

Leftover syrup from canned fruit: can also be frozen to avoid wasting it. Pour into a rigid container, cover, label and freeze until required.

T

Tagliatelle
see **Pasta**

Tangelo*
This dessert fruit from the citrus family is a cross between a tangerine and a pomelo (whose other name is grapefruit). Prepare, freeze and thaw as for **Orange**.
*Not available in Australia.

Tangerine (Aust. Mandarin)
see also **Fruit** for information on packing

For convenience, freeze seedless ones if possible, otherwise you will lose a lot of juice when removing pips (seeds) before freezing.

TO FREEZE: peel, remove pith, leave whole or divide into segments. (Remove pips (seeds) if necessary.) Pack in light syrup.

TO THAW: leave in container in the refrigerator until just thawed but still slightly frosted. (For faster thawing, remove from container and thaw at room temperature.) Use for desserts, in fresh fruit salads, with icecream, or sponge cake and cream.
STORAGE TIME: 12 months.

Tansy *(Tanacetum vulgare)*
An old-fashioned herb which is rarely used in cooking nowadays, and therefore not worth freezing.

Tape, Freezer
see page 235

Tarragon *(Artemisia dracunculus)*
An aromatic herb growing to a height of 46–75 cm/18–30 inches, tarragon has a distinctive spicy fragrance. It is invaluable in cooking chicken and for flavouring sauces and stuffings. Tarragon may be successfully frozen as an alternative method of preservation to drying. When growing in the garden, keep the flower heads from forming, or they will rob the leaves of nourishment.

TO FREEZE: pick young shoots continually throughout the growing season. Wash if necessary under cold running water, shake dry, then put bunches directly into freezer bags, seal, label and freeze. Or pick the larger leaves individually, chop finely, freeze in ice cube trays until solid, then pack cubes in bags. Or blanch sprigs or leaves in boiling water for 30 seconds, drain and cool under cold running water, then pat dry and pack in bags. For large quantities to be used in sauces at a later date, purée freshly picked whole young sprigs in an electric blender with a little water, press into small rigid containers, cover, label and freeze. Or freeze in ice cube trays.

TO THAW: crumble bunches or sprigs while still frozen and add to sauces or stuffings. Add frozen cubes to any game, kidney or liver dish, to sauces, particularly sauce Béarnaise, and soups. Or leave cubes to thaw in a strainer for a few minutes at room temperature, then toss with buttered mushrooms or new potatoes just before serving.
STORAGE TIME: 3 months (unblanched sprigs); 5 months (blanched sprigs); 8–10 months (cubes).

To freeze tarragon sauce: purée whole young sprigs and leaves in an electric blender with a little water, then stir into a cooled white sauce. Pour into a rigid container, cover, label and freeze.

TO THAW: unwrap and put into a heavy saucepan, then reheat gently from frozen on top of the stove, adding more liquid if the mixture is too thick. Do not boil or the pungency of the herb will be lost.
STORAGE TIME: 6 months.

To freeze tarragon butter: chop freshly picked leaves finely, then blend into butter with salt and pepper to taste. Form into a roll, wrap in aluminium foil, then overwrap in a freezer bag, seal, label and freeze. Cut off frozen slices as required, or cut the roll into convenient-sized portions (25–50 g/1–2 oz/2–4 tablespoons), wrap individually in foil, then pack together in a freezer bag.
STORAGE TIME: 4 months.

Tart
see **Pastry & Pastry-based Dishes**

Tea
It is quite useful to have a quantity of iced tea in the freezer, especially during the summer months when fruit cups and punches are likely to be served.

TO FREEZE: strain strong cold tea into ice cube trays, freeze until solid, transfer cubes to trays and open (flash) freeze for approximately 2 hours. Pack in freezer bags, seal, label and return to freezer. Add frozen cubes to drinks as required.
STORAGE TIME: 6 months.

Tarragon can be frozen in ice cube trays, or as tarragon sauce or butter.

Below left: Freeze iced tea cubes to add to summer drinks and punches.

Storage Times – Tea

Tomatoes can be frozen whole for future use in composite dishes like Ratatouille (see page 181), or as delicious homemade tomato juice.

Temperature
see page 229

Terrine
see **Pâté & Terrine**

Thawing
see also individual entries for precise thawing instructions

How long frozen food takes to thaw depends on its density, shape and size, but in general, up to 12 hours or overnight is more than adequate. The method of thawing can also vary, either in the refrigerator or at room temperature, wrapped or unwrapped. Certain foods such as frozen vegetables or prepared items like burgers, fish fingers, raw pastry dishes and pizzas are more enjoyable cooked from frozen without thawing, and are perfectly safe to eat.

However, some raw foods *must* be thawed before cooking. This is to avoid any possible health risk due to heat not penetrating right through the food and thus destroying any dormant food-poisoning organisms that might be present. Large whole fish and raw whole poultry must be treated in this way because their body cavities can harbour harmful bacteria. So too must boned and rolled joints (cuts) of meat (unstuffed), because organisms can be transferred to the inner surface of the meat during the boning and rolling process.

Thawing can be accelerated if necessary, but this should be avoided if possible. Leave fish, meat and poultry in their wrappings and stand in lukewarm (not hot) water, or hold under cold running water.

Soft juicy fruits such as raspberries and strawberries are best served slightly icy inside; because of their natural high water content they tend to collapse if thawed completely.

Thawing
1 Whole poultry and large fish must be completely thawed before cooking.
2 Hamburgers can be cooked straight from frozen.

Thyme (Common — *Thymus vulgaris*; Lemon — *Thymus x citriodorus*)
These are the two most valued of all the many thymes in cooking, familiar in Italy, Spain and throughout southern Europe, and growing 20–30 cm/8–12 inches high. The two thymes are closely related, highly pungent and an essential part of a bouquet garni. Common thyme is used mainly in casseroles and stuffings; lemon thyme is more subtle and imparts a fruity flavour to such diverse dishes as baked custard, fish cakes and meatballs. Dried leaves are more aromatic than fresh thyme, but quickly become musty and cannot be matched with fresh or frozen sprigs.
TO FREEZE: wash small sprigs under cold running water only if absolutely necessary, shake dry, then pack immediately in freezer bags, seal, label and freeze. Or blanch sprigs in boiling water for 1 minute, drain, cool under cold running water, then shake dry and pack in bags.
TO THAW: use frozen or thawed sprigs in casseroles, fish dishes, meat loaves and soups, or sprinkle crumbled frozen leaves over mushrooms, tomatoes and root vegetables. Always use sparingly.
STORAGE TIME: 6 months.

Tomato
Tomatoes cannot be used as a salad vegetable after freezing, but they will be invaluable for use in cooking or as tomato juice, purée or sauce. Freeze only firm but ripe, medium-sized fruit.
To freeze whole: wipe and remove stalks but do not skin, then pack in small quantities in freezer bags, seal, label and freeze.
TO THAW: leave in wrappings for 2 hours at room temperature, then use in cooking as for fresh tomatoes.

To freeze tomato juice: wipe and remove stalks, cut tomatoes into quarters. Simmer in their own juice for 5 to 10 minutes until skins have softened. Strain through a nylon sieve, season with salt, pepper and sugar to taste, then cool and pack in small quantities in rigid containers. Cover, label and freeze.
TO THAW: leave in containers in the refrigerator until required consistency for use.
To freeze tomato purée: prepare as for *Tomato juice* above, return sieved tomato juice to the saucepan and simmer until reduced to desired thickness. Remove from the heat, cool rapidly, then pour into small rigid containers, leaving 1.25 cm/½ inch headspace.
TO THAW: as for *Juice* above.
To freeze tomato sauce: prepare as for *Purée* above, adding finely chopped onions and seasonings.
TO THAW: as for *Juice* above. Use with pasta dishes.
See also recipes for *Tomato Soup, Creamed Tomatoes* and *Ratatouille*.
STORAGE TIME: 12 months.

Tray Meals and T.V. Dinners
These are available commercially and can be bought in a wide variety of different dishes, usually a combination of meat or poultry in a sauce or gravy and one or two vegetables. Follow manufacturers' directions for storage times, thawing and reheating instructions. It is possible to make up this type of meal at home, using special compartmented aluminium foil trays, but care and thought must be given to choosing foods that require the same thawing, reheating and storage treatment, and the time this takes will probably outweigh the convenience of such meals.

Trotter, Pig's
see **Pork**

1

2

Trout, River

Trout may be divided into two types — migratory and non-migratory. For the migratory sea fish, see **Salmon Trout**. The smaller lake and river trout is excellent fried, grilled (broiled), poached or smoked. Only freeze fish that has just been caught.

To freeze river trout: clean and wash very thoroughly to remove traces of muddy flavour. Pat dry, pack in freezer bags, then seal, label and freeze.

TO THAW: unwrap and cook from frozen.

STORAGE TIME: 3 months.

Truffle

The prized fungus that grows on the roots of beeches and oaks in certain parts of France and Italy, is packed in tins (cans) or jars and exported to be sold as one of the most expensive foods in the world. Any partially opened containers should be transferred to a rigid container, covered with Madeira and stored in the refrigerator.

To freeze fresh truffles: peel, sauté in butter and Madeira until almost cooked, then cool and pack in rigid containers or freezer bags. Cover or seal, label and freeze.

TO THAW: leave at room temperature for 2 hours, then reheat on top of stove until just boiling. Canned or fresh truffles can also be frozen in a prepared dish, according to recipe used.

STORAGE TIME: 3 months.

Truffle, Chocolate

see recipe

Tuna

Tuna or tunny is a large fish of the mackerel family, most commonly found tinned (canned) in oil. The fish grows to a length of approximately 3 metres/10 feet and can weigh 450 kg/1000 lb.

To freeze fresh tuna: cut into steaks, then pack in freezer bags, seal, label and freeze.

TO THAW: unwrap and leave for 2 hours in the refrigerator, then grill (broil) or poach.

STORAGE TIME: 3 months.

Turbot

A large European flatfish, diamond-shaped and often weighing up to 22 kg/50 lb, turbot has a very good flavour. Smaller fish are known as chicken turbot. The fish is too large for freezing whole.

TO FREEZE: cut into steaks, then pack in freezer bags, seal, label and freeze.

TO THAW: unwrap and leave for 2 hours in the refrigerator, then bake, fry or poach, and serve with an anchovy, cream, lobster or shrimp sauce.

STORAGE TIME: 3 months.

Turkey

see **Poultry**

Turnip

Freeze only small, young, quickly grown turnips.

TO FREEZE: trim off tops and roots, then peel thinly. Leave whole and blanch in boiling water for 1 minute, or dice and blanch in boiling water for 2 minutes. Drain, then cool rapidly in iced water, drain, pat dry and pack in freezer bags. Seal, label and freeze.

TO THAW: unwrap and put frozen turnips in boiling salted water. Bring back to the boil, cover and simmer for 5 to 10 minutes, depending on size. Drain and serve hot, tossed in butter and seasonings to taste. Or leave in container (remove for faster thawing) and thaw at room temperature for approximately 2 hours, then heat gently in butter and sugar.

To freeze turnip purée: cook in boiling salted water until tender, drain, then leave to cool slightly. Mash, purée in an electric blender or work in a Mouli-légumes (foodmill), leave until completely cold, then pack in rigid containers. Cover, label and freeze.

TO THAW: remove from container and reheat from frozen in a double boiler with butter and seasonings to taste.

STORAGE TIME: 12 months.

Turtle

The turtle is an enormous animal unsuitable for home preparation. Turtles are cooked live to make soup, but if their flesh is put into cold storage it is of little use on thawing.

Temperature – Upright Freezer

Ugli Fruit*

see also **Fruit** for information on packing

The puffy and wrinkled skin of the ugli fruit, one of the citrus fruits grown mainly in Jamaica, hides the combined taste of grapefruit, oranges and tangerines. Ugli fruit store well in the freezer and can be used in fresh fruit salads with icecream, in sauces (both sweet and sweet-and-sour), and as a garnish for cakes and desserts.

TO FREEZE: grate or shred off outer peel, removing all pith and any strands. Divide into segments, open (flash) freeze on trays until solid, then pack in freezer bags, seal, label and return to freezer. Or remove skin from segments and/or slices, pack dry with sugar or pack in light syrup.

TO THAW: leave in wrappings (or remove for faster thawing) for approximately 2 hours at room temperature.

STORAGE TIME: 12 months.

*Not available in Australia.

Upright Freezer

see page 228

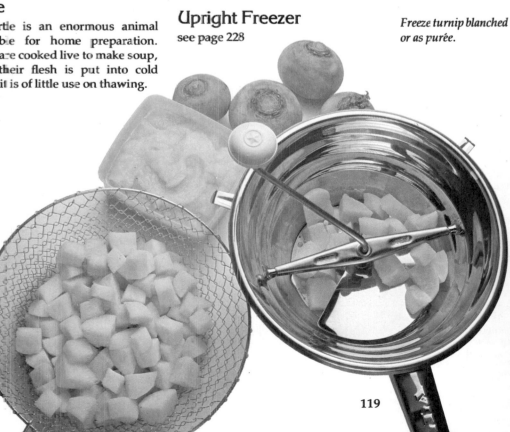

Freeze turnip blanched or as purée.

Cuts From a Side of Veal (U.K.)*

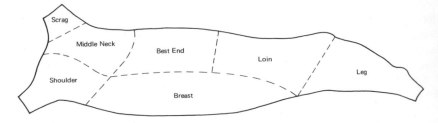

Cuts From a Side of Veal (U.S.)*

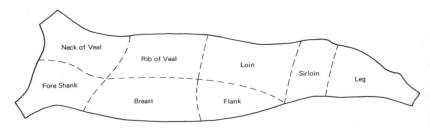

Vacuum Pack

This is the commercial method of packing food to exclude all air. Vacuum-packed goods, especially bacon and cured meats, have a longer freezer storage life than similar items packed in normal freezer wrappings. See also **Bacon & Cured Pork.**

Variety Meats

see **Meat, Fresh**

Veal

Veal does not keep well, and should be frozen within 2 or 3 days of killing.

Choosing

Many butchers do not keep veal

Cuts From a Side of Veal (Australia)

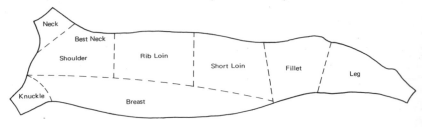

Cut	Approximate weight range (based on 21.5 kg/ 48 lb carcass)		Ways of butchering	Type of meat and cooking
	kg	lb		

Leg	4	9	(a) Two joints (cuts)
			   1. Fillet end
			   2. Knuckle end
			 (b) Fillet end sliced for escalopes
				The fillet is the tenderest cut of veal and the most expensive. It is a top-quality roasting cut, or can be thinly sliced for escalopes. The knuckle end can be braised whole or the meat can be cubed for pies or stews. The bone makes excellent jellied stock

Loin	1.5	3	(a) Joint (cut) on the bone (b) Boned for stuffing and rolling (c) Loin chops	Top quality roasting meat. Chops can be fried, grilled. (broiled) or sautéed
Best End (Rib of Veal)	1	2	(a) Small joint on the bone (b) Cutlets	Medium-quality meat for braising or slow roasting. Cutlets are best braised or casseroled
Breast	675g	1½	(a) Boned and cubed for casseroles and pies (b) If large enough, boned for stuffing and rolling	Lean but coarse-textured meat which needs slow, moist cooking. Stuffed breast can be boiled, braised, pot roasted or stewed
Shoulder	2.5	5½	(a) Boned for stuffing and rolling (b) Oyster cut for neat roast and remainder cubed for pies and stews	A difficult joint (cut) to carve, therefore it is usually boned and rolled. Medium-quality meat for braising and slow roasting. Also very good meat for pies
Middle Neck and Scrag (Neck of Veal)	1.5	3	(a) If large, middle neck can be left in one piece (b) Divided into cutlets	Coarse-textured meat with good flavour if cooked slowly. Middle neck can be stuffed and braised or slow roasted. Cutlets need slow, moist cooking

regularly in stock, but will order it for you when required. Veal is a very young, lean meat containing a lot of gelatinous connective tissue, but no gristle and hardly any fat. The flesh should look moist, fine in texture and pale pink in colour. Veal that is not fresh takes on a dry, brownish look and may become mottled. Two kinds of veal are sold that are suitable for freezing, one from the very tender, pale-coloured but expensive milk-fed calves*, and the other from calves that have been grass-fed. The veal from grass-fed calves is slightly darker in colour and less tender, although many people consider it has more flavour.

*Not available in Australia.

Buying

Veal is not normally available ready-frozen from freezer centres, but can be ordered as a side, forequarter or hindquarter from a butcher specializing in meat for freezing. Tell the

*Because of the wide range of sizes in veal carcasses, methods of butchering are varied. In a small carcass the leg can be removed and rest of the carcass (i.e. loin, best end (rib of veal), shoulder, neck and breast) can be boned, rolled and tied. The roll is then cut into convenient-sized pieces.

butcher whether you require milk-fed or grass-fed veal, and the approximate size of calf.

Freezer Space Needed

Allow 56 litres/2 cu ft of space for every 9 kg/20 lb veal on the bone, but half this space for boneless veal.

Weight Range of Whole Carcass (U.K.)

Bobby calves: from 3 to 10 days old and weighing 11–18 kg/25–40 lb. Although seemingly cheaper, the ratio of bone to meat in a bobby calf is very high, and the meat has had no time to develop flavour. Bobby veal is not recommended for freezing, except for use in meat pies and stock.
Medium calves: grass-fed calves of several weeks old, weighing 18–36 kg/40–80 lb. The veal from these more mature calves is likely to prove more satisfactory for freezing.
Fat or milk-fed calves: specially reared calves weighing up to 90 kg/200 lb. and yielding very tender but expensive meat. They can be imported (usually hindquarters only) or home-produced.

Weight Range of Whole Carcass (U.S.)

Vealers: From 8 to 12 weeks old and weighing 66–90 kg/150–200 lb. These small calves are entirely milk-fed and very expensive.
Calves: These are the calves who have gone out to graze on grass and grain. They are left until approximately 6 months old and slaughtered when they weigh approximately 160–180 kg/350–400 lb.

Packaging and Freezing

Because veal is so lean, it is especially important to pack it carefully and protect it from the drying effect of cold air in the freezer. See **Meat, Fresh.**
THAWING AND COOKING: see **Meat, Fresh.**
STORAGE TIME: Joints (large cuts) and chops — up to 6 months. Pie (stewing) veal and offal (variety meat/fancy meat) — up to 3 months.

Veal Bones

Veal bones make rich, jellied stock. Use very promptly after purchase or freeze for future use as for **Beef** *Beef Bones.*

Vegetable(s)

see **individual names**

Vegetable Oyster

see **Salsify**

Venison

see **Game**

1

2

Verbena *(Lippia citriodora)*

prepare, freeze and thaw as for **Balm, Lemon**

Vermicelli

see **Pasta**

Vine Leaves

These are generally pickled, and are not satisfactory frozen on their own. However, they can be frozen successfully as dolmades.
To freeze dolmades: boil fresh vine leaves in salted water until tender, then drain and leave to cool. Put a spoonful of cooked savoury stuffing mixture (minced (ground) beef, herbs, onions, rice, spices, etc.) on each leaf and fold into a parcel. Squeeze tightly so that they stay firm and will not unfold. Open (flash) freeze on trays until solid, or wrap individually in aluminum foil or cling film. Pack in freezer bags or rigid containers. Seal or cover, label and freeze.
TO THAW: leave in wrappings at room temperature until partially thawed but not too soft, then unwrap and put gently into a shallow pan with a squeeze of lemon juice. Pour in sufficient tomato juice to half cover them, cover the pan and simmer very gently for approximately 30 minutes. Remove from the heat and leave until cool or completely cold before serving with natural yogurt.
STORAGE TIME: 6 months.

Vitamins

Loss of vitamins, B and C in particular, is slight during freezing. In fact, the greatest loss of vitamins is likely to occur while food is being prepared prior to freezing, especially with vegetables. Vitamin loss may also occur during cooling, therefore all food should be cooled very quickly.

Vol-au-vent

see **Pastry & Pastry-based Dishes**

3

4

Vine Leaves
1 *Spooning savoury filling onto cooked vine leaves.*
2 *Folding leaves over filling to form dolmades.*
3 *Packing open-frozen or individually wrapped dolmades into rigid freezer containers.*
4 *Serve dolmades with tomato sauce and yogurt.*

Waffle

Both homemade and commercially prepared waffles can be frozen successfully. For best results they should be absolutely fresh, yet quite cold before freezing.

TO FREEZE: pack in original container or in a freezer bag, interleaved with freezer film, seal, label and freeze.

TO THAW: unwrap, place on a baking sheet and bake from frozen in a fairly hot oven (190°C/375°F or Gas Mark 5) for approximately 10 minutes. Or unwrap and reheat from frozen under the grill (broiler). Serve hot with butter and maple syrup or honey.

STORAGE TIME: 2 months.

Water Chestnut

The very crisp fruit of the water plant resembles the other chestnut in shape and size. They have a long storage life on a shelf when purchased in a tin (can) and therefore it is not necessary to freeze them, other than as part of a prepared dish when they will store satisfactorily, and may lose only a little crispness.

Centre: Freeze whitebait in freezer bags, then unwrap and thaw for 1 hour before cooking and serving as for fresh.

Below: Freeze waffles interleaved with freezer film, heat through from frozen and serve as for fresh waffles.

Watercress

Although watercress cannot be used as a salad vegetable or garnish after being frozen, it is excellent frozen as Montpellier butter, or if used to make into a soup. Or it can be made into a soup before freezing (see recipe for *Watercress Soup*).

TO FREEZE: wash and dry thoroughly, then simmer gently in a little butter for 10 minutes. Remove from the heat, leave to cool, then pack in rigid containers, cover, label and freeze.

TO THAW: remove from container and use from frozen as for fresh watercress, allowing a little extra cooking time.

To freeze watercress (Montpellier) butter: wash thoroughly and discard stalks. Dry the leaves, pressing out any liquid in a cloth, then chop finely. Blend into fresh butter a little at a time until required strength and colour, then add salt and pepper to taste. Chill in the refrigerator until manageable, then wrap between sheets of greaseproof (waxed) paper and roll into a cylindrical shape. Wrap in aluminium foil and freeze until solid, then pack in a freezer bag, seal, label and return to freezer. Cut off slices as required, using a knife dipped in hot water.

STORAGE TIME: 6 months.

Water Ice

see **Ice(s)/Icecream**

Watermelon

see **Melon**

Whale

Whale steaks may be frozen, but the flesh is closer to beef than it is to fish.

TO FREEZE: pack steaks in freezer bags, interleaving each one with cling film. Seal, label and freeze.

TO THAW: unwrap and leave for 6 hours in the refrigerator, then soak for 1 hour in 2 × 5 ml spoons/2 teaspoons bicarbonate of soda (baking soda) to 1 litre/2 pints/5 cups water. Rinse well, then marinate for 2 hours in a liquid of three parts water to one part vinegar. Drain, then cut across the grain in thin steaks approximately 1.25 cm/½ inch thick. Sprinkle with lemon juice and tenderize by beating. Fry, braise or stew as for beef.

STORAGE TIME: 3 months.

Whelk*

Prepare and freeze this large mollusc as for **Periwinkle**. It does, however, tend to toughness and is never used in recipes.

TO THAW: leave in containers for 4 hours in the refrigerator, then dress with vinegar, salt and pepper.

STORAGE TIME: 1 month.

*Not available in Australia.

Whitebait

The young of the herring and sprat which are traditionally deep-fried whole in hot oil or fat and served as a first course or a light luncheon dish.

TO FREEZE: rinse well in very cold water, then pat dry and pack in freezer bags, seal, label and freeze.

TO THAW: unwrap and leave for 1 hour in the refrigerator, then coat in flour and deep-fry in hot oil or fat, shaking the basket gently to separate fish. Drain well, then dip again in hot oil or fat.

Serve immediately with salt and lemon slices.

STORAGE TIME: 3 months.

White Cabbage

see **Cabbage**

Whitecurrant

see **Currant**

Whitefish

An important American fish which flourishes in lakes.

TO FREEZE: wash and clean, pat dry, then leave whole or fillet. Wrap fish or fillets individually in cling film, then pack several together in a freezer bag. Seal, label and freeze.

TO THAW: unwrap and leave for 6 hours in the refrigerator, then remove bones. Season, rub with butter and bake or grill (broil).

STORAGE TIME: 3 months.

Whiting

While the flesh of this fish, similar in size to a herring, is rather tasteless, it is light and easily digested and popular for invalid food.

TO FREEZE: clean, remove backbone, then pack in freezer bags. Seal, label and freeze.

TO THAW: unwrap and bake, fry or grill (broil) from frozen.

STORAGE TIME: 3 months.

Whitloof

see **Chicory**

Widgeon

see **Game**

Wild Boar

see **Game**, *Boar*

Wild Duck

see **Game**

Wine

see **Drink(s)**

Winkle

see **Periwinkle**

Witch

see **Sole**

Woodchuck

see **Game**

Woodcock

see **Game**

Wood Pigeon

see **Game**, *Pigeon*

Wrapping

see **Packaging** (page 232)

Yam

see **Sweet Potato**

Yeast

Fresh yeast can be stored in the freezer and is extremely useful if you do a lot of baking — fresh yeast will not keep well by any other method of storing, and is not always available in the shops. Buy yeast in bulk — 225 g / ½ lb packs are a useful size — and cut into 15 g / ½ oz or 25 g / 1 oz cubes, if not cut already.

TO FREEZE: wrap each cube individually in aluminium foil or cling film, then pack cubes together in a freezer bag or rigid container, seal or cover, label and freeze.

TO THAW: leave wrapped cubes for approximately 30 minutes at room temperature, then use as for fresh yeast. Or frozen yeast can be coarsely grated if required immediately.

STORAGE TIME: 1 month.

Yogurt

Homemade yogurt will not freeze satisfactorily as it will separate and become acidic on thawing. Commercially prepared plain yogurt will freeze for short periods, although some brands may separate. Ready-frozen yogurts have stabilizers added, which prevent separation. Fruit yogurts will freeze, although there is some risk that they will separate, depending on the brand. If separation does occur, brisk whisking will probably restore the yogurt to its original texture. Freeze yogurt in the carton in which it was bought and thaw slowly in the refrigerator for best results. It is worth experimenting with different brands of yogurt — fruit and natural — to find one that will keep successfully in your freezer.

STORAGE TIME: 6 weeks (fruit yogurts only), 2 weeks (natural).

Zucchini

see **Courgette**

Waffle – Zucchini

Divide fresh yeast into usable quantities for freezing. When required thaw or grate and use to make a Savarin (see page 220), Chelsea Buns (see page 210) or any other yeast product.

Freezer Recipes

Soups and Appetizers

Cream of Cauliflower Soup is illustrated below, with French Onion Soup shown opposite.

Tomato Soup

A good homemade tomato soup is so different from the canned variety that it is hard to believe they are the same dish. Make this at the end of the summer when fresh garden tomatoes are in abundance.

Metric/Imperial

25 g/1 oz butter
2 potatoes, peeled and diced
2 onions, peeled and finely chopped
1 kg/2 lb tomatoes, skinned and roughly chopped
2 sprigs fresh parsley
1 sprig fresh basil
1×5 ml spoon/1 teaspoon sugar
Salt and freshly ground pepper
600 ml/1 pint chicken stock or water
TO FINISH:
300 ml/½ pint milk
2×15 ml spoons/2 tablespoons fresh single cream
1×15 ml spoon/1 tablespoon freshly chopped parsley

American

2 tablespoons butter
2 potatoes, peeled and diced
2 onions, peeled and finely chopped
2 lb tomatoes, skinned and roughly chopped
2 sprigs fresh parsley
1 sprig fresh basil
1 teaspoon sugar
Salt and freshly ground pepper
2½ cups chicken stock or water
TO FINISH:
1¼ cups milk
2 tablespoons light cream
1 tablespoon freshly chopped parsley

Melt the butter in a heavy saucepan. Add the potatoes and onions, cover with a lid and cook gently for 5 minutes. Add the tomatoes, parsley, basil, sugar and salt and pepper to taste. Cover again and cook gently for another 5 minutes. Stir in the stock or water and simmer for 20 to 25 minutes or until the vegetables are tender. Remove from the heat, discard parsley and basil sprigs, then leave to cool. Purée in an electric blender or work through a sieve or Mouli-légumes (foodmill) until the soup is quite smooth. Taste for seasoning and adjust if necessary.

TO FREEZE: pour into a rigid container, cover, label and freeze. Or pour soup into a freezer bag-lined preformer (forming container) and freeze until solid. Remove from preformer (container), seal, label and return to freezer.

TO THAW: put frozen soup into a heavy saucepan with the milk. Reheat gently on top of the stove, stirring occasionally.

TO SERVE: taste for seasoning, then pour hot soup into warmed tureen or individual soup bowls. Swirl with cream and sprinkle with parsley.

Cream of Cauliflower Soup

Simple cauliflower soup is ideal for a winter dinner party or even a family weekend lunch. Serve with squares of cheese on toast.

Metric/Imperial

Butter for frying
1 large onion, peeled and finely chopped
1 medium-sized cauliflower, washed and divided into florets
900 ml/1½ pints chicken stock
Pinch of ground mace
Salt and ground white pepper
TO FINISH:
300 ml/½ pint milk
150 ml/¼ pint fresh single cream
1×1.25 ml spoon/¼ teaspoon ground mace (optional)
Fried or toasted croûtons
Freshly chopped parsley

American

Butter for frying
1 large onion, peeled and finely chopped
1 medium-sized cauliflower, washed and divided into florets
3¾ cups chicken stock
Pinch of ground mace
Salt and ground white pepper
TO FINISH:
1½ cups milk
⅔ cup light cream
¼ teaspoon ground mace (optional)
Fried or toasted croûtons
Freshly chopped parsley
Serves 4 to 6

Melt a knob of butter in a saucepan and, when foaming, add the onion and fry gently until soft and golden. Add the cauliflower, stock, mace, and salt and pepper to taste. Bring to the boil, stirring, then lower the heat, half cover with a lid and simmer gently for about 20 to 25 minutes or until the cauliflower is tender. Remove from the heat, taste for seasoning and leave to cool. Purée in an electric blender or work through a sieve or Mouli-légumes (foodmill) until the soup is very smooth.

TO FREEZE: pour into a rigid container, cover, label and freeze. Or pour the soup into a freezer bag-lined preformer (forming container) and freeze until solid. Remove from preformer (container), seal, label and return to freezer.

TO THAW: unwrap frozen soup and

put into a heavy saucepan with the milk. Reheat gently, on top of the stove, stirring occasionally, then stir in the cream and heat through without boiling.

TO SERVE: taste for seasoning, then pour hot soup into warmed tureen or individual soup bowls. Sprinkle with mace, if liked, and top with croûtons and a little chopped parsley. Serve immediately.

French Onion Soup

Keep a quantity of French Onion Soup in the freezer for impromptu supper meals – reheated and topped with sizzling Gruyère toasts, it makes a meal in itself.

Metric/Imperial
Butter for frying
1×15 ml spoon/1 tablespoon olive or vegetable oil
¾ kg/1½ lb onions, peeled and thinly sliced into rings
38 g/1½ oz flour
1 litre/2 pints well-flavoured beef stock
Salt and freshly ground black pepper
TO FINISH:
1–2 garlic cloves, crushed
4 rounds of French bread
50 g/2 oz Gruyère cheese, grated

American
Butter for frying
1 tablespoon olive or vegetable oil
1½ lb onions, peeled and thinly sliced into rings
6 tablespoons flour
5 cups well-flavoured beef stock
Salt and freshly ground black pepper
TO FINISH:
1–2 garlic cloves, crushed
4 rounds of French bread
½ cup grated Gruyère cheese

Heat a knob of butter and the oil in a saucepan and, when foaming, add the onions. Cover and fry very gently for 15 to 20 minutes, stirring occasionally, until soft and golden. Stir in the flour and cook gently for another 2 minutes, stirring constantly.

Gradually stir in the stock and bring to the boil. Season to taste. Lower the heat, cover with a lid and simmer gently for 20 minutes. Remove from heat. Leave to cool.

TO FREEZE: pour into a rigid container, cover, label and freeze. Or pour the soup into a freezer bag-lined preformer (forming container) and freeze until solid. Remove from preformer (container), seal, label and return to freezer.

TO THAW: unwrap frozen soup and put into a heavy saucepan with 2 × 15 ml spoons/2 tablespoons water. Reheat gently on top of the stove, stirring occasionally. Once thawed, stir in the garlic and bring soup to the boil, stirring constantly. Taste for seasoning. Pour into individual soup bowls.

TO SERVE: toast the French bread on both sides. Top each round with grated Gruyère and float in individual soup bowls. Put under a preheated hot grill (broiler) for 2 minutes or until the cheese melts and is bubbling. Serve immediately.

Tomato Soup
Cream of Cauliflower Soup
French Onion Soup

Scallop and Artichoke Soup

The delicate and subtle flavours of Jerusalem artichokes and scallops blend particularly well to make this soup.

Metric/Imperial

Butter for frying

1 onion, peeled and finely chopped

700 g/1½ lb Jerusalem artichokes, peeled and chopped

600 ml/1 pint chicken stock

Salt and freshly ground pepper

2 scallops/250 g (Tasmanian) scallops, removed from the shells and cleaned

75 ml/⅛ pint white wine

75 ml/⅛ pint water

TO FINISH:
150 ml/¼ pint milk

2×15 ml spoons/2 tablespoons fresh single cream

1×15 ml spoon/1 tablespoon freshly chopped parsley

American

Butter for frying

1 onion, peeled and finely chopped

1½ lb Jerusalem artichokes, peeled and chopped

2½ cups chicken stock

Salt and freshly ground pepper

8 sea scallops

⅓ cup white wine

⅓ cup water

TO FINISH:
⅔ cup milk

2 tablespoons light cream

1 tablespoon freshly chopped parsley

Melt a knob of butter in a large saucepan. Add the onion and artichokes, cover with a lid and cook gently for 5 minutes. Stir in the stock and season to taste. Half cover with a lid and simmer for 20 to 25 minutes or until the artichokes are tender.

Remove from the heat, leave to cool slightly, then purée in an electric blender or work through a sieve or Mouli-légumes (foodmill).

Poach the scallops in the white wine and water for 2 to 4 minutes until they are just tender. Remove from the heat. Slice the scallops thinly and add to the soup with their cooking liquid. Taste for seasoning, then leave to cool.

TO FREEZE: pour into a rigid container, cover, label and freeze. Or pour soup into a freezer bag-lined preformer (forming container) and freeze until solid. Remove from preformer (container), seal, label and return to freezer.

TO THAW: leave in container overnight in refrigerator or for 3 to 4 hours at room temperature, then reheat soup very gently with the milk in a heavy saucepan, stirring occasionally. Do not let the soup boil, or the scallops will become tough.

TO SERVE: taste for seasoning, stir in cream then pour hot soup into warmed tureen or individual soup bowls. Sprinkle with parsley.

Ham and Pea Soup is shown in the tureen and soup bowl at the back of the photograph, with Scallop and Artichoke Soup in the foreground.

Scallop and
Artichoke Soup
Ham and Pea
Soup

Ham and Pea Soup

*The Dutch, who call this dish
Erwtensoep, can be seen eating it at
almost any time of the day in the open air
or in the cafés. Like all the hearty meat
soups, it can be served as a snack, a first
course or a meal in itself.*

Metric/Imperial

½ kg/1 lb whole or split dried green
peas, soaked overnight in cold water

1 large knuckle of bacon soaked
overnight in cold water
or
1 pig's trotter *and* 225 g/½ lb smoked
pork or bacon, in the piece

1 onion, peeled and finely chopped

3 celery stalks, scrubbed and finely
chopped

1 potato, peeled and diced

3 litres/5 pints water

Freshly ground black pepper

Fried or toasted croûtons, to finish

American

1 lb whole or split dried green peas,
soaked overnight in cold water

1 large smoked ham hock, soaked
overnight in cold water
or
1 pig's foot *and* ½ lb Canadian bacon,
in the piece

1 onion, peeled and finely chopped

3 celery stalks, scrubbed and finely
chopped

1 potato, peeled and diced

3 quarts water

Freshly ground black pepper

Fried or toasted croûtons, to finish

Drain the peas and put them in a large
saucepan with the drained knuckle of
bacon (ham hock) or the pig's trotter
(foot) and the smoked pork or (Canadian) bacon. Add the onion, celery,
potato and water. Bring to the boil,
cover with a lid and simmer for 3
hours. Remove from the heat and
take the meat from the pan. Discard
any fat and bone, dice the meat and
return to the soup. Taste for seasoning and add pepper only (the smoked
meats are salty enough). Cool.

TO FREEZE: pour into a rigid container, cover, label and freeze. Or
pour soup into a freezer bag-lined
preformer (forming container) and
freeze until solid. Remove from preformer (container), seal, label and
return to freezer.

TO THAW: unwrap frozen soup and
put into a heavy saucepan with
2 × 15 ml spoons/2 tablespoons
water. Reheat gently on top of the
stove for approximately 1 hour, stirring occasionally.

TO SERVE: taste for seasoning, pour
hot soup into warmed tureen or soup
bowls and add croûtons.

Scotch Broth is on the left of the illustration with Goulash Soup in the centre and Cock-a-leekie Soup on the right.

Cock-a-leekie Soup

This traditional Scottish soup makes a sustaining winter meal served with crusty bread (homemade if possible) to soak up every last drop.

Metric/Imperial

½ kg/1 lb stewing beef, in one piece
1¾ litres/3 pints water
1 small boiling fowl
1½ kg/3 lb leeks (white and pale green parts only), washed
1 bay leaf
Salt and freshly ground pepper
½ kg/1 lb prunes, soaked overnight in cold water, then stoned
½ kg/1 lb potatoes, peeled and thickly sliced

American

1½ lb beef shank
7½ cups water
1 small boiling fowl
3 lb leeks (white and pale green parts only), washed
1 bay leaf
Salt and freshly ground pepper
1 lb prunes, soaked overnight in cold water, then stoned
1 lb potatoes, peeled and thickly sliced

Serves 6 to 8

Put the beef in a large saucepan with the water and bring slowly to the boil. Skim with a slotted spoon, cover with a lid and simmer for 30 minutes. Add boiling fowl, two of the leeks and the bay leaf. Season to taste. Simmer very gently, so that the water barely moves in the pan, for 2½ to 3 hours, or until the meat and boiling fowl are tender.

Remove the beef and boiling fowl from the pan and leave to cool slightly. Remove the leeks and discard.

Add the prunes and potato slices to the pan and increase the heat slightly so that the liquid is bubbling. Slice (shred) the beef (discarding bones). Take the chicken meat off the bones and cut it into serving pieces. Chop the remaining leeks and add to the pan with the beef and chicken. Simmer for anotper 5 to 10 minutes, or until the leeks and potatoes are just cooked. Remove from the heat, taste for seasoning and leave to cool.

TO FREEZE: pour into a rigid container, cover, label and freeze. Or pour soup into a freezer bag-lined preformer (forming container) and freeze until solid. Remove from preformer (container), seal, label and return to freezer.

TO THAW: leave in wrappings over-night in the refrigerator, or for 3 to 4 hours at room temperature. Unwrap and heat gently in a heavy saucepan on top of the stove, stirring occasionally. Bring to the boil.

TO SERVE: taste for seasoning, then place pieces of beef and chicken with some prunes and vegetables in each bowl. Pour over the hot soup and serve immediately.

Goulash Soup

The best possible soup for a really cold winter day, especially as you can turn it into a main dish by adding cooked potatoes just before serving.

Metric/Imperial

1×15 ml spoon/1 tablespoon flour
2×5 ml spoons/2 teaspoons paprika
Salt and freshly ground pepper
225 g/½ lb shin of beef, cut into small cubes
25 g/1 oz lard or vegetable oil
2 onions, peeled and thinly sliced
2 garlic cloves, peeled and finely chopped
1×15 ml spoon/1 tablespoon tomato purée (paste)
1 litre/2 pints beef stock or water
TO FINISH: 2 large potatoes, peeled and thickly sliced *or* 1 red or green pepper (capsicum), cored, seeded and cut into strips *or* 100 g/¼ lb mushrooms, cleaned and thickly sliced *and* 150 ml/¼ pint cultured soured cream

American

1 tablespoon flour
2 teaspoons sweet paprika
Salt and freshly ground pepper
½ lb shin of beef, cut into small cubes
2 tablespoons lard or vegetable oil
2 onions, peeled and thinly sliced
2 garlic cloves, peeled and finely chopped
1 tablespoon tomato paste
5 cups beef stock or water
TO FINISH: 2 large potatoes, peeled and thickly sliced *or* 1 red or green pepper, cored, seeded and cut into strips *or* ¼ lb mushrooms, cleaned and thickly sliced *and* ⅔ cup sour cream

Mix the flour gently with the paprika and salt and pepper to taste. Use this to coat the meat. Heat the lard or oil in a heavy saucepan and brown the meat lightly on all sides. Add the onions and garlic, cover and cook gently until the onions are soft. Add any remaining seasoned flour, then stir in the tomato purée (paste) and the stock or water. Cover with a lid and simmer very gently for 2 hours or until the meat is tender. Remove from the heat, taste for seasoning and leave to cool.

TO FREEZE: pour into a rigid container, cover, label and freeze. Or pour soup into a freezer bag-lined preformer (forming container) and freeze until solid. Remove from the preformer (container), seal, label and return to freezer.

TO THAW: unwrap frozen soup and put into a heavy saucepan with 2 × 15 ml spoons/2 tablespoons water. Reheat gently on top of the stove, stirring occasionally. Add the potatoes and cook for 15 to 20 minutes or until tender; or add the pepper or mushrooms and cook for 5 minutes.

TO SERVE: taste for seasoning, pour into warmed tureen or individual soup bowls, top with the sour(ed) cream and serve immediately.

Scotch Broth

This classic Scottish soup is made with lamb and barley, and flavoured with root vegetables. There are many versions, some including sliced leeks, shredded cabbage, diced turnips, or dried split peas.

Metric/Imperial
2 whole breasts of lamb
1 litre/2 pints water
3 onions, peeled
3 carrots, peeled
50 g/2 oz pearl barley
2 parsnips, peeled and diced
Salt and freshly ground pepper
1×15 ml spoon/1 tablespoon freshly chopped parsley, to finish

American
2 whole breasts of lamb
5 cups water
3 onions, peeled
3 carrots, peeled
¼ cup pearl barley
2 parsnips, peeled and diced
Salt and freshly ground pepper
1 tablespoon freshly chopped parsley, to finish

Put the breasts of lamb into a large saucepan, add the water and bring gently to the boil. Skim any scum that rises to the surface. Add 1 onion, 1 carrot and the pearl barley and simmer for 1½ hours or until the meat is tender and almost falls off the bones. Remove the meat from the pan and discard the onion and carrot.

Dice the remaining onions and carrots and add to the pan with the parsnips. Season to taste and simmer for another 20 to 25 minutes or until the vegetables are tender.

Meanwhile, when the meat is cool enough to handle, strip it off the bones and return the meat to the pan. Remove from the heat, taste for seasoning and leave to cool. Chill overnight in the refrigerator, then skim off and discard all the fat on the surface.

TO FREEZE: spoon into a rigid container, cover, label and freeze. Or pour soup into a freezer bag-lined preformer (forming container) and freeze until solid. Remove from preformer (container), seal, label and return to freezer.

TO THAW: unwrap frozen soup and put into a heavy saucepan. Reheat gently on top of the stove for 30 to 40 minutes, stirring occasionally.

TO SERVE: taste for seasoning, then sprinkle with the parsley.

Mushroom and Onion Soup is illustrated in the left-hand photograph, with Watercress Soup in the centre and Chilled Avocado Soup on the right.

Mushroom and Onion Soup

This soup is perfect for a dinner party. Make some now and freeze for a special occasion.

Metric/Imperial
Butter for frying
1/4 kg/1/2 lb mushrooms, cleaned and finely chopped
1 large onion, peeled and finely chopped
1×15 ml spoon/1 tablespoon flour
1 litre/2 pints chicken stock
1 bouquet garni (parsley and thyme sprigs, 1 bay leaf)
Salt and freshly ground black pepper
TO FINISH: 150 ml/1/4 pint milk
150 ml/1/4 pint fresh single cream
Freshly chopped parsley

American
Butter for frying
1/2 lb mushrooms, cleaned and finely chopped
1 large onion, peeled and finely chopped
1 tablespoon flour
5 cups chicken stock
1 bouquet garni (parsley and thyme sprigs, 1 bay leaf)
Salt and freshly ground black pepper
TO FINISH: 2/3 cup milk
2/3 cup light cream
Freshly chopped parsley
Serves 4 to 6

Melt a knob of butter in a saucepan. Add the mushrooms and onion, cover and cook gently for 5 minutes. Stir in the flour and continue cooking for another 2 minutes, stirring constantly. Gradually stir in the stock and bring to the boil, stirring. Add the bouquet garni, and salt and pepper to taste. Lower the heat, half cover with a lid and simmer gently for 20 minutes. Remove from the heat and discard bouquet garni. Taste for seasoning, then leave soup to cool.

TO FREEZE: pour into a rigid container, cover, label and freeze. Or pour soup into a freezer bag-lined preformer (forming container) and freeze until solid. Remove from preformer (container), seal, label and return to freezer.

TO THAW: unwrap frozen soup and put into a heavy saucepan with the milk. Reheat gently on top of the stove, stirring occasionally, then add cream and heat through without boiling.

TO SERVE: taste for seasoning, then pour into warmed tureen or individual soup bowls and sprinkle with chopped parsley.

Chilled Avocado Soup

Ripe avocados will not keep long, especially in warm summer weather, but if you make them into an iced soup they will keep up to 2 months in the freezer.

Metric/Imperial
3 medium-sized ripe avocados
Juice of 1 lemon
600 ml/1 pint chicken stock
150 ml/1/4 pint natural yogurt
Dash of Tabasco sauce
Salt and ground white pepper
TO FINISH: Approx. 150 ml/1/4 pint milk
Few chopped spring onions

American
3 medium-sized ripe avocados
Juice of 1 lemon
2 1/2 cups chicken stock
2/3 cup natural yogurt
Dash of Tabasco sauce
Salt and ground white pepper
TO FINISH: Approx. 2/3 cup milk
Few chopped scallions

Cut the avocados in half with a sharp, stainless steel knife. Remove the stones (pits) and scoop out the flesh into a bowl. Chop roughly, then mash the lemon juice into the flesh with a fork. Add the remaining ingredients, excet the milk and spring onions (scallions). Purée in an electric blender or work through a nylon sieve until the soup is quite smooth. Taste for seasoning and adjust if necessary.

TO FREEZE: freeze immediately after making to prevent discoloration. Pour into a rigid container, cover, label and freeze. Or pour soup into a freezer bag-lined preformer (forming container) and freeze until solid. Remove from preformer (container), seal, label and return to freezer.

TO THAW: leave in container for approximately 6 to 8 hours in the refrigerator, whisking occasionally to prevent separation. Stir in enough milk to make the consistency of the soup like single (light) cream.

TO SERVE: taste for seasoning, pour into a chilled tureen or individual soup bowls and sprinkle with chopped spring onions (scallions).

Watercress Soup

Make this soup in spring or early summer when watercress is young and tender. It can be served hot or chilled.

Metric/Imperial
Butter for frying
2 onions, peeled and finely chopped
2 potatoes, peeled and diced
2 bunches (100 g/1/4 lb) watercress, washed and picked off the stalks
600 ml/1 pint chicken stock
Salt and freshly ground pepper
TO FINISH: 300 ml/1/2 pint milk
Sprig watercress

American
Butter for frying
2 onions, peeled and finely chopped
2 potatoes, peeled and diced
2 bunches watercress, washed and picked off the stalks
2½ cups chicken stock
Salt and freshly ground pepper
TO FINISH: 1¼ cups milk
Sprig watercress

Melt a knob of butter in a large saucepan. Add the onions and potatoes, cover with a lid and cook gently for 5 minutes. Add half the watercress and cook for another 5 minutes. Stir in the stock, and season to taste. Half cover with a lid and simmer for 20 to 25 minutes or until the vegetables are tender. Remove from the heat and leave to cool. Purée in an electric blender or work through a sieve or Mouli-légumes (foodmill). Chop the remaining watercress roughly and add to the soup. Alternatively, blend the soup again briefly with the remaining watercress.

TO FREEZE: pour into a rigid container, cover, label and freeze. Or pour soup into a freezer bag-lined preformer (forming container) and freeze until solid. Remove from preformer (container), seal, label and return to freezer.

TO THAW: put frozen soup into a heavy saucepan with the milk. Reheat gently on top of the stove, stirring occasionally. If you wish to serve the soup chilled, thaw overnight in the refrigerator, or for 4 to 5 hours at room temperature, then stir in the cold milk.

TO SERVE: taste for seasoning, then pour into a tureen or individual soup bowls (warmed if you are serving the soup hot) and top with a sprig of watercress.

pour the soup into a freezer bag-lined preformer (forming container) and freeze until solid. Remove from preformer (container), seal, label and return to freezer.

TO THAW: leave in container overnight in the refrigerator, then stir in enough milk to make a pouring consistency. Keep refrigerated until serving time.

TO SERVE: add cream and taste for seasoning. Pour soup into chilled tureen or individual soup bowls and sprinkle with chives. Serve with hot Herb or Garlic Bread (pages 62 and 59). Vichyssoise can also be served hot: put the frozen soup into a saucepan (preferably non-stick) with 400 ml/¾ pint/2 cups milk and reheat gently until very hot. Taste for seasoning. Check consistency and add more milk if necessary. Serve hot, swirled with cream and sprinkled with chopped parsley.

Spanish Summer Soup

Make this soup in the middle of summer while peppers (capsicums) are plentiful – and when the freezer is fairly full: because the milk is added at serving time, the soup uses very little space in the freezer.

Metric/Imperial
2×15 ml spoons/2 tablespoons vegetable oil
50 g/2 oz butter
2 large onions, peeled and finely chopped
2 large green peppers (capsicums), cored, seeded and finely chopped
38 g/1½ oz flour
600 ml/1 pint well-flavoured homemade chicken stock
Salt and freshly ground black pepper
TO FINISH: 400 ml/¾ pint milk
4×15 ml spoons/4 tablespoons fresh single cream

American
2 tablespoons vegetable oil
¼ cup butter
2 large onions, peeled and finely chopped
2 large green peppers, cored, seeded and finely chopped
6 tablespoons flour
2½ cups well-flavoured homemade chicken stock
Salt and freshly ground black pepper
TO FINISH: 2 cups milk
4 tablespoons light cream

The photograph above shows Vichyssoise sprinkled with snipped chives; opposite is Spanish Summer Soup garnished with a swirl of cream.

Vichyssoise

A classic iced summer soup which makes an ideal first course at a dinner party on a warm evening. It is also delicious as a light lunch served with Herb Bread (see page 62). Vichyssoise freezes very well and as leeks are in plentiful supply during cold weather it is a good idea to make this soup when they are in season and freeze it until the hot weather arrives.
If preferred, it can be served hot, sprinkled with parsley instead of chives.

Metric/Imperial
Butter for frying
½ kg/1 lb potatoes, peeled and diced
4 leeks (white and pale green parts only), washed and chopped
400 ml/¾ pint chicken stock
Pinch of cayenne pepper
Salt and ground white pepper
TO FINISH: Approx. 400 ml/¾ pint milk
4×15 ml spoons/4 tablespoons fresh single cream
2×15 ml spoons/2 tablespoons snipped chives

American
Butter for frying
1 lb potatoes, peeled and diced
4 leeks (white and pale green parts only), washed and chopped
2 cups chicken stock
Pinch of cayenne pepper
Salt and ground white pepper
TO FINISH: Approx. 2 cups milk
4 tablespoons light cream
2 tablespoons finely cut chives

Melt a knob of butter in a saucepan. Add the potatoes and leeks, cover and cook gently for 5 minutes. Stir in the stock, bring to the boil, then lower the heat. Stir in the cayenne pepper, and salt and pepper to taste. Half cover with a lid and simmer for 20 to 25 minutes or until the vegetables are tender. Remove from the heat, taste for seasoning and leave to cool. Purée in an electric blender or work through a sieve or Mouli-légumes (foodmill) until the soup is very smooth.

TO FREEZE: pour into a rigid container, cover, label and freeze. Or

Heat the oil and butter in a pan and, when foaming, add the onions and peppers (capsicums). Cover with a lid and cook gently, shaking the pan occasionally, for 5 minutes or until the vegetables are soft and lightly coloured. Stir in the flour with a wooden spoon and cook for another minute. Gradually stir in the stock, bring to the boil, then lower the heat. Add salt and pepper to taste, half cover with a lid and simmer for 20 to 25 minutes or until the vegetables are tender. Remove from the heat, taste for seasoning and leave to cool. Purée in an electric blender or work through a sieve or Mouli-légumes (foodmill) until the soup is smooth.

TO FREEZE: pour into a rigid container, cover, label and freeze. Or pour the soup into a freezer bag-lined preformer (forming container) and freeze until solid. Remove from preformer, seal, label and return to freezer.

TO THAW: unwrap frozen soup and put into a heavy saucepan with 2×15 ml spoons/2 tablespoons water. Reheat gently on top of the stove, stirring occasionally. Gradually stir in the milk and heat through.

TO SERVE: taste for seasoning, pour hot soup into warmed tureen or individual soup bowls and swirl cream on top. If you like, this soup may be served cold: thaw overnight in the refrigerator, then stir in cold milk and taste for seasoning. Swirl with cream just before serving.

Lebanese Cucumber Soup

This is a refreshing soup for a hot day, very quickly made with good homemade chicken stock from the freezer, and tangy natural yogurt. There are many variations of the popular Middle Eastern recipe but they are all always served cold.

Metric/Imperial
400 ml/¾ pint chicken stock
150 ml/¼ pint tomato juice
300 ml/½ pint natural yogurt
150 ml/¼ pint fresh single cream
1 garlic clove, peeled
Salt and freshly ground pepper
TO FINISH:
1 small cucumber, peeled, diced and drained
1 hard-boiled egg, finely chopped
1×15 ml spoon/1 tablespoon finely chopped fresh mint

American
2 cups chicken stock
⅔ cup tomato juice
1¼ cups natural yogurt
⅔ cup light cream
1 garlic clove, peeled
Salt and freshly ground pepper
TO FINISH:
1 small cucumber, peeled, diced and drained
1 hard-cooked egg, finely chopped
1 tablespoon finely chopped fresh mint

Combine all the soup ingredients in an electric blender, with salt and pepper to taste, and purée until smooth. Taste for seasoning, then chill in the refrigerator for at least 30 minutes.

TO FREEZE: pour soup into a freezer bag-lined preformer (forming container) and freeze until solid. Remove from preformer (forming container). Overwrap in a freezer bag, seal, label and return to freezer.

TO THAW: leave in wrappings for 6 to 8 hours in the refrigerator. Blend again briefly if the soup has separated.

TO SERVE: taste for seasoning. Stir the cucumber, egg and mint into the soup and pour into chilled tureen or individual soup bowls.

Individual Mushroom Quiches are on the left of the photograph, with Greek Spinach Puffs in the centre and Onions à la Grecque on the right.

Individual Mushroom Quiches

These individual mushroom tartlets are best served hot, and three or four make a filling start to a meal. The quantities below will make approximately 36 tartlets. Take as many out of the freezer as you require for each meal.

Metric/Imperial

FOR THE PASTRY:

225 g/½ lb flour

1×2.5 ml spoon/½ teaspoon salt

1×5 ml spoon/1 teaspoon icing sugar

150 g/5 oz butter, cut into small pieces

75 ml/scant ⅛ pint iced water

FOR THE FILLING:
50 g/2 oz butter

450 g/1 lb button mushrooms, washed and thinly sliced

1 large mild onion (preferably Spanish), peeled and finely chopped

Squeeze of lemon juice

Salt and freshly ground pepper

1×15 ml spoon/1 tablespoon flour

150 ml/¼ pint fresh double cream

1 egg, lightly beaten

1×15 ml spoon/1 tablespoon sherry

American

FOR THE PASTRY:
2 cups flour

½ teaspoon salt

1 teaspoon confectioners' sugar

⅔ cup butter, cut into small pieces

¼ cup iced water

FOR THE FILLING:
¼ cup butter

1 lb small mushrooms, washed and thinly sliced

1 large mild onion (preferably Bermuda), peeled and finely chopped

Squeeze of lemon juice

Salt and freshly ground pepper

1 tablespoon flour

⅔ cup heavy cream

1 egg, lightly beaten

1 tablespoon sherry

To make the pastry, sift the flour, salt and icing (confectioners') sugar into a mixing bowl. Add the butter and rub into the flour with the fingers until the mixture resembles fine breadcrumbs. Using a palette knife, stir in enough iced water to draw the mixture together. Form into a ball, wrap in aluminium foil and chill in the refrigerator for at least 30 minutes.

Roll out the chilled dough on a floured board and use to line individual tartlet or patty tins (pans) or small aluminium foil flan cases. Prick well with a fork and chill for 30 minutes in the refrigerator. Fill with foil and beans and bake blind in a hot oven (230°C/450°F or Gas Mark 8) for 10 minutes. Remove foil and beans, then leave to cool.

For the filling, melt the butter in a saucepan, add the mushrooms and onion and cook gently until soft. Add the lemon juice, and salt and pepper to taste. Sprinkle in the flour and cook gently for a few minutes, stirring constantly. Remove from the heat and leave to cool. Stir the cream into the egg, add the sherry and beat well with a fork. Stir this mixture into the cooled mushroom mixture, blend well and taste for seasoning.

Fill the cold tartlet cases with the mushroom mixture.

TO FREEZE: open (flash) freeze filled tartlets in their tins (pans) or cases on trays until solid, then remove from the tins (pans), put in a rigid container, cover, label and freeze. If you have used foil flan cases, wrap well in cling film or foil, label and freeze.

TO THAW: unwrap the tartlets and bake from frozen in a hot oven (230°C/450°F or Gas Mark 8) for 10 minutes, then reduce the heat to fairly hot (190°C/375°F or Gas Mark 5) and bake for another 20 to 30 minutes, or until the mixture has set and is lightly browned on top.

TO SERVE: serve hot or cold. Garnish the dish with watercress.

Onions à la Grecque

The Greek-style preparation of adding olive oil, tomato flavouring and red wine to onions gives this dish a piquant flavour.

Metric/Imperial

150 ml/¼ pint water

150 ml/¼ pint red wine

Juice of ½ lemon

4×15 ml spoons/4 tablespoons olive oil

2×15 ml spoons/2 tablespoons tomato purée (paste)

2×15 ml spoons/2 tablespoons sugar

1 sprig fresh rosemary

Salt and freshly ground pepper

½ kg/1 lb pickling onions, blanched and peeled

1×15 ml spoon/1 tablespoon freshly chopped parsley, to finish

American

⅔ cup water

⅔ cup red wine

Juice of ½ lemon

4 tablespoons olive oil

2 tablespoons tomato paste

2 tablespoons sugar

1 sprig fresh rosemary

Salt and freshly ground pepper

1 lb baby white onions, blanched and peeled

1 tablespoon freshly chopped parsley, to finish

Put all the ingredients, except the onions and parsley, into a wide shallow saucepan and bring slowly to the boil, stirring well. Add the onions, cover with a lid and simmer very gently for 20 to 30 minutes or until the onions are tender but not too soft when pierced with a skewer. Lift the onions out carefully with a slotted spoon and transfer to a bowl. Bring the cooking liquid to the boil again and boil rapidly, uncovered, for 5 to 10 minutes or until reduced by nearly half. Remove from the heat, taste for seasoning, then strain over the onions and leave to cool.

TO FREEZE: pour into a rigid container, cover, label and freeze. Or pour into a freezer bag-lined preformer (forming container) and freeze until solid. Remove from preformer (forming container), seal, label and return to freezer.

TO THAW: leave in wrappings overnight in the refrigerator, or for 4 to 5 hours at room temperature.

TO SERVE: remove wrappings, transfer to a serving dish, sprinkle with the parsley and serve cold.

Greek Spinach Puffs

A small supply in the freezer of these light and crisp savouries is invaluable, as they make an excellent first course for a dinner or, if made quite small, can also be served with cocktails. Make and deep-fry them ahead of time, so that they only need reheating when guests are about to arrive. The fila or strudel pastry can be bought at most good delicatessens or Middle Eastern stores, and it can be stored in the freezer for several months if wrapped in a freezer bag.

Metric/Imperial
½ kg/1 lb fresh spinach, well washed, *or* 225 g/½ lb frozen spinach
50 g/2 oz butter
100 g/¼ lb feta, Gruyère, Parmesan or Cheddar cheese, grated
1×1.25 ml spoon/¼ teaspoon grated nutmeg
1 small egg, lightly beaten
Salt and freshly ground pepper
225 g/½ lb fila or strudel pastry
Oil for deep-fat frying
Watercress or lettuce (optional), to finish

American
1 lb fresh spinach, well washed, *or* 1×10 oz package frozen spinach
¼ cup butter
1 cup grated feta, Gruyère, Parmesan or Cheddar cheese
¼ teaspoon grated nutmeg
1 egg, lightly beaten
Salt and freshly ground pepper
½ lb fila or strudel leaves
Oil for deep-fat frying
Watercress or lettuce (optional), to finish

Cook the spinach, adding 2×5 ml spoons/2 teaspoons water if necessary for frozen spinach, none for fresh, until it is just tender. Remove from the heat and transfer to a bowl. Press out any water. Chop spinach finely, then stir in a small knob of the butter, the cheese, nutmeg and egg, and seasoning to taste. Melt the remaining butter. Spread out the first sheet of fila or strudel pastry and keep the rest covered with a damp cloth. Brush pastry lightly with some of the melted butter. Cut it into long strips, each 5 cm/2 inches or 7.5 cm/3 inches wide, depending on whether the puffs are to be served for cocktails or made larger. Place 1 × 5 ml spoon/1 teaspoon of the spinach and egg mixture 2.5 cm/1 inch from the top of the first strip. Fold the top of the pastry over diagonally to form a small triangle, so that the top edge now lies over the side edge, and the filling is completely covered. Fold this triangle down again, so that the top edge of the strip is now straight again. Continue folding the triangle over onto itself until the whole strip has been used up. This should ensure that all the edges have been closed at least once. Continue in the same way with the rest of the pastry, brushing each strip first with butter, until all have been used up.

Deep-fry the puffs in hot oil until they are golden brown. Drain each puff on kitchen paper towels when it is cooked, then leave to cool.

TO FREEZE: put the puffs in a rigid container, cover, label and freeze.

TO THAW: put frozen puffs on a baking sheet and bake in a hot oven (220°C/425°F or Gas Mark 7) for 10 or 15 minutes, depending on their size.

TO SERVE: serve very hot, with a garnish of watercress or lettuce, if you like.

The illustration shows, from left to right, Kipper Pâté garnished with a twist of lemon, Smoked Haddock Mousse finished with egg, parsley and aspic, and Baked Smokies topped with sliced tomatoes.

Smoked Haddock Mousse

The flavour of the smoked haddock is lightened by the addition of mayonnaise and cream in this delicate mousse.

Metric/Imperial

½ kg/1 lb smoked haddock
600 ml/1 pint milk
1 onion, peeled and quartered
50 g/2 oz butter
50 g/2 oz flour
15 g/½ oz gelatine
75 ml/scant ⅛ pint water
150 ml/¼ pint mayonnaise
75 ml/scant ⅛ pint fresh double cream, lightly whipped
Salt and freshly ground pepper
TO FINISH: 1 hard-boiled egg, sliced
Few sprigs of fresh parsley
300 ml/½ pint aspic jelly (optional)

American

1 lb smoked haddock
2½ cups milk
1 onion, peeled and quartered
¼ cup butter
½ cup flour
1 envelope unflavored gelatin
⅓ cup water
⅔ cup mayonnaise
⅓ cup heavy cream, lightly whipped
Salt and freshly ground pepper
TO FINISH: 1 hard-cooked egg
Few sprigs of fresh parsley
1¼ cups aspic jelly (optional)

Place the haddock in a wide saucepan (preferably non-stick) and add the milk and onion. Bring to the boil, cover with a lid and remove from the heat. Leave for 30 minutes, then lift out the fish and flake the flesh, removing all the skin and bones. Strain the cooking liquid and reserve.

Melt the butter in a clean saucepan, add the flour and cook over a low heat for 2 minutes, stirring constantly. Stir in the reserved cooking liquid and, when the sauce has thickened, bring to the boil. Remove from the heat, stir in the flaked fish and leave to cool.

Sprinkle the gelatin(e) over the water, leave for 5 minutes until spongy, then heat gently until dissolved. Stir into the haddock mixture. Fold in the mayonnaise and the cream and season to taste. Grease a 1 litre/2 pint/5 cup freezerproof dish. Spoon in the mixture and leave to set.

TO FREEZE: wrap the dish in cling film, then overwrap in a freezer bag, seal, label and freeze.

TO THAW: unwrap, cover loosely and thaw overnight in refrigerator or for 4 to 5 hours at room temperature.

TO SERVE: decorate top of mousse with slices of hard-boiled egg and sprigs of parsley. If you like, pour over some aspic (jelly), then leave for 1 hour in the refrigerator until set.

Kipper Pâté

A firm favourite for a dinner party first course, Kipper Pâté freezes well. Serve with toast.

Metric/Imperial

Unsalted butter for frying
225 g/½ lb kipper fillets
225 g/½ lb cream cheese, softened
1 garlic clove, crushed
1×15 ml spoon/1 tablespoon grated or creamed horseradish
Juice of ½ lemon
Freshly ground black pepper
Lemon twist, to finish

American

Unsalted butter for frying
½ lb kipper fillets
½ lb cream cheese, softened
1 garlic clove, crushed
1 tablespoon grated or creamed horseradish
Juice of ½ lemon
Freshly ground black pepper
Lemon twist, to finish

Melt a knob of butter in a frying pan. Add the kipper fillets and fry gently for 10 minutes or until the fish is soft and will flake easily with a fork. Remove from the pan, leave to cool, then remove any skin and large bones. Put the kipper flesh in a bowl and mash with a fork. With a wooden spoon, beat in the remaining ingredients, adding black pepper to taste. Beat until the pâté is quite smooth.

TO FREEZE: spoon into an aluminium foil container, cover, then overwrap in a freezer bag, seal, label and freeze.

TO THAW: leave in wrappings overnight in the refrigerator, or for approximately 5 hours at room temperature.

TO SERVE: transfer to a serving bowl, garnish with a lemon twist and chill for 30 minutes before serving.

Baked Smokies

Some of the best smoked fish are Arbroath smokies from Scotland: whole young haddocks smoked over a fire of oak chips to a dark tarry colour. They are moist and tender and have an incomparably rich flavour. Baked smokies makes an exceptionally good and unusual first course for a winter dinner menu, or can be served as a main dish for a family meal.

Metric/Imperial

2 Arbroath smokies, or ¾ kg/1½ lb smoked haddock or mackerel
2 onions, peeled and finely chopped
Freshly ground pepper
225 g/½ lb tomatoes, sliced
300 ml/½ pint fresh double cream
25 g/1 oz hard cheese, grated

American

2 Arbroath smokies, or 1½ lb smoked haddock, mackerel or whitefish
2 onions, peeled and finely chopped
Freshly ground pepper
½ lb tomatoes, sliced
1¼ cups heavy cream
¼ cup grated Cheddar cheese

Flake the flesh of the fish and put half in a foil dish or freezerproof casserole. Sprinkle with half the chopped

onion. Season with pepper to taste, and repeat with the remaining fish and onions. Cover with the sliced tomatoes, pour in the cream and sprinkle the cheese on top.

TO FREEZE: wrap the dish well in aluminium foil, overwrap in a freezer bag, seal, label and freeze.

TO THAW: unwrap, then place the frozen dish in a hot oven (220°C/425°F or Gas Mark 7) and bake for 20 minutes. Lower the oven temperature to moderate (180°C/350°F or Gas Mark 4) and bake for another 30 to 40 minutes, or until the top is lightly browned and the dish is thoroughly hot.

TO SERVE: serve very hot, straight from the cooking dish.

The photograph below shows Crab Soufflé on the left and Smoked Trout Pâté on the right. Devilled Prawns (Shrimp) are illustrated opposite.

Smoked Trout Pâté

For a special occasion, line the bowl of this rich pâté with smoked salmon and turn it out before serving, or roll a spoonful of the pâté in a slice of smoked salmon for each serving. Serve with thin slices of brown bread and butter or with very thin hot toast.

Metric/Imperial

4–5 smoked trout (approx. ¾ kg/1½ lb), skinned and boned
150 ml/¼ pint fresh double cream
1×15 ml spoon/1 tablespoon creamed horseradish
100 g/¼ lb smoked salmon (optional)
Few sprigs of watercress, to finish

American

4–5 smoked trout (approx. 1½ lb), skinned and boned
⅔ cup heavy cream
1 tablespoon prepared horseradish
¼ lb smoked salmon (optional)
Few sprigs of watercress, to finish

Put the trout flesh in an electric blender with the cream and horseradish. Blend until well mixed, but not necessarily completely smooth. Spoon into a freezerproof dish, lined with smoked salmon if you like.
TO FREEZE: wrap the dish in cling film, then overwrap in aluminium foil or a freezer bag. Seal, label and freeze.
TO THAW: leave in wrappings overnight in the refrigerator or for 4 to 5 hours at room temperature.
TO SERVE: unwrap and serve as suggested above. Garnish with watercress.

Devilled Prawns (Shrimp)

This is a quick and easy dish to make. Freeze it for dinner parties or for when unexpected guests arrive.

Metric/Imperial

2×15 ml spoons/2 tablespoons olive or vegetable oil
1 large onion, peeled and finely chopped
1 garlic clove, crushed with 1×2.5 ml spoon/½ teaspoon salt
½ kg/1 lb tomatoes, skinned, quartered and seeded
1×15 ml spoon/1 tablespoon tomato purée (paste)
1×2.5 ml spoon/½ teaspoon sugar
1×2.5 ml spoon/½ teaspoon Tabasco sauce
2×5 ml spoons/2 teaspoons Worcestershire sauce
2×15 ml spoons/2 tablespoons dry white wine
Freshly ground black pepper
350 g/¾ lb fresh shelled prawns
TO FINISH:
225 g/½ lb long-grain white rice, boiled and drained
2×15 ml spoons/2 tablespoons freshly chopped parsley

American

2 tablespoons olive or vegetable oil
1 large onion, peeled and finely chopped
1 garlic clove, crushed with ½ teaspoon salt
1 lb tomatoes, skinned, quartered and seeded
1 tablespoon tomato paste
½ teaspoon sugar
½ teaspoon Tabasco sauce
2 teaspoons Worcestershire sauce
2 tablespoons dry white wine
Freshly ground black pepper
1 lb fresh small shrimp, shelled
TO FINISH:
1 cup long-grain white rice, boiled and drained
2 tablespoons freshly chopped parsley

Heat the oil in a pan, then put in the onion and garlic and fry gently until soft and lightly coloured. Stir in the tomatoes, tomato purée (paste), sugar, Tabasco and Worcestershire sauces, wine, and black pepper to taste. Bring to the boil, stirring, then lower the heat, half cover with a lid and simmer gently for 8 to 10 minutes or until the tomatoes are soft but still retain their shape. Stir in the prawns (shrimp) and heat through. Remove from the heat, taste for seasoning, and leave to cool.
TO FREEZE: pour into a boil-in-the-bag or freezer bag-lined preformer (forming container) and freeze until solid. Remove from preformer (container). Overwrap in a freezer bag, seal, label and freeze (return to freezer).
TO THAW: if using a boil-in-the-bag, remove overwrapping, put bag in a pan of boiling water and boil for 15 minutes. Or turn out of freezer bag and reheat gently from frozen in a heavy saucepan on top of the stove, stirring constantly.
TO SERVE: taste for seasoning, then arrange on a bed of freshly boiled rice and sprinkle with parsley.

Crab Soufflé

Frozen crabmeat is well worth keeping in the freezer, since the season for fresh crabmeat is so short. This soufflé makes a luxurious first course for a dinner, or an impromptu supper dish.

Metric/Imperial
100 g/¼ lb butter
50 g/2 oz flour
400 ml/¾ pint milk
4 egg yolks
275 g/10 oz frozen crabmeat, thawed
150 ml/¼ pint fresh double cream
2×15 ml spoons/2 tablespoons sherry
50 g/2 oz Parmesan, Gruyère, or sharp Cheddar cheese, grated
Salt and freshly ground pepper
5 egg whites
25 g/1 oz flaked almonds

American
½ cup butter
½ cup flour
2 cups milk
4 egg yolks
10 oz frozen crabmeat, thawed
⅔ cup heavy cream
2 tablespoons sherry
½ cup grated Parmesan, Gruyère or sharp Cheddar cheese
Salt and freshly ground pepper
5 egg whites
¼ cup slivered almonds

Melt the butter in a heavy saucepan. Add the flour and cook over a low heat for five minutes, stirring constantly. Stir in the milk slowly and continue to cook gently until the sauce thickens. Bring to the boil, then remove from the heat. Beat in the egg yolks one at a time, then stir in the crabmeat, cream, sherry and half the grated cheese, with salt and pepper to taste. Beat the egg whites until they stand in peaks, then fold into the mixture. Butter a 3 pint/1.5 litre/7½ cup soufflé dish or individual ramekin dishes and pour in the crab mixture. Sprinkle with the remaining grated cheese and the almonds. Bake in a fairly hot oven (190°C/375°F or Gas Mark 5) for 35 to 40 minutes for the large soufflé, 15 to 20 minutes for the small ones. The mixture should be well risen and browned on top, but still creamy in the centre.

TO SERVE: serve immediately, straight from the cooking dish.

Salmon and Prawn (Shrimp) Quiches are illustrated in the left-hand photograph; Calamares Salad and Taramasalata on the right.

Salmon and Prawn (Shrimp) Quiches

These individual quiches make an unusual first course for a dinner party or they can be served as picnic or buffet party fare with a selection of salads and French bread.

Metric/Imperial

FOR THE PASTRY:
275 g/10 oz flour

Pinch of salt

175 g/6 oz butter or margarine, cut into small pieces

1 egg yolk

Water to mix

FOR THE FILLING:
225 g/8 oz can red salmon (skin and bones discarded), drained and flaked

100 g/¼ lb cooked shelled prawns, roughly chopped

100 g/¼ lb cream cheese, softened

3 eggs, beaten

150 ml/¼ pint milk

Juice of ½ lemon

1×1.25 ml spoon/¼ teaspoon cayenne pepper

Salt and freshly ground black pepper

Freshly chopped parsley, to finish

American

FOR THE PASTRY:
2½ cups flour

Pinch of salt

¾ cup butter or margarine, cut into small pieces

1 egg yolk

Water to mix

FOR THE FILLING:
½ lb can red salmon (skin and bones discarded), drained and flaked

¼ lb cooked shelled shrimp, roughly chopped

¼ lb cream cheese, softened

3 eggs, beaten

⅔ cup milk

Juice of ½ lemon

¼ teaspoon cayenne pepper

Salt and freshly ground black pepper

Freshly chopped parsley, to finish

Makes 6 individual quiches

To make the pastry, sift the flour and salt into a mixing bowl. Add the butter or margarine and rub into the flour with the fingers until the mixture resembles fine breadcrumbs. Stir in the egg yolk and enough water to draw the mixture together. Transfer to a lightly floured board and knead the dough briefly until smooth. Wrap in aluminium foil and chill in the refrigerator for at least 30 minutes. Lightly grease six 13 cm/5 inch shallow (or 7.5 cm/3 inch deep) fluted flan cases (tart pans) with removable bases. Place on baking sheets. Roll out the dough on a floured board and use to line the flan cases (tart pans). Chill for at least 15 minutes in the refrigerator.

Meanwhile make the filling. Put the salmon and prawns (shrimp) into a large mixing bowl and stir in the remaining ingredients, with salt and pepper to taste. Stir well to combine. Pour the filling into the prepared pastry cases.

TO FREEZE: freeze on the baking sheets until solid. Remove from the freezer, leave for a few minutes at room temperature, then carefully ease quiches out of flan cases (tart pans). Wrap in aluminium foil, then overwrap in a freezer bag, seal, label and return to freezer.

TO THAW: unwrap, replace quiches in flan cases (tart pans) and place on baking sheets. Cover with foil, then bake from frozen in a fairly hot oven (190°C/375°F or Gas Mark 5) for 45 minutes. Remove foil and bake for another 15 minutes or until brown.

TO SERVE: remove from oven and leave for 10 minutes. Remove from cases (pans), transfer to serving platter and sprinkle with chopped parsley before serving.

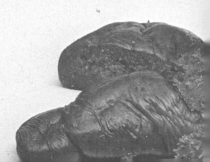

Taramasalata

Serve with hot toast or Pita (see page 93) as a first course or as a dip, or spread on canapés to serve with cocktails.

Metric/Imperial

225 g/½ lb smoked cod's roe, fresh or from a jar or can
2 slices stale white bread
1 small garlic clove, peeled
Juice of ½ lemon
150 ml/¼ pint olive oil
2×15 ml spoons/2 tablespoons cold water
Freshly ground black pepper

American

½ lb fresh smoked cod's roe, or 1×8 oz jar tarama
2 slices stale white bread
1 small garlic clove, peeled
Juice of ½ lemon
⅔ cup olive oil
2 tablespoons cold water
Freshly ground black pepper

Skin the cod's roe if necessary. Soak the bread briefly in a little cold water and squeeze out well. Put the cod's roe, bread, garlic and lemon juice in an electric blender and purée until smooth. Continue working blender on low speed, adding the olive oil slowly until it has all been absorbed, then slowly blend in the cold water to make a lighter consistency. Season to taste with the pepper.

TO FREEZE: spoon the mixture into a freezerproof bowl, cover in cling film or aluminium foil, then overwrap in a freezer bag, seal, label and freeze.

TO THAW: leave in wrappings overnight in the refrigerator, or for 4 to 5 hours at room temperature.

TO SERVE: unwrap, transfer to a serving dish and serve chilled as suggested above.

Calamares Salad

Calamares, squid or inkfish, are becoming widely available from good fishmongers or fish markets. Carefully cooked they are extremely tender and tasty, and make an unusual first course.

Metric/Imperial

¾ kg/1½ lb fresh squid
2×15 ml spoons/2 tablespoons olive oil
1 large onion, peeled and cut into thin rings
1 garlic clove, peeled and finely chopped
150 ml/¼ pint white wine
150 ml/¼ pint water
1 sprig fresh parsley
1 strip lemon peel
1 bay leaf
Salt and freshly ground pepper
Pinch each of dried marjoram, rosemary and thyme
Juice of ½ lemon
1×15 ml spoon/1 tablespoon freshly chopped parsley to finish

American

1½ lb fresh squid
2 tablespoons olive oil
1 large onion, peeled and cut into thin rings
1 garlic clove, peeled and finely chopped
⅔ cup white wine
⅔ cup water
1 sprig fresh parsley
1 strip lemon peel
1 bay leaf
Salt and freshly ground pepper
Pinch each of dried marjoram, rosemary and thyme
Juice of ½ lemon
1 tablespoon freshly chopped parsley, to finish

Wash and skin the squid. Remove the long transparent backbone and clean the inside. Remove the head with its inkbags, and push out the hard core at the centre of the tentacles. Cut the body into rings about 1.25 cm/½ inch wide. Leave the tentacles whole if they are quite small, otherwise cut into 2.5 cm/1 inch lengths. Heat the oil in a shallow saucepan. Add the onion rings and garlic and cook for 1 minute. Add the squid and remaining ingredients, except the lemon juice and chopped parsley, cover and simmer for approximately 1 hour, or until tender. Lift the squid out of the pan and put aside in a bowl. Boil the cooking liquid for 10 minutes to reduce slightly. Discard the parsley sprig, lemon peel and bay leaf, then pour the liquid over the squid. Add the lemon juice, taste for seasoning and leave to cool.

TO FREEZE: pour into a freezer bag-lined preformer (forming container) and freeze until solid. Remove from preformer (container), overwrap in a freezer bag, seal, label and return to freezer.

TO THAW: leave in wrappings overnight in the refrigerator, or for 4 to 5 hours at room temperature.

TO SERVE: unwrap, transfer to a serving dish and sprinkle with the parsley. Serve chilled.

Pork Terrine and Chicken Vol-au-vents are illustrated below.

Chicken Vol-au-vents

Vol-au-vents, or literally "puffs of wind", are as light and airy as their name implies. They can be made in any size — one large round for a family meal; or medium-sized individual cases to be used as elegant first courses for dinner parties; or tiny ones which are delicious served as cocktail snacks. The pastry cases, sometimes called patty shells, can be bought ready cooked, needing only to be heated before serving; or they are available uncooked and commercially frozen in various sizes. You can also make your own from puff pastry. Always reheat or bake the cases just before serving, and heat the filling separately, so the pastry stays crisp.

The filling given here will fill 12 medium-sized vol-au-vent cases. This will serve 12 as a first course, or 6 as a light main course.

Metric/Imperial
25 g/1 oz butter
25 g/1 oz flour
150 ml/¼ pint chicken stock
300 ml/½ pint fresh single cream
1×15 ml spoon/1 tablespoon sherry
Salt and freshly ground pepper
225 g/½ lb cooked chicken meat, finely diced

American
2 tablespoons butter
¼ cup flour
⅔ cup chicken stock
1¼ cups light cream
1 tablespoon sherry
Salt and freshly ground pepper
½ lb cooked chicken meat, finely diced

Melt the butter in a saucepan. Add the flour and cook very gently for a few minutes, stirring well. Stir in the chicken stock and, when this is smooth, bring to the boil. Add the cream and the sherry, and season to taste. Add the chicken, mix well, then remove from the heat and leave to cool.

TO FREEZE: pour into a rigid container, cover, label and freeze. Or pour into a freezer bag-lined pre-former (forming container) and freeze until solid. Remove from preformer (forming container), seal, label and return to freezer.

TO THAW: unwrap frozen sauce and put into a heavy saucepan. Reheat gently on top of the stove, stirring occasionally. Add 1×15 ml spoon/1 tablespoon water or stock, if necessary.

TO SERVE: taste the hot sauce for seasoning, then spoon into heated vol-au-vent cases and serve.

Chicken Liver Pâté

The quickest of all the pâtés to make, this is also one of the most universally liked. Serve with crusty French bread or very thin hot toast, or spoon into tiny hot vol-au-vents or pastry cases and serve with cocktails.

Metric/Imperial
225 g/½ lb chicken livers
100 g/¼ lb butter
1×15 ml spoon/1 tablespoon brandy
1×15 ml spoon/1 tablespoon port, sherry or Madeira
1 garlic clove, peeled
Salt and freshly ground pepper
1 bay leaf

American
½ lb chicken livers
½ cup butter
1 tablespoon brandy
1 tablespoon port, sherry or Madeira
1 garlic clove, peeled
Salt and freshly ground pepper
1 bay leaf

Clean the chicken livers, cutting out any greenish parts or veins. Melt 25 g/1 oz/2 tablespoons of the butter in a frying pan. Put in the livers and cook them gently for 5 minutes, turning them from time to time; the liver should be cooked on the outside, but still pink, though not raw, on the inside. Transfer the livers to an electric blender, mincer or Mouli-légumes (foodmill) and pour the brandy into the frying pan. Increase the heat and let the brandy bubble for 1 minute, stirring with a wooden spoon to loosen any sediment in the pan. Pour this into the blender. Add the port, sherry or Madeira and the garlic clove and blend until the mix-

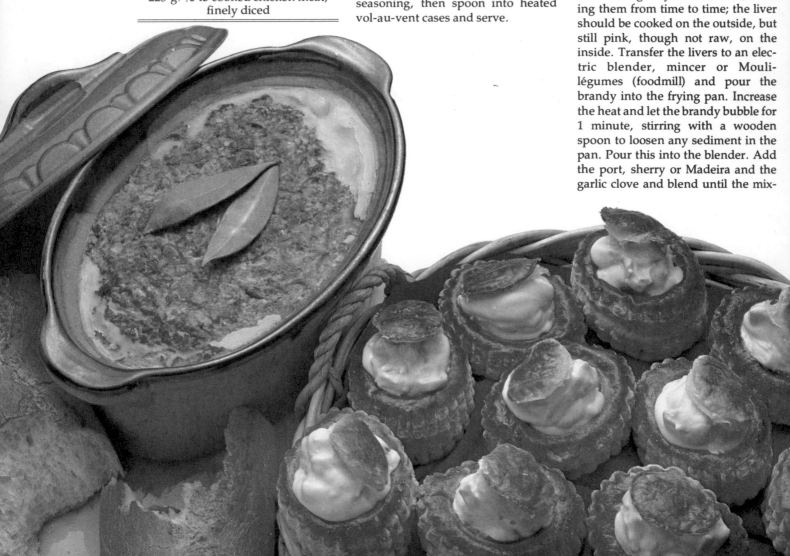

ture is smooth. Or work livers through the mincer or Mouli-légumes (foodmill) and add the alcohol and garlic afterwards. Beat in another 50 g/2 oz/4 tablespoons butter and season to taste in a bowl. Spoon the mixture into a small freezerproof terrine, pâté or soufflé dish or crock, and smooth the top. Melt the remaining 25 g/1 oz/2 tablespoons butter in a clean pan. Place the bay leaf on top of the pâté and pour over the melted butter. Leave to set.

TO FREEZE: wrap the terrine or dish (crock) in cling film, then overwrap in aluminium foil, label and freeze.

TO THAW: leave in wrappings overnight in the refrigerator, or for 4 to 5 hours at room temperature.

TO SERVE: remove wrappings and serve as suggested above.

Pork Terrine

This robust, well-flavoured pork pâté makes an excellent first course, but can also be the centrepiece for a summer lunch or picnic, served with salad, crusty French bread and a bottle of red wine. It is not too expensive to make, and freezes well so you can always have at least one good impromptu meal on hand.

Metric/Imperial

1¼ kg/2½ lb belly pork, skinned, boned and minced
225 g/½ lb pig's liver, fat and ducts removed
1 onion, peeled and very finely chopped
2 garlic cloves, peeled and finely chopped
1×15 ml spoon/1 tablespoon chopped rosemary, fresh or dried
1 egg
2×15 ml spoons/2 tablespoons brandy
Salt and freshly ground pepper
Butter for frying
2 bay leaves, to finish

American

2½ lb ground pork, half fat and half lean
½ lb pig's liver, fat and ducts removed
1 onion, peeled and very finely chopped
2 garlic cloves, peeled and finely chopped
1 tablespoon chopped rosemary, fresh or dried
1 egg
2 tablespoons brandy
Salt and freshly ground pepper
Butter for frying
2 bay leaves, to finish

Work the pork and liver together through the fine blade of the mincer (grinder). Add the onion, garlic and rosemary. Beat the egg lightly with the brandy and mix into the meat. Season generously. Fry a small spoon of the mixture in a little butter to taste for seasoning.

Spoon the mixture into a large freezerproof terrine or soufflé dish (1 litre/2 pints/5 cups), or into two smaller ones. Bake in a hot oven (220°C/425°F or Gas Mark 7) for 15 minutes, then reduce the heat to fairly hot (190°C/375°F or Gas Mark 5) and bake for another 1 to 1½ hours, or until the meat has shrunk away from the sides of the dish and the juice is clear. Remove from oven, place a weight on top of the pâté and leave to cool.

TO FREEZE: wrap well in cling film, then overwrap in a freezer bag. Seal, label and freeze.

TO THAW: leave in wrappings for 20 to 24 hours in the refrigerator or for 6 to 7 hours at room temperature.

TO SERVE: garnish with bay leaves and serve from the terrine.

Country-style Pâté

It is always useful to keep at least one pâté in the freezer, either for use as an easy first course to a meal which requires last minute attention, or for a picnic or lunch with French bread and a glass of red wine.

Metric/Imperial

350 g/¾ lb piece boned ham shank
2×15 ml spoons/2 tablespoons clear honey
6 black peppercorns
6 juniper berries
1×5 ml spoon/1 teaspoon freshly chopped thyme or 1×2.5 ml spoon/½ teaspoon dried thyme
100 g/¼ lb pork fat
100 g/¼ lb pork sausagemeat
50 g/2 oz fresh white breadcrumbs
1 small onion, peeled and finely chopped
1×2.5 ml spoon/½ teaspoon ground allspice
1 egg
4×15 ml spoons/4 tablespoons dry wine, sherry or fresh lemon juice
Salt and freshly ground black pepper
8 rashers streaky bacon

American

¾ lb piece boned, cured ham shank
2 tablespoons honey
6 black peppercorns
6 juniper berries
1 teaspoon freshly chopped thyme or ½ teaspoon dried thyme
¼ lb pork fat
¼ lb loose pork sausagemeat
1 cup fresh white breadcrumbs
1 small onion, peeled and finely chopped
½ teaspoon ground allspice
1 egg
4 tablespoons dry wine, sherry or fresh lemon juice
Salt and freshly ground black pepper
8 strips bacon

Serves 6 to 8

Put the ham, honey, peppercorns, juniper berries and thyme in a large saucepan and add water to cover the ham. Bring to the boil, then lower the heat, cover with a lid and simmer gently for approximately 1 hour or until the ham is tender. Remove from the pan and leave to cool. Mince (grind) the ham finely with the pork fat into a mixing bowl and stir in the remaining ingredients (except the bacon and seasoning) until combined. Season to taste with pepper, adding salt carefully if the ham is salty.

Flatten the bacon with the blade of a knife and use to line the base and sides of a greased 1 litre/2 pint/5 cup ovenproof dish or loaf tin (pan). Spoon in the pâté mixture, pressing down well with a spoon. Cover the top of the pâté with aluminium foil. Put into a roasting tin (pan) half filled with hot water and bake in a warm oven (160°C/325°F or Gas Mark 3) for 2 hours. Remove from roasting tin (pan) and put heavy weights (cans or a brick) on top of pâté. Leave until completely cold.

TO FREEZE: remove foil, turn pâté out and wrap in a double thickness of laminated freezer paper. Overwrap in a freezer bag, seal, label and freeze.

TO THAW: unwrap and cover loosely. Thaw overnight in the refrigerator, then remove from refrigerator 1 to 2 hours before serving to allow to come to room temperature.

TO SERVE: arrange, bacon side up, on serving platter with 1 or 2 slices cut. Garnish with watercress sprigs, tomato quarters, lettuce leaves or lemon wedges.

Main-course Dishes

Beef in Beer is
illustrated below, with
Boeuf Bourguignonne
shown opposite.

Beef in Beer

*This unusual recipe for beef and vegetables
cooked in beer actually improves with
freezing and reheating.
Serve with boiled or mashed potatoes
and a seasonal green vegetable.*

Metric/Imperial
Vegetable oil for frying
2 medium-sized onions, peeled and sliced
4 celery stalks, scrubbed and roughly chopped
2 large carrots, peeled and sliced
¾–1 kg/1½–2 lb chuck steak, trimmed of fat and cut into large chunks
Flour for coating
Salt and freshly ground black pepper
400 ml/¾ pint light ale (Aust lager)
1 bouquet garni (parsley and thyme sprigs, 1 bay leaf)
Freshly chopped parsley, to finish

American
Vegetable oil for frying
2 medium-sized onions, peeled and sliced
4 celery stalks, scrubbed and roughly chopped
2 large carrots, peeled and sliced
1½–2 lb chuck steak, trimmed of fat and cut into large chunks
Flour for coating
Salt and freshly ground black pepper
1 pint beer
1 bouquet garni (parsley and thyme sprigs, 1 bay leaf)
Freshly chopped parsley, to finish

Heat 2 tablespoons of oil in a flame-proof casserole, add the vegetables and cook gently for 5 minutes or until lightly coloured. Remove from the casserole with a slotted spoon and set aside.

Coat the steak in flour, seasoned with salt and pepper to taste. Put into the casserole a few pieces at a time, with a little more oil if necessary. Cook the meat quickly on all sides over high heat until all are browned. Return vegetables to the casserole, stir in the light ale (lager/beer) and add the bouquet garni. Bring to the boil, stirring.

Cover the casserole and transfer to a cool oven (150°C/300°F or Gas Mark 2) to cook for 2 to 2½ hours or until the meat is tender. Stir a little water into the stew if it becomes dry during cooking. When the meat is tender, remove casserole from oven, discard bouquet garni, taste for seasoning, then leave to cool.

TO FREEZE: turn into a foil container or foil-lined casserole, cover and freeze. If using casserole, remove foil package when solid and overwrap in a freezer bag, seal, label and return to freezer.

TO THAW: reheat the frozen stew in covered foil container or replace in casserole. Heat in a fairly hot oven (200°C/400°F or Gas Mark 6) for 1¼ hours or until bubbling.

TO SERVE: taste for seasoning, then transfer to a serving dish or serve straight from casserole, sprinkled with plenty of chopped parsley.

Boeuf Bourguignonne

*The classic French casserole Boeuf
Bourguignonne makes an ideal main
course when entertaining, either for a
dinner party occasion or, if made in larger
quantities, for a buffet.*

Metric/Imperial
38 g/1½ oz beef or pork dripping or lard
175 g/6 oz streaky bacon, rinds removed and bacon diced
¾–1 kg/1½–2 lb chuck steak, trimmed of fat and cut into large chunks
2×15 ml spoons/2 tablespoons flour
300 ml/½ pint Burgundy or other full-bodied red wine
Approx. 150 ml/¼ pint beef stock
4 carrots, peeled and sliced
1 bouquet garni (parsley and thyme sprigs, 1 bay leaf)
Salt and freshly ground black pepper
12–16 small onions, blanched and peeled
225 g/½ lb button mushrooms, cleaned
2×15 ml spoons/2 tablespoons freshly chopped parsley, to finish

American
3 tablespoons beef or pork drippings or oil
6 oz bacon in the piece, rind removed and bacon diced
1½–2 lb chuck or round steak, trimmed of fat and cut into large chunks
2 tablespoons flour
1¼ cups Burgundy or other full-bodied red wine
Approx. ⅔ cup beef stock
4 carrots, peeled and sliced
1 bouquet garni (parsley and thyme sprigs, 1 bay leaf)
Salt and freshly ground black pepper

12–16 baby onions, blanched and peeled

½ lb button mushrooms, cleaned

2 tablespoons freshly chopped parsley, to finish

Melt the fat in a large pan. Put in the bacon and fry until crisp and lightly browned. Remove bacon from the pan with a slotted spoon and put into an ovenproof casserole.

Put the beef in the pan, a few pieces at a time, and brown quickly on all sides over high heat. Transfer to the casserole with a slotted spoon. Brown the remaining pieces.

Sprinkle the flour over the fat remaining in the pan and cook until browned, stirring constantly with a wooden spoon. Gradually stir in the wine and stock and bring to the boil, stirring. Pour over the meat in the casserole, add the carrots and bouquet garni and season to taste.

Cover the casserole and cook in a warm oven (160°C/325°F or Gas Mark 3) for 1½ hours, adding a little extra stock during cooking if necessary. Add the onions and mushrooms and continue cooking for another 30 minutes or until the meat and vegetables are tender. Remove from the oven, taste for seasoning and leave to cool.

TO FREEZE: turn into a rigid container or foil-lined casserole, cover and freeze. If using casserole, remove foil package when solid and overwrap in a freezer bag, seal, label and return to freezer.

TO THAW: unwrap and replace in casserole. Cover and leave overnight in the refrigerator, then reheat in a fairly hot oven (200°C/400°F or Gas Mark 6) for 40 minutes or until bubbling and heated through, stirring occasionally. Or reheat the food from frozen in the casserole, allowing approximately 1¼ hours in a fairly hot oven.

TO SERVE: taste for seasoning, sprinkle with chopped parsley and serve with freshly boiled noodles and a tossed mixed salad.

Beef Olives

Beef olives, or beef birds, as this dish is sometimes called, are individual parcels of meat wrapped around a stuffing. They are interesting enough to serve at a dinner party, yet not so expensive that they cannot make an unusual family meal.

Metric/Imperial

1 kg/2 lb piece of beef (rump or skirt), trimmed of fat

Salt and freshly ground pepper

100 g/¼ lb fresh breadcrumbs

2 onions, peeled and finely chopped

225 g/½ lb mushrooms, cleaned, trimmed and finely chopped

Finely grated rind of 1 lemon

100 g/¼ lb fresh parsley, chopped

1 egg, lightly beaten

2×15 ml spoons/2 tablespoons beef dripping or oil

25 g/1 oz flour

150 ml/¼ pint beef stock

1 garlic clove, peeled and crushed

1×15 ml spoon/1 tablespoon prepared French mustard

American

2 lb very thinly sliced round steak or top round

Salt and freshly ground pepper

1½ cups fresh breadcrumbs

2 onions, peeled and finely chopped

½ lb mushrooms, cleaned, trimmed and finely chopped

Finely grated rind of 1 lemon

2 cups finely chopped parsley

1 egg, lightly beaten

2 tablespoons beef drippings or oil

¼ cup flour

⅔ cup beef stock

1 garlic clove, peeled and crushed

1 tablespoon prepared French mustard

If necessary, cut the beef into thin slices. Place these between two sheets of greaseproof (waxed) paper and beat them until very thin. Sprinkle each slice with salt and pepper to taste. Mix the breadcrumbs with the onions, mushrooms, lemon rind and parsley, then season lightly and bind together with the egg. Place a spoonful of this filling on each slice of beef, roll up and secure with a wooden toothpick or tie with string or thread. Heat the dripping(s) or oil in a flameproof casserole. Quickly brown each of the beef olives on all sides. Remove them from the pan with a slotted spoon. Sprinkle in the flour and cook for a few minutes until it begins to turn dark brown. Slowly stir in the stock, then add the garlic. Return the beef olives to the pan. Half cover with a lid and simmer for 40 to 50 minutes or until the meat is tender. Remove from the heat, stir in the mustard and leave to cool.

TO FREEZE: pour into an aluminium foil container, cover and freeze, or pour into a freezer bag-lined preformer (forming container), freeze until solid, then remove preformer (container). Overwrap in a freezer bag, seal, label and return to freezer.

TO THAW: unwrap and reheat from frozen in a heavy saucepan or flameproof casserole on top of the stove for 30 to 40 minutes. Add a little stock or water if necessary and turn the beef olives over in the sauce from time to time.

TO SERVE: taste for seasoning and serve hot with potatoes or rice, and salad.

The photograph shows Swedish Hamburgers on the left and Steak and Kidney Pie on the right.

Swedish Hamburgers

The addition of beetroot (beets) and capers to these hamburgers makes a very different flavour. You can either serve them in the traditional way with raw onion rings, tomato slices and lettuce in a hamburger bun or crusty roll, or top them with fried eggs.

Metric/Imperial

¾ kg/1½ lb lean minced beef

1 small onion, peeled and finely chopped

1×15 ml spoon/1 tablespoon capers, drained and finely chopped

2 medium-sized cooked beetroot, peeled and finely chopped

1 large potato, boiled, skinned and mashed with 1×15 ml spoon/1 tablespoon butter and 2×15 ml spoons/2 tablespoons fresh double cream

Salt and freshly ground black pepper

1 egg, beaten

Flour for coating

Vegetable or cooking oil for frying

American

1½ lb lean ground beef

1 small onion, peeled and finely chopped

1 tablespoon capers, drained and finely chopped

2 medium-sized cooked beets, peeled and finely chopped

1 large potato, boiled, skinned and mashed with 1 tablespoon butter and 2 tablespoons heavy cream

Salt and freshly ground black pepper

1 egg, beaten

Flour for coating

Vegetable or cooking oil for frying

Put the beef, onion, capers, beetroot (beets) and potato in a large bowl and mix well together. Season to taste with salt and pepper and bind the mixture with the egg. Shape into four large flat patties with floured hands.

TO FREEZE: open (flash) freeze on a tray until solid, then wrap each hamburger individually in aluminium foil and pack together in a freezer bag. Seal, label and return to freezer.

TO THAW: heat 4 spoons of oil in a large frying pan. Unwrap the hamburgers and fry frozen for approximately 10 minutes on each side or until cooked through and golden brown.

TO SERVE: remove from pan with a slotted spoon and serve immediately with garnishes of your choice.

Steak and Kidney Pie

Steak and kidney pie, made with oysters as they do at the Savoy Hotel in London, can be a grand dish. There is no need to use the very best steak, however, as the preliminary slow cooking will ensure that the meat is tender.

Metric/Imperial

½–¾ kg/1–1½ lb beef steak (rump, skirt or chuck/Aust topside or round), trimmed and cut into cubes

225 g/½ lb ox kidney, cored and cut into cubes

50 g/2 oz flour

Salt and freshly ground pepper

50 g/2 oz butter

1×15 ml spoon/1 tablespoon oil

2 onions, peeled and roughly chopped

300 ml/½ pint beef stock

1 bay leaf

1×1.25 ml spoon/¼ teaspoon dried marjoram

2 whole cloves

6–12 oysters, shelled with liquid reserved (optional)

1×15 ml spoon/1 tablespoon dry or medium sherry

Few drops Worcestershire or Tabasco sauce

FOR THE PASTRY:
50 g/2 oz butter, softened

25 g/1 oz lard or shortening, softened

100 g/¼ lb flour

Pinch of salt

75 ml/scant ⅛ pint iced water

Swedish Hamburgers
Steak and Kidney Pie

American

1–1½ lb beef steak (rump, round or chuck), trimmed and cut into cubes
½ lb beef kidney, cored and cut into cubes
½ cup flour
Salt and freshly ground pepper
¼ cup butter
1 tablespoon oil
2 onions, peeled and roughly chopped
1¼ cups beef stock
1 bay leaf
¼ teaspoon dried marjoram
2 whole cloves
6–12 oysters, shucked with liquid reserved (optional)
1 tablespoon dry or medium sherry
Few drops Worcestershire or Tabasco sauce
FOR THE PASTRY: ¼ cup butter, softened
2 tablespoons lard or shortening, softened
1 cup flour
Pinch of salt
⅓ cup iced water

Coat the steak and kidney in the flour, well seasoned with salt and pepper. Put the butter and oil in a flameproof casserole and heat gently until the butter has melted. Add the onions and cook until golden. Add the meat and sear it quickly on all sides. Sprinkle in any remaining seasoned flour, cook for 1 minute, then slowly stir in the stock. Add the bay leaf, marjoram and cloves. Add the oysters and their liquid (if using), the sherry and sauce, then cover with a lid and simmer on top of the stove or bake in a moderate oven (180°C/350°F or Gas Mark 4) for approximately 1 hour or until the meat is tender. Remove from the heat, discard the bay leaf and cloves, taste for seasoning and leave to cool.

Meanwhile, make the pastry: blend the butter and lard or shortening together and divide into four portions. Sift the flour and salt into a bowl and rub in one-quarter of the fat. Mix to a firm dough with the water. Knead lightly on a floured board and roll out to a large rectangle. Spread the rectangle of dough with another quarter of the fat to within 2.5 cm/1 inch of the edges. Fold in three and press the edges to seal. Wrap in aluminium foil and put in the refrigerator to rest for 15 minutes.

Roll out again into the rectangle and spread with the third quarter of fat. Fold, seal and chill. Repeat the rolling, spreading and folding once more, using the last of the fat.

When the meat has cooled, transfer to a 1 litre/2 pint/5 cup freezerproof or aluminium foil pie dish. Roll out the dough, cut off a strip and press it around the moistened rim of the dish. Moisten the strip of dough with water, then cover with the remaining dough and press down the edges firmly. Trim off excess. Make a few incisions in the top to form air vents, and decorate with pastry leaves.

TO FREEZE: wrap the pie dish in cling film, then overwrap in aluminium foil or a freezer bag. Seal, label and freeze.

TO THAW: unwrap the pie and bake from frozen in a hot oven (220°C/425°F or Gas Mark 7) for 30 minutes, then reduce the heat to moderate (180°C/350°F or Gas Mark 4) and bake for another 30 minutes, or until a skewer inserted into an incision is hot to the touch when withdrawn.

TO SERVE: serve hot straight from the cooking dish. Cut the pastry into wedges and place a wedge on each plate with some filling beside it. Can be served with Brussels sprouts.

Rogan Gosht is illustrated on this page, with Beef Goulash on the opposite page.

Beef Goulash

The classic Hungarian goulash is an exciting combination of beef and tomatoes spiced with paprika and topped with sour(ed) cream. Different regions of Hungary have their own variations of this recipe. Some include peppers, others use veal but they all contain paprika. Serve with noodles tossed in butter and a crisp green salad.

Metric/Imperial

25 g/1 oz beef dripping or lard

1 large onion, peeled and chopped

¾–1 kg/1½–2 lb chuck steak, trimmed of fat and cut into large chunks

Flour for coating

Salt and freshly ground black pepper

1×5 ml spoon/1 teaspoon caraway seeds

1×15 ml spoon/1 tablespoon paprika

½ kg/1 lb tomatoes, skinned, seeded and chopped

400 ml/¾ pint beef stock

2×15 ml spoons/2 tablespoons tomato purée (paste)

½ kg/1 lb potatoes, peeled and diced

TO FINISH:
150 ml/¼ pint cultured soured cream, at room temperature

Freshly chopped parsley or snipped chives

American

2 tablespoons beef drippings or oil

1 large onion, peeled and chopped

1½–2 lb chuck steak, trimmed of fat and cut into large chunks

Flour for coating

Salt and freshly ground black pepper

1 teaspoon caraway seeds

1 tablespoon sweet paprika

1 lb tomatoes, skinned, seeded and chopped

2 cups beef stock

2 tablespoons tomato paste

1 lb potatoes, peeled and diced

TO FINISH:
⅔ cup sour cream, at room temperature

Freshly chopped parsley or finely cut chives

Melt the fat in a flameproof casserole. Add the onion and fry gently for 5 minutes or until soft. Meanwhile, coat the beef in flour seasoned with salt and pepper to taste. Add to the casserole a few pieces at a time and cook until all the meat is browned. Add a little more fat to the pan if necessary. Sprinkle over the caraway seeds and paprika and cook for 2 minutes. Stir in the tomatoes, stock and tomato purée (paste). Bring to the boil, stirring. Cover the casserole and transfer to a cool oven (150°C/300°F or Gas Mark 2) to cook for 1½ hours. Stir in the diced potatoes and continue cooking for 1 hour or until the meat and potatoes are tender. Stir a little water or more beef stock into the goulash if it becomes dry during the cooking time. When the meat and potatoes are tender, remove casserole from oven, taste for seasoning, then leave to cool.

TO FREEZE: turn into a foil container or foil-lined casserole, cover and freeze. If using casserole, remove foil package when solid and overwrap in a freezer bag, seal, label and return to freezer.

TO THAW: remove packaging and reheat frozen goulash in covered foil container or replace in casserole. Heat in a fairly hot oven (200°C/400°F or Gas Mark 6) for 1¼ hours or until bubbling.

TO SERVE: remove from oven and taste for seasoning. Leave for 5 minutes, then transfer to a serving dish if necessary. Spoon over sour(ed) cream and sprinkle with parsley or chives. The sour(ed) cream may be served separately, sprinkled with a little paprika, if you like.

Rogan Gosht

This spicy Indian curry combines beef and onions in a rich tomato sauce. It can also be made with lamb — in which case use the tender, lean meat from the fillet end of the leg and cook for 1 to 1½ hours.

Metric/Imperial

Butter for frying

2 large onions, peeled and finely chopped

1 garlic clove, peeled and crushed

1×5 ml spoon/1 teaspoon finely chopped fresh root (green) ginger, or 1×2.5 ml spoon/½ teaspoon ground ginger

¾–1 kg/1½–2 lb chuck steak, trimmed of fat and cut into cubes

1×15 ml spoon/1 tablespoon ground turmeric

1×15 ml spoon/1 tablespoon ground coriander

2×5 ml spoons/2 teaspoons ground cumin

1×2.5 ml spoon/½ teaspoon chilli powder, or to taste

Salt and freshly ground black pepper

397 g/14 oz can tomatoes, puréed

300 ml/½ pint beef stock

4 lemon wedges, to finish (optional)

American
Butter for frying
2 large onions, peeled and finely chopped
1 garlic clove, peeled and crushed
1 teaspoon finely chopped fresh ginger, or ½ teaspoon ground ginger
1½–2 lb chuck steak, trimmed of fat and cut into cubes
1 tablespoon ground turmeric
1 tablespoon ground coriander
2 teaspoons ground cumin
½ teaspoon chili powder, or to taste
Salt and freshly ground black pepper
1 large can tomatoes, puréed
1¼ cups beef stock
4 lemon wedges, to finish (optional)

Melt a knob of butter in a flameproof casserole. Add the onions, garlic and ginger and fry gently until soft. Stir in the meat and spices, with salt and pepper to taste, and continue to fry until the meat is browned on all sides, stirring constantly. Take care that the spices do not burn. Stir in the puréed tomatoes and beef stock and bring to the boil.

Lower the heat, cover with a lid and simmer very gently for approximately 2 hours or until the beef is tender, stirring occasionally. Remove from the heat, taste for seasoning and leave to cool.

TO FREEZE: turn into a foil-lined casserole, cover and freeze until solid, then remove foil package and overwrap in a freezer bag, seal, label and return to freezer.

TO THAW: unwrap and replace in casserole. Cover and leave overnight in the refrigerator, then reheat in a fairly hot oven (200°C/400°F or Gas Mark 6) for approximately 40 minutes or until bubbling and heated through, stirring occasionally. Or reheat the food from frozen in the casserole, allowing approximately 1¼ hours in a fairly hot oven.

TO SERVE: arrange curry on a bed of freshly boiled rice on a hot serving platter. Garnish with lemon wedges, if you like, and serve with side dishes of your choice such as mango chutney, lime pickle, tomato and banana salad and cucumber with yogurt and mint.

Beef Goulash
Rogan Gosht

151

The photograph opposite shows Spring Casserole with the vegetables arranged around the meat before it is carved.

Spring Casserole

Make this with young, tender spring vegetables and new baby lamb.

Metric/Imperial
25 g/1 oz butter
1×15 ml spoon/1 tablespoon oil
1 small leg or shoulder of lamb (approx. 1½282 kg/3–4 lb)
1 garlic clove, peeled and cut in half
225 g/½ lb button onions, blanched and peeled
25 g/1 oz flour
600 ml/1 pint chicken or beef stock
1 sprig fresh rosemary
Salt and freshly ground pepper
225 g/½ lb small turnips, peeled
225 g/½ lb baby carrots, peeled
225 g/½ lb small new potatoes, peeled
225 g/½ lb broad beans, shelled
225 g/½ lb peas, shelled

American
2 tablespoons butter
1 tablespoon oil
1 small leg or shoulder of lamb (approx. 3–4 lb)
1 garlic clove, peeled and cut in half
½ lb baby white onions, blanched and peeled
¼ cup flour
2½ cups chicken or beef stock
1 sprig fresh rosemary
Salt and freshly ground pepper
½ lb small turnips, peeled
½ lb baby carrots, peeled
½ lb small new potatoes, peeled
½ lb lima beans, shelled
½ lb peas, shelled

Put the butter and oil in a large flameproof casserole and heat gently until the butter has melted. Meanwhile, rub the lamb all over with the cut garlic clove. Brown the meat on all sides in the butter and oil, then remove from the casserole and set aside. Put the onions in the casserole, brown quickly, then remove with a slotted spoon and set aside also. Sprinkle in the flour and cook until pale golden brown, stirring constantly. Slowly stir in the stock to make a smooth sauce, then return the meat to the casserole. Crush the garlic clove and add to the casserole with the rosemary, and seasoning to taste. Cover with a lid and simmer for 1 hour. Add the turnips, carrots and potatoes and simmer for 15 minutes. Return the onions to the casserole,

add the beans and peas, and simmer for another 10 minutes. Remove from the heat, taste for seasoning and leave to cool.

If serving immediately continue to simmer until the vegetables are just tender and present the meat whole, surrounded by the vegetables, before carving.

TO FREEZE: carve the lamb into thick slices, place in an aluminium foil or rigid container, add the vegetables and sauce, cover, label and freeze. Or put everything into a freezer bag-lined preformer (forming container) and freeze until solid. Remove pre-former (container), seal, label and return to freezer.

TO THAW: leave in wrappings overnight in the refrigerator, or for 5 hours at room temperature, then unwrap and transfer to a large flameproof casserole. Add a little water, cover with a lid and simmer on top of the stove until all the vegetables are just tender. Do not let the vegetables get too soft.

TO SERVE: taste for seasoning, and serve on a warmed serving dish or platter which allows all the vegetables to be seen.

Meatballs Napoli

Serve with freshly cooked spaghetti or tagliatelli and a crisp green salad.

Metric/Imperial
¾ kg/1½ lb lean minced beef
2 small onions, peeled and very finely chopped
1 garlic clove, peeled and crushed
4×15 ml spoons/4 tablespoons dried breadcrumbs
1 egg, beaten
1×5 ml spoon/1 teaspoon dried basil
1×5 ml spoon/1 teaspoon dried oregano
Salt and freshly ground black pepper
Approx 4×15 ml spoons/4 tablespoons flour, for coating
1×1.25 ml spoon/¼ teaspoon cayenne pepper
Olive oil for frying
397 g/14 oz can tomatoes, puréed or sieved
150 ml/¼ pint chicken stock
1×15 ml spoon/1 tablespoon red wine vinegar
1×5 ml spoon/1 teaspoon sugar
2×15 ml spoons/2 tablespoons grated Parmesan cheese, to finish

American
1½ lb lean ground beef
2 small onions, peeled and very finely chopped
1 garlic clove, peeled and crushed
4 tablespoons dried breadcrumbs
1 egg, beaten
1 teaspoon dried basil
1 teaspoon dried oregano
Salt and freshly ground black pepper
Approx. ¼ cup flour, for coating
¼ teaspoon cayenne pepper
Olive oil for frying
1 large can tomatoes, puréed or sieved
⅔ cup chicken stock
1 tablespoon red wine vinegar
1 teaspoon sugar
2 tablespoons grated Parmesan cheese, to finish

Mix the beef with half the onions, the garlic and breadcrumbs, then stir in the egg to combine. Season with half the basil and oregano, and salt and pepper to taste, and stir well.

Roll into approximately 30 to 34 small balls with floured hands, then coat in the flour seasoned with the cayenne pepper.

Heat 2 tablespoons of oil in a flameproof casserole. Put in some of the meatballs and brown on all sides. Add more oil and meatballs until they are all browned. Drain.

Put the remaining onion in the casserole, with a little more oil if necessary, and fry gently until golden. Add the tomatoes, chicken stock, the remaining basil and oregano, the wine vinegar and sugar. Season to taste. Bring to the boil, stirring constantly, then lower the heat and return the meatballs to the casserole. Cover and transfer to a warm oven (160°C/325°F or Gas Mark 3) to cook for 45 minutes. Remove from the oven, and leave to cool.

TO FREEZE: pack into an aluminium foil container, cover, then overwrap in a freezer bag, seal, label and freeze.

TO THAW: remove overwrapping and reheat from frozen in covered foil container in a fairly hot oven (200°C/400°F or Gas Mark 6) for approximately 1 hour or until meatballs are heated through.

TO SERVE: taste for seasoning, then arrange meatballs and tomato sauce in a hot serving dish on top of freshly cooked spaghetti tossed in butter. If you like, arrange the meatballs around the edge of the dish and pour the sauce over the spaghetti in the centre. Top with grated Parmesan.

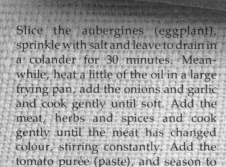

Moussaka

The classic Mediterranean Moussaka is made with minced (ground) lamb and aubergines (eggplant) covered with a light, white sauce.

Metric/Imperial

4 aubergines (eggplant)

Salt

150 ml/¼ pint oil

2 onions, peeled and thinly sliced

2 garlic cloves, peeled and finely chopped

¾–1 kg/1½–2 lb lean minced lamb, or half quantities each of lean minced lamb and lean minced beef

1×5 ml spoon/1 teaspoon fresh, or 1×2.5 ml spoon/½ teaspoon dried oregano, or rosemary and thyme

1×5 ml spoon/1 teaspoon ground cinnamon, or 1×2.5 ml spoon/½ teaspoon ground allspice

2×15 ml spoons/2 tablespoons tomato purée (paste)

Salt and freshly ground pepper

FOR THE SAUCE:
25 g/1 oz butter

25 g/1 oz flour

400 ml/¾ pint milk

1×1.25 ml spoon/¼ teaspoon grated nutmeg

Salt and freshly ground pepper

2 eggs, lightly beaten

American

4 large eggplant

Salt

⅔ cup oil

2 onions, peeled and thinly sliced

2 garlic cloves, peeled and finely chopped

1½–2 lb lean ground lamb, or half quantities each of lean ground lamb and lean ground beef

1 teaspoon fresh, or ½ teaspoon dried, oregano, or rosemary and thyme

1 teaspoon ground cinnamon, or ½ teaspoon ground allspice

2 tablespoons tomato paste

Salt and freshly ground pepper

FOR THE SAUCE:
2 tablespoons butter

¼ cup flour

2 cups milk

¼ teaspoon grated nutmeg

Salt and freshly ground pepper

2 eggs, lightly beaten

Slice the aubergines (eggplant), sprinkle with salt and leave to drain in a colander for 30 minutes. Meanwhile, heat a little of the oil in a large frying pan, add the onions and garlic and cook gently until soft. Add the meat, herbs and spices and cook gently until the meat has changed colour, stirring constantly. Add the tomato purée (paste), and season to taste. Remove from the heat and leave to cool.

Rinse the aubergine (eggplant) slices and pat dry on kitchen paper towels. Heat some of the remaining oil in another frying pan. Add the aubergine (eggplant) slices, a few at a time, and fry until they are golden brown on both sides. Add more oil as necessary. Leave to drain on kitchen paper towels. When all the aubergine (eggplant) slices have been fried, put a layer of them in a 1½ litre/3 pint/2 quart freezerproof or baking foil dish. Follow with a layer of the meat mixture, and repeat until all the meat and aubergines (eggplant) have been used up, finishing with a layer of aubergines (eggplant).

To make the sauce: melt the butter in a clean saucepan. Add the flour and cook over a very low heat for a few minutes without allowing to brown, stirring constantly. Add the milk very slowly, a cupful at a time, and stir until smooth before adding any more. Bring to the boil, stirring, then lower the heat and simmer until the sauce thickens. Add the nutmeg, and season to taste. Remove from the heat. Stir a little of the hot sauce into the eggs, then add this gradually to the remaining sauce, stirring well after each addition. Pour over the moussaka in the dish. Leave to cool.
TO FREEZE: wrap the dish in cling film, then overwrap in aluminium foil, label and freeze.
TO THAW: unwrap and reheat from frozen in a hot oven (220°C/425°F or Gas Mark 7) for 20 minutes, then reduce the heat to moderate (180°C/350°F or Gas Mark 4), and continue cooking for another 40 to 50 minutes or until the dish is heated through and lightly browned on top.
TO SERVE: serve hot straight from the cooking dish.

Normandy Pork

Normandy is famous for its apples, and for the cider and Calvados (apple brandy) that are brewed and distilled from them. Norman cooking can be exceedingly rich, but like all good peasant cuisines, it is also very adaptable. This dish can be made more — or less — extravagant, as you like: it is delicious at its richest, made with fillet (tenderloin) of pork, choice eating apples, Calvados and thick cream; but it is just as good made with a less expensive cut of meat, cooking apples, cider and yogurt.

Metric/Imperial

100 g/¼ lb pork fat, diced

1 large onion, peeled and finely chopped

1 kg/2 lb skinned and boned pork (fillet or tenderloin, loin, shoulder, or lean end of belly), cut into strips

½ kg/1 lb apples

2×15 ml spoons/2 tablespoons Calvados, or 4×15 ml spoons/4 tablespoons cider

300 ml/½ pint fresh double cream, single cream, cultured soured cream or yogurt

Salt and freshly ground pepper

American

¼ lb pork fat, cut into dice

1 large onion, peeled and finely chopped

2 lb boned pork (tenderloin, loin or shoulder), cut into strips

1 lb apples

2 tablespoons Calvados or Applejack or 4 tablespoons hard cider

1¼ cups heavy cream, light cream, sour cream or yogurt

Salt and freshly ground pepper

Fry the pork fat in a flameproof casserole until the pieces are crisp and all the fat has run. Pour off all but 2×15 ml spoons/2 tablespoons of the fat, add the onion and cook gently. Add the meat and brown rapidly.

Peel, core and chop the apples finely. Add to the casserole, cover with a lid and simmer for 20 to 30 minutes or until the meat is tender and the apples have cooked to a thick sauce. Increase the heat, add the Calvados, Applejack, or cider and let it bubble for 1 minute. Pour in the cream or yogurt and cook gently until the sauce has thickened, stirring continuously. Remove from the heat, season to taste and leave to cool.
TO FREEZE: pour into an aluminium foil or rigid container, cover, label and freeze. Or pour into a freezer bag-lined preformer (forming container) and freeze until solid. Remove pre-former (container), seal, label and return to freezer.
TO THAW: unwrap and reheat gently from frozen in a heavy saucepan or flameproof casserole on top of the stove for 30 to 40 minutes. Add a little water or cider if necessary.
TO SERVE: serve hot.

Boiled Leg of Lamb in Caper Sauce

This is an unusual and tasty way of cooking lamb which has the added advantage that the meat does not shrink, as it tends to do when roasted.

Metric/Imperial

1 leg of lamb (approx. 1½–2 kg/3–4 lb)
1 onion, peeled and roughly chopped
1 carrot, peeled and roughly chopped
1 bouquet garni (parsley, marjoram, rosemary sprigs and 1 bay leaf)
50 g/2 oz butter
50 g/2 oz flour
2×15 ml spoons/2 tablespoons fresh double cream
1×15 ml spoon/1 tablespoon green capers
Salt and freshly ground pepper

American

1 leg of lamb (approx. 3–4 lb)
1 onion, peeled and roughly chopped
1 carrot, peeled and roughly chopped
1 bouquet garni (parsley, marjoram, rosemary sprigs and 1 bay leaf)
¼ cup butter
½ cup flour
2 tablespoons heavy cream
1 tablespoon capers
Salt and freshly ground pepper

Put the leg of lamb in a large sauce-pan, add enough cold water to cover, and bring to the boil. Skim with a slotted spoon, then add the onion, carrot and bouquet garni. Half cover with a lid and simmer for 1½ to 2 hours or until the meat is tender when pierced with a skewer. (The meat should still be pink in the centre, but not red; when pricked with the skewer the juice should flow clear.) Take the meat out of the pan and carve into thick slices. Strain the cooking liquid into a measuring jug.

Melt the butter in a clean pan. Add the flour and cook over a gentle heat for 2 minutes, stirring well. Do not allow to colour. Slowly stir in approximately 600 ml/1 pint/2½ cups of the strained cooking liquid to make a fairly thick sauce. Add the cream and capers, with a little of their pickling juice, and season to taste.
TO FREEZE: put the slices of meat in aluminium foil or rigid container and pour over the sauce. Cover, label and freeze. Or pour into a freezer bag-lined preformer (forming container) and freeze until solid. Remove pre-former (container), seal, label and return to freezer.
TO THAW: unwrap and put into a heavy saucepan or flameproof casserole. Reheat gently from frozen for 30 to 40 minutes on top of the stove, adding 1×15 ml spoon/1 tablespoon water and stirring occasionally.
TO SERVE: taste sauce for seasoning. Put into a warmed serving dish and serve with creamed potatoes and a green vegetable or salad.

Moussaka
Normandy Pork
Boiled Leg of Lamb in Caper Sauce

Illustrated from left to right are Hungarian Pork with Sauerkraut accompanied by a dish of sour(ed) cream, Polish Meat Loaf and Pork Pie.

Pork Pie

The traditional English pork pie, wrapped in pastry and baked in the classic fluted, hinged oval mould, is rarely made at home nowadays. Yet a slice of the pie, with its mosaic pattern set in a frame of jellied stock, is pleasing to the eye and palate. Any loaf tin, hinged or not, will be adequate to bake the pie.

Metric/Imperial

½ kg/1 lb skinned and boned pork, cut from shoulder, neck, spare ribs or lean end of belly

225 g/½ lb bacon in the piece, rind and any bones removed

Salt and freshly ground pepper

1×5 ml spoon/1 teaspoon freshly chopped sage or marjoram *or* 1×2.5 ml spoon/½ teaspoon dried sage or marjoram

4–6 rashers streaky bacon, rinds removed

FOR THE PASTRY:
450 g/1 lb flour

1×5 ml spoon/1 teaspoon salt

1×5 ml spoon/1 teaspoon icing sugar

150 ml/¼ pint water

100 g/¼ lb lard, cut into pieces

TO FINISH:
1 egg yolk

1×15 ml spoon/1 tablespoon water

300 ml/½ pint good homemade stock, made from pork or veal bones, including 1 trotter or knuckle of veal

American

1 lb boned pork

½ lb bacon in the piece, rind and any bones removed

Salt and freshly ground pepper

1 teaspoon freshly chopped sage or marjoram *or* ½ teaspoon dried sage or marjoram

4–6 strips bacon, rinds removed

FOR THE PASTRY:
4 cups flour

1 teaspoon salt

1 teaspoon confectioners' sugar

⅔ cup water

½ cup lard, cut into pieces

TO FINISH:
1 egg yolk

1 tablespoon water

1¼ cups good homemade stock, made from pork or veal bones, including 1 pig's foot or knuckle of veal

Work half the pork and half the piece of bacon through a mincer (grinder) and season to taste. Cut the remaining meat into small cubes. Fry gently

in its own fat until brown, then sprinkle with the herbs. Remove from the heat, season liberally, and leave to cool.

Meanwhile make the pastry: sift the flour, salt and sugar into a large bowl. Put the water in a saucepan and bring to the boil. Add the lard and, when melted, pour slowly onto the flour mixture. Beat well until the mixture is smooth and comes away from the sides of the bowl. Leave to cool.

Grease a ½ kg/1 lb pie tin (pan). Roll out dough on a floured board and use two-thirds of it to line the tin (pan). Line the dough with the bacon rashers (strips). Put half the minced (ground) meat into the tin (pan), cover with the cubed meat and finish with a second layer of minced (ground) meat. Cover with the remaining dough, making a raised edge, and seal well with a little water. Make a hole in the centre and put a small paper or foil funnel (chimney) into it to keep the hole open during baking. Bake in a warm oven (160°C/325°F or Gas Mark 3) for 1½ to 2 hours or until the top is lightly browned and a skewer inserted in the hole is hot to the touch when withdrawn. Remove from the oven and leave to cool for 1 hour, then gently remove the pie from the tin (pan).

Beat the egg yolk with the water. Brush over the pie and return to the warm oven for 10 to 15 minutes to set the glaze. If the stock has jellied, put it in a saucepan and heat gently until melted. Pour it into the pie through the hole in the centre, using as much as the pie will hold. The meat will have shrunk during the cooking, leaving spaces at the sides and top. Leave the pie to cool and set.

TO FREEZE: wrap in cling film, then overwrap in aluminium foil or a freezer bag. Seal, label and freeze.
TO THAW: bake from frozen in a fairly hot oven (200°C/400°F or Gas Mark 6) for 30 minutes until the pastry is crisp. Remove from the oven and leave for 3 to 4 hours to finish thawing.
TO SERVE: slice thickly and serve cold with a salad and beer, lager or cider.

Hungarian Pork with Sauerkraut

This is an excellent dish for a winter buffet supper. It can be eaten with a fork, it is warming, unusual, and not too expensive. Serve with crusty black bread and chilled white wine, cider or lager (light beer).

Metric/Imperial

1×15 ml spoon/1 tablespoon oil

½ kg/1 lb onions, peeled and chopped

2 garlic cloves, peeled and finely chopped

700 g–1 kg/1½282 lb skinned and boned pork (belly, shoulder or spare rib), diced

700 g–1 kg/1½–2 lb fresh sauerkraut

1×15 ml spoon/1 tablespoon paprika

1×15 ml spoon/1 tablespoon caraway seeds (optional)

½ kg/1 lb tomatoes, skinned and roughly chopped

Salt and freshly ground black pepper

TO FINISH:
25 g/1 oz flour

1×15 ml spoon/1 tablespoon water

150 ml/¼ pint cultured soured cream

American
1 tablespoon oil
1 lb onions, peeled and chopped
2 garlic cloves, peeled and finely chopped
1½–2 lb boned pork, cut into dice
1½–2 lb fresh sauerkraut
1 tablespoon paprika
1 tablespoon caraway seeds (optional)
1 lb tomatoes, skinned and roughly chopped
Salt and freshly ground black pepper
TO FINISH:
¼ cup flour
1 tablespoon water
⅔ cup sour cream

Heat the oil in a large flameproof casserole, add the onions and garlic and cook until soft and golden. Increase the heat, add the meat and sear quickly on all sides. Add the sauerkraut, paprika, caraway seeds (if using) and the tomatoes. Stir well, season to taste, cover and simmer for 1½ hours or until the meat and sauerkraut are really tender. Remove from the heat, taste for seasoning and leave to cool.

TO FREEZE: if you can spare the flameproof casserole, freeze the pork and sauerkraut in the casserole. Otherwise, pour into an aluminium foil container and cover. Or pour into a freezer bag-lined preformer (forming container), freeze until solid, then remove preformer (container). Overwrap casserole, container or bag in a freezer bag, seal, label and freeze (return to freezer).

TO THAW: unwrap and put into a heavy saucepan or flameproof cas-

serole. Reheat gently from frozen on top of the stove for approximately 1 hour, adding 1×15 ml spoon/1 tablespoon water, if necessary, and stirring occasionally. Mix the flour and water to a smooth paste in a cup and, when the dish is really hot, stir in and cook for 5 minutes, stirring constantly.

TO SERVE: taste for seasoning, stir in the sour(ed) cream and serve very hot, straight from the casserole.

Polish Meat Loaf

This veal and mushroom loaf is basted with sour(ed) cream while baking, and the resulting moist mixture lends itself to successful freezing. Serve hot or cold.

Metric/Imperial
1 kg/2 lb minced lean veal, or half quantities each of minced lean veal and minced lean beef
1 onion, peeled and finely chopped
1 garlic clove, peeled and finely chopped
225 g/½ lb mushrooms, cleaned and finely chopped
100 g/¼ lb fresh white breadcrumbs
75 ml/scant ⅛ pint dry white wine
1 egg, lightly beaten
Salt and freshly ground pepper
1×1.25 ml spoon/¼ teaspoon grated nutmeg
150 ml/¼ pint cultured soured cream
150 ml/¼ pint stock
Sliced tomatoes, gherkins or pickled cucumbers, to finish

American
2 lb ground lean veal, or half quantities each of ground lean veal and ground lean beef
1 onion, peeled and finely chopped
1 garlic clove, peeled and finely chopped
½ lb mushrooms, cleaned and finely chopped

1½ cups fresh white breadcrumbs
⅓ cup dry white wine
1 egg, lightly beaten
Salt and freshly ground pepper
¼ teaspoon grated nutmeg
⅔ cup sour cream
⅔ cup stock
Sliced tomatoes, gherkins or sweet-sour cucumbers, to finish

Put the meat in a large bowl with the onion, garlic, mushrooms and breadcrumbs. Mix well until thoroughly combined. Beat the wine into the egg with salt and pepper to taste. Add the nutmeg, then stir into the meat and breadcrumbs to make a stiff mixture. Shape into a loaf and place in a large roasting pan. Pour over the sour(ed) cream and roast in a fairly hot oven (200°C/400°F or Gas Mark 6) for 40 to 50 minutes or until the meat is cooked and a light crust is formed, basting from time to time.

Remove the meat from the pan and place in a deep aluminium foil dish. Transfer the roasting pan to the top of stove, pour in the stock and stir well to loosen any sediment. Strain over the meat. Leave to cool.

TO FREEZE: cover the dish, then overwrap in aluminium foil, label and freeze.

TO THAW: to serve hot, bake the meat loaf from frozen in its wrapped foil dish in a hot oven (220°C/425°F or Gas Mark 7) for 20 minutes, then reduce the heat to fairly hot (190°C/375°F or Gas Mark 5) and bake for another 30 to 40 minutes or until the loaf is heated through. Slit open the foil wrapping for the last 15 minutes to allow the top to become crisp. To serve cold, leave in wrappings overnight in the refrigerator or for 5 to 6 hours at room temperature.

TO SERVE: unwrap and transfer to a serving dish. Garnish with sliced tomatoes, gherkins or pickled sweet-sour cucumber, if you like.

Coq au Vin garnished with triangles of fried bread is shown opposite.

Coq au Vin

This is a classic dinner party dish, which can be prepared well in advance for a special occasion and stored in the freezer. Follow with a green salad tossed in French dressing.

Metric/Imperial

1 roasting chicken (1¾–2 kg/3½–4 lb/Aust. size 15 to 20), jointed
50 g/2 oz flour
Salt and freshly ground pepper
50 g/2 oz butter
2×15 ml spoons/2 tablespoons oil
100 g/¼ lb green bacon in the piece, rind removed and diced
½ kg/1 lb button onions, blanched and peeled
2 garlic cloves, peeled and finely chopped
1×15 ml spoon/1 tablespoon tomato purée (paste)
1×5 ml spoon/1 teaspoon sugar
2×15 ml spoons/2 tablespoons brandy
½ bottle full-bodied red wine
1 bouquet garni (parsley, marjoram and rosemary sprigs, 1 bay leaf)
225 g/½ lb button mushrooms, wiped
TO FINISH:
Triangles of bread, fried until crisp and golden in a mixture of oil and butter
Bunch of watercress (optional)

American

1 roasting chicken (3½–4 lb), cut into 6 pieces
½ cup flour
Salt and freshly ground pepper
¼ cup butter
2 tablespoons oil
¼ lb bacon in the piece, rind removed and diced
1 lb baby white onions, blanched and peeled
2 garlic cloves, peeled and finely chopped
1 tablespoon tomato paste
1 teaspoon sugar
2 tablespoons brandy
½ bottle full-bodied red wine
1 bouquet garni (parsley, marjoram and rosemary sprigs, 1 bay leaf)
½ lb small mushrooms, wiped
TO FINISH:
Triangles of bread, fried until crisp and golden in a mixture of oil and butter
Bouquet of watercress (optional)

Coat the pieces of chicken in the flour, well seasoned with salt and pepper. Put the butter and oil in a flameproof casserole and heat gently until the butter has melted. Add the chicken pieces and brown quickly on all sides. Remove the chicken from the casserole and set aside. Add the bacon, onions and garlic and cook gently until golden brown. Sprinkle in any remaining flour, add the tomato purée (paste) and the sugar, and stir well.

Return the chicken pieces to the casserole. Warm the brandy, pour it over the chicken and set it alight. Allow it to flame well for 1 minute, then douse the flames with the wine. Add the bouquet garni, cover the casserole and simmer over a low heat for 30 to 40 minutes or until the chicken is tender. Add the mushrooms and simmer for another 15 minutes. Remove from the heat, taste for seasoning and leave to cool.

TO FREEZE: if you can spare the flameproof casserole, freeze the coq au vin in the casserole. Otherwise, pour into an aluminium foil container and cover. Or pour into a freezer bag-lined preformer (forming container), freeze until solid, then remove preformer (container). Overwrap casserole, container or bag in a freezer bag, seal, label and freeze (return to freezer).

TO THAW: leave in wrappings overnight in the refrigerator, or for at least 4 to 5 hours at room temperature. Unwrap and put into a heavy saucepan or flameproof casserole. Reheat gently on top of the stove, stirring occasionally.

TO SERVE: taste for seasoning and serve very hot with triangles of fried bread, and watercress if liked.

Country Chicken and Mushroom Pie

Traditional meat pies make wholesome and filling meals in next to no time. Make a batch of pies all at once to keep on hand for family suppers.

Metric/Imperial

1 roasting chicken (1½ kg/3 lb/Aust. size 15)
2 onions, peeled
2 carrots, peeled and roughly chopped
6 black peppercorns
1 bouquet garni (parsley and thyme sprigs, 1 bay leaf)
Salt
50 g/2 oz butter
225 g/½ lb mushrooms, cleaned and thinly sliced
25 g/1 oz flour
150 ml/¼ pint dry white wine
4×15 ml spoons/4 tablespoons fresh single cream
1×5 ml spoon/1 teaspoon freshly chopped tarragon, or 1×2.5 ml spoon/½ teaspoon dried tarragon
Freshly ground black pepper
TO FINISH:
225 g/½ lb frozen puff pastry, thawed
1 egg, beaten, for glazing

Coq au Vin
**Country Chicken
and Mushroom
Pie**

American

1 roasting chicken (3 lb)
2 onions, peeled
2 carrots, peeled and roughly chopped
6 black peppercorns
1 bouquet garni (parsley and thyme sprigs, 1 bay leaf)
Salt
¼ cup butter
½ lb mushrooms, cleaned and thinly sliced
¼ cup flour
⅔ cup dry white wine
4 tablespoons light cream
1 teaspoon freshly chopped tarragon or ½ teaspoon dried tarragon
Freshly ground black pepper
TO FINISH: ½ lb frozen puff pastry, or patty shells, thawed
1 egg, beaten, for glazing

Put the chicken in a large saucepan. Quarter one of the onions and add to the pan with the carrots, peppercorns, bouquet garni, and salt to taste. Barely cover the chicken with water and bring to the boil. Lower the heat, cover with a lid and simmer gently for 1 hour or until the chicken is tender. Remove pan from the heat and leave chicken to cool in the cooking liquid. Remove chicken from pan, strain cooking liquid and reserve. Take chicken meat from bones and cut into bite-sized pieces, discarding any skin.

Melt the butter in a frying pan. Chop the remaining onion finely and add to the pan. Fry gently until soft and golden, then add the mushrooms and fry for another 2 minutes. Sprinkle in the flour and cook for 1 minute, stirring, then stir in 150 ml/¼ pint/⅔ cup of the reserved cooking liquid and the white wine. Bring slowly to the boil, stirring, then simmer for 2 minutes until the sauce thickens. Remove from the heat, add the cream and tarragon, and salt and pepper to taste. Fold the chicken pieces into the sauce and transfer to a 1 litre/2 pint/5 cup freezerproof or aluminium foil pie dish. Leave until cold.

TO FREEZE: wrap in aluminium foil or a freezer bag, seal, label and freeze.

TO THAW: leave in wrappings for 12 hours in the refrigerator, then unwrap and put pie funnel in centre of pie dish. Roll out the pastry or patty shells on a floured board, dampen the edge of the pie dish with water and press on a strip of pastry to cover edge. Cover the filling with the remaining pastry, pressing down firmly to seal. Trim the edges with a sharp knife and use trimmings to decorate the top of pie. Brush the pastry with the beaten egg. Bake on a preheated baking sheet in a fairly hot oven (200°C/400°F or Gas Mark 6) for 30 minutes or until the pie is heated through and bubbling, and the pastry is golden brown.

TO SERVE: serve hot, straight from the pie dish, with a green vegetable.

The dish illustrated here is Hare Casserole.

Hare Casserole

This is a mellow, autumnal dish and an unusual main course to give guests at a dinner party. The marinating and slow cooking of the hare gives it a rich aromatic flavour which is complemented by the fresh herbs in the forcemeat (stuffing) balls, already prepared and frozen separately. Serve with baked or creamed potatoes, some quince or crab apple jelly, and a good winter salad. Rabbit may be substituted for the hare in this casserole, in which case the cooking time will be approximately 2 hours.

Metric/Imperial

1 hare, jointed

6 garlic cloves, peeled and cut in halves

6 bay leaves

Thinly pared rind of 1 lemon

150 ml/¼ pint, plus 1×15 ml spoon/1 tablespoon, olive oil

1 bottle full-bodied red wine

75 g/3 oz flour

Salt and freshly ground black pepper

1×5 ml spoon/1 teaspoon ground cloves

25 g/1 oz butter

FOR THE FORCEMEAT (STUFFING) BALLS:
100 g/¼ lb fresh white breadcrumbs

1×15 ml spoon/1 tablespoon freshly chopped parsley

1×5 ml spoon/1 teaspoon freshly chopped marjoram, or 1×2.5 ml spoon/½ teaspoon dried marjoram

1×5 ml spoon/1 teaspoon freshly chopped thyme, or 1×2.5 ml spoon/½ teaspoon dried thyme

Salt and freshly ground pepper

Finely grated rind of 1 lemon

1 egg

2×15 ml spoons/2 tablespoons milk

25 g/1 oz butter, melted

Oil and butter for frying

American

1 hare, cut up

6 garlic cloves, peeled and cut in halves

6 bay leaves

Thinly pared rind of 1 lemon

⅔ cup, plus 1 tablespoon, olive oil

1 bottle full-bodied red wine

¾ cup flour

Salt and freshly ground black pepper

1 teaspoon ground cloves

2 tablespoons butter

FOR THE FORCEMEAT (STUFFING) BALLS:
1½ cups fresh white breadcrumbs

1 tablespoon freshly chopped parsley

1 teaspoon freshly chopped marjoram or ½ teaspoon dried marjoram

1 teaspoon freshly chopped thyme or ½ teaspoon dried thyme

Salt and freshly ground pepper

Finely grated rind of 1 lemon

1 egg

2 tablespoons milk

2 tablespoons melted butter

Oil and butter for frying

Cut all the meat off the bones of the hare. Put into a large bowl with the garlic, bay leaves, lemon rind, 150 ml/¼ pint/⅔ cup olive oil and the red wine. Leave to marinate for 8 to 12 hours, turning the meat from time to time.

The following day, mix the flour with salt and pepper to taste, and the cloves. Drain the pieces of meat, reserving the marinade, and roll them in the seasoned flour. Put the butter and the remaining oil in a flameproof casserole and heat gently until the butter has melted. Add the meat and brown each piece quickly on all sides. Lift out the meat with a slotted spoon and set aside. Sprinkle in any remaining seasoned flour, cook for 1 minute, then strain the marinade and stir it in slowly. When the sauce is smooth, raise the heat and bring to the boil. Return the pieces of meat to the

casserole, cover and transfer to a cool oven (150°C/300°F or Gas Mark 2) to cook for 5 to 6 hours, by which time there should be a rich amalgam of tender meat and thick sauce. Remove from the heat, taste for seasoning and leave to cool.

TO FREEZE: if you can spare the flameproof casserole, freeze the hare and sauce in the casserole. Otherwise, pour into an aluminium foil container and cover. Or pour into a freezer bag-lined preformer (forming container), freeze until solid, then remove preformer (container). Overwrap casserole, container or bag in a freezer bag, seal, label and freeze (return to freezer).

TO THAW: leave in wrappings overnight in the refrigerator, or for 4 to 5 hours at room temperature. Unwrap and put into a heavy saucepan or flameproof casserole. Reheat gently for approximately 1 hour on top of the stove, stirring occasionally. If you

wish to reheat the dish straight from frozen, add 2×15 ml spoons/2 tablespoons water and reheat very gently, stirring occasionally.

TO SERVE: taste for seasoning and serve straight from the casserole. Add sizzling hot forcemeat (stuffing) balls at the last moment.

TO MAKE THE FORCEMEAT (STUFFING) BALLS: mix the breadcrumbs with the parsley, marjoram, thyme, salt and pepper to taste, and lemon rind. Beat the egg lightly with the milk and the melted butter and stir into the breadcrumbs. Roll the mixture into walnut-sized balls.

TO FREEZE: open (flash) freeze until solid, then put in a freezer bag. Seal, label and return to freezer.

TO THAW: unwrap and fry the balls from frozen in a mixture of hot oil and butter until they are crisp and golden brown.

TO SERVE: drop the balls into the casserole just before serving.

Chicken with Tarragon

The aromatic, slightly bitter taste of the tarragon gives this dish its characteristic flavour. Make it in spring and early summer when fresh tarragon is available; it will retain its flavour in the freezer. If you have access to plenty of fresh tarragon, freeze some so that you can make the dish at any time of the year. Do not try to use dried tarragon, which does not have nearly the same savour. To prepare, freeze and thaw tarragon, see page 117.

Metric/Imperial
1 roasting chicken (1¾–2 kg/3½–4 lb/ Aust. size 15 to 20), trussed
6 sprigs fresh tarragon
75 g/3 oz butter
2×15 ml spoons/2 tablespoons oil
1 onion, peeled and finely chopped
1 carrot, peeled and finely chopped
Salt and freshly ground pepper
Approx. 300 ml/½ pint chicken stock
25 g/1 oz flour
2×15 ml spoons/2 tablespoons dry sherry

American
1 roasting chicken (3½–4 lb), trussed
6 sprigs fresh tarragon
⅓ cup butter
2 tablespoons oil
1 onion, peeled and finely chopped
1 carrot, peeled and finely chopped
Salt and freshly ground pepper
Approx. 1¼ cups chicken stock
¼ cup flour
2 tablespoons dry sherry

Stuff the chicken with three sprigs of the tarragon and 25 g/1 oz/2 tablespoons of the butter. Put half the remaining butter and the oil in a flameproof casserole, just large enough to hold the chicken, and heat gently until the butter has melted. Add the chicken and brown gently on all sides. Remove the chicken and set aside. Add the onion and carrot to the casserole and cook gently until soft. Return the chicken to the casserole and season to taste. Cover tightly and transfer to a moderate oven (180°C/350°F or Gas Mark 4) to cook for 1 to 1½ hours, or until the chicken is tender, basting from time to time.

Remove from the oven, cut the chicken into serving pieces and set aside. Strain the cooking liquid into a measuring jug and make up to 600 ml/1 pint/2½ cups with chicken stock.

Melt the remaining 25 g/1 oz/2 tablespoons butter in the casserole. Sprinkle in the flour and cook over a gentle heat for 2 minutes, without allowing to brown, stirring well slowly. Stir in the reserved liquid, bring to the boil, then season to taste and add the sherry. Chop the leaves of the remaining tarragon sprigs finely, then add to the pan. Remove from the heat and allow to cool.

TO FREEZE: if you can spare the flameproof casserole, freeze the chicken and sauce in the casserole. Otherwise, place the chicken in a large aluminium foil container, pour over the sauce and cover with a lid. Or put into a freezer bag-lined preformer (forming container), freeze until solid, then remove preformer (container). Overwrap casserole, container or bag in a freezer bag as the smell of the tarragon can be very pervasive. Seal, label and freeze (return to freezer).

TO THAW: leave in wrappings overnight in the refrigerator, or for 5 to 6 hours at room temperature. Unwrap and put into a heavy saucepan or flameproof casserole. Reheat gently, turning the chicken occasionally.

TO SERVE: taste for seasoning and serve hot with new potatoes. Follow with a green salad tossed in French dressing.

Pigeons with Grapes are illustrated on the left of the photograph with Pheasant in Cream and Brandy Sauce on the right. The pheasants have been left whole and are accompanied by the sauce.

Pigeons with Grapes

Wood pigeons and grapes become ready for the table at about the same time, and in France during the vendange *these and other game birds are often cooked with grapes. The strong flavour of pigeons mingles beautifully with the sweet but slightly astringent taste of the fruit, and the two textures complement each other particularly well.*

Metric/Imperial
50 g/2 oz butter
2 large onions, peeled and finely chopped
4 pigeons, trussed
2×15 ml spoons/2 tablespoons 'marc' or brandy
½ kg/1 lb seedless grapes, peeled
Salt and freshly ground pepper
Few whole grapes, to garnish

American
¼ cup butter
2 large onions, peeled and finely chopped
4 pigeons, trussed
2 tablespoons brandy
1 lb seedless grapes, peeled
Salt and freshly ground pepper
Few whole grapes, to garnish

Melt the butter in a flameproof casserole just large enough to hold the pigeons comfortably side by side. Add the onions and cook gently until soft. Increase the heat, add the pigeons and brown them on all sides. Warm the 'marc' or brandy, pour it over the pigeons and set alight. When the flames have died down, remove the pigeons. Add the grapes, stir well, then replace the pigeons, breast down to keep them moist, on the bed of onion and grapes. Cover with a lid and simmer over a low heat for 1½ to 2½ hours until the pigeons are tender. (The time taken can vary tremendously with the age and toughness of the birds.) Remove from the heat, season to taste and leave until completely cold.

TO FREEZE: if you can spare the flameproof casserole, freeze the pigeons and grapes in the casserole. Otherwise, pour into an aluminium foil or rigid container, cover, label and freeze. Or pour into a freezer bag-lined preformer (forming container), freeze until solid, then remove preformer (container). Overwrap casserole, container or bag in a freezer bag, seal, label and freeze (return to freezer).

TO THAW: leave in wrappings overnight in the refrigerator, or for 5 to 6 hours at room temperature. Unwrap, transfer to a heavy saucepan or flameproof casserole and reheat gently on top of the stove.
TO SERVE: taste for seasoning, and serve hot.

Pheasant in Cream and Brandy Sauce

This is the most unashamedly luxurious dish, fit for the grandest of dinner parties.

Metric/Imperial
2 pheasants, plucked, drawn and trussed
25 g/1 oz butter
1×15 ml spoon/1 tablespoon oil
2×15 ml spoons/2 tablespoons brandy
2 onions, peeled and finely chopped
2 carrots, peeled and finely chopped
1 bay leaf
1 sprig fresh thyme
300 ml/½ pint fresh double cream
Salt and freshly ground pepper
Bunch of watercress, to finish

American
2 pheasants, plucked, drawn and trussed
2 tablespoons butter
1 tablespoon oil
2 tablespoons brandy
2 onions, peeled and finely chopped
2 carrots, peeled and finely chopped
1 bay leaf
1 sprig fresh thyme
1¼ cups heavy cream
Salt and freshly ground pepper
Bouquet of watercress, to finish

Wipe the pheasants inside and out with kitchen paper towels. Put the butter and oil in a flameproof casserole and heat gently until the butter has melted. Brown the pheasants quickly on all sides. Warm the brandy, pour it over the pheasants and set alight. When the flames have died down, add the onions, carrots, bay leaf and thyme, cover with a lid and cook over a low heat for approximately 1 hour, or until the pheasants are tender, when pierced with a skewer. Remove the bay leaf, stir in the cream, mix well and bring briefly to the boil. Remove from the heat, taste for seasoning. If serving immediately, arrange the whole birds

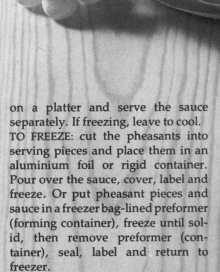

on a platter and serve the sauce separately. If freezing, leave to cool.
TO FREEZE: cut the pheasants into serving pieces and place them in an aluminium foil or rigid container. Pour over the sauce, cover, label and freeze. Or put pheasant pieces and sauce in a freezer bag-lined preformer (forming container), freeze until solid, then remove preformer (container), seal, label and return to freezer.
TO THAW: leave in wrappings overnight in the refrigerator, or for 4 to 5 hours at room temperature. Unwrap, transfer to a heavy saucepan or flameproof casserole and reheat gently on top of the stove, stirring occasionally.
TO SERVE: taste for seasoning and transfer to a warmed serving platter. Garnish with watercress and serve with triangular-shaped croûtes or game (potato) chips, and salad.

Liver à la Crème

Cooked in sour(ed) cream, liver does not lose its delicate flavour or moist texture.

Metric/Imperial
50 g/2 oz butter
1×15 ml spoon/1 tablespoon oil
¾–1 kg/1½–2 lb calf's or pig's liver, cut into thin strips
½ kg/1 lb onions, peeled and finely chopped
300 ml/½ pint cultured soured cream
Finely grated rind of 1 lemon
2×15 ml spoons/2 tablespoons freshly chopped parsley
Salt and freshly ground pepper

Kidney and Mushroom Casserole

Kidneys make a simple and economical dish, which is nonetheless delicious enough to serve at a dinner party. Serve with rice, followed by a salad.

Liver à la Crème (American)

American
¼ cup butter
1 tablespoon oil
1½–2 lb calf's or pig's liver, cut into thin strips
1 lb onions, peeled and finely chopped
1¼ cups sour cream
Finely grated rind of 1 lemon
2 tablespoons freshly chopped parsley
Salt and freshly ground pepper

Put the butter and oil in a deep frying pan or flameproof casserole and heat gently until the butter has melted. Add the liver and brown quickly on all sides. Remove with a slotted spoon and set aside. Add the onions to the pan and cook gently until soft. Return the liver to the pan, together with the juice that will have run from it, then stir in the sour(ed) cream, lemon rind and parsley. Mix well together and season to taste. Remove from the heat immediately and leave to cool.

TO FREEZE: pour into an aluminium foil or rigid container, cover, label and freeze. Or pour into a freezer bag-lined preformer (forming container), freeze until solid, then remove pre-former (container), seal, label and return to freeze.

TO THAW: leave in wrappings to thaw partially for at least 2 hours at room temperature, then unwrap, put into a heavy saucepan and reheat gently, turning occasionally. Add 1×15 ml spoon/1 tablespoon sour(ed) cream or yogurt if necessary.

TO SERVE: taste for seasoning and serve hot, with potatoes or rice.

Kidney and Mushroom Casserole

Metric/Imperial
¾–1 kg/1½–2 lb pig's, lamb's or calf's kidneys, skin and cores removed
75 g/3 oz butter
1×15 ml spoon/1 tablespoon oil
½ kg/1 lb button onions, blanched and peeled, or large onions, peeled and quartered
½ kg/1 lb button mushrooms, cleaned
4×15 ml spoons/4 tablespoons port or Madeira
150 ml/¼ pint cultured soured cream
Salt and freshly ground pepper
1×15 ml spoon/1 tablespoon freshly chopped parsley, to finish

American
1½–2 lb lamb's or veal kidneys, skin and cores removed
⅓ cup butter
1 tablespoon oil
1 lb baby white onions, blanched and peeled, or large onions, peeled and quartered
1 lb small mushrooms, cleaned
4 tablespoons port or Madeira
⅔ cup sour cream
Salt and freshly ground pepper
1 tablespoon freshly chopped parsley, to finish

Cut the kidneys into thick slices. Put the butter and oil in a flameproof casserole and, when the butter has melted, add the kidneys. Cook gently until they have coloured on all sides, stirring constantly. Remove from the casserole with a slotted spoon and set aside. Add the onions to the casserole and brown quickly, then remove with a slotted spoon and set aside also. Add the mushrooms to the casserole and cook until soft, then remove with a slotted spoon and set aside. Pour the port or Madeira into the casserole, increase the heat and let the liquid bubble for 1 minute. Return the kidneys, onions and mushrooms to the casserole, cover with a lid and simmer for approximately 15 minutes or until the kidneys are tender. Stir in the sour(ed) cream, remove from the heat, taste for seasoning and leave to cool.

TO FREEZE: pour into an aluminium foil or rigid container, cover, label and freeze. Or pour into a freezer bag-lined preformer (forming container), freeze until solid, then remove pre-former (container), seal, label and return to freezer.

TO THAW: leave in wrappings overnight in the refrigerator, or for 4 to 5 hours at room temperature, then unwrap and transfer to a heavy saucepan or flameproof casserole. Add a little water, cover with a lid and reheat gently, stirring occasionally. Be careful not to overcook the kidneys or they will toughen.

TO SERVE: taste for seasoning, then arrange on a bed of freshly boiled rice. Sprinkle with parsley and serve very hot. A crisp green salad can be served with the kidneys or as a separate course afterwards.

Pigeons with Grapes

Pheasant in Cream and Brandy Sauce

Liver à la Crème

Kidney and Mushroom Casserole

Spaghetti alla Bolognese

The photograph on this page shows Spaghetti alla Bolognese. Canelloni is illustrated opposite.

Bolognese sauce keeps very well in the freezer and is worth making in large quantities, especially when home-grown tomatoes are plentiful. It can be used in a number of dishes — as a stuffing for cannelloni, in lasagne and moussaka, or with spaghetti as in this recipe.

Metric/Imperial

2×15 ml spoons/2 tablespoons olive oil

1 medium-sized onion, peeled and finely chopped

1 garlic clove, peeled and crushed

100 g/¼ lb unsmoked bacon, rinds removed and chopped

2 celery stalks, scrubbed and finely chopped

1 carrot, peeled and grated

1 green or red pepper (capsicum), cored, seeded and chopped

½ kg/1 lb lean minced beef

2×15 ml spoons/2 tablespoons tomato purée (paste)

350 g/¾ lb tomatoes, skinned and chopped

300 ml/½ pint beef stock and 150 ml/¼ pint dry red or white wine, or 450 ml/¾ pint beef stock

1×5 ml spoon/1 teaspoon freshly chopped oregano, or 1×2.5 ml spoon/½ teaspoon dried oregano

1×5 ml spoon/1 teaspoon freshly chopped basil, or 1×2.5 ml spoon/½ teaspoon dried basil

½ bay leaf, crushed

1×5 ml spoon/1 teaspoon brown sugar

Salt and freshly ground black pepper

TO FINISH:
350 g/¾ lb spaghetti

50 g/2 oz freshly grated Parmesan cheese

American

2 tablespoons olive oil

1 medium-sized onion, peeled and finely chopped

1 garlic clove, peeled and crushed

¼ lb unsalted pork fat back, chopped

2 celery stalks, scrubbed and finely chopped

1 carrot, peeled and grated

1 green or red pepper, cored, seeded and chopped

1 lb lean ground beef

2 tablespoons tomato paste

¾ lb tomatoes, skinned and chopped

1¼ cups beef stock and ⅔ cup dry red or white wine, or 2 cups beef stock

1 teaspoon freshly chopped oregano or ½ teaspoon dried oregano

1 teaspoon freshly chopped basil, or ½ teaspoon dried basil

½ bay leaf, crushed

1 teaspoon brown sugar

Salt and freshly ground black pepper

TO FINISH:
¾ lb spaghetti

½ cup freshly grated Parmesan cheese

Heat the oil in a saucepan, add the onion, garlic, bacon or pork fat, celery, carrot and pepper (capsicum). Fry gently for 5 minutes or until soft. Add the beef and cook gently until browned, breaking the meat up and stirring with a wooden spoon. Add the remaining ingredients, with salt and pepper to taste. Bring to the boil, stirring, then lower the heat, cover with a lid and simmer gently for 40 to 45 minutes, stirring occasionally. Remove from the heat, taste for seasoning and leave to cool.

TO FREEZE: pour into a freezer bag-lined preformer (forming container) and freeze until solid. Remove from preformer (container), overwrap in a freezer bag, seal, label and return to freezer.

TO THAW: unwrap frozen sauce and put into a heavy saucepan with

2 × 15 ml spoons/2 tablespoons water. Reheat gently on top of the stove, stirring occasionally.

TO SERVE: cook the spaghetti in boiling salted water for 12 to 15 minutes or until *al dente* (tender but firm to the bite). Drain well and arrange in a circle on a hot serving platter. Taste the Bolognese sauce for seasoning, then spoon into the centre of spaghetti and serve immediately, with Parmesan cheese handed separately.

Cannelloni

Cannelloni can be made very quickly using Bolognese sauce from the freezer, and it is useful both as a first or main course. If serving as a main course, allow two cannelloni per person with salads, fresh French bread and a bottle of red Italian wine. Allow one cannelloni per person if serving as a first course.

Metric/Imperial
Salt
1×15 ml spoon/1 tablespoon vegetable oil
8 sheets of wide lasagne
½ quantity of Bolognese sauce (see opposite)
FOR THE CHEESE SAUCE: 25 g/1 oz butter
25 g/1 oz flour
300 ml/½ pint hot milk
1×1.25 ml spoon/¼ teaspoon ground mace
Freshly ground black pepper
50 g/2 oz Cheddar cheese, grated
TO FINISH: 2×15 ml spoons/2 tablespoons grated Parmesan cheese
1×15 ml spoon/1 tablespoon butter, cut into small pieces

American
Salt
1 tablespoon vegetable oil
8 pieces of wide lasagne
½ quantity of Bolognese sauce (see opposite)
FOR THE CHEESE SAUCE: 2 tablespoons butter
¼ cup flour
1¼ cups hot milk
¼ teaspoon ground mace
Freshly ground black pepper
½ cup grated Cheddar cheese
TO FINISH: 2 tablespoons grated Parmesan cheese
1 tablespoon butter, cut into small pieces

Bring a large pan of salted water to the boil and stir in the vegetable oil. Cook half the lasagne for 8 to 10 minutes or until *al dente* (tender but firm to the bite). Lift out and pat dry with a clean tea (dish) towel or kitchen paper towels. Repeat this process with the remaining lasagne.

Put a spoonful of Bolognese sauce on each sheet (piece) of lasagne and roll up. Grease a freezerproof baking dish or foil dish and pack the cannelloni into it tightly.

TO PREPARE THE SAUCE: melt the butter in a saucepan, stir in the flour and cook for 1 to 2 minutes, stirring constantly. Remove from the heat and gradually add the milk, stirring vigorously. When all the milk is incorporated, return to the heat and bring to the boil, stirring constantly. Lower the heat, add the mace, salt and pepper to taste and the grated cheese. Simmer gently for a few minutes until the sauce is thick, stirring constantly. Coat the cannelloni with the sauce, then leave to cool.

TO FREEZE: wrap in a freezer bag or aluminium foil, overwrap in a freezer bag, seal, label and freeze.

TO THAW: unwrap and bake from frozen in a fairly hot oven (200°C/400°F or Gas Mark 6) for approximately 1 hour or until heated through and bubbling.

TO SERVE: sprinkle the cannelloni with the Parmesan cheese, dot with butter and put under a preheated hot grill (broiler) for a few minutes or until the top is golden brown. Serve immediately.

Spaghetti alla Bolognese Cannelloni

Macaroni and Cheese Casserole is on the left of the photograph above, with Pizza on the right. Tarte aux Oignons is illustrated opposite.

Macaroni and Cheese Casserole

A well-made macaroni and cheese casserole makes a delicious and filling meal. It can be made in advance and kept in the freezer ready for a family meal and even packaged in individual portions. Use a fairly strong cheese for the best flavour, and do not overcook the macaroni.

Metric/Imperial

50 g/2 oz butter or margarine
50 g/2 oz flour
600 ml/1 pint milk
175 g/6 oz Cheddar or other hard cheese, grated
Salt and freshly ground pepper
100 g/¼ lb cut macaroni
25 g/1 oz dried breadcrumbs
15 g/½ oz butter, cut into small pieces, to finish

American

¼ cup butter or margarine
½ cup flour
2½ cups milk
1½ cups grated Cheddar or other hard cheese
Salt and freshly ground pepper
¼ lb elbow macaroni
¼ cup dried breadcrumbs
1 tablespoon butter, cut into small pieces, to finish

Melt the butter or margarine in a saucepan, add the flour and cook over a very low heat for a few minutes until the mixture turns quite liquid, stirring constantly. Add the milk very slowly, a cupful at a time, and stir until smooth before adding any more. Bring to the boil, stirring, then lower the heat and simmer until the sauce thickens. Add all but 2×15 ml spoons/2 tablespoons of the cheese. Stir until it has melted, then remove from the heat, season to taste and leave to cool. Cook the macaroni according to package directions in plenty of boiling salted water until just tender. Drain, rinse in cold water and drain again.

Butter a freezerproof baking dish or foil dish. Put in a layer of the macaroni and pour over a thick layer of sauce. Repeat and finish with a layer of the sauce. Mix the remaining cheese with the breadcrumbs and sprinkle on top.

TO FREEZE: open (flash) freeze until solid, then wrap the dish well in cling film and overwrap in aluminium foil or a freezer bag. Seal, label, and return to freezer.

TO THAW: unwrap, dot with the butter, then reheat from frozen in a fairly hot oven (200°C/400°F or Gas Mark 6) for 1 hour or until heated through and bubbling.

TO SERVE: serve hot, straight from the cooking dish, accompanied by a green salad.

Pizza

Pizza is an invaluable standby to keep in the freezer. It can be served at any time and made in any size —large enough for a family meal or summer lunch, or small enough for a quick meal or snack for one.

The topping lends itself to infinite variation, but tomatoes and cheese are essential, and the ingredients given below make the classic Neapolitan pizza. Make a few when you are making bread (see page 208). The quantities given below make three 23 cm/9 inch pizzas.

Metric/Imperial

½ kg/1 lb white bread dough (approx. ⅕ quantity given on p.208)
½ kg/1 lb tomatoes, thinly sliced
2×50 g/1¾ oz tins anchovy fillets, drained
Pinch of dried marjoram
Pinch of dried basil
100 g/¼ lb mozzarella, or other soft cheese, thinly sliced
Freshly ground black pepper
50 g/2 oz black olives, halved and stoned
Olive oil for sprinkling

American

1 lb white bread dough (approx. ⅕ quantity given on p.208)
1 lb tomatoes, thinly sliced
2×1¾ oz cans flat anchovies, drained

Pinch of dried marjoram

Pinch of dried basil

¼ lb mozzarella, or other soft cheese, thinly sliced

Freshly ground black pepper

½ cup black olives, halved and pitted

Olive oil for sprinkling

Spread the dough as thinly as possible on well-oiled baking sheets, pizza pans, or flat foil dishes. Cover completely with the tomato slices. Make a lattice of anchovies on top, then sprinkle on the marjoram and basil. Arrange the cheese slices over the pizza, sprinkle with pepper and top with olives.

TO FREEZE: open (flash) freeze until solid, then remove from baking sheets, pans or dishes and wrap pizzas individually in cling film. Overwrap in aluminium foil or freezer bag or rigid container, seal or cover, label and return to freezer.

TO THAW: unwrap and return pizzas to baking sheets, pans or dishes. Bake from frozen in a very hot oven (230°C/450°F or Gas Mark 8) for 10 minutes. Remove from oven, sprinkle liberally with olive oil and return to the oven for another 15 to 20 minutes, depending on size.

TO SERVE: cut into wedges and serve sizzling hot.

American
FOR THE PASTRY:
1 cup flour
Pinch of salt
¼ cup butter, cut into small pieces
1 egg yolk
Approx. 1 tablespoon ice-cold water
FOR THE FILLING:
2 tablespoons olive or corn oil
1 tablespoon butter
1 lb onions, peeled and thinly sliced
1 tablespoon flour
1 whole egg, beaten
1 egg yolk, beaten
⅔ cup light cream
Salt and freshly ground black pepper

Sift the flour and salt into a mixing bowl. Add the butter and rub into the flour with the fingers until the mixture resembles fine breadcrumbs. Using a palette knife, stir in the egg yolk and enough water to draw the mixture together. Transfer to a lightly floured board and knead the dough briefly until smooth. Wrap in aluminium foil and chill in the refrigerator for at least 30 minutes.

Roll out the chilled dough on a floured board to a circle large enough to line an 18 cm/7 inch flan ring, or pie pan with removable base. Chill in the refrigerator for another 15 minutes.

Meanwhile, prepare the filling: heat the oil and butter in a frying pan and, when foaming, add the onions and fry very gently for 15 minutes or until soft and golden. Sprinkle over the flour and cook for another 5 minutes. Transfer to a bowl and stir in the egg, egg yolk and cream. Season with salt and plenty of freshly ground black pepper. Pour prepared filling into chilled dough and bake in a fairly hot oven (200°C/400°F or Gas Mark 6) for 20 to 25 minutes or until filling is just set and golden brown. Remove from oven and leave to cool.

TO FREEZE: open (flash) freeze until solid, then remove flan ring or pie pan, wrap tart in cling film, then overwrap in a freezer bag, seal, label and freeze.

TO THAW: unwrap and reheat tart from frozen in a moderate oven (180°C/350°F or Gas Mark 4) for 30 to 40 minutes or until heated through. If tart is to be served cold, leave to thaw for approximately 4 hours at room temperature.

TO SERVE: leave hot tart to rest for approximately 10 minutes before serving. Cut into wedges to serve.

Tarte aux Oignons

Onion tart makes a really delicious light main course for a lunch or supper meal, served with a selection of salads and French bread. The secret of making a good quiche lies in not overbaking — the filling should be just set, though still creamy.

Metric/Imperial
FOR THE PASTRY:
100 g/¼ lb flour
Pinch of salt
50 g/2 oz butter, cut into small pieces
1 egg yolk
Approx. 1×15 ml spoon/1 tablespoon ice-cold water
FOR THE FILLING:
2×15 ml spoons/2 tablespoons olive or corn oil
1×15 ml spoon/1 tablespoon butter
½ kg/1 lb onions, peeled and thinly sliced
1×15 ml spoon/1 tablespoon flour
1 whole egg, beaten
1 egg yolk, beaten
150 ml/¼ pint fresh single cream
Salt and freshly ground black pepper

Fish Pie

This is an excellent luncheon or supper dish, which needs no accompaniment other than a green salad. While it is best made with fresh fish, it can be made equally well with frozen fish.

Metric/Imperial	American
1 kg/2 lb filleted white fish (such as cod, haddock or hake)	2 lb boneless white fish (such as cod, haddock or hake)
400 ml/¾ pint milk	2 cups milk
400 ml/¾ pint water	2 cups water
1 onion, peeled and cut in half	1 onion, peeled and cut in half
1 bay leaf	1 bay leaf
1 blade of mace or pinch of ground mace	1 blade of mace or pinch of ground mace
50 g/2 oz butter	¼ cup butter
75 g/3 oz flour	¾ cup flour
300 ml/½ pint fish stock, made from fish trimmings	1¼ cups fish stock, made from fish trimmings
1 medium-sized tin condensed mushroom soup	1×10½ oz can condensed mushroom soup
Salt and freshly ground pepper	Salt and freshly ground pepper
100 g/¼ lb fresh prawns, shelled	¼ lb fresh shrimp, shelled
2×15 ml spoons/2 tablespoons freshly chopped parsley	2 tablespoons freshly chopped parsley
½–¾ kg/1–1½ lb mashed potatoes	1–1½ lb mashed potatoes
50 g/2 oz dried breadcrumbs	½ cup dried breadcrumbs
25 g/1 oz butter, to finish	2 tablespoons butter, to finish

Put the fish in a wide saucepan, cover with the milk and water and add the onion, bay leaf and blade or pinch of mace. Bring slowly to the boil,

remove from the heat, cover with a lid and leave to cool. The fish will be cooked by the time it has cooled. Lift out the fish, flake it and remove any remaining bones. Strain the cooking liquid and reserve.

Melt the butter in a clean saucepan, add the flour and cook for 2 minutes without allowing to brown, stirring constantly. Slowly stir in the strained cooking liquid and the fish stock. Add the mushroom soup, stir well until blended and season to taste. Bring to the boil, stirring continuously. Gently stir in the prawns (shrimp), flaked fish and the parsley. Pour into a 1½ litre/3 pint/2 quart freezer-proof or aluminium foil dish, cover with the mashed potatoes and sprinkle with the breadcrumbs. Leave to cool.

TO FREEZE: wrap the dish in cling film, then overwrap in aluminium foil or a freezer bag. Seal, label and freeze.

TO THAW: unwrap, dot with the butter and bake from frozen in a hot oven (220°C/425°F or Gas Mark 7) for 20 minutes, then reduce the heat to moderate (180°C/350°F or Gas Mark 4) and bake for another 20 to 30 minutes or until the fish is hot when tested with a skewer.

TO SERVE: serve very hot, straight from the cooking dish.

Koulibiac

This is an excellent way of keeping salmon in the freezer, ready to serve at very little notice. It is also a good recipe for using leftovers from a whole salmon, as it uses relatively little fish for each serving. A large koulibiac (double the quantities given here) makes an unusual dish for a buffet supper, and for a really splendid centrepiece, make it in the shape of a large fish (see below).

Metric/Imperial
50 g/2 oz butter
1 large onion, peeled and finely chopped
225 g/½ lb mushrooms, cleaned and finely chopped
225 g/½ lb long-grain white rice, boiled and drained
50 g/2 oz flaked almonds, lightly toasted
½ kg/1 lb cooked salmon, flaked
1×5 ml spoon/1 teaspoon finely chopped preserved ginger (optional)
1×15 ml spoon/1 tablespoon chopped raisins (optional)
1×15 ml spoon/1 tablespoon lemon juice
Salt and freshly ground pepper
350 g/¾ lb frozen puff pastry, thawed
1 egg yolk, lightly beaten with a little water, to glaze
FOR THE SAUCE:
300 ml/½ pint fresh single cream
150 ml/¼ pint fish or chicken stock
2 shallots, peeled and finely chopped
1×15 ml spoon/1 tablespoon freshly chopped mixed herbs (parsley, chives, fennel, tarragon)
1×5 ml spoon/1 teaspoon prepared French mustard
Squeeze of lemon juice
Salt and freshly ground pepper

American
¼ cup butter
1 large onion, peeled and finely chopped
½ lb mushrooms, cleaned and finely chopped
1¼ cups long-grain white rice, boiled and drained
¼ cup shredded almonds, lightly toasted
1 lb cooked salmon, flaked
1 teaspoon finely chopped candied ginger (optional)
1 tablespoon chopped raisins (optional)
1 tablespoon lemon juice
Salt and freshly ground pepper
¾ lb frozen puff pastry, thawed
1 egg yolk, lightly beaten with a little water, to glaze
FOR THE SAUCE:
1¼ cups light cream
⅔ cup fish or chicken stock
2 shallots, peeled and finely chopped
1 tablespoon freshly chopped mixed herbs (parsley, chives, fennel, tarragon)
1 teaspoon prepared French mustard
Squeeze of lemon juice
Salt and freshly ground pepper

Melt the butter in a saucepan. Add the onion and cook until soft, then add the mushrooms and cook until soft. Increase the heat briefly to evaporate the liquid. Put into a mixing bowl with the rice, almonds, salmon, the ginger and raisins (if using) and the lemon juice. Mix well together and season to taste. Divide the pastry into two portions, one slightly smaller than the other. Roll the smaller piece out on a floured board and, if you like, cut it into the shape of a fish. Place on a foil-covered baking sheet. Pile the salmon mixture on top, leaving a 2.5 cm/1 inch margin all round. Roll out the second piece of pastry to a slightly larger rectangle and, if you are making a fish-shaped koulibiac, cut this into a rather larger fish than the first. Place carefully over the top of the filling, fold over and seal the edges well, moistening with a little water. Make a few incisions in the top to form air vents, and decorate with pastry to use up any scraps. Brush all over with the egg glaze.

TO FREEZE: open (flash) freeze until solid, then remove from the baking sheet, wrap well in cling film, overwrap in aluminium foil, seal, label and return to freezer.

TO THAW: unwrap the koulibiac, place on a greased baking sheet and bake from frozen in a hot oven (220°C/425°F or Gas Mark 7) for 30 minutes, then reduce the heat to moderate (180°C/350°F or Gas Mark 4) and bake for another 40 to 50 minutes or until the pastry is golden brown, and the filling is hot when tested by a skewer inserted into an air vent.

TO SERVE: make the sauce by boiling the cream and stock in a saucepan for 5 minutes until thick, then stir in the remaining ingredients, and season to taste. Transfer the koulibiac to a warmed serving platter and serve hot. Pour the sauce into a sauce boat and serve separately.

Fish Pie with its topping of mashed potatoes and breadcrumbs is illustrated to the left of Koulibiac and its accompanying sauce.

Petits Pois Française
are illustrated on this
page. Peas in Sauce
are shown in the lower
photograph opposite,
with Swiss-style
Potato Cake in the top
right-hand corner.

Ways with Vegetables

Petits Pois Française

*The addition of mint, lettuce and onions
makes frozen peas more interesting.*

Metric/Imperial

2×15 ml spoons/2 tablespoons butter
1 lettuce heart, washed and shredded
Approx. 12 small spring onions, topped and tailed
1×5 ml spoon/1 teaspoon sugar
1×15 ml spoon/1 tablespoon freshly chopped mint
Salt and freshly ground black pepper
½ kg/1 lb frozen petits pois

American

2 tablespoons butter
1 Romaine lettuce heart, washed and shredded
Approx. 12 small scallions, trimmed
1 teaspoon sugar
1 tablespoon freshly chopped mint
Salt and freshly ground black pepper
1×20 oz package frozen peas

Melt the butter in a pan and add the lettuce and spring onions (scallions) with the sugar, mint and salt and pepper to taste. Simmer gently for 10 minutes. Add the petits pois (peas), cover with a lid and simmer gently for 3 to 5 minutes or until the peas are tender. Remove from the heat, taste for seasoning and transfer to a warmed serving dish. Serve immediately.

Peas in Sauce

This is a good way to turn commercially frozen peas into a dish worth serving on its own, as the French sometimes do, after the main course.

Metric/Imperial

150 ml/¼ pint water
50 g/2 oz butter
50 g/2 oz ham or bacon (rinds and bone removed), very finely chopped
½ kg./1 lb frozen peas or petits pois
Salt and freshly ground pepper
1×5 ml spoon/1 teaspoon sugar
Pinch of grated nutmeg
15 g/½ oz flour
150 ml/¼ pint milk or fresh single cream
Freshly chopped parsley, to finish

American

⅔ cup water
¼ cup butter
2 oz ham or Canadian bacon, very finely chopped
2×10 oz packages frozen peas or petits pois
Salt and freshly ground pepper
1 teaspoon sugar
Pinch of grated nutmeg
2 tablespoons flour
⅔ cup milk or light cream
Freshly chopped parsley, to finish

Put the water and butter in a saucepan and bring to the boil. Add the ham or bacon and the peas, cover with a lid and cook for 10 minutes or until just tender. Add salt and pepper to taste, the sugar and nutmeg. Put the flour into a cup, add a little of the cooking liquid and stir until quite smooth. Slowly stir this into the pan, then add the milk or cream and bring to the boil, stirring constantly. Cook until the sauce is smooth. Lower the heat and cook for 2 minutes. Taste for seasoning, sprinkle in the parsley and serve hot.

Swiss-style Potato Cake

This is an unusual way to serve potatoes. It makes a very quick meal with grilled (broiled) or fried sausages or chops because it can be served 30 minutes after coming out of the freezer.

Metric/Imperial
1 kg/2 lb potatoes in their jackets, boiled for 10 minutes, drained, cooled and peeled
50 g/2 oz Gruyère cheese, grated
75 g/3 oz butter
1 medium-sized onion, peeled and finely chopped
Salt and freshly ground black pepper
Few parsley sprigs, to finish (optional)

American
2 lb potatoes in their skins, boiled for 10 minutes, drained, cooled and peeled
½ cup grated Gruyère cheese
⅓ cup butter
1 medium-sized onion, peeled and finely chopped
Salt and freshly ground black pepper
Few parsley sprigs, to finish (optional)

Petits Pois Française
Peas in Sauce
Swiss-style Potato Cake

Grate the potatoes into a mixing bowl, using the coarse side of the grater. Stir in the grated cheese, then set aside. Melt 1 tablespoon of the butter in a frying pan and, when foaming, add the onion. Fry gently until soft and golden, then add the onion to the potato and cheese mixture. Add salt and pepper to taste. Clean the frying pan and line it with a piece of aluminium foil. Shape potato mixture into a circle in the foil.
TO FREEZE: fold over foil and freeze mixture until solid. Lift out foil, overwrap in a freezer bag, seal, label and return to freezer.
TO THAW: melt the remaining butter in the frying pan and, when foaming, put in the unwrapped frozen potato cake. Cook gently for 15 minutes on each side until the cake is golden brown and cooked through. Turn once only during cooking.
TO SERVE: invert a serving platter over the potato cake and turn out.

Potato and Cheese Casserole is illustrated with Vichy Carrots. Austrian Red Cabbage is shown opposite.

Potato and Cheese Casserole

This makes a substantial family meal and needs only a salad or green vegetable as an accompaniment.

Metric/Imperial

1 kg/2 lb potatoes, peeled
½ kg/1 lb onions, peeled and thinly sliced
225 g/½ lb Cheddar cheese, thinly sliced, or 100 g/¼ lb Cheddar cheese and 100 g/¼ lb blue cheese, both thinly sliced
25 g/1 oz butter, cut into small pieces
Salt and freshly ground pepper
300 ml/½ pint milk

American

6 medium potatoes, peeled
3 medium onions, peeled and thinly sliced
½ lb Cheddar cheese, thinly sliced, or ¼ lb Cheddar cheese and ¼ lb blue cheese, both thinly sliced
2 tablespoons butter, cut into small pieces
Salt and freshly ground pepper
1¼ cups milk

Slice the potatoes very thinly on a mandoline or with the thinnest blade of an electric slicer, and leave for 15 minutes in cold water to rinse off some of the starch. Pat dry with kitchen paper towels. Butter a 1 litre/2 pint/5 cup freezerproof casserole or aluminium foil dish and put in a layer of potato slices. Cover with a layer of onions, then with a layer of cheese. Dot with a little butter and season to taste. Repeat these layers until all the ingredients are used up, finishing with a layer of potatoes.

Put the milk in a saucepan and bring to the boil, then pour over the ingredients in the casserole. Put the dish on a baking sheet and bake in a fairly hot oven (190°C/375°F or Gas Mark 5) for 40 minutes or until the potatoes are tender when pierced with a skewer. Remove from the oven and leave to cool.

TO FREEZE: cover in cling film, then overwrap in aluminium foil or a freezer bag. Seal, label and freeze.

TO THAW: unwrap and reheat from frozen in a hot oven (220°C/425°F or Gas Mark 7) for 20 minutes, then reduce the heat to fairly hot (190°C/375°F or Gas Mark 5) and cook for another 30 to 40 minutes until the dish is heated through and the top golden brown.

TO SERVE: serve hot, straight from the cooking dish.

Vichy Carrots

This way of cooking carrots brings out their delicate sweetness and is just as good a cooking method for older carrots as it is for tender new ones. A delicious accompaniment for roast beef.

Metric/Imperial

¾ kg/1½ lb carrots, scraped, left whole if new, cut into rings if old
300 ml/½ pint water
25 g/1 oz sugar
50 g/2 oz butter
Salt and freshly ground pepper
TO FINISH:
1×15 ml spoon/1 tablespoon freshly chopped parsley
2×15 ml spoons/2 tablespoons fresh double cream (optional)

American

1½ lb carrots, scraped, left whole if new, cut into rings if old
1¼ cups water
2 tablespoons sugar
¼ cup butter
Salt and freshly ground pepper
TO FINISH:
1 tablespoon freshly chopped parsley
2 tablespoons heavy cream (optional)

Put all the ingredients, with salt and pepper to taste, in a heavy saucepan. Stir to combine, then cover with a lid and cook over gentle heat for 15 to 30 minutes or until the carrots are just tender. (The time taken will vary according to the age of the carrots.) Remove the lid, raise the heat and boil rapidly until most, but not all, the

liquid has evaporated. Remove from the heat, taste for seasoning and leave to cool.

TO FREEZE: pour into a rigid container, cover, label and freeze. Or pour into a freezer bag-lined preformer (forming container) and freeze until solid. Remove preformer (container), seal, label and return to freezer.

TO THAW: unwrap and reheat gently from frozen in a saucepan on top of the stove, stirring occasionally.

TO SERVE: taste for seasoning, pour over the cream, if using, and sprinkle with the parsley.

Austrian Red Cabbage

The piquant taste of this braised red cabbage dish combines well with game, poultry and pork dishes. When you are pressed for time and want to concentrate your cooking on the main course, take this out of the freezer already prepared.

Metric/Imperial

1 small red cabbage, washed, trimmed and thinly sliced
1 large onion, peeled and thinly sliced
1 large cooking apple, peeled, cored and sliced
4×15 ml spoons/4 tablespoons chicken stock
2×15 ml spoons/2 tablespoons wine or cider vinegar
1×15 ml spoon/1 tablespoon sugar
Few whole cloves, crushed
Salt and freshly ground black pepper
TO FINISH:
1×15 ml spoon/1 tablespoon butter
Few parsley sprigs (optional)

American

1 red cabbage, washed, trimmed and thinly sliced
1 large onion, peeled and thinly sliced
1 large cooking apple, peeled, cored and sliced
4 tablespoons chicken stock
2 tablespoons wine or cider vinegar
1 tablespoon sugar
Few whole cloves, crushed
Salt and freshly ground black pepper
TO FINISH:
1 tablespoon butter
Few parsley sprigs (optional)

Put the cabbage, onion and apple in an ovenproof casserole dish and pour over the stock and vinegar. Sprinkle over the sugar and crushed cloves, then add salt and pepper to taste. Stir well to mix. Cover with a lid or buttered aluminium foil and bake in a moderate oven (180°C/350°F or Gas Mark 4) for 1 to 1½ hours or until the cabbage is very tender. Remove from the oven, taste for seasoning and leave to cool.

TO FREEZE: pour into a rigid container, cover, label and freeze.

TO THAW: leave in container for 4 to 5 hours at room temperature, then remove from container and reheat gently with the butter in a heavy saucepan on top of the stove, stirring occasionally. Be careful not to let the cabbage stick to the bottom of the pan.

TO SERVE: taste for seasoning, transfer to a serving dish and garnish with parsley, if you like. Serve hot.

Potato and Cheese Casserole
Vichy Carrots
Austrian Red Cabbage

Indian Cauliflower

An interesting and spicy way of cooking cauliflower, it transforms this vegetable into a dish which can stand on its own. Always overwrap this dish before freezing, to prevent cross-flavouring.

The photograph opposite shows Indian Cauliflower in the rectangular serving dish, with Broccoli in Cheese Sauce in the round casserole. The small dish of yogurt is to serve with the cauliflower.

Metric/Imperial

1 onion, peeled and quartered

3–4 garlic cloves, peeled

25 g/1 oz fresh root (green) ginger, peeled

4×15 ml spoons/4 tablespoons water

4×15 ml spoons/4 tablespoons oil

1×2.5 ml spoon/½ teaspoon ground turmeric

2 tomatoes, skinned and chopped

1×1.25 ml spoon/¼ teaspoon cayenne pepper

2×5 ml spoons/2 teaspoons ground coriander

1×5 ml spoon/1 teaspoon ground cumin

2×5 ml spoons/2 teaspoons salt

Freshly ground pepper

Pinch of ground cinnamon

1 whole cardamom pod, split

Juice of ½ lemon

1 cauliflower, washed and divided into florets

Yogurt, to finish

American

1 onion, peeled and quartered

3–4 garlic cloves, peeled

2 inch piece of fresh ginger, peeled

4 tablespoons water

4 tablespoons oil

½ teaspoon ground turmeric

2 tomatoes, skinned and chopped

¼ teaspoon cayenne pepper

2 teaspoons ground coriander

1 teaspoon ground cumin

2 teaspoons salt

Freshly ground pepper

Pinch of ground cinnamon

1 whole cardamom, split

Juice of ½ lemon

1 cauliflower, washed and divided into florets

Yogurt, to finish

Put the onion, garlic, ginger and water into an electric blender and purée until smooth. Heat the oil in a shallow pan, add the contents of the blender and the remaining ingredients, except the cauliflower and yogurt. Cook gently for 5 minutes, adding a little water if the mixture begins to stick to the bottom of the pan. Add the cauliflower and stir well to coat every floret in the sauce. Cover with a lid and cook gently for 15 to 20 minutes or until the cauliflower is just tender. Remove from the heat, taste for seasoning and leave to cool.

TO FREEZE: place in an aluminium foil container and cover. Or pour into a freezer bag-lined preformer (forming container), freeze until solid, then remove preformer (container). Overwrap container or bag in a freezer bag, seal, label and freeze (return to freezer).

TO THAW: leave in wrappings overnight in the refrigerator, or for 2 to 3 hours at room temperature, then unwrap and reheat gently in a heavy saucepan on top of the stove, stirring occasionally.

TO SERVE: taste for seasoning and serve hot with a side dish of yogurt.

Baked Cucumber

Raw cucumber does not freeze successfully because of the very high water content, but when baked, cucumber not only freezes beautifully, but also acquires a subtly different and quite distinctive taste. It is excellent served with fish, and combines particularly well with Mushrooms in Sour(ed) Cream, (page 176).

Metric/Imperial

1 large or 2 medium-sized cucumbers, peeled

Salt

Pinch of sugar

Few drops of wine vinegar

1×15 ml spoon/1 tablespoon freshly chopped herbs (chives, mint, parsley, tarragon)

Freshly ground pepper

50 g/2 oz butter, cut into small pieces

American

1 large or 2 medium-sized cucumbers, peeled

Salt

Pinch of sugar

Few drops of wine vinegar

1 tablespoon freshly chopped herbs (chives, mint, parsley, tarragon)

Freshly ground pepper

¼ cup butter, cut into small pieces

Cut the cucumber(s) into quarters lengthwise, discard the seeds and cut the flesh into 1.5 cm/½ inch lengths. Put into a bowl and sprinkle with plenty of salt, the sugar and wine vinegar. Leave for at least 30 minutes to extract the moisture. Drain, place in an ovenproof dish, then sprinkle with the herbs and a little pepper. Dot with the butter and bake in a hot oven (220°C/425°F or Gas Mark 7) for 30 minutes. Remove from the oven and leave to cool.

TO FREEZE: pour into a rigid container, cover, label and freeze. Or pour into a freezer bag-lined preformer (forming container) and freeze until solid. Remove preformer (container), seal, label and return to freezer.

TO THAW: unwrap, put into heavy saucepan and reheat gently from frozen on top of the stove, stirring occasionally.

TO SERVE: taste for seasoning and serve hot.

Broccoli in Cheese Sauce

Broccoli is one of the best of the commercially frozen vegetables. Cooked as in this recipe, it makes a substantial side dish and can be made with either fresh broccoli and then frozen, or with frozen broccoli.

Metric/Imperial

¾ kg/1½ lb fresh broccoli, trimmed and divided into florets, or 2×283 g/10 oz packages frozen broccoli

25 g/1 oz butter

25 g/1 oz flour

300 ml/½ pint milk

Salt and white pepper

Pinch of grated nutmeg

50 g/2 oz Cheddar cheese, grated

1×15 ml spoon/1 tablespoon dried breadcrumbs

15 g/½ oz butter, cut into small pieces, to finish

American

1½-lb bunch fresh broccoli, trimmed and divided into florets, or 2×10 oz packages frozen broccoli spears

2 tablespoons butter

¼ cup flour

1¼ cups milk

Salt and white pepper

Pinch of grated nutmeg

½ cup grated Cheddar cheese

1 tablespoon dried breadcrumbs

1 tablespoon butter, cut into small pieces, to finish

Cook the broccoli in the minimum of boiling salted water for 10 to 15 minutes, or according to directions on package, then remove with a slotted spoon, reserving the cooking liquid, and put in a freezerproof or aluminium foil dish. Melt the butter in a clean saucepan, add the flour and cook over a very low heat for a few minutes without allowing to brown, stirring constantly. Add the milk very slowly, a little at a time, and stir until smooth before adding any more. Bring to the boil, stirring, then lower the heat and simmer until the sauce thickens. Stir in 1×15 ml spoon/1 tablespoon of the reserved broccoli cooking liquid, seasoning to taste, the nutmeg and half the grated cheese. Pour the sauce over the broccoli. Mix the remainder of the cheese with the breadcrumbs and sprinkle on top. Leave to cool.

TO FREEZE: wrap the dish in cling film, then overwrap in aluminium foil or a freezer bag. Seal, label and freeze.

TO THAW: unwrap, dot with the butter and bake from frozen in a fairly hot oven (190°C/375°F or Gas Mark 5) for 30 minutes or until heated through and a golden crust has formed.

TO SERVE: if you are making the dish for serving immediately and not for the freezer, keep all the ingredients hot and place quickly under a hot grill (broiler) to brown on top. Serve hot.

Purée of Brussels Sprouts

This purée has a lovely bright but delicate green colour. It is an excellent way of freezing sprouts, but is equally good freshly made with frozen sprouts.

Metric/Imperial
¾ kg/1½ lb Brussels sprouts, washed and trimmed
2×15 ml spoons/2 tablespoons fresh single cream
25 g/1 oz butter
Salt and freshly ground pepper
Pinch of grated nutmeg
2×15 ml spoons/2 tablespoons fresh double cream, to finish

American
1½ lb Brussels sprouts, washed and trimmed
2 tablespoons light cream
2 tablespoons butter
Salt and freshly ground pepper
Pinch of grated nutmeg
2 tablespoons heavy cream, to finish

Cook the Brussels sprouts in plenty of boiling salted water until they are just tender (this will take 10 to 20 minutes, depending on their age). Drain, then put into an electric blender or Mouli-légumes (foodmill), with the single (light) cream and the butter, and purée until smooth. Transfer to a bowl and season to taste, using plenty of pepper. Stir in the nutmeg, then leave to cool.

TO FREEZE: pour into a rigid container, cover, label and freeze. Or pour into a freezer bag-lined pre-former (forming container) and freeze until solid. Remove preformer (container), seal, label and return to freezer.

TO THAW: unwrap and reheat gently from frozen in a heavy saucepan on top of the stove, stirring occasionally.

TO SERVE: taste for seasoning, stir in the double (heavy) cream and serve very hot.

Mushrooms in Sour(ed) Cream can be seen in the bottom left-hand corner of the photograph opposite, with Courgette (Zucchini) Ragoût to the right and Onions Braised in Cider at the top.

Mushrooms in Sour(ed) Cream

Serve as an accompaniment to fish or poultry, as a filling for pancakes (crêpes), omelettes or vol-au-vent (puff pastry) cases, or quite simply piled onto hot buttered toast to make an unusual snack or first course.

Metric/Imperial
50 g/2 oz butter
2 onions, peeled and finely chopped
½ kg/1 lb mushrooms, trimmed, wiped and thinly sliced
Squeeze of lemon juice
150 ml/¼ pint cultured soured cream
Salt and freshly ground black pepper

American
¼ cup butter
2 onions, peeled and finely chopped
1 lb mushrooms, trimmed, wiped and thinly sliced
Squeeze of lemon juice
⅔ cup sour cream
Salt and freshly ground black pepper

Melt the butter in a heavy saucepan, add the onions and cook gently until soft. Add the mushrooms and the lemon juice and cook, uncovered, over a gentle heat for 10 minutes or until the mushrooms are quite soft and their liquid has evaporated. Stir in the sour(ed) cream, reheat without boiling, then remove from the heat. Taste for seasoning and leave to cool. If serving immediately, the sour(ed) cream can simply be poured over the hot mushrooms in the serving dish, if preferred.

TO FREEZE: pour into a rigid container, cover, label and freeze. Or pour into a freezer bag-lined preformer (forming container) and freeze until solid. Remove from preformer (container), seal, label and return to freezer.

TO THAW: unwrap and heat very gently from frozen in a saucepan on top of the stove, stirring occasionally.

TO SERVE: taste for seasoning and serve hot, as suggested above.

Courgette (Zucchini) Ragoût

This way of cooking courgettes (zucchini) gives them a rich and mellow flavour. It can be served as a side dish or, with the addition of eggs, can be made into a light supper dish.

When in season, marrow (summer squash) can be used for this dish and is just as delicious as courgettes (zucchini).

Peel the marrow (summer squash), discard the seeds and pith, and cut the flesh into cubes before adding to the onions and garlic with the tomatoes.

Metric/Imperial
25 g/1 oz butter
1×15 ml spoon/1 tablespoon oil
2 onions, peeled and chopped
1 garlic clove, peeled and finely chopped
700 g/1½ lb courgettes (zucchini), peeled and sliced
225 g/½ lb tomatoes, skinned and roughly chopped
Salt and freshly ground pepper
4 eggs, lightly beaten, to finish (optional)

American
2 tablespoons butter
1 tablespoon oil
2 onions, peeled and chopped
1 garlic clove, peeled and finely chopped
1½ lb zucchini, peeled and sliced
½ lb tomatoes, skinned and roughly chopped
Salt and freshly ground pepper
4 eggs, lightly beaten, to finish (optional)

Put the butter and oil in a heavy saucepan or flameproof casserole and heat gently until the butter has melted. Add the onions and garlic and cook until soft. Add the slices of courgette (zucchini) and the tomatoes, then cover with a lid and simmer for 20 to 30 minutes or until tender. Remove from the heat, season to taste and leave to cool.

TO FREEZE: pour into a freezer bag-lined preformer (forming container), freeze until solid, then remove preformer (container). Overwrap in a freezer bag, seal, label and return to freezer.

TO THAW: unwrap and reheat gently from frozen in a heavy saucepan on top of the stove, stirring occasionally.

TO SERVE: taste for seasoning and serve hot as a side dish. Or stir in the eggs and cook over a gentle heat until they begin to set. Serve with toast or fried bread.

Onions Braised in Cider

Use the very large, mild onions (Spanish or Bermuda, if available) to make this unusual side dish. Do not freeze this dish in a rigid plastic container or it will be impossible to remove the smell of the onions from the plastic.

Metric/Imperial
2×15 ml spoons/2 tablespoons oil
4–6 very large onions, peeled
300 ml/½ pint cider
1 bay leaf
1 sprig fresh rosemary
Salt and freshly ground pepper

American
2 tablespoons oil
4–6 very large onions, peeled
1¼ cups hard cider
1 bay leaf
1 sprig fresh rosemary
Salt and freshly ground pepper

Heat the oil in a heavy saucepan or flameproof casserole, large enough to hold the onions side by side. Add the onions and pour over the cider. Add the bay leaf and rosemary, and salt and pepper to taste, then half cover with a lid and simmer for 30 to 40 minutes or until the onions are tender, but not too soft.

Lift the onions out with a slotted spoon and place them in an aluminium foil dish. Bring the liquid left in the pan to the boil, then boil rapidly to reduce to a thin, syrupy consistency. Strain over the onions and leave to cool.

TO FREEZE: cover the foil dish or open (flash) freeze until solid, then wrap in cling film. Overwrap in aluminium foil or a freezer bag, then seal, label and freeze (return to freezer).

TO THAW: unwrap the onions, return to the saucepan or casserole and reheat gently from frozen on top of the stove, stirring occasionally.

TO SERVE: taste for seasoning, then transfer to a warmed dish with a slotted spoon. Boil the liquid in the pan quickly to reduce to a thick syrup and pour over the onions before serving.

Courgette (Zucchini) and Cheese Casserole

This delicate vegetable is particularly good combined with a mild cheese. Cooked in this way it makes a delicious side dish, or served with the potato casserole given on page 172, a complete vegetarian meal.

Metric/Imperial

50 g/2 oz butter

¾ kg/1½ lb courgettes (zucchini), washed and thickly sliced

1×15 ml spoon/1 tablespoon freshly chopped basil

1×5 ml spoon/1 teaspoon lemon juice

Salt and freshly ground pepper

175 g/6 oz mozzarella or other soft cheese, thinly sliced

50 g/2 oz dried breadcrumbs

American

¼ cup butter

1½ lb zucchini, washed and thickly sliced

1 tablespoon freshly chopped basil

1 teaspoon lemon juice

Salt and freshly ground pepper

6 oz mozzarella or other soft cheese, thinly sliced

½ cup dried breadcrumbs

Melt half the butter in a deep frying pan, add the courgettes (zucchini) and cook for 10 minutes or until just tender. Remove from the heat, sprinkle with the basil, lemon juice, and salt and pepper to taste. Mix well to combine.

Butter a freezerproof casserole or an aluminium foil dish. Put in half the courgettes (zucchini), cover with half the cheese and repeat. Fry the breadcrumbs in the remaining butter until golden brown, then spread on top of the casserole and leave to cool.

TO FREEZE: wrap the dish in cling film and overwrap in aluminium foil or a freezer bag. Seal, label and freeze.

TO THAW: unwrap and bake from frozen in a moderate oven (180°C/350°F or Gas Mark 4) for 35 to 40 minutes or until heated through and crisp on top.

TO SERVE: serve hot, straight from the cooking dish.

Leek Pie

*The mild onion flavour of leeks
is frozen in pastry in this lunch, brunch,
or family supper dish.*

Metric/Imperial

275 g/10 oz prepared shortcrust
pastry (made with 275 g/10 oz flour)

350 g/¾ lb leeks (white and pale
green parts only), washed and cut
into 2.5 cm/1 inch lengths

50 g/2 oz butter

2 egg yolks

2×15 ml spoons/2 tablespoons fresh
double cream

Salt and freshly ground pepper

American

2½ cups prepared pie pastry (made
with 2½ cups flour)

¾ lb leeks (white and pale green
parts only), washed and cut into
1 inch lengths

¼ cup butter

2 egg yolks

2 tablespoons heavy cream

Salt and freshly ground pepper

Line a 20 cm/8 inch flan tin (pan) or
aluminium foil pie dish with two-
thirds of the pastry. Put the leeks and
butter in a saucepan with 1×15 ml
spoon/1 tablespoon water, cover and
cook over gentle heat until the leeks
begin to soften. Remove from the
heat. Beat the egg yolks into the
cream and stir this mixture into the
leeks. Season to taste and leave to
cool.

Pour the leek mixture into the
pastry case and cover with the
remaining pastry. Dampen the edges
with a little water and press together
to seal. Make a few incisions in the
top to form air vents.

TO FREEZE: wrap in cling film, then
overwrap in aluminium foil or in a
freezer bag. Seal, label and freeze.

TO THAW: unwrap and bake from
frozen in a very hot oven
(230°C/450°F or Gas Mark 8) for 30
minutes, then reduce the heat to
moderate (180°C/350°F or Gas Mark
4) and bake for another 20 to 30
minutes or until the top is lightly
browned.

TO SERVE: cut into wedges and serve
very hot.

Leek Salad

*The piquant flavour of this dish makes an
unusual salad to serve with cold meat or as
a first course. When freezing leeks, keep
some in whole lengths for making this
dish: trim them of the beards and dark
green tops, leaving the white and pale
green parts only, then wash thoroughly
and pack in a freezer bag or foil container.*

Metric/Imperial

350 g/¾ lb frozen leeks (see above)

150 ml/¼ pint cultured soured cream

1 small garlic clove, peeled and
crushed

1×5 ml spoon/1 teaspoon creamed
horseradish

1×5 ml spoon/1 teaspoon brown
sugar

2×15 ml spoons/2 tablespoons wine
vinegar

Salt and freshly ground pepper

Paprika pepper, to finish

American

¾ lb frozen leeks (see above)

⅔ cup sour cream

1 small garlic clove, peeled and
crushed

1 teaspoon prepared horseradish

1 teaspoon brown sugar

2 tablespoons wine vinegar

Salt and freshly ground pepper

Paprika pepper, to finish

Cook the leeks from frozen in the
minimum of boiling salted water for
15 minutes or until just tender. Drain
and place in a deep serving dish. Mix
together the remaining ingredients,
with salt and pepper to taste, and
pour over the leeks. Leave to marinate for at least 1 hour in the
refrigerator, then sprinkle with a little
paprika to add colour just before
serving.

**Courgette
(Zucchini) and
Cheese Casserole
Leek Pie
Leek Salad**

*Courgette (Zucchini)
and Cheese Casserole
is on the right of this
photograph, with Leek
Pie in the centre and
the ingredients for
Leek Salad on the left.*

Peperonata

Peperonata is illustrated below, with Ratatouille shown opposite.

This is a good method of freezing peppers (capsicums) and tomatoes – two salad vegetables that do not freeze well in their raw state, yet are usually inexpensive and plentiful in the summer. Serve hot as a vegetable dish, to accompany roast or grilled (broiled) meats, or chilled as a first course with thinly sliced brown bread and butter or hot crusty French bread.

Metric/Imperial

Butter and olive oil for frying

1 medium-sized onion, peeled and finely chopped

4 large red peppers (capsicums), cored, seeded and cut in strips

6 large tomatoes, skinned, quartered and seeded

1×5 ml spoon/1 teaspoon sugar

Salt and freshly ground black pepper

2×15 ml spoons freshly chopped parsley, to finish

American

Butter and olive oil for frying

1 medium-sized onion, peeled and finely chopped

4 large red peppers, cored, seeded and cut in strips

6 large tomatoes, skinned, quartered and seeded

1 teaspoon sugar

Salt and freshly ground black pepper

2 tablespoons freshly chopped parsley, to finish

Heat a knob of butter and 2 tablespoons of oil in a saucepan and, when foaming, add the onion. Cook gently until soft and transparent. Add the peppers (capsicums), cover with a lid and simmer very gently for 15 minutes. Add the tomatoes and sugar, and salt and pepper to taste. Replace the lid and continue to simmer gently for another 15 minutes or until the vegetables make a thick purée. Remove from the heat, taste for seasoning and leave to cool.

TO FREEZE: spoon into a rigid container, cover, label and freeze. Or spoon into a freezer bag-lined preformer (forming container), freeze until solid, then remove preformer (container), seal, label and return to freezer.

TO THAW: if serving hot, unwrap and reheat gently from frozen in a heavy saucepan on top of the stove. Add 2×15 ml spoons/2 tablespoons water and stir occasionally. If serving chilled, leave to thaw for 4 to 5 hours at room temperature or overnight in the refrigerator.

TO SERVE: taste for seasoning and transfer hot peperonata to a warmed serving dish. Sprinkle with the chopped parsley and serve immediately. If serving as a first course, taste for seasoning, chill in the refrigerator for 30 minutes, then sprinkle with the chopped parsley before serving.

Creamed Tomatoes

Tomatoes are usually served in a salad, or added to other dishes as a flavouring. Here is a way of serving them hot on their own, with baked fish or roast poultry.

Metric/Imperial

¾ kg/1½ lb tomatoes, skinned and roughly chopped

50 g/2 oz butter

25 g/1 oz flour

Salt and freshly ground pepper

25 g/1 oz brown sugar

1×15 ml spoon/1 tablespoon freshly chopped basil (optional)

150 ml/¼ pint fresh double cream

American

1½ lb tomatoes, skinned and roughly chopped

¼ cup butter

¼ cup flour

Salt and freshly ground pepper

3 tablespoons brown sugar

1 tablespoon freshly chopped basil (optional)

⅔ cup heavy cream

Put the tomatoes in a heavy saucepan with the butter and cook gently until they begin to soften. Dredge with the flour and add salt and pepper to taste, the sugar and basil (if using). Simmer, uncovered, until the tomatoes are quite soft and all the liquid has evaporated, stirring occasionally. Stir in the cream and remove from the heat. Taste for seasoning and leave to cool.

TO FREEZE: pour into a rigid container, cover, label and freeze. Or pour into a freezer bag-lined preformer (forming container), freeze until solid, then remove preformer (container), seal, label and return to freezer.

TO THAW: unwrap and reheat gently from frozen in a heavy saucepan on top of the stove, stirring occasionally.

TO SERVE: taste for seasoning and serve hot.

Ratatouille

Make plenty of this flavourful vegetable casserole during the summer months while tomatoes, courgettes (zucchini), peppers (capsicums) and aubergines (eggplant) are plentiful. Ratatouille is a treat during the winter when garden-fresh vegetables are either not available, or are terribly expensive.

Metric/Imperial
1 large aubergine (eggplant), sliced
Salt
4×15 ml spoons/4 tablespoons olive oil
2 medium-sized onions, peeled and thinly sliced
1 garlic clove, peeled and crushed
¾ kg/1½ lb ripe tomatoes, skinned, seeded and quartered
½ kg/1 lb courgettes (zucchini), sliced
1 large green pepper (capsicum), cored, seeded and thinly sliced
1 large red pepper (capsicum), cored, seeded and thinly sliced
Freshly ground black pepper
Freshly chopped parsley, to finish

American
1 large eggplant, sliced
Salt
4 tablespoons olive oil
2 medium-sized onions, peeled and thinly sliced
1 garlic clove, peeled and crushed
1½ lb ripe tomatoes, skinned, seeded and quartered
1 lb zucchini, sliced
1 large green pepper, cored, seeded and thinly sliced
1 large red pepper, cored, seeded and thinly sliced
Freshly ground black pepper
Freshly chopped parsley, to finish

Sprinkle the aubergine (eggplant) slices with salt and leave to drain for 30 minutes in a colander. Wash and dry well with kitchen paper towels. Heat the oil in a large saucepan, add the onions, garlic and tomatoes and cook gently for 3 to 4 minutes until the juices flow from the tomatoes. Add the remaining vegetables, and salt and pepper to taste. Stir well. Bring to the boil, stirring constantly, then lower the heat, cover with a lid and cook gently, stirring occasionally, for at least 30 minutes or until the vegetables are soft. Remove from the heat, taste for seasoning and leave until completely cold.
TO FREEZE: pour into a freezer bag-lined preformer (forming container) and freeze until solid. Remove from preformer (container), overwrap in a freezer bag, seal, label and return to freezer

TO THAW: if serving hot, unwrap ratatouille and reheat gently from frozen in a heavy saucepan on top of the stove. Add 2×15 ml spoons/2 tablespoons water and stir occasionally. If the ratatouille is to be served chilled as a first course, leave to thaw for 4 to 5 hours at room temperature. Chill for 30 minutes in the refrigerator before serving.
TO SERVE: taste for seasoning, sprinkle with chopped parsley, and serve hot as a vegetable dish to accompany grilled (broiled) or roast meat or fish. Serve chilled as a first course.

Braised Jerusalem Artichokes

The availability of Jerusalem artichokes varies, so cook them when you can get them – they are usually to be found in specialist greengrocers and markets. They are particularly good with venison or other game and red meat.

Metric/Imperial
50 g/2 oz butter
25 g/1 oz sugar
½ kg/1 lb Jerusalem artichokes, peeled
225 g/½ lb button onions, blanched and peeled
Salt and freshly ground pepper

American
¼ cup butter
2 tablespoons sugar
1 lb Jerusalem artichokes, peeled
½ lb baby white onions, blanched and peeled
Salt and freshly ground pepper

Melt the butter in a heavy saucepan or flameproof casserole, add the sugar and stir well. Add the artichokes and onions, stir to coat in the butter and sugar mixture, then cover with a lid and cook over a very low heat for 20 to 30 minutes or until the artichokes are just beginning to become tender. Remove from the heat, season to taste and leave to cool.
TO FREEZE: spoon into a rigid container, cover, label and freeze. Or spoon into a freezer-lined preformer (forming container), freeze until solid, then remove preformer (container), seal, label and return to freezer.
TO THAW: unwrap, place in an ovenproof casserole, cover and bake from frozen in a moderate oven (180°C/350°F or Gas Mark 4) for 30 to 40 minutes.
TO SERVE: taste for seasoning and serve hot, straight from the casserole.

Aubergine (Eggplant) Galette is illustrated below, with Stuffed Peppers (Capsicums) in the centre and Stuffed Aubergines (Eggplant) opposite.

Aubergine (Eggplant) Galette

Soft and creamy, this casserole of aubergines (eggplant), tomatoes and cream cheese makes a perfect accompaniment to roast lamb or shish kebab. It makes an impressive vegetable dish to serve at a dinner party and as it can be prepared completely before freezing it will leave you free to concentrate on other parts of the meal.

Metric/Imperial

2 large aubergines (eggplant), sliced

Salt

Butter and vegetable oil for frying

1 large onion, peeled and thinly sliced

350 g/¾ lb tomatoes, skinned, chopped and seeded

1×5 ml spoon/1 teaspoon freshly chopped basil, or 1×2.5 ml spoon/½ teaspoon dried basil

1×15 ml spoon/1 tablespoon freshly chopped parsley

Freshly ground black pepper

175 g/6 oz cream cheese, softened with 2×15 ml spoons/2 tablespoons milk

2×15 ml spoons/2 tablespoons grated Parmesan cheese

2×15 ml spoons/2 tablespoons dried breadcrumbs

1×15 ml spoon/1 tablespoon butter, cut into small pieces, to finish

American

2 large eggplant, sliced

Salt

Butter and vegetable oil for frying

1 large onion, peeled and thinly sliced

¾ lb tomatoes, skinned, chopped and seeded

1 teaspoon freshly chopped basil, or ½ teaspoon dried basil

1 tablespoon freshly chopped parsley

Freshly ground black pepper

6 oz cream cheese, softened with 2 tablespoons milk

2 tablespoons grated Parmesan cheese

2 tablespoons dried breadcrumbs

1 tablespoon butter, cut into small pieces, to finish

Sprinkle the aubergine (eggplant) slices with salt and leave to drain in a colander for 30 minutes. Wash and dry well with kitchen paper towels. Heat a knob of butter and a tablespoon oil in a large frying pan and, when foaming, add enough aubergine (eggplant) slices to cover the bottom of the pan. Fry until browned on both sides, then remove from the pan with a slotted spoon and drain on kitchen paper towels. Fry the remaining aubergine (eggplant) slices in this way, adding more butter and oil when necessary. Set aside.

Fry the onion until golden in the same pan. Stir in the tomatoes, basil, parsley, and salt and pepper to taste. Cook gently for 5 to 10 minutes until the mixture begins to soften. Remove from the heat and taste for seasoning.

Divide the aubergines (eggplant) into three equal portions and put one in the bottom of a freezerproof baking dish or aluminium foil container. Divide the tomato mixture into two and put one on top of the aubergines (eggplant). Spoon half of the cream cheese on top of the tomatoes. Repeat these layers once more, finishing with a layer of aubergines (eggplant). Mix the Parmesan cheese and breadcrumbs together and sprinkle over the dish. Leave until cold.

TO FREEZE: cover with aluminium foil, then overwrap in a freezer bag. Seal, label and freeze.

TO THAW: remove freezer bag. Reheat gently from frozen in the covered dish or container in a moderate oven (180°C/350°F or Gas Mark 4) for 30 minutes. Remove foil, dot with butter and continue cooking until the topping is golden brown and the casserole is bubbling.

TO SERVE: serve hot, straight from the casserole.

Stuffed Peppers (Capsicums)

This makes a substantial family supper dish served with hot Herb Bread (see page 62) and a salad or two.

Metric/Imperial

4 large green peppers (capsicums), cored and seeded

Vegetable oil for frying

1 small onion, peeled and very finely chopped

100 g/¼ lb mushrooms, wiped and very finely chopped

225 g/½ lb lean minced beef

2 tomatoes, skinned, seeded and chopped

1×15 ml spoon/1 tablespoon tomato purée (paste)

1×2.5 ml spoon/½ teaspoon dried mixed herbs

Salt and freshly ground black pepper

50 g/2 oz long-grain white rice, boiled and drained

TO FINISH:
50 g/2 oz Cheddar cheese, grated

1×15 ml spoon/1 tablespoon butter, cut into 4 pieces

American

4 large green peppers, cored and seeded

Vegetable oil for frying

1 small onion, peeled and very finely chopped

¼ lb mushrooms, wiped and very finely chopped

½ lb lean ground beef

2 tomatoes, skinned, seeded and chopped

1 tablespoon tomato paste

½ teaspoon dried mixed herbs

Salt and freshly ground black pepper

⅓ cup long-grain white rice, boiled and drained

TO FINISH:
½ cup grated Cheddar cheese

1 tablespoon butter, cut into 4 pieces

Blanch the peppers (capsicums) by dropping into boiling salted water and bringing back to the boil. Drain and refresh under cold running water. Pat dry with kitchen paper towels. Heat 2 tablespoons of oil in a pan. Add the onion and mushrooms and fry until soft. Add the minced (ground) beef and fry until browned, stirring constantly. Stir in the tomatoes, tomato purée (paste), mixed herbs, and salt and pepper to taste. Add enough water to moisten the mixture. Bring to the boil, then lower the heat, half cover with a lid and simmer gently for 15 to 20 minutes. Remove the pan from the heat. Stir in the rice, mix well to combine and taste for seasoning. Leave to cool, then spoon into prepared pepper (capsicum) cases.

TO FREEZE: wrap each pepper (capsicum) individually in aluminium foil, then overwrap in a freezer bag, seal, label and freeze.

TO THAW: remove freezer bag. Stand peppers (capsicums) wrapped in foil in a small, deep ovenproof dish. Bake in a fairly hot oven (200°C/400°F or Gas Mark 6) for 45 minutes.

TO SERVE: remove foil, sprinkle top of each pepper (capsicum) with the grated cheese and dot with butter. Return to the oven and continue cooking for 10 to 15 minutes or until the cheese is bubbling. Transfer to a warmed serving dish and serve immediately. If preferred, the cheese topping can be omitted.

Stuffed Aubergines (Eggplant)

This stuffed vegetable makes a most unusual first course or main dish accompaniment. Freeze each aubergine (eggplant) half individually so that you can take out of the freezer as few or as many as you need.

Metric/Imperial
2 even-sized aubergines (eggplant)
Butter for frying
1 small onion, peeled and finely chopped
100 g/¼ lb mushrooms, wiped and finely chopped
4 large tomatoes, skinned, chopped and seeded
50 g/2 oz fresh white breadcrumbs
Finely grated rind and juice of 1 lemon
1×5 ml spoon/1 teaspoon freshly chopped oregano or 1×2.5 ml spoon/½ teaspoon dried oregano
Salt and freshly ground black pepper
½–1 egg, beaten
3×15 ml spoons/3 tablespoons olive oil
Lettuce leaves, to finish

American
2 even-sized eggplant
Butter for frying
1 small onion, peeled and finely chopped
¼ lb mushrooms, wiped and finely chopped
4 large tomatoes, skinned, chopped and seeded
1 cup fresh white breadcrumbs
Finely grated rind and juice of 1 lemon
1 teaspoon freshly chopped oregano or ½ teaspoon dried oregano
Salt and freshly ground black pepper
½–1 egg, beaten
3 tablespoons olive oil
Lettuce leaves, to finish

Cut the aubergines (eggplant) in halves lengthwise and scoop out most of the flesh with a small metal spoon, being careful not to split the skin. Chop the flesh very finely and set aside in a large mixing bowl.

Melt a knob of butter in a pan and, when foaming, add the onion and cook gently until soft and transparent. Add the mushrooms and tomatoes and cook for a few minutes until the juices run. Transfer to the mixing bowl. Add the breadcrumbs, lemon rind and juice, oregano, and salt and pepper to taste. Stir well to combine, then add enough egg to bind the mixture.

Spoon the mixture into the aubergine (eggplant) cases and put into an ovenproof dish. Pour over the oil, cover with a lid or aluminium foil and bake in a moderate oven (180°C/350°F or Gas Mark 4) for 35 minutes or until cooked through. Remove from the oven and leave in the dish until completely cold.

TO FREEZE: put aubergine (eggplant) halves on a tray, open (flash) freeze until solid, then wrap each half individually in aluminium foil. Overwrap in a freezer bag, seal, label and return to freezer.

TO THAW: unwrap the aubergines (eggplant) and put in an ovenproof dish. Cover with a lid or aluminium foil and bake from frozen in a moderate oven (180°C/350°F or Gas Mark 4) for 45 minutes or until the stuffing is heated through and bubbling.

TO SERVE: arrange lettuce leaves on a serving platter and sprinkle with salt and pepper. Put aubergine (eggplant) halves in a circle on the lettuce and serve immediately.

Aubergine (Eggplant) Galette
Stuffed Peppers (Capsicums)
Stuffed Aubergines (Eggplant)

Chicory (Endive) au Gratin is illustrated in the foreground of the photograph opposite, with Spinach Soufflé standing behind.

Spinach Quiche

This is one of those invaluable dishes which can be served hot or cold, as a first course or main dish, summer or winter, and is as appropriate at a formal occasion as at a summer picnic.

Metric/Imperial

275 g/10 oz prepared shortcrust pastry (made with 275 g/10 oz flour)

¾ kg/1½ lb fresh spinach, washed and roughly chopped, or 1×350 g/12 oz package frozen whole leaf spinach

50 g/2 oz butter

2 eggs, lightly beaten

2×15 ml spoons/2 tablespoons fresh double cream

225 g/½ lb ricotta, curd or light cream cheese

50 g/2 oz Parmesan cheese, grated

1×1.25 ml spoon/¼ teaspoon grated nutmeg

Salt and freshly ground pepper

American

2½ cups prepared pie pastry (made with 2½ cups flour)

1½ lb fresh spinach, washed and roughly chopped, or 1×10 oz package frozen whole leaf spinach

¼ cup butter

2 eggs, lightly beaten

2 tablespoons heavy cream

½ lb ricotta, curd or light cream cheese

½ cup grated Parmesan cheese

¼ teaspoon grated nutmeg

Salt and freshly ground pepper

Line a 25 cm/10 inch flan ring or aluminium foil tin (pie pan) with the pastry. Prick well with a fork, line with foil and fill with dried beans. Bake blind in a hot oven (220°C/425°F or Gas Mark 7) for 10 minutes, then remove from the oven, remove beans and foil and leave to cool.

Meanwhile, put the spinach and butter in a saucepan (without water), cover with a lid and cook for 8 to 10 minutes or until just tender. Remove the lid, increase the heat and cook until any excess moisture has evaporated, stirring constantly. Transfer to a bowl. Beat the eggs and cream into the ricotta, curd or cream cheese and stir this into the spinach. Add the Parmesan cheese and the nutmeg, and salt and pepper to taste. Pour into the cooled flan case.

TO FREEZE: open (flash) freeze until solid, then remove from the flan ring, if you like. Place in a rigid container and cover with a lid, or wrap in cling film, then overwrap in aluminium foil or a freezer bag and seal. Label and return to freezer.

TO THAW: unwrap and return to flan ring (if using). Bake from frozen in a very hot oven (230°C/450°F or Gas Mark 8) for 15 minutes, then reduce the heat to fairly hot (190°C/375°F or Gas Mark 5) and bake for another 20 to 30 minutes or until the mixture has set and a light golden brown crust has formed.

TO SERVE: leave to rest for 5 minutes, then remove flan ring (if using) or foil dish and transfer to a serving platter. Serve hot or cold.

Spinach Soufflé

Spinach is one of the best vegetables to freeze, and commercially frozen spinach is usually excellent and a great time-saver. This recipe is quickly made with frozen spinach, and makes a delicate and unusual first course for dinner, or a light main dish.

Metric/Imperial

50 g/2 oz butter

100 g/¼ lb frozen spinach

150 ml/¼ pint fresh single cream

4 egg yolks

100 g/¼ lb Cheddar cheese, grated

Salt and freshly ground pepper

5 egg whites

American

¼ cup butter

¼ lb frozen spinach

⅔ cup light cream

4 egg yolks

1 cup grated Cheddar cheese

Salt and freshly ground pepper

5 egg whites

Melt the butter in a saucepan, add the spinach and cook from frozen for 10 minutes or until just thawed. Purée in an electric blender or Mouli-légumes (foodmill) until smooth, then transfer to a bowl. Beat the cream into the egg yolks and stir into the spinach together with the grated cheese. Season to taste. Beat the egg whites until stiff, then fold into the spinach and egg mixture. Butter a 1 litre/2 pint/5 cup soufflé dish. Spoon in the spinach mixture and bake in a fairly hot oven (190°C/375°F or Gas Mark 5) for 30 to 35 minutes or until the soufflé has risen and formed a crust. The centre should still be quite creamy.

TO SERVE: serve immediately, straight from the soufflé dish.

Celeriac Purée

Celeriac, the edible root of a variety of celery, varies in size from that of an apple to that of a coconut. Look for firm roots with no signs of mushiness.
A tasty and original alternative to mashed potatoes, Celeriac Purée is particularly good with game or poultry. Make this dish when celeriac is at its peak.

Metric/Imperial

1 medium-sized celeriac (approx. ½ kg/1 lb), peeled and thickly sliced

150 ml/¼ pint chicken or beef stock

2 medium-sized potatoes, peeled and diced

50 g/2 oz butter

Salt and freshly ground pepper

TO FINISH:
2×15 ml spoons/2 tablespoons fresh double cream

1×15 ml spoon/1 tablespoon freshly chopped parsley

American

1 medium-sized celeriac (approx. 1 lb), peeled and thickly sliced

⅔ cup chicken or beef stock

2 medium-sized potatoes, peeled and diced

¼ cup butter

Salt and freshly ground pepper

TO FINISH:
2 tablespoons heavy cream

1 tablespoon freshly chopped parsley

Blanch the celeriac in boiling salted water for 5 minutes, then drain and put in a heavy saucepan with the stock. Cover and cook over a gentle heat for 10 minutes, then add the potatoes. Cover with a lid and cook for another 10 to 15 minutes or until the vegetables are tender and the stock has been absorbed. If there is still a lot of liquid, uncover and boil rapidly to evaporate.

Remove from the heat, then mash with a potato masher or a fork. Blend in the butter and season to taste. Leave to cool.

TO FREEZE: spoon into a rigid container, cover, label and freeze. Or spoon into a freezer-lined preformer (forming container), freeze until solid, then remove preformer (container), seal, label and return to freezer.

TO THAW: unwrap and reheat from frozen in a heavy saucepan or flame-proof casserole on top of the stove, stirring occasionally. Add a little water if necessary.

TO SERVE: stir in the cream and parsley, taste for seasoning and serve hot.

Chicory (Endive) au Gratin

Firm white heads of chicory (endive) are made into a light but nourishing dish with the addition of ham and cheese.

Metric/Imperial
6–8 heads of chicory (Aust. endive), washed and trimmed
6–8 rashers smoked bacon, rinds removed, or 6–8 slices ham
25 g/1 oz butter
25 g/1 oz flour
300 ml/½ pint milk
100 g/¼ lb Cheddar, Gruyère or Parmesan cheese, grated
1×5 ml spoon/1 teaspoon prepared French mustard
2×15 ml spoons/2 tablespoons fresh double cream (optional)
Salt and freshly ground pepper

American
6–8 heads of endive, washed and trimmed
6–8 strips bacon, rinds removed, or 6–8 slices ham
2 tablespoons butter
¼ cup flour
1¼ cups milk
1 cup grated Cheddar, Gruyère or Parmesan cheese
1 teaspoon prepared French mustard
2 tablespoons heavy cream (optional)
Salt and freshly ground pepper

Blanch the chicory (endive) in boiling water for 10 minutes, then drain and leave to cool. Wrap each head in a rasher (strip) of bacon or slice of ham. Butter a shallow freezerproof baking dish or foil dish and put the chicory (endive) into the dish, packing them close together.

Melt the butter in a clean saucepan, add the flour and cook over a very low heat for a few minutes, without allowing to brown, stirring constantly. Add the milk very slowly, a little at a time, and stir until smooth before adding any more. Bring to the boil, stirring, then lower the heat and stir in all but 1×15 ml spoon/1 tablespoon of the grated cheese, the mustard, cream (if using), and salt and pepper to taste. Pour over the chicory (endive) and sprinkle on the remaining cheese. Leave to cool.

TO FREEZE: wrap the dish in cling film, then overwrap in aluminium foil or a freezer bag. Seal, label and freeze.

TO THAW: unwrap and bake from frozen in a hot oven (220°C/425°F or Gas Mark 7) for 20 minutes, then reduce the heat to moderate (180°C/350°F or Gas Mark 4) and bake until heated through and browned on top. If necessary, brown quickly under the grill (broiler) to finish.

TO SERVE: serve bubbling hot, straight from the dish.

Spinach Quiche
Spinach Soufflé
Celeriac Purée
Chicory (Endive) au Gratin

The photograph below shows Mixed Vegetable Medley. Opposite are Bean Salad and Sweet and Sour Beetroot (Beets).

Bean Salad

Use frozen French or runner beans when making this dish. It is a delicious alternative to serving them hot, and brings out their flavour particularly well.

Metric/Imperial

½ kg/1 lb frozen French or runner beans

1 small onion, peeled and very finely chopped

1×15 ml spoon/1 tablespoon wine vinegar

3×15 ml spoons/3 tablespoons oil

Squeeze of lemon juice

Salt and freshly ground pepper

1×1.25 ml spoon/¼ teaspoon sugar

Freshly chopped dill or parsley (optional), to finish

American

1 lb frozen French-style green beans

1 small onion, peeled and very finely chopped

1 tablespoon wine vinegar

3 tablespoons oil

Squeeze of lemon juice

Salt and freshly ground pepper

¼ teaspoon sugar

Freshly chopped dill or parsley (optional), to finish

Cook the beans in boiling salted water for 10 minutes or until just tender. Drain and place in a shallow dish or salad bowl. Sprinkle with the onion. Whisk together the remaining ingredients to make a French dressing and pour over the beans and onion. Mix well and leave until cold. Sprinkle with dill or parsley, if using, just before serving.

Sweet and Sour Beetroot (Beets)

Cooked hot beetroot (beets) make an unusual vegetable and they are a welcome change from the more usual ways of using beetroot (beets) in salads or borshch. This dish is particularly good with roast pork.

Metric/Imperial

25 g/1 oz sugar

150 ml/¼ pint wine vinegar

1×15 ml spoon/1 tablespoon flour (mixed to a paste with 2×15 ml spoons/2 tablespoons water)

½ kg/1 lb cooked beetroot, skinned and sliced

1×2.5 ml spoon/½ teaspoon dried dill

Salt and freshly ground black pepper

Knob of butter, to finish (optional)

American

2 tablespoons sugar

⅔ cup wine vinegar

1 tablespoon flour (mixed to a paste with 2 tablespoons water)

1 lb cooked beets, skinned and sliced

½ teaspoon dried dill

Salt and freshly ground black pepper

Knob of butter, to finish (optional)

Put the sugar, wine vinegar and flour paste into a saucepan and bring slowly to the boil, stirring constantly. Lower the heat and simmer gently for a few minutes until the mixture thickens. Add the beetroot (beet) slices, dill, and salt and pepper to taste. Turn them carefully in the sauce so that they are evenly coated, then cover with a lid and simmer very gently for 10 minutes. Remove from the heat, taste for seasoning and leave to cool.

TO FREEZE: put into a rigid container, cover, label and freeze.

TO THAW: unwrap and reheat gently from frozen in a covered heavy saucepan on top of the stove. Add 2×15 ml spoons/2 tablespoons water and cook for 30 minutes, stirring occasionally and carefully to separate the beetroot (beet) slices.

TO SERVE: taste for seasoning and transfer to a warmed serving dish. Put the knob of butter on top, if liked, and serve immediately.

Mixed Vegetable Medley

It is not necessary to have all the vegetables listed for this recipe: use whatever is in season or what you have to hand — the results will be just as good. If you do substitute vegetables of your own choice, be sure they are ones that freeze well.

Metric/Imperial

1 medium-sized aubergine (eggplant), sliced

Salt

Vegetable oil for frying

1 large onion, peeled and finely chopped

1 green pepper (capsicum), cored, seeded and sliced into rings

4 medium-sized courgettes (zucchini), sliced into rings

100 g/¼ lb mushrooms, wiped and chopped

225 g/½ lb tomatoes, skinned, quartered and chopped, or 1×225 g/8 oz can tomatoes

150 ml/¼ pint chicken stock
2×15 ml spoons/2 tablespoons tomato purée (paste)
1×5 ml spoon/1 teaspoon dried mixed herbs (basil, oregano and thyme)
1×15 ml spoon/1 tablespoon freshly chopped parsley
Freshly ground black pepper
TO FINISH: 2×15 ml spoons/2 tablespoons chicken stock or water
2 large potatoes, parboiled, skinned and thinly sliced
1×15 ml spoon/1 tablespoon butter, cut into small pieces

American
1 medium-sized eggplant, sliced
Salt
Vegetable oil for frying
1 large onion, peeled and finely chopped
1 green pepper, cored, seeded and sliced into rings
4 medium-sized zucchini, sliced into rings

¼ lb mushrooms, wiped and chopped
½ lb tomatoes, skinned, quartered and chopped, or 1×½ lb can tomatoes
⅔ cup chicken stock
2 tablespoons tomato paste
1 teaspoon dried mixed herbs (basil, oregano and thyme)
1 tablespoon freshly chopped parsley
Freshly ground black pepper
TO FINISH:
2 tablespoons chicken stock or water
2 large potatoes, parboiled, skinned and thinly sliced
1 tablespoon butter, cut into small pieces

Sprinkle the aubergine (eggplant) slices with salt and leave to drain in a colander for 30 minutes. Wash and dry well with kitchen paper towels. Set aside. Heat 2 tablespoons of oil in a large flameproof casserole, add the onion and green pepper (capsicum) and fry gently until soft and lightly coloured. Add the remaining vegetables and cook gently for 5 minutes,

stirring constantly. Stir in the remaining ingredients, with salt and pepper to taste, cover with a lid and simmer gently for 30 minutes or until the vegetables are soft.

Remove from the heat, taste for seasoning, adjust if necessary, and leave the vegetables to cool.

TO FREEZE: pour vegetables into a rigid container, cover, label and freeze. Or pour into a freezer bag-lined preformer (forming container). Freeze until solid, remove preformer (container), seal, label and return to freezer.

TO THAW: unwrap and reheat gently in a flameproof casserole on top of the stove with the chicken stock or water, stirring occasionally.

Taste for seasoning, then put the sliced potatoes in a layer on top of the vegetables, dot with butter and bake in a fairly hot oven (200°C/400°F or Gas Mark 6) for 20 to 25 minutes or until the potatoes are crisp and golden brown.

TO SERVE: serve hot, straight from the casserole, as a vegetable accompaniment to roast or grilled (broiled) meats, poultry or sausages.

Bean Salad

Sweet and Sour Beetroot (Beets)

Mixed Vegetable Medley

Desserts and Puddings

Gooseberry Fool is in the foreground of the photograph opposite, with Iced Raspberry Soufflé to the right and Lemon Soufflé behind.

Iced Raspberry Soufflé

An iced soufflé is lighter than an icecream and does not melt so quickly; therefore, it is particularly suitable for a buffet party. Make it in the summer with fresh raspberries, or in the winter with frozen raspberry purée. Do not keep in the freezer for more than 1 to 2 weeks.

Metric/Imperial

½ kg/1 lb raspberries

4 egg whites

225 g/½ lb caster sugar

300 ml/½ pint fresh double cream, lightly whipped

TO FINISH:

150 ml/¼ pint fresh double cream

Few whole fresh or frozen raspberries

American

1 pint raspberries

4 egg whites

1 cup sugar

1¼ cups heavy cream, lightly whipped

TO FINISH:

⅔ cup heavy cream

Few whole fresh or frozen raspberries

Serves 6 to 8

Purée the raspberries in a blender, then pass them through a nylon sieve, or put the raspberries through a Mouli-légumes (foodmill). Beat the egg whites until stiff, then slowly beat in the sugar, a spoonful at a time. Beat in the raspberry purée, then fold in the cream. Pour the mixture into a freezerproof bowl or soufflé dish.
TO FREEZE: open (flash) freeze until solid, then wrap in cling film and overwrap in aluminium foil or a freezer bag. Seal, label and return to freezer.
TO THAW: thaw in wrappings for 1 hour in the refrigerator.
TO SERVE: unwrap and decorate with rosettes of whipped cream and whole raspberries.

Lemon Soufflé

It is always a good idea to keep a refreshing lemon dessert such as this in the freezer.

Metric/Imperial

Finely grated rind of 2 lemons

4×15 ml spoons/4 tablespoons lemon juice

3 eggs, separated

75 g/3 oz caster sugar

1×15 ml spoon/1 tablespoon powdered gelatine

4×15 ml spoons/4 tablespoons water

300 ml/½ pint fresh double cream

TO FINISH:

150 ml/¼ pint fresh double cream

Approx. 12 ratafia biscuits

American

Finely grated rind of 2 lemons

4 tablespoons lemon juice

3 eggs, separated

6 tablespoons sugar

1 envelope unflavored gelatin

4 tablespoons water

1¼ cups heavy cream

TO FINISH:

⅔ cup heavy cream

Approx. 12 graham crackers

Serves 6

First prepare a 600 ml/1 pint/2½ cup freezerproof soufflé dish: cut a strip of doubled greaseproof (waxed) paper long enough to go around the outside of the dish (overlapping by 2.5–5 cm/1–2 inches) and 5–7.5 cm/2–3 inches higher than the dish. Tie this securely around the outside of the dish with string. Brush the inside of the paper above the rim very lightly with melted butter.
Put the lemon rind and juice, egg yolks and sugar into a heatproof bowl and stand over a pan of hot water. Beat with a rotary beater or whisk until thick. Sprinkle the gelatin(e) over the water in a small heatproof bowl. Leave until spongy, then place bowl in a pan of hot water and stir over low heat until the gelatin(e) has dissolved. Leave to cool slightly, then stir into the lemon mixture. Remove from heat and leave until half set.
Whip the cream until it is thick, then fold into the soufflé mixture. Beat the egg whites until stiff, fold in, then spoon into the prepared soufflé dish. Chill in the refrigerator for at least 4 hours or until set.
TO FREEZE: open (flash) freeze until solid, then wrap in cling film and overwrap in aluminium foil or a freezer bag. Seal, label and return to freezer.

TO THAW: leave in wrappings for 4 to 5 hours at room temperature.
TO SERVE: unwrap, remove paper collar carefully, then press some finely crushed ratafias (graham crackers) onto the sides of the soufflé. Decorate the top with piped whipped cream and whole ratafias or other decorative biscuits (cookies).

Gooseberry Fool

The gooseberry season is lamentably short, but this classic English dish keeps beautifully in the freezer.

Metric/Imperial

½ kg/1 lb gooseberries, washed but not topped and tailed

75 ml/⅛ pint water

100–175 g/4–6 oz sugar

250 ml/scant ½ pint milk or single cream

2 egg yolks

1×5 ml spoon/1 teaspoon cornflour

150 ml/¼ pint fresh double cream, lightly whipped

Macaroons or sponge fingers, to serve

American

1 lb gooseberries, washed but not trimmed

⅓ cup water

½–¾ cup sugar

1¼ cups milk or light cream

2 egg yolks

1 teaspoon cornstarch

⅔ cup heavy cream, lightly whipped

Macaroons or ladyfingers, to serve

Put the gooseberries in a saucepan with the water and sugar to taste. Poach the fruit gently until very soft, then push through a nylon sieve. Leave to cool.
Meanwhile, heat the milk or cream. Beat the egg yolks lightly in a heatproof bowl with the cornflour (cornstarch), then pour the milk over. Place the bowl over a pan of simmering water and stir until the custard thickens enough to coat the back of the spoon. Remove from the heat and leave to cool. Mix the gooseberry purée into the custard and taste for sweetness. Leave until cold, stirring occasionally, then fold in the double (heavy) cream.
TO FREEZE: pour into a rigid container, cover, label and freeze.
TO THAW: leave in container for 3 to 4 hours at room temperature.
TO SERVE: stir if necessary, transfer to serving dishes and serve chilled, with macaroons or sponge (lady) fingers.

Chocolate Mousse is illustrated below. Iced Honey and Brandy Mousse is in individual ramekins in the foreground of the photograph opposite, with Rhubarb Suédoise on the right and Strawberry Mousse in the soufflé dish behind.

Rhubarb Suédoise

This is a good way of cooking rhubarb for children, because it takes away some of the fruit's natural acidity. To make the dessert into a special treat, decorate it with whipped cream after unmoulding, then finish with baby meringues.

Metric/Imperial

½ kg/1 lb rhubarb, washed and cut into 2.5 cm/1 inch lengths
225 g/½ lb sugar
25 g/1 oz cornflour
2×15 ml spoons/2 tablespoons water
1×15 ml spoon/1 tablespoon caster sugar, to finish

American

1 lb rhubarb, washed and cut into 1 inch lengths
1 cup sugar
2 tablespoons cornstarch
2 tablespoons water
1 tablespoon sugar, to finish

Put the rhubarb in a bowl, cover it with the sugar, then leave for at least 1 hour to draw out the juice. Put the rhubarb and juice in a saucepan, add as much water as is needed just to cover the rhubarb and bring to the boil. Cover and simmer for 20 to 30 minutes or until the rhubarb is very soft and has almost disintegrated. Mix the cornflour (cornstarch) to a smooth paste with the water. Pour this into the pan and boil for 5 minutes until the initial cloudiness disappears and the rhubarb mixture thickens, stirring constantly. Taste for sweetness. Rinse a freezerproof mould out in cold water, pour in the rhubarb, then leave until set.

TO FREEZE: wrap in cling film, then overwrap in aluminium foil or a freezer bag. Seal, label and freeze.

TO THAW: leave in wrappings for 4 to 5 hours at room temperature.

TO SERVE: unwrap and unmould onto a serving platter. (If difficult to unmould, wrap mould briefly in a towel that has been rung out in hot water — the suédoise should then slip out easily.) Sprinkle with sugar just before serving or decorate as suggested above.

Chocolate Mousse

Chocolate Mousse is a good desert to freeze because it keeps its creamy texture even after freezing and thawing, and individual pots or cups can be tucked neatly into corners of the freezer.

Metric/Imperial

225 g/½ lb plain chocolate, broken into pieces
2×15 ml spoons/2 tablespoons water
4 eggs, separated
1×15 ml spoon/1 tablespoon brandy (optional)
TO FINISH:
150 ml/¼ pint fresh double cream
50 g/2 oz chocolate, grated

American

8 squares (8 oz) semisweet chocolate, broken into pieces
2 tablespoons water
4 eggs, separated
1 tablespoon brandy (optional)
TO FINISH:
⅔ cup heavy cream
2 squares (2 oz) semisweet chocolate, grated

Put the chocolate pieces and water in a heatproof bowl over a pan of hot water and heat gently until the chocolate melts. Remove from the pan and leave to cool for 1 to 2 minutes. Stir the egg yolks into the melted chocolate one at a time, then stir in the brandy, if using. Beat the egg whites until stiff, then fold carefully into the chocolate mixture.

TO FREEZE: spoon mousse into four individual freezerproof ramekins, or one large freezerproof dish. Wrap in freezer bags, seal, label and freeze.

TO THAW: unwrap and leave for 2 to 3 hours in the refrigerator.

TO SERVE: sprinkle with the grated chocolate and pipe rosettes of whipped cream on top of the mousse, or around the edge of the dish.

Strawberry Mousse

Can be made with fresh strawberries or frozen strawberry purée.

Metric/Imperial

½ kg/1 lb strawberries
15 g/½ oz powdered gelatine
2×15 ml spoons/2 tablespoons water
Juice of 1 lemon
150 g/5 oz caster sugar
2 egg whites
150 ml/¼ pint fresh double cream, lightly whipped
TO FINISH:
150 ml/¼ pint fresh double cream
5 whole strawberries

American

1 lb strawberries
1 envelope unflavored gelatin
2 tablespoons water
Juice of 1 lemon
⅔ cup sugar
2 egg whites
⅔ cup heavy cream, lightly whipped
TO FINISH:
⅔ cup heavy cream
5 whole strawberries

First prepare a 600 ml/1 pint/2½ cup freezerproof soufflé dish: cut a strip of doubled greaseproof (waxed) paper long enough to go around the outside of the dish (overlapping by 2.5–5 cm/1–2 inches, and 5–7.5 cm/2–3 inches higher than the dish). Tie this securely around the outside of the dish. Brush the inside of the paper above the rim with melted butter.

Purée the strawberries in an electric blender or work through a Mouli-légumes (foodmill), or large sieve. Sprinkle the gelatin(e) over the water in a small saucepan and leave for 5 minutes until spongy. Place over a low heat to dissolve. Add the lemon juice and the sugar, then stir until the sugar has dissolved. Stir this into the strawberry purée and taste for sweetness — the mixture should be a little oversweet at this point. Leave to cool and thicken a little. Whip the egg whites until stiff, fold into the strawberry mixture, then fold in the cream. Spoon into the prepared soufflé dish and chill in the refrigerator until set.

TO FREEZE: open (flash) freeze until solid, then wrap in cling film and overwrap in foil or a freezer bag. Seal, label and return to freezer.

TO THAW: leave in wrappings for 4 to 5 hours at room temperature.

TO SERVE: unwrap, remove the paper collar carefully, then decorate with whipped cream and strawberries.

Iced Honey and Brandy Mousse

Luxurious and rich, this iced mousse is quickly made with an electric beater.

Metric/Imperial	American
3 eggs, separated	3 eggs, separated
2×15 ml spoons/2 tablespoons honey	2 tablespoons honey
2×15 ml spoons/2 tablespoons lemon juice	2 tablespoons lemon juice
2×15 ml spoons/2 tablespoons brandy	2 tablespoons brandy
2×15 ml spoons/2 tablespoons water	2 tablespoons water
150 ml/¼ pint fresh double cream, lightly whipped	⅔ cup heavy cream, lightly whipped
Langue de chats biscuits or fan wafers, to serve	Langue de chats cookies or fan wafers, to serve
	Serves 6

Beat the egg yolks, honey, lemon juice, brandy and water together with an electric beater until the mixture is thick and light and has doubled or tripled in volume. Beat the egg whites until stiff, then fold into the egg yolk mixture with the cream. Pour into a ½ litre/1 pint/2½ cup freezerproof soufflé or glass dish, or into individual ramekin dishes.

TO FREEZE: open (flash) freeze until solid, then wrap in cling film and overwrap in aluminium foil or a freezer bag. Seal, label and return to freezer.

TO THAW: do not thaw, but serve frozen.

TO SERVE: serve from dish(es), with biscuits or wafers.

This photograph illustrates, from left to right, Grape Jelly (Mold), Peach and Grape Crème Brûlée and Chocolate Mocha Bavarian Cream.

Grape Jelly (Mold)

This jelly (mold) looks most attractive if made in a ring mould and is the exception to the rule that a jelly (mold) should not be frozen. Pile the extra grapes into the centre just before serving.

Metric/Imperial

300 ml/½ pint water
15 g/½ oz powdered gelatine
175 g/6 oz sugar
Thinly pared rind and juice of 1 orange
Thinly pared rind and juice of 1 lemon
300 ml/½ pint red or white wine
225 g/½ lb black or green grapes, peeled, halved and seeded
TO FINISH: Extra black or green grapes
Fresh double cream, lightly whipped

American

1¼ cups water
1 envelope unflavored gelatin
¾ cup sugar
Thinly pared rind and juice of 1 orange
Thinly pared rind and juice of 1 lemon
1¼ cups red or white wine
½ lb black or green grapes, peeled, halved and seeded
TO FINISH: Extra black or green grapes
Heavy cream, lightly whipped

Put 4×15 ml spoons/4 tablespoons of the water in a small bowl, sprinkle over the gelatin(e) and leave for 5 minutes until spongy. Put the remaining water into a small saucepan with the sugar and orange and lemon rind. Stir to dissolve the sugar, then bring to the boil and boil for 3 minutes. Remove from the heat and stir in the gelatin(e) until dissolved. Leave to cool, then add the wine and the orange and lemon juice. Rinse a 900 ml/1½ pint/4 cup freezerproof jelly (gelatin) mould in cold water, then put the grapes in the bottom. Strain the jelly (gelatin) mixture into the mould and leave to set.

TO FREEZE: wrap in cling film, then overwrap in aluminium foil or a freezer bag. Seal, label and freeze.

TO THAW: leave in wrappings for 3 to 4 hours at room temperature.

TO SERVE: unmould onto a chilled serving platter, decorate with extra grapes and lightly whipped cream, or serve the cream separately.

Peach and Grape Crème Brûlée

Peaches keep extremely well in the freezer, and this is one of the simplest, yet most effective ways of serving them. Choose ripe but firm fruit for best results.

Metric/Imperial

6 small peaches, peeled, halved, stoned and sliced
225 g/½ lb seedless grapes, washed
50 g/2 oz caster sugar
2×15 ml spoons/2 tablespoons brandy (optional)
150–300 ml/¼–½ pint fresh double cream, stiffly whipped
TO FINISH: 50–75 g/2–3 oz brown sugar
Macaroons or langues de chats biscuits, to serve (optional)

American

6 small peaches, peeled, halved, pitted and sliced
½ lb seedless grapes, washed
¼ cup sugar
2 tablespoons brandy (optional)
⅔–1¼ cups heavy cream, stiffly whipped
TO FINISH: ⅓–½ cup brown sugar
Macaroons or langues de chats cookies, to serve (optional)

Put the peach slices and grapes into 4–6 individual freezerproof ramekin dishes and mix together gently. Sprinkle with the sugar and brandy (if using), then cover completely with the cream to seal in the fruit. (The amount of cream will vary according to the number of dishes used — it should be at least 1.25 cm/½ inch thick.)

TO FREEZE: open (flash) freeze until solid, then wrap in cling film and overwrap in aluminium foil or a freezer bag. Seal, label and return to freezer.

TO THAW: unwrap and sprinkle the frozen dessert with brown sugar so that the cream is completely covered with a thin layer of the sugar. Place under a very hot grill (broiler) for a few minutes until all the sugar has melted and forms a hard crust on top. Remove from the heat and leave to thaw for 4 to 5 hours at room temperature.

TO SERVE: serve in the dishes, with macaroons or langues de chats handed separately if liked.

Chocolate Mocha Bavarian Cream

Lighter than a mousse and creamier than a soufflé, this has a velvety texture and subtle flavour that is quite irresistible.

Metric/Imperial

4 eggs, separated
100 g/¼ lb caster sugar
1×2.5 ml spoon/½ teaspoon cornflour
400 ml/¾ pint milk
75 g/3 oz plain or bitter eating chocolate, broken into pieces
15 g/½ oz powdered gelatine
2×15 ml spoons/2 tablespoons strong black liquid coffee
2×15 ml spoons/2 tablespoons orange-flavoured liqueur (optional)
150 ml/¼ pint fresh double cream, lightly whipped
Grated chocolate (optional), to finish

American

4 eggs, separated
½ cup sugar
½ teaspoon cornstarch
2 cups milk
3 squares (3 oz) semisweet chocolate, broken into pieces
1 envelope unflavored gelatin
2 tablespoons strong black liquid coffee
2 tablespoons orange-flavored liqueur (optional)
⅔ cup heavy cream, lightly whipped
Grated chocolate (optional), to finish

Serves 6

Beat the egg yolks with half the sugar and the cornflour (cornstarch) until light and fluffy. Scald the milk, add the chocolate and stir until it has melted. Pour slowly onto the egg mixture, stirring constantly, then return the mixture to the pan and heat gently without allowing to boil. Stir constantly until the mixture has thickened enough to coat the back of the spoon. Remove from the heat.

Sprinkle the gelatin(e) over the coffee in a small bowl and leave for 5 minutes until spongy. Then place in a pan of hot water to dissolve completely. Stir into the custard mixture. Stir in the liqueur and leave to cool, stirring occasionally. Beat the egg whites until stiff, then beat in the remaining sugar and fold into the cooled custard. Fold in the cream lightly. Pour into a freezerproof bowl, soufflé dish or individual dishes and leave to set.

TO FREEZE: wrap in cling film, then overwrap in aluminium foil or a freezer bag. Seal, label and freeze.

TO THAW: unwrap, cover loosely and leave at room temperature for 4 to 5 hours if in large bowl, 2 to 3 hours in individual dishes.

TO SERVE: decorate with grated chocolate, if you like.

Grape Jelly (Mold)

Peach and Grape Crème Brûlée

Chocolate Mocha Bavarian Cream

Tarte Française

A classic French dessert, this apple flan is glazed with apricot jam. Make it in the autumn when cooking apples are in plentiful supply.

Tarte Française is illustrated below, with Upside-down Toffee Apple Tart shown opposite.

Metric/Imperial

FOR THE PASTRY:
150 g/6 oz flour

Pinch of salt

75 g/3 oz butter, cut into small pieces

2 egg yolks

1×15 ml spoon/1 tablespoon caster sugar

FOR THE FILLING:
¾ kg/1½ lb cooking apples

Juice of 1 lemon

50 g/2 oz caster sugar, or to taste

50 g/2 oz butter, cut into small pieces

TO FINISH:
4×15 ml spoons/4 tablespoons apricot jam, sieved

2×15 ml spoons/2 tablespoons lemon juice

American

FOR THE PASTRY:
1½ cups flour

Pinch of salt

⅓ cup butter, cut into small pieces

2 egg yolks

1 tablespoon sugar

FOR THE FILLING:
1½ lb cooking apples

Juice of 1 lemon

¼ cup sugar, or to taste

¼ cup butter, cut into small pieces

TO FINISH:
4 tablespoons apricot jam, strained

2 tablespoons lemon juice

Sift the flour and salt onto a marble slab or board. Make a well in the centre and add the butter, egg yolks and sugar. Draw the flour into the centre with the fingers and work all the ingredients together until a soft dough is formed. Transfer to a lightly floured board, and knead the dough briefly until smooth. Wrap in aluminium foil and chill for at least 30 minutes in the refrigerator.

Butter a 23 cm/9 inch fluted flan tin (tart pan), and press in the chilled dough. Prick the base with a fork. Chill in the refrigerator for 15 minutes.

Meanwhile, peel, core and slice the apples thinly. Sprinkle with the lemon juice to prevent discoloration. Arrange the apple slices, overlapping, in the flan case. Sprinkle with the sugar (the amount needed will depend on the tartness of the apples), then dot with butter. Bake on a preheated baking sheet in a fairly hot oven (190°C/375°F or Gas Mark 5) for 30 minutes or until the apples are cooked through and the pastry is golden. Remove from the oven and leave to cool.

TO FREEZE: open (flash) freeze until solid, then remove carefully from tin (pan). Cover with cling film and overwrap in aluminium foil or a freezer bag. Seal, label, and return to freezer.

TO THAW: unwrap flan and return to tin (pan). Reheat from frozen in a fairly hot oven (200°C/400°F or Gas Mark 6) for approximately 20 minutes or until heated through. Cover with aluminium foil if the flan becomes too brown during reheating. Remove from the oven, leave to cool slightly, then remove from flan tin (pan).

TO SERVE: put jam and lemon juice in a saucepan and heat gently, stirring constantly with a wooden spoon. Brush over warm apple flan and leave until set before serving.

Blackberry and Apple Pie

Blackberry and apple pies are a must for the freezer — both fruits freeze well and are in season for such a short time each year. The pie can also be made with frozen blackberries and apples, if you like, and is delicious served with cream or icecream.

Metric/Imperial

FOR THE PASTRY:
225 g/½ lb flour

Pinch of salt

50 g/2 oz lard or shortening, cut into small pieces

50 g/2 oz butter or margarine, cut into small pieces

1×15 ml spoon/1 tablespoon caster sugar

Approx. 2×15 ml spoons/2 tablespoons cold water

FOR THE FILLING:
225 g/½ lb blackberries, washed with stalks removed

½ kg/1 lb cooking apples

Finely grated rind and juice of ½ lemon

100 g/¼ lb caster sugar, or to taste

2×15 ml spoons/2 tablespoons flour

American

FOR THE PASTRY:
2 cups flour

Pinch of salt

¼ cup shortening, cut into small pieces

¼ cup butter or margarine, cut into small pieces

1 tablespoon sugar

Approx. 2 tablespoons cold water

FOR THE FILLING:
½ lb blackberries, washed with stalks removed

1 lb tart or cooking apples

Finely grated rind and juice of ½ lemon

½ cup sugar, or to taste

2 tablespoons flour

Sift the flour and salt into a mixing bowl, add the fats and rub into the flour with the fingers until the mixture resembles fine breadcrumbs. Using a palette knife, stir in the sugar and enough water to draw the mixture together. Transfer to a lightly floured board and knead the dough briefly until smooth. Wrap in aluminium foil and chill in the refrigerator for at least 30 minutes.

Divide the dough in two and roll out half on a floured board to a circle large enough to fit the base of a 20 cm/8 inch pie dish (pan) or plate lined with aluminium foil. Chill in the refrigerator for 15 minutes.

Meanwhile, put the blackberries in a mixing bowl. Peel, core and slice the apples. Fold into the blackberries with the lemon rind and juice, then add the sugar (the amount needed will depend on the tartness of the apples) and flour. Spoon the fruit mixture into the pastry case. Roll out the remaining dough to a circle for the lid. Lay it over the filling, pressing down and sealing the edges with water. Flute the edges with your fingers or crimp with the prongs of a fork.

TO FREEZE: open (flash) freeze until

solid, then remove from pie dish (pan) or plate by carefully lifting up foil. Cover in cling film, then over-wrap in aluminium foil or a freezer bag. Seal, label and return to freezer.
TO THAW: unwrap pie and return to pie dish (pan) or plate. Bake from frozen in a hot oven (220°C/425°F or Gas Mark 7) for 30 minutes, then make a slit in the top of pastry with a knife and cover pie with foil. Reduce the heat to fairly hot (190°C/375°F or Gas Mark 5) and bake for another 40 to 50 minutes or until a skewer inserted into the top of pie pierces tender apples. Remove the foil from the pie for the last 10 to 15 minutes of cooking to crisp up the pastry.
TO SERVE: sprinkle with (caster) sugar and leave to rest for 5 to 10 minutes.

Upside-down
Toffee Apple Tart

*Let the children make this tart – it will be
as much fun for them to make as
it will be good to eat later.*

Metric/Imperial
FOR THE PASTRY: 100 g/¼ lb flour
Pinch of salt
1×15 ml spoon/1 tablespoon icing sugar
50 g/2 oz butter, cut into small pieces
1 egg yolk, lightly beaten with 1×2.5 ml spoon/½ teaspoon vinegar
1×15 ml spoon/1 tablespoon iced water
FOR THE FILLING: 100 g/¼ lb sugar
1×15 ml spoon/1 tablespoon water
25 g/1 oz butter
½ kg/1 lb cooking or dessert apples
Fresh single cream, to serve

American
FOR THE PASTRY: 1 cup flour
Pinch of salt
1 tablespoon confectioners' sugar
¼ cup butter, cut into small pieces
1 egg yolk, lightly beaten with ½ teaspoon vinegar
1 tablespoon iced water
FOR THE FILLING: ½ cup sugar
1 tablespoon water
2 tablespoons butter
1 lb tart or cooking or dessert apples
Light cream, to serve

Make the pastry as for Plum Tart (page 197) and chill in the refrigerator for at least 30 minutes. Meanwhile, put the sugar, water and half the butter in a small saucepan and heat gently until the mixture has melted and turned golden brown. Pour immediately into a buttered 23 cm/9 inch aluminium foil or metal cake tin (pan) and tilt until the bottom of the tin is all covered. Leave until completely set.

Peel and core the apples and cut into thin slices. Arrange the slices, overlapping, in circles on top of the toffee base. Dot with the remaining butter. Roll out the chilled dough to a circle large enough to cover the apple slices. Place it on top of them and seal the edges to the lip of the tin (pan) with a little water. Prick the dough with a fork.
TO FREEZE: open (flash) freeze until solid, then wrap in cling film and overwrap in aluminium foil or a freezer bag. Seal, label and return to freezer.
TO THAW: unwrap and bake the tart from frozen in a hot oven (220°C/425°F or Gas Mark 7) for 40 to 50 minutes, or until pale golden brown.
TO SERVE: remove from the oven, leave to cool for a few minutes, then loosen the edges of the pastry and turn upside-down onto a warmed serving platter, being careful not to spill any juice. The toffee should have come away from the base of the tin (pan) and have sunk into the apples and pastry. Serve single (light) cream separately.

Illustrated from left to right are Plum Tart, Pears in Red Wine, and Orange Salad accompanied by cream and brandy snaps.

Orange Salad

Make this refreshing dessert in the winter when oranges are really plentiful. As an alternative to the brandy or liqueur suggested below, use gin — the flavour is unusual and surprisingly good.

Metric/Imperial
6 Navel or other juicy oranges
100 g/¼ lb sugar
2×15 ml spoons/2 tablespoons brandy or orange-flavoured liqueur
TO SERVE: Fresh single cream
Brandy snaps

American
6 Navel or other juicy oranges
½ cup sugar
2 tablespoons brandy or orange-flavored liqueur
TO SERVE: Light cream
Brandy snaps

Pare the rind off one orange very thinly, taking care not to include any of the pith. Cut the rind into very fine strips. Peel all the oranges thickly with a very sharp knife, removing all the pith and as much of the inner skin and pith as possible. Divide the oranges into segments and cut away all the skin encasing the segments, keeping the pieces of orange flesh intact. Remove any pips (seeds). Put the skinned orange segments in a bowl. Put the sugar and fine strips of orange rind in a heavy saucepan and heat gently, until the sugar has turned golden brown and begins to bubble, stirring occasionally. Pour this quickly over the oranges. It will be set to a hard toffee crust at first, then dissolve in the juice of the oranges. Taste for sweetness and add the brandy or liqueur.

TO FREEZE: transfer to a rigid container, cover, label and freeze.
TO THAW: leave in container for 4 to 5 hours at room temperature.
TO SERVE: transfer to a glass or china serving dish. Serve cream and brandy snaps separately.

Pears in Red Wine

Pears cannot be frozen successfully raw, but cooked in this way they not only freeze well, they also look extremely decorative when served. Do not use over-ripe pears for this dessert or they may disintegrate and spoil the look of the finished dish.

Metric/Imperial
½ kg/1 lb dessert or good cooking pears
100 g/¼ lb sugar
150 ml/¼ pint water
Approx. 150 ml/¼ pint red wine
Strip of orange peel
Fresh double cream, lightly whipped with Kirsch, to serve (optional)

American
4 medium-sized dessert or good cooking pears
½ cup sugar
⅔ cup water
Approx. ⅔ cup red wine
Strip of orange peel
Heavy cream, lightly whipped with Kirsch, to serve (optional)

Peel the pears, but do not remove their stalks (stems). Put the sugar and water in a saucepan just large enough to hold the pears side by side. Heat gently until the sugar has dissolved, stirring constantly, then bring to the boil and boil for 3 minutes. Put the pears in the pan, pour over enough red wine just to cover the pears, add the orange peel and poach very gently until the pears are just soft. (The poaching time will vary from 15 to 45 minutes according to the ripeness and size of the pears.)

Lift the pears out with a slotted spoon and transfer to a small bowl. Bring the liquid in the pan to the boil, then boil rapidly to reduce by about half. Strain over the pears and leave them to cool in the syrup, turning them from time to time so that they become evenly coloured. Discard the orange peel.

TO FREEZE: transfer the pears and syrup to a rigid container, cover, label and freeze.
TO THAW: leave in container for 5 to 6 hours at room temperature.
TO SERVE: transfer to a serving dish and serve with the whipped cream handed separately, if you like.

Plum Tart

This open tart freezes particularly well, and the contrast of the sweet pastry and the tartness of the plums is especially delicious. It is best made with small, purple-skinned, yellow-fleshed plums.

Metric/Imperial

FOR THE PASTRY:
150 g/6 oz flour

Pinch of salt

1×15 ml spoon/1 tablespoon icing sugar

75 g/3 oz butter, cut into small pieces

2 egg yolks, lightly beaten with 1×5 ml spoon/1 teaspoon vinegar

1×15 ml spoon/1 tablespoon iced water

FOR THE FILLING:
2×15 ml spoon/2 tablespoons biscuit or cake crumbs

700 g/1½ lb plums, washed, halved and stoned

75 g/3 oz caster sugar

1×2.5 ml spoon/½ teaspoon ground cinnamon

25 g/1 oz flaked almonds

Fresh double cream, lightly whipped with sugar to taste, to serve (optional)

American

FOR THE PASTRY:
1½ cups flour

Pinch of salt

1 tablespoon confectioners' sugar

⅓ cup butter, cut into small pieces

2 egg yolks, lightly beaten with 1 teaspoon vinegar

1 tablespoon iced water

FOR THE FILLING:
2 tablespoons cookie or cake crumbs

1½ lb plums, washed, halved and pitted

⅓ cup sugar

½ teaspoon ground cinnamon

2 tablespoons slivered almonds

Heavy cream, lightly whipped with sugar to taste, to serve (optional)

Sift the flour, salt and icing (confectioners') sugar onto a marble slab or board. Make a well in the centre and add the butter. Pour in the egg and vinegar mixture. Work all the ingredients together with a palette knife until the mixture resembles fine crumbs. Sprinkle on the iced water, then transfer to a lightly floured board and knead the dough briefly until smooth. Wrap in aluminium foil and chill in the refrigerator for at least 30 minutes.

Roll out the chilled dough and use to line a 23 cm/9 inch flan tin (tart pan) or aluminium foil tin (pie pan). Prick well with a fork. Line with foil and fill with dried beans. Bake blind in a hot oven (220°C/425°F or Gas Mark 7) for 10 minutes. Remove from the oven, remove beans and foil and sprinkle the biscuit (cookie) or cake crumbs evenly over the pastry. Arrange the plums in circles on top, slightly overlapping, with skin sides uppermost. Mix the sugar and cinnamon together, sprinkle evenly over the plums, then scatter over the almonds. Return to the hot oven and bake for 30 to 40 minutes or until the plums are just soft and cooked. Remove from the oven and taste for sweetness. Sprinkle on a little more sugar if necessary, then leave to cool.
TO FREEZE: wrap in cling film, then overwrap in aluminium foil or a freezer bag. Seal, label and freeze.
TO THAW: unwrap and bake the tart from frozen in a hot oven (220°C/425°F or Gas Mark 7) for 30 minutes or until the pastry is crisp. Remove from the oven and leave to thaw further at room temperature, if necessary.
TO SERVE: serve cold, with sweetened whipped cream handed separately, if liked.

Continental Baked Cheesecake is illustrated above, with Treacle Tart shown opposite.

Uncooked Cheesecake

This is a light dessert cheesecake which makes a good ending for a buffet supper.

Metric/Imperial

50 g/2 oz butter

225 g/½ lb digestive biscuits, finely crushed

350 g/¾ lb cream cheese, softened

75 g/3 oz caster sugar

2 eggs, separated

Finely grated rind and juice of 1 lemon

15 g/½ oz powdered gelatine

2×15 ml spoons/2 tablespoons water

300 ml/½ pint fresh double cream, lightly whipped

50 g/2 oz plain or bitter eating chocolate, grated, to finish

American

¼ cup butter

½ lb digestive biscuits or graham crackers, finely crushed

¾ lb cream cheese, softened

⅓ cup sugar

2 eggs, separated

Finely grated rind and juice of 1 lemon

1 envelope unflavored gelatin

2 tablespoons water

1¼ cups heavy cream, lightly whipped

2 squares (2 oz) semisweet chocolate, grated, to finish

Continental Baked Cheesecake

This cheesecake is best served with coffee after a dinner party. Offer small portions at first — it is deceptively creamy and rich. An extra-special way to serve it is to cover the top with halves of seedless grapes: lay the grapes cut sides down and sprinkle with plenty of sugar just before serving.

Metric/Imperial

225 g/½ lb digestive biscuits

50 g/2 oz butter or margarine, melted

½ kg/1 lb cream cheese, softened

2×15 ml spoons/2 tablespoons thick honey

50 g/2 oz brown sugar

Pinch of salt

2 eggs, beaten

Ground cinnamon, to finish

American

½ lb digestive biscuits or graham crackers

¼ cup butter or margarine, melted

2×8 oz packages cream cheese, softened

2 tablespoons thick honey

⅓ cup brown sugar

Pinch of salt

2 eggs, beaten

Ground cinnamon, to finish

Put the biscuits (crackers) between two sheets of greaseproof (waxed) paper and crush finely with a rolling pin. Put in a mixing bowl, pour in the melted butter or margarine and stir to combine.

Using a metal spoon, press the crumb mixture into the base and sides of a greased 18 cm/7 inch loose-bottomed cake tin (springform pan). Chill in the refrigerator for 30 minutes or until quite firm.

Meanwhile, prepare the filling. Cream the cheese, honey, sugar and salt together in a bowl, then beat in the eggs one at a time until the mixture is light and fluffy.

Pour the prepared filling into the chilled crumb base and bake in a cool oven (150°C/300°F or Gas Mark 2) for 45 to 60 minutes or until the filling is set.

Turn off the oven and leave the cheesecake inside the oven until it is completely cold.

TO FREEZE: open (flash) freeze until solid, then remove from the tin (pan). Wrap in cling film, then overwrap in a freezer bag. Seal, label and return to freezer.

TO THAW: unwrap, place on a serving dish and leave overnight in the refrigerator or for 4 to 5 hours at room temperature.

TO SERVE: sprinkle the top of the cheesecake liberally with ground cinnamon or cover with grapes as described above.

Melt the butter in a small saucepan, remove from the heat and stir in the biscuit (cracker) crumbs. Pour into a 25 cm/10 inch loose-bottomed cake tin (springform pan) and press down evenly to cover the base. Bake in a fairly hot oven (190°C/375°F or Gas Mark 5) for 10 minutes. Remove from the oven and leave to cool.

Beat the cream cheese with the sugar and egg yolks until the mixture is light and fluffy, then stir in the lemon rind. Sprinkle the gelatin(e) over the water in a pan, leave for 5 minutes until spongy, then heat gently until dissolved. Stir in the lemon juice, then beat the gelatin(e) mixture into the cream cheese mixture. Beat the egg whites until stiff, fold into the mixture, then fold in the cream. Pour mixture into the tin (pan) and leave to set.

TO FREEZE: open (flash) freeze until solid, then remove from the tin (pan). Wrap in cling film, then overwrap in aluminium foil or a freezer bag. Seal, label and return to freezer.

TO THAW: unwrap, place on a serving dish and leave overnight in the refrigerator or for 4 to 5 hours at room temperature.

TO SERVE: sprinkle the top of cheesecake with grated chocolate before serving.

Treacle Tart

This version of the classic English tart is a little less sweet than some, but if you really like the teeth-sticking variety, mix a little black treacle (molasses) with the syrup.

Metric/Imperial
FOR THE PASTRY:
150 g/6 oz flour
Pinch of salt
1×15 ml spoon/1 tablespoon icing sugar
75 g/3 oz butter, cut into small pieces
2 egg yolks, lightly beaten with 1×5 ml spoon/1 teaspoon vinegar
1×15 ml spoon/1 tablespoon iced water
FOR THE FILLING:
40 g/1½ oz fine fresh white breadcrumbs
225 ml/8 fl oz golden syrup
Finely grated rind and juice of ½ lemon
Fresh single or double cream, to serve

American
FOR THE PASTRY:
1½ cups flour
Pinch of salt
1 tablespoon confectioners' sugar
⅓ cup butter, cut into small pieces
2 egg yolks, lightly beaten with 1 teaspoon vinegar
1 tablespoon iced water
FOR THE FILLING:
½ cup fine fresh white breadcrumbs
1 cup golden or light corn syrup
Finely grated rind and juice of ½ lemon
Light or heavy cream, to serve

Make the pastry as for Plum Tart (page 197), and chill in the refrigerator at least for 30 minutes. Roll out the chilled dough and use to line a 20 cm/8 inch flan tin (tart pan), reserving leftover dough for decoration. Prick well with a fork, line with foil and fill with dried beans. Bake blind in a hot oven (220°C/425°F or Gas Mark 7) for 10 minutes. Remove from the oven, remove baking beans and foil and leave to cool.

Mix together the breadcrumbs, syrup and lemon rind and juice and pour this into the cooled flan case. Make a trellis over the top with the reserved strips of dough.

TO FREEZE: open (flash) freeze until solid, then wrap in cling film and overwrap in aluminium foil or a freezer bag. Seal, label and return to freezer.

TO THAW: unwrap and bake the tart from frozen in a hot oven (220°C/425°F or Gas Mark 7) for 20 minutes. Reduce the heat to fairly hot (190°C/375°F or Gas Mark 5) and bake for another 30 to 40 minutes or until the top of the pastry is pale golden brown.

TO SERVE: serve hot or cold, with cream handed separately.

The photograph opposite shows Lemon Mille-feuille Gâteau in the foreground with Charlotte Malakoff on the pedestal behind.

Lemon Mille-feuille Gâteau

Made with frozen puff pastry, this gâteau can be prepared very quickly if necessary. You can also freeze the completed gâteau, if you like.

Metric/Imperial

350–375 g/12–13 oz frozen puff pastry, thawed

4×15 ml spoons/4 tablespoons lemon curd (see page 224)

Juice of ½ lemon

300 ml/½ pint fresh double cream, lightly whipped

25 g/1 oz icing sugar

Crystallized lemon slices, to finish (optional)

American

Approx. ¾ lb frozen puff pastry, thawed

4 tablespoons lemon cheese (see page 224)

Juice of ½ lemon

1¼ cups heavy cream, lightly whipped

3 tablespoons confectioners' sugar

Crystallized lemon slices, to finish (optional)

Roll out the puff pastry and, using a dinner plate as a guide, cut into three rounds of approximately 23 cm/9 inch diameter. Cut remaining pastry into pastry leaves. Place on greased baking sheets, prick and bake in a hot oven (220°C/425°F or Gas Mark 7) for 10 minutes, or until the pastry has risen and is pale golden brown. (The pastry leaves will need less time than the rounds.) Remove from the oven and leave to cool.

Fold the lemon curd (cheese) and a few drops of the lemon juice into the whipped cream, and use to sandwich together the pastry rounds. Stir the remaining lemon juice into the icing (confectioners') sugar and use at once to ice the top of the gâteau. Decorate with the pastry leaves and the crystallized lemon slices.

TO FREEZE: open (flash) freeze until solid, then place carefully in a rigid container, tin or cardboard box. Cover, label and return to freezer.

TO THAW: remove from the container and transfer to a serving platter. Leave to thaw for 3 to 4 hours at room temperature.

TO SERVE: serve still slightly chilled, and cut into slices with a serrated-edged knife.

Charlotte Malakoff

Serve it on its own, or with tart fruit, such as raspberries or redcurrants, to counteract the sweetness of the charlotte and to provide a pleasing colour contrast.

Metric/Imperial

2×15 ml spoons/2 tablespoons orange-flavoured liqueur

1×15 ml spoon/1 tablespoon water

12–15 crisp sponge fingers

125 g/¼ lb unsalted butter

125 g/¼ lb caster sugar

125 g/¼ lb ground almonds

Finely grated rind of ½ orange

150 ml/¼ pint fresh double cream, lightly whipped

225 g/½ lb fresh or frozen raspberries or redcurrants, whole or puréed, to finish (optional)

American

2 tablespoons orange-flavored liqueur

1 tablespoon water

12–15 crisp ladyfingers

½ cup unsalted butter

½ cup sugar

⅔ cup ground almonds

Finely grated rind of ½ orange

⅔ cup heavy cream, lightly whipped

½ pint box fresh or frozen raspberries, whole or puréed, to finish (optional)

Line the bottom of 900 ml/1½ pint/2 pint charlotte mould or freezerproof soufflé dish with a round of grease-proof (waxed) paper. Mix half the liqueur with the water, then dip the sponge (lady) fingers briefly into this mixture and use to line the mould or dish, keeping the sugared side against the dish. Stand the fingers side by side in an upright position, around the inside of the mould.

Cream the butter and sugar together until light and fluffy, then add the ground almonds, orange rind and remaining liqueur. Fold in the cream lightly, then spoon the mixture into the lined mould or dish. Smooth over the top. Trim tops of biscuits (cookies), if necessary.

TO FREEZE: cover with cling film or aluminium foil, then overwrap in a freezer bag, seal, label and freeze.

TO THAW: unwrap, cover loosely and leave for 5 to 6 hours at room temperature.

TO SERVE: unmould onto a serving dish, surround with whole fruit or pour over fruit purée, or serve this separately.

Crêpes Suzette are illustrated above. Opposite, the Chocolate Sauce can be seen being poured over the Profiteroles.

Chestnut Pancakes (Crêpes)

Sweet pancakes (crêpes) go well after a light main course. The crêpes and filling can be frozen separately, or the dessert can be prepared completely and frozen. It is then ready to serve after thawing.

Metric/Imperial
FOR THE PANCAKE (CRÊPE) BATTER: 100 g/¼ lb flour
Pinch of salt
1×15 ml spoon/1 tablespoon icing sugar
1 egg, lightly beaten with 1 egg yolk
300 ml/½ pint milk
1×15 ml spoon/1 tablespoon brandy
1×15 ml spoon/1 tablespoon melted butter
Oil for frying
Dash of soda water
FOR THE FILLING: 1×15 ml spoon/1 tablespoon strong black liquid coffee
2×15 ml spoons/2 tablespoons rum or brandy
225 g/8 oz can sweetened chestnut purée
300 ml/½ pint fresh double cream, lightly whipped
Icing sugar, to finish

American
FOR THE CRÊPE BATTER: 1 cup flour
Pinch of salt
1 tablespoon confectioners' sugar
1 egg, lightly beaten with 1 egg yolk
1¼ cups milk
1 tablespoon brandy
1 tablespoon melted butter
Oil for frying
Dash of soda water
FOR THE FILLING: 1 tablespoon strong black liquid coffee
2 tablespoons rum or brandy
½ lb can sweetened chestnut purée
1¼ cups heavy cream, lightly whipped
Confectioners' sugar, to finish

Sift the flour, salt and icing (confectioners') sugar into a mixing bowl. Make a well in the centre, add the eggs, then gradually add half the milk. Beat vigorously with a wooden spoon, incorporating the flour gradually to make a smooth batter. Stir in the remaining milk, the brandy and the melted butter. Transfer to a jug or measuring cup for easy pouring and leave to stand in a cool place for at least 30 minutes.

Add a little more milk if necessary to make the batter the consistency of double (heavy) cream. Heat a little oil in a pancake (crêpe) or frying pan until very hot. Whisk the soda water into the batter, then pour a little (2×15 ml spoons/2 tablespoons) into the pan. Tilt the pan quickly so that the batter runs over the bottom. Cook over high heat until the underneath of the pancake (crêpe) is golden brown, then turn the pancake (crêpe) over and cook the other side until golden brown. Slide the pancake (crêpe) out of the pan onto a wire rack to cool. Repeat this method with the remaining batter, making 12 pancakes (crêpes) in all. Leave to cool.

Blend the coffee and half the rum or brandy into the chestnut purée. Whip the remaining rum or brandy into the cream, then fold half the cream into the chestnut purée. Spread this mixture onto each pancake (crêpe), roll up and place side by side in a freezerproof serving dish. Cover with the remaining cream.

TO FREEZE: open (flash) freeze until solid, then wrap in cling film and overwrap in foil or a freezer bag. Seal, label and return to freezer.

TO THAW: unwrap and leave for 4 to 5 hours at room temperature.

TO SERVE: dredge with little icing (confectioners') sugar before serving.

Crêpes Suzette

It is said that the first time Crêpes Suzette were heated at the table in a chafing dish, the liqueurs accidentally caught fire, but the embarrassed young chef served them anyway — to the Prince of Wales. The characteristic orange-flavoured sauce has been a classic ever since. Interleaved with greaseproof (waxed) paper, crêpes can be taken from the freezer as needed.

Metric/Imperial
FOR THE CRÊPE BATTER: 100 g/¼ lb flour
Pinch of salt
2 eggs, beaten
300 ml/½ pint milk
1×15 ml spoon/1 tablespoon melted butter
Oil or butter for frying
FOR THE SAUCE: 100 g/¼ lb caster sugar
Finely grated rind and juice of 2 oranges
2×15 ml spoons/2 tablespoons brandy
2×15 ml spoons/2 tablespoons Curaçao or orange-flavoured liqueur
1 slice of orange, to finish (optional)

American
FOR THE CRÊPE BATTER:
1 cup flour
Pinch of salt
2 eggs, beaten
1¼ cups milk
1 tablespoon melted butter
Oil or butter for frying
FOR THE SAUCE:
½ cup sugar
Finely grated rind and juice of 2 oranges
2 tablespoons brandy
2 tablespoons Curaçao or orange-flavored liqueur
1 slice of orange, to finish (optional)

Make the crêpe batter. Cook the crêpes and leave until cold as for Chestnut Pancakes (Crêpes), see opposite.

TO FREEZE: stack the crêpes, one on top of the other, interleaving each one with oiled greaseproof (waxed) paper. Put into freezer bags, seal, label and freeze.

TO THAW: unwrap crêpes and spread out individually. Leave to thaw for 20 to 30 minutes at room temperature. Heat a little oil or butter in a frying pan and reheat crêpes gently for ½ minute on each side, one at a time. Fold each crêpe into four to make a wedge-shape and keep warm while cooking remainder.

TO SERVE: make the sauce. Heat the sugar in a large frying pan, and cook over low heat until pale golden. Stir in the orange rind and juice with a wooden spoon, then add folded crêpes to the pan. Stir in the brandy and Curaçao or liqueur, heat for 1 minute and ignite if wished. Garnish with a twisted slice of orange, if you like, and serve immediately.

Profiteroles with Chocolate Sauce

Profiteroles can be frozen individually, so you can take out as many as you need. If you freeze the chocolate sauce as well there will be very little work to do at the last moment.

Metric/Imperial
FOR THE CHOUX PASTRY:
150 ml/¼ pint water
50 g/2 oz butter
Pinch of salt
65 g/2½ oz flour, sifted
2–3 eggs, beaten
FOR THE CHOCOLATE SAUCE:
1×5 ml spoon/1 teaspoon cornflour
150 ml/¼ pint milk
100 g/¼ lb brown sugar
50 g/2 oz plain chocolate, broken into pieces
Knob of butter
FOR THE FILLING:
150 ml/¼ pint fresh double cream, whipped with 1×15 ml spoon/1 tablespoon caster sugar

American
FOR THE CHOUX PASTRY:
⅔ cup water
¼ cup butter
Pinch of salt
⅔ cup flour, sifted
2–3 eggs, beaten
FOR THE CHOCOLATE SAUCE:
1 teaspoon cornstarch
⅔ cup milk
⅔ cup brown sugar
2 squares (2 oz) semisweet chocolate, broken into pieces
Knob of butter
FOR THE FILLING:
⅔ cup heavy cream, whipped with 1 tablespoon sugar

To make the choux pastry: put the water, butter and salt in a saucepan and heat gently until the butter has melted. Bring to the boil. Immediately remove the pan from the heat and quickly beat in the flour all at once. Continue beating for 2 minutes until the mixture draws away from the sides of the pan and forms a ball. Leave to cool slightly, then beat in the eggs one at a time until the dough is smooth and shiny. Add enough egg to make a mixture that just falls from the spoon — all the last egg may not be needed. Put the mixture into a large piping (pastry) bag fitted with a 1.25 cm/½ inch plain nozzle (tube) and pipe approximately 20 mounds onto a greased baking sheet. Allow room between each one for expansion during cooking. Bake just above the centre of a fairly hot oven (200°C/400°F or Gas Mark 6) for approximately 20 minutes or until the profiteroles are golden brown. Remove from the oven and make a slit in the side of each profiterole so that the steam can escape. Leave on a wire rack until completely cold.

Meanwhile, make the chocolate sauce. Blend the cornflour (cornstarch) with a little of the milk, then put in a saucepan with the remaining milk and the sugar. Stir over a gentle heat until the sugar has dissolved, then increase the heat and bring to the boil. Boil briskly for 2 minutes, without stirring. Remove from the heat and stir in the chocolate and butter until melted. Leave to cool.

TO FREEZE: open (flash) freeze profiteroles on trays until solid, then pack carefully into freezer bags. Seal, label and return to freezer. Pour chocolate sauce into a rigid container, cover, label and freeze.

TO THAW: unwrap frozen profiteroles, place on baking sheets and reheat in a moderate oven (180°C/350°F or Gas Mark 4) for approximately 10 minutes until heated through. Leave to cool. Tip frozen chocolate sauce into a saucepan and reheat gently, stirring occasionally.

TO SERVE: pipe or spoon the whipped cream into the profiteroles. Pile on a serving dish and dribble over hot chocolate sauce.

Baked Alaska

This makes a spectacular ending to a meal. Have it ready in the freezer, then pop it in the oven at the last moment, just before serving. It is best not to keep it in the freezer for more than 1 to 2 days. You can always make the Alaska with different flavoured icecream, substituting appropriate liqueur for the marsala. In this case, use a little less liqueur and dilute it with a little water before sprinkling over the sponge cake.

Metric/Imperial
100 g/¼ lb trifle sponges or sponge cake, cut into 1.25 cm/½ inch thick slices
150 ml/¼ pint marsala
600 ml/1 pint vanilla or strawberry icecream, slightly softened
3 egg whites
75 g/3 oz caster sugar
TO FINISH: 2×15 ml spoons/2 tablespoons brandy
1×15 ml spoon/1 tablespoon caster sugar

American
¼ lb sponge cake, cut into ½ inch thick slices
⅔ cup marsala
1¼ pints vanilla or strawberry icecream, slightly softened
3 egg whites
⅓ cup sugar
TO FINISH: 2 tablespoons brandy
1 tablespoon sugar
Serves 6

Line the bottom and sides of a shallow ovenproof serving dish with the cake slices. Sprinkle with half the marsala. Blend the remaining marsala into the icecream, then spoon onto the sponge, leaving at least a 2.5 cm/1 inch margin all around. Smooth the top and sides, then put in the freezer. Meanwhile, beat the egg whites until stiff, then slowly beat in the sugar to make a smooth meringue mixture. Remove serving dish from freezer and spread meringue mixture carefully over the icecream and sponge, right up to the edge of the dish to seal it completely.

TO FREEZE: open (flash) freeze until solid, then, if you are preparing the Alaska more than a few days ahead, wrap loosely with aluminium foil or freezer tissue, label and return to freezer. Do not wrap tightly or the meringue will collapse.

TO THAW: remove wrapping, if used, and bake from frozen in a hot oven (220°C/425°F or Gas Mark 7) for 10 minutes or until the meringue has browned slightly. Meanwhile, warm the brandy.

TO SERVE: sprinkle with sugar, then pour the brandy over the meringue topping. Set alight and bring flaming to the table. Serve immediately.

Orange Sherbet

This is an ideal dinner party dessert, especially if the sherbet is served in the orange shells. Serve with thin wafers or langues de chats biscuits (cookies).

Metric/Imperial
600 ml/1 pint plus 4×15 ml spoons/4 tablespoons water
225 g/½ lb sugar
1×15 ml spoon/1 tablespoon powdered gelatine
6–8 large Navel or other juicy oranges
1 egg white
Angelica, to finish

American
2½ cups plus 4 tablespoons water
2 cups sugar
1 envelope unflavored powdered gelatin
6–8 large Navel or other juicy oranges
1 egg white
Candied angelica, to finish
Serves 6 to 8

Put the 600 ml/1 pint/2½ cups water and the sugar in a saucepan and heat gently until the sugar has dissolved, stirring occasionally. Bring to boil, then boil for 5 minutes. Meanwhile, sprinkle the gelatin(e) over the remaining water and leave until spongy. Remove sugar syrup from heat, stir in the gelatin(e) mixture and leave to cool.

Cut the tops off the oranges and carefully scoop out the juice and flesh with a teaspoon, discarding any pips (seeds) and being careful to keep the shells intact if you are serving the sherbet in them. Purée the orange juice and flesh in an electric blender, then push through a sieve to extract the juice; there should be 300 ml/½ pint/1¼ cups. If not, add extra water to make this quantity. When the sugar mixture is quite cool, stir in the orange juice, then pour into an ice-tray or metal tin (pan).

TO FREEZE: put in freezer for 1 to 2 hours or until mixture becomes mushy. Remove from freezer and beat well. Beat the egg white until stiff, then fold into sherbet. Return to the tray or tin (pan), wrap in aluminium foil or a freezer bag, cover or seal, label and return to freezer.

TO THAW: unwrap and leave to stand for a maximum of 10 minutes at room temperature.

TO SERVE: scoop onto individual plates immediately after thawing while sherbet is fairly soft in texture. If wishing to serve sherbet in orange shells, wash these thoroughly after scooping out flesh and juice, then pat dry and cut the bottoms level so that the oranges will stand upright. Spoon prepared sherbet into shells after adding egg white, piling it above the top of shells. Put any remaining sherbet in tray or tin (pan) and return to freezer as above. Stand oranges in an upright position on a tray, freeze for approximately 2 hours until solid, then wrap oranges individually in freezer bags. Seal, then stand in a rigid container, cover, label and return to freezer. Thaw as above. Decorate with angelica. Serve extra sherbet in a bowl for 'second helpings'.

Cassata

This moulded icecream dessert is filled with fruit and nuts. Use homemade icecream or a top-quality commercially prepared variety.

Metric/Imperial
600 ml/1 pint chocolate icecream, slightly softened
400 ml/¾ pint strawberry icecream or water ice, slightly softened
150 ml/¼ pint fresh double cream
15 g/½ oz icing sugar
25 g/1 oz candied peel, finely chopped
25 g/1 oz sultanas, chopped
15 g/½ oz candied angelica, chopped
50 g/2 oz red glacé cherries, chopped
15 g/½ oz almonds, blanched and cut into slivers

American

1¼ pints chocolate icecream, slightly softened
1 pint strawberry icecream or sherbet, slightly softened
⅔ cup heavy cream
1¼ tablespoons confectioners' sugar
2 tablespoons finely chopped candied peel
2 tablespoons chopped golden raisins
1 tablespoon chopped candied angelica or candied green cherries
¼ cup candied red cherries, chopped
2 tablespoons slivered almonds
Serves 6 to 8

Line a chilled 1 litre/2 pint/5 cup metal bowl, mould or pudding basin with the chocolate ice cream. Put in the freezer until hard, then smooth in the strawberry icecream, water ice, or sherbet to form another layer, approximately 1.25 cm/½ inch thick, leaving a well in the centre. Return to the freezer until hard. Lightly whip the cream with the icing (confectioners') sugar, fold in the chopped fruit and nuts, then fill the centre well of the mould with this mixture. Smooth over the top.

TO FREEZE: cover with cling film or aluminium foil, then overwrap in a freezer bag, seal, label and freeze.

TO THAW: leave in wrappings for 30 minutes in the refrigerator.

TO SERVE: turn out of the mould onto a chilled serving platter: wrap the mould briefly in a towel that has been rung out in hot water — the cassata should slip out of the mould immediately. If it is melted on the outside, return to the freezer for 10 minutes to harden before serving.

Brown Bread Icecream

This old-fashioned icecream is made with leftover stale bread, and is amazingly good.

Metric/Imperial

50 g/2 oz butter
75 g/3 oz breadcrumbs, made from stale brown bread
175 g/6 oz sugar
4 egg yolks
300 ml/½ pint milk or fresh single cream
2×15 ml spoons/2 tablespoons sweet sherry
300 ml/½ pint fresh double cream, lightly whipped

American

¼ cup butter
1 cup breadcrumbs, made from stale wholewheat bread
¾ cup sugar
4 egg yolks
1¼ cups milk or light cream
2 tablespoons cream sherry
1¼ cups heavy cream, lightly whipped

Melt the butter in a pan, add the breadcrumbs and fry until crisp. Sprinkle on half the sugar and continue to fry until the sugar has caramelized, stirring constantly. Pour onto a wooden board, leave to cool, then crush into fine crumbs with a rolling pin.

Beat the egg yolks with the remaining sugar until light and fluffy. Scald the milk or single (light) cream and pour slowly onto the yolk and sugar mixture, beating constantly. Return to the pan and heat gently without allowing to boil. Stir constantly until the mixture has thickened enough to coat the back of the spoon. Remove from the heat and leave to cool. When cool, stir in the breadcrumbs and sherry, then fold in the double (heavy) cream.

TO FREEZE: pour into a rigid container and freeze rapidly, either in the ice-making compartment of the refrigerator, or in the quick-freezing part of the freezer. After 1 hour, or when the mixture begins to set, stir well with a fork to distribute the crumbs evenly. Transfer to a freezer-proof dish, cover with aluminium foil, label and return to freezer.

TO THAW: remove from freezer, wrap the dish with a towel that has been rung out in hot water, then unmould onto a chilled platter. Smooth the sides with a metal spatula and return to freezer for 10 minutes, then transfer to the refrigerator for 30 minutes.

TO SERVE: scoop or cut into wedges and serve on chilled plates.

Christmas Plum Pudding

It is a good idea to freeze your Christmas pudding since there is then no risk of mould forming on top.

Metric/Imperial

100 g/¼ lb self-raising flour
1×5 ml spoon/1 teaspoon mixed spice
1×1.25 ml spoon/¼ teaspoon salt
100 g/¼ lb fresh white breadcrumbs
100 g/¼ lb shredded beef suet
100 g/¼ lb dark brown sugar
350 g/¾ lb seedless raisins
100 g/¼ lb sultanas
100 g/¼ lb currants
100 g/¼ lb candied peel, finely chopped
50 g/2 oz blanched almonds, finely chopped
2 large cooking apples, peeled, cored and coarsely chopped
Finely grated rind and juice of ½ lemon
2 eggs, beaten
150 ml/¼ pint beer
Approx. 2×15 ml spoons/2 tablespoons brandy, sherry or milk
Brandy butter or whipped fresh double cream, to serve

American

1 cup flour, sifted with 1½ teaspoons baking powder
½ teaspoon ground allspice
½ teaspoon ground cinnamon
¼ teaspoon salt
2 cups fresh white breadcrumbs
⅔ cup ground beef suet
⅔ cup dark brown sugar
2 cups seedless raisins
¾ cup golden raisins
¾ cup currants
½ cup candied peel, finely chopped
½ cup blanched almonds, finely chopped
2 large cooking apples, peeled, cored and coarsely chopped
Finely grated rind and juice of ½ lemon
2 eggs, beaten
⅔ cup beer
Approx. 2 tablespoons brandy, sherry or milk
Hard sauce or whipped heavy cream, to serve

Make 2 puddings:
1×1 litre/1 quart/5 cup; and 1×½ litre/1 pint/2½ cup

Sift the flour into a bowl with the spices and salt. Stir in the breadcrumbs, suet and sugar, the dried fruit and peel, nuts and apples. Mix well together. Beat in the lemon rind and juice and eggs, then the beer, and enough brandy, sherry or milk to make a consistency that just drops from the spoon. Stir well to combine. Divide the mixture between heatproof pudding basins or soufflé dishes. Cover the tops of puddings with circles of greased greaseproof (parchment) paper, then put a piece of cloth or aluminium foil around the top of the basins, with a pleat in the centre, and tie securely around the rims with string. Place the basins in the top of a double boiler or steamer, or in a large pan of gently bubbling water, and steam for 4 to 5 hours, adding more water from time to time during cooking to keep the level up. Remove the basins carefully from the pan and leave until quite cold.
TO FREEZE: turn the puddings out of the basins and wrap well in aluminium foil. Overwrap in freezer bags, seal, label and freeze.
TO THAW: unwrap the puddings and replace in the basins. Leave to thaw overnight at room temperature. Cover the tops with aluminium foil, then re-steam for 2 to 3 hours.
TO SERVE: turn out onto a warmed serving dish, decorate with sprigs of holly, pour warmed brandy over and set alight. Serve with brandy butter (hard sauce) or whipped cream.

Soft Fruit Pudding

Soft fruits are in season for such a short time, so make this dessert after a day's berry picking. Use fresh fruit, fruit from the freezer, or a mixture of both.

Metric/Imperial

¾ kg/1½ lb mixed soft fruits (blackberries, raspberries, redcurrants or blackcurrants), washed and hulled
175 g/6 oz caster sugar, or to taste
100–175 g/4–6 oz crustless stale white bread, cut into thin slices
150 ml/¼ pint fresh double cream, to serve

American

1½ lb mixed soft fruits (blackberries, raspberries, blueberries), washed and hulled
¾ cup sugar, or to taste
4–6 oz crustless stale white bread, cut into thin slices
⅔ cup heavy cream, to serve

Put the soft fruit and sugar in a saucepan (the amount of sugar needed will depend on the tartness of the fruit). Cook gently for 5 minutes or until the sugar has dissolved and the fruit is soft. Taste for sweetness. Line the base and sides of a 900 ml/1½ pint/1 quart aluminium foil basin or metal bowl with the bread slices, reserving 2 or 3 slices for the top. Pour the poached fruit into the basin and put the reserved bread slices on the top, pressing down firmly. Cover the top of the basin with a plate or saucer and put heavy weights, cans or a brick on top. Leave overnight in the refrigerator.
TO FREEZE: remove weights and plate or saucer. Cover basin with aluminium foil, overwrap in a freezer bag, seal, label and freeze.
TO THAW: unwrap and leave for 6 to 8 hours at room temperature.
TO SERVE: turn pudding out onto serving platter and serve double (heavy) cream separately.

Christmas Plum Pudding
Soft Fruit Pudding

Christmas Plum Pudding is illustrated opposite, with Soft Fruit Pudding shown below.

207

Baked Goods and Family Treats

Two loaves of White Bread can be seen opposite, with a loaf of Wholewheat Bread between them, and Doughnuts in the foreground. The 'bumpy' white loaf at the back is formed by shaping the dough into four separate oblongs and placing them side-by-side in the tin.

White Bread

It is worth making quite a batch of bread and freezing the spare loaves. They will emerge as newly-baked from the freezer.

Metric/Imperial
25 g/1 oz fresh (compressed) yeast
¾ litre/1½ pints lukewarm water
1½ kg/3 lb strong plain flour
2×5 ml spoons/2 teaspoons salt
50 g/2 oz lard

American
2 packages compressed fresh yeast or 2 envelopes dried yeast
3½ cups lukewarm water
3½ quarts (14 cups) white flour
2 teaspoons salt
¼ cup lard
Makes approximately four 450 g/1 lb loaves

Dissolve the yeast in the water, then leave in a warm place for 10 minutes. Sift the flour and salt into a large bowl and rub in the lard. Make a well in the centre and pour in the yeast mixture slowly, working in the flour to produce a firm dough which leaves the bowl clean. Transfer the dough to a floured board and knead until firm and elastic. Grease the bowl and return dough to it, cover with a clean, dampened tea (dish) towel and leave to rise in a warm place for 1 hour or until doubled in bulk.

Knead the dough again on a floured board for 5 minutes to knock out the air until smooth. Cover and leave to rise again in a warm place for 30 minutes. Divide the dough into as many parts as you wish to make loaves, and either shape into loaves and place on a greased baking sheet or place in greased loaf tins (pans). Leave to rise again in a warm place for another 30 minutes or until the tops of the loaves begin to flatten slightly.

Bake in a very hot oven (230°C/450°F or Gas Mark 8) for 30 to 50 minutes or until the loaves are brown on top, and sound hollow when tapped on the bottom (see Wholewheat Bread). Remove from the tins, transfer to a wire rack and leave to cool.

TO FREEZE: wrap in aluminium foil, then overwrap in a freezer bag, seal, label and freeze.

TO THAW: leave in wrappings for 4 to 5 hours at room temperature. Or bake from frozen in foil wrapping in a very hot oven (230°C/450°F or Gas Mark 8) for 30 minutes, then remove from oven and leave to cool.

TO SERVE: as soon as possible.

Wholewheat Bread

One of the beauties of freezing is that bread can be taken out as and when it is needed; this way you need never have to eat stale bread.

Metric/Imperial
15 g/½ oz fresh (compressed) yeast
300 ml/½ pint lukewarm milk and water, mixed
225 g/½ lb wholewheat flour
225 g/½ lb strong plain flour, sifted
1×5 ml spoon/1 teaspoon salt
38 g/1½ oz cracked wheat, to finish

American
1 cake fresh yeast or 1 envelope dried yeast
1¼ cups lukewarm milk and water, mixed
2 cups wholewheat flour
2 cups all-purpose flour, sifted
1 teaspoon salt
¼ cup cracked wheat, to finish

Dissolve the yeast in a few tablespoons of the milk and water, then leave in a warm place for 10 minutes. Put flours and the salt in a large, warmed bowl and stir well to combine. Make a well in the centre and pour in the yeast mixture and the remaining milk and water. Mix together with a wooden spoon until a soft dough is formed, then transfer to a floured board and knead for 10 minutes or until smooth. Return the dough to the greased bowl, cover with a clean dampened tea (dish) towel and leave to rise in a warm place for 1 hour or until doubled in bulk.

Knead the dough again on a floured board for 5 minutes to knock out the air. Shape the dough and put into a well-greased, warmed 1 kg/2 lb 8½ × 4½ × 2½-inch loaf tin (pan) or place on a greased baking sheet. Leave to rise again in a warm place until the dough rises to the top of the tin (pan).

Brush the top of the dough with a little milk and water, then sprinkle with the cracked wheat. Bake in a hot oven (225°C/425°F or Gas Mark 7) for 30 to 40 minutes or until the loaves are brown on top. Remove from the tin (pan) and knock the bottom of the loaf with your knuckles — the bread is ready if it sounds hollow. (If not cooked, return loaf to the oven, putting directly onto oven shelf, and cook for another few minutes.) Remove from the oven, transfer to a wire rack, and leave to cool.

TO FREEZE: wrap in aluminium foil, then overwrap in a freezer bag, seal, label and freeze.

TO THAW: leave in wrappings for 4 hours at room temperature. Thawed bread may be 'refreshed' in foil wrapping in a fairly hot oven (200°C/400°F or Gas Mark 6) for 15 minutes.

Doughnuts

Doughnuts can be taken from the freezer and served within 10 minutes. Because they are refreshed in the oven they are as good as when they are freshly baked.

Metric/Imperial
15 g/½ oz fresh (compressed) yeast
150 ml/¼ pint lukewarm milk
225 g/½ lb strong plain flour
1×2.5 ml spoon/½ teaspoon salt
1×15 ml spoon/1 tablespoon butter or margarine, cut into small pieces
1×15 ml spoon/1 tablespoon caster sugar
Red fruit jam (optional)
Oil for deep-fat frying
Caster sugar, to finish

American
1 cake fresh yeast or 1 envelope dried yeast
scant ⅔ cup lukewarm milk
2 cups flour
½ teaspoon salt
1 tablespoon butter or margarine, cut into small pieces
1 tablespoon sugar
Red fruit jam (optional)
Oil for deep-fat frying
Sugar, to finish

Dissolve the yeast in a little of the milk, then leave in a warm place for 10 minutes. Sift the flour and salt into a warm bowl, add the butter or margarine and rub into the flour with the fingers. Stir in the sugar. Make a well in the centre and pour in the yeast mixture, adding enough of the remaining warm milk to form a smooth dough. Knead the dough for a few minutes on a lightly floured board, but do not allow to become sticky. Return to the greased bowl, cover with a clean dampened tea (dish) towel and leave to rise in a warm place for 1 hour or until doubled in bulk.

Transfer the dough to a floured board and knead lightly to knock out the air. Roll out into a piece approximately 1.25 cm/½ inch thick. Cut into 12 to 14 rounds with a 6.5 cm/2½ inch round biscuit (cookie) cutter. If wishing to make ring doughnuts, cut a hole in the middle of each round of dough with a 2.5 cm/1 inch cutter. Or to make jam doughnuts, flatten each round of dough and put 1×5 ml spoon/1 teaspoon jam in the centre of each. Fold the edges up and roll the dough into a ball, enclosing and sealing the jam in the centre. Put the rounds on greased baking sheets, leaving room for expansion, and leave to rise in a warm place for approximately 20 minutes.

Heat the oil in a deep fat fryer until the temperature reaches 180–190°C /350–375°F on a deep-frying thermometer. Fry the doughnuts a few at a time in the hot oil until they rise to the surface and are golden brown and puffy. Remove from the fryer with a slotted spoon and drain on kitchen paper towels. Leave until cold.
TO FREEZE: pack in a single layer in aluminium foil or freezer bags, seal, label and freeze.
TO THAW: unwrap, place on a baking sheet and reheat from frozen in a fairly hot oven (200°C/400°F or Gas Mark 6) for 5 to 8 minutes or until hot.
TO SERVE: toss in plenty of sugar and serve immediately.

White Bread

Wholewheat Bread

Doughnuts

Chelsea Buns are illustrated on this page and Scones (Baking Powder Biscuits) can be seen opposite.

Mince Pies

Store these in the freezer for the festive period when there is so much cooking to do. Mince pies can be reheated from frozen and served fresh and warm within minutes.

Metric/Imperial
225 g/½ lb flour
Pinch of salt
150 g/5 oz butter or margarine, cut into small pieces
1×15 ml spoon/1 tablespoon caster sugar
Approx. 3×15 ml spoons/3 tablespoons water
Approx. 350 g/¾ lb mincemeat (fruit mince)
TO FINISH: 1 egg, beaten
Icing sugar for dusting

American
2 cups flour
Pinch of salt
⅔ cup butter or margarine, cut into small pieces
1 tablespoon sugar
Approx. 3 tablespoons water
Approx. 1½ cups mincemeat
TO FINISH: 1 egg, beaten
Confectioners' sugar for sprinkling
Makes approximately 12 mince pies

Sift the flour and salt into a mixing bowl, add the butter or margarine and rub into the flour with the fingers until the mixture resembles fine breadcrumbs. Using a palette knife, stir in the sugar and enough water to draw the mixture together. Transfer to a lightly floured board and knead the dough briefly until smooth. Wrap in aluminium foil and chill in the refrigerator for at least 30 minutes.

Roll out the chilled dough on a floured board. Cut 12 circles using a 7.5 cm/3 inch round fluted biscuit (cookie) cutter, and 12 circles using a 6.5 cm/2½ inch cutter. Lightly grease a tray of deep patty tins (muffin cups) and line with the larger circles of dough. Divide the mincemeat (fruit mince) equally among them. Moisten the edges of the dough with water, then top with the remaining circles, sealing well. Make a small hole with a skewer in the top of each pie.

TO FREEZE: open (flash) freeze until solid, then remove pies from tins (cups) and put into a rigid container.
TO THAW: return frozen pies to the tins (cups), brush with the beaten egg and bake in a fairly hot oven (200°C/400°F or Gas Mark 6) for 20 minutes or until brown.
TO SERVE: remove pies from tins (cups), sprinkle with icing (confectioners') sugar and serve hot.
N.B. If you like, you can cook the mince pies before freezing. Cook as above, cool, pack and freeze, then reheat from frozen on a baking sheet in a fairly hot oven for approximately 10 minutes or until heated through.

Chelsea Buns

Homemade Chelsea buns are simply out of this world, and deep-frozen ones taste just as good as they did on the day they were baked.

Metric/Imperial
350 g/¾ lb strong plain flour
1×2.5 ml spoon/½ teaspoon salt
1×5 ml spoon/1 teaspoon mixed spice
38 g/1½ oz butter, margarine or lard
15 g/½ oz fresh (compressed) yeast, or 3×5 ml spoons/3 teaspoons dried yeast and 1×5 ml spoon/1 teaspoon sugar
Approx. 150 ml/¼ pint lukewarm milk
1 egg, beaten
3×15 ml spoons/3 tablespoons caster sugar
50 g/2 oz butter
50 g/2 oz demerara sugar
50 g/2 oz currants or sultanas
FOR THE SUGAR SYRUP: 50 g/2 oz sugar
2×15 ml spoons/2 tablespoons water

American
3 cups flour
½ teaspoon salt
½ teaspoon ground allspice
½ teaspoon ground cinnamon
3 tablespoons butter, margarine or shortening
1 cake fresh yeast, or 1 envelope dried yeast and 1 teaspoon sugar
Approx. ⅔ cup lukewarm milk
1 egg, beaten
3 tablespoons sugar
¼ cup butter
⅓ cup light brown sugar
⅓ cup currants or golden raisins
FOR THE SUGAR SYRUP: ¼ cup sugar
2 tablespoons water

Sift the flour, salt and half the mixed spice (allspice and cinnamon) into a warm mixing bowl. Work in the fat with the fingers. Dissolve the yeast in a little of the warm milk. (If using dried yeast, stir the sugar into the warm milk, then sprinkle over the dried yeast.) Leave in a warm place for 10 minutes or until frothy. Stir the egg and sugar into the flour, then make a well in the centre and gradually add the yeast and remaining milk, mixing with the hands until a soft dough is formed. If the dough is too dry, add a little more warm milk. Knead the dough on a lightly floured board until smooth. Return to the greased bowl, cover with a clean dampened tea (dish) towel and leave in a warm place for ¾ to 1 hour or until doubled in bulk.

Transfer dough to a floured board and roll out 1.25 cm/½ inch thick into an oblong shape, approximately 30 cm/12 inches × 23 cm/9 inches. Melt the butter in a small pan, then brush over the dough. Mix together the sugar, fruit and remaining spice and sprinkle over the butter. Roll up the dough from the long end like a Swiss (jelly) roll, dampening the edges and pressing down firmly to seal. Cut the roll into 10 to 12 slices, using a very sharp knife dipped in warm water and cutting with a sawing motion. Grease a roasting pan, and lay the slices in it, cut sides up. Cover and leave in a warm place for 30 to 45 minutes or until well risen.

Bake in a hot oven (220°C/425°F or Gas Mark 7) for 15 to 20 minutes or until browned on top. Remove from the oven, transfer to a wire rack and leave to cool.

TO FREEZE: wrap Chelsea buns in a single layer in aluminium foil, then overwrap in a freezer bag, seal, label and freeze.

TO THAW: remove overwrapping, put foil package on a baking sheet and reheat in a fairly hot oven (200°C/400°F or Gas Mark 6) for 10 to 15 minutes or until hot. Meanwhile, make a sugar syrup as for Savarin (page 220). Remove foil package from the oven, unwrap and transfer buns to a wire rack. Brush with the prepared sugar syrup, then leave to cool slightly.

TO SERVE: Separate the buns from each other, split and butter.

Scones (Baking Powder Biscuits)

Scones, like their American counterpart, baking powder biscuits, freeze well after baking. Next time someone pops in unexpectedly for tea, fetch a few scones out of the freezer — they can be on the table within 15 minutes.

Metric/Imperial
225 g/½ lb self-raising flour
Pinch of salt
50 g/2 oz butter, cut into small pieces
50 g/2 oz caster sugar
Approx. 150 ml/¼ pint milk

American
2 cups flour, sifted with 1 tablespoon baking powder
Pinch of salt
¼ cup butter, cut into small pieces
¼ cup sugar
Approx. ⅔ cup milk

Sift the flour and salt into a mixing bowl. Add the butter, then work into the flour with the fingers until the mixture resembles fine breadcrumbs. Stir in the sugar, then gradually stir in the milk until a soft dough is formed. Turn the dough out onto a floured board and knead lightly until smooth. Roll out until approximately 1.75 cm/¾ inch thick, then stamp into 12 to 15 rounds with a 5 cm/2 inch round biscuit (cookie) cutter. Put the rounds on a preheated greased baking sheet and bake in a hot oven (220°C/425°F or Gas Mark 7) for 10 minutes or until the scones are well risen and golden. Remove from the oven, transfer to a wire rack and leave to cool.

TO FREEZE: wrap in a single layer in aluminium foil, then overwrap in a freezer bag, seal, label and freeze.

TO THAW: remove overwrapping, put foil package on a baking sheet and reheat in a moderate oven (180°C/350°F or Gas Mark 4) for 10 minutes or until hot.

TO SERVE: split and butter while still warm, and serve with homemade jam and whipped cream.

Mince Pies
Chelsea Buns
Scones (Baking Powder Biscuits)

211

Scotch Gingerbread

This is a moist, sticky gingerbread, marvellous for tea on a cold day, or for a children's party.

Metric/Imperial

125 g/¼ lb butter or margarine

175 g/6 oz black treacle

50 g/2 oz golden syrup

125 g/¼ lb dark brown sugar

6×15 ml spoons/6 tablespoons milk

2 eggs, lightly beaten

225 g/½ lb flour

Large pinch of salt

1×5 ml spoon/1 teaspoon bicarbonate of soda

1×15 ml spoon/1 tablespoon ground ginger

1×5 ml spoon/1 teaspoon ground cinnamon

25 g/1 oz blanched almonds, flaked

American

½ cup butter or margarine

½ cup molasses

¼ cup golden or light corn syrup

⅔ cup dark brown sugar

6 tablespoons milk

2 eggs, lightly beaten

2 cups flour

Large pinch of salt

1 teaspoon baking soda

1 tablespoon ground ginger

1 teaspoon ground cinnamon

3 tablespoons slivered almonds

Melt the butter or margarine, treacle or molasses, syrup and brown sugar in a small saucepan over gentle heat, stirring until well blended. Remove from the heat and leave to cool a little, then blend in the milk and eggs.

Sift the flour into a bowl with the salt, soda, ginger and cinnamon, then pour the contents of the pan slowly into the centre and beat with a wooden spoon until the batter is smooth. Grease a 20 cm/8 inch square cake tin (pan) and line with greased greaseproof (waxed) paper. Pour in the batter. Sprinkle with the flaked almonds.

Bake in a warm oven (160°C/325°F or Gas Mark 3) for 1 hour or until a skewer inserted in centre of cake comes out clean. Remove from pan, leave to cool for 10 minutes, then turn out onto a wire rack and leave to cool completely.

TO FREEZE: wrap in cling film, then overwrap in aluminium foil or a freezer bag, seal, label and freeze.

TO THAW: unwrap and leave for 3 to 4 hours at room temperature.

TO SERVE: slice or cut into squares before serving.

Pastry Cream Slices and Horns

These professional-looking confections can be made very quickly with frozen puff pastry or patty shells. If you have no cornet-shaped moulds, the pastry can be rolled around cannelloni moulds or a homemade version made with heavy-duty aluminium foil.

Metric/Imperial

225 g/½ lb frozen puff pastry, thawed for 30 minutes at room temperature

1 egg white, lightly beaten

25 g/1 oz sugar

TO FINISH:
1×15 ml spoon/1 tablespoon red jam (optional)

150 ml/¼ pint fresh double or whipping cream, lightly whipped

American

½ lb frozen puff pastry or patty shells, thawed for 30 minutes at room temperature

1 egg white, lightly beaten

2 tablespoons sugar

TO FINISH:
1 tablespoon red jam (optional)

⅔ cup heavy cream, lightly whipped

To make slices: roll out the pastry thinly on a floured board, then cut into strips 2.5 cm/1 inch wide, 5 cm/2 inches long. Brush with the egg white and sprinkle liberally with sugar.

To make horns: roll out pastry a little thinner than for slices; then cut into long strips 1.5 cm/½ inch wide and roll around metal cornet-shaped moulds. Brush with egg white, then sprinkle with sugar.

Place slices or horns on baking sheets and bake in a hot oven (220°C/425°F or Gas Mark 7) for 10 to 15 minutes or until the pastry has risen and is pale brown, turning the horns over after 10 minutes. Do not leave in the oven too long, or the sugar will burn. Remove from the oven, transfer to a wire rack, and leave to cool for 10 to 15 minutes. Remove cornet moulds used.

TO SERVE: split the slices, then sandwich together with jam (if using) and lightly whipped cream. Fill the horns with jam and cream. Serve as soon as possible, or refrigerate until serving time.

Brownies

An old-time favourite, Brownies need no introduction on either side of the Atlantic. They keep beautifully moist and fresh in the freezer.

Metric/Imperial

75 g/3 oz butter

75 g/3 oz caster sugar

1 egg, lightly beaten

100 g/¼ lb flour

Pinch of salt

1×1.25 ml spoon/¼ teaspoon baking powder

75 g/3 oz plain chocolate, melted in 1×15 ml spoon/1 tablespoon milk

75 g/3 oz shelled walnuts, roughly chopped (optional)

American

⅓ cup butter

⅓ cup sugar

1 egg, lightly beaten

1 cup flour

Pinch of salt

¼ teaspoon baking powder

3 squares (3 oz) semisweet chocolate melted in 1 tablespoon milk

½ cup shelled walnuts, roughly chopped (optional)

Cream the butter and sugar together until light and fluffy, then beat in the egg. Sift the flour together with the salt and baking powder and beat into the mixture, then stir in the melted chocolate and the walnuts (if using). Grease a 20 cm/8 inch square deep cake tin (pan) and pour in the mixture. Bake in a moderate oven (130°C/350°F or Gas Mark 4) for 25 to 30 minutes or until a skewer inserted in centre of cake comes out clean. Remove from the oven, leave to cool for 10 minutes, then cut into squares while still warm and leave to cool completely.

TO FREEZE: place in a rigid container, box or tin, or leave in the baking tin (pan). Cover or wrap, label and freeze.

TO THAW: leave in container for 1 hour at room temperature.

TO SERVE: serve with tea, as a snack or with icecream for dessert.

Madeleines

These are Marcel Proust's delicate little teacakes, a bite of which, dipped in tea, brought back the memory of his childhood. For the authentic shape, they should be baked in fluted, shell-shaped tins, but ordinary bun (muffin) or patty tins (tartlet pans) will do just as well. They emerge from the freezer, ready to eat within 40 minutes, as crisp and light as newly baked.

Metric/Imperial

2 eggs, separated

125 g/¼ lb caster sugar

125 g/¼ lb unsalted butter, melted and cooled

125 g/¼ lb flour, sifted

Juice of ½ lemon

American

2 eggs, separated

½ cup sugar

½ cup unsalted butter, melted and cooled

1 cup flour, sifted

Juice of ½ lemon

Makes 24

Beat the egg yolks with the sugar until the mixture is thick and light. Beat in the butter, then the flour and lemon juice. Beat the egg whites until stiff, then fold into the cake mixture. Put heaped teaspoonsful of the mixture into buttered madeleine moulds and bake in a fairly hot oven (190°C/375°F or Gas Mark 5) for 20 to 25 minutes or until just beginning to brown at the edges. Remove from the oven, leave to cool in moulds for 5 to 10 minutes, then transfer carefully (they are quite fragile) to a wire rack to cool completely.

TO FREEZE: pack in a rigid container, box or tin, cover, label and freeze.

TO THAW: leave in container at room temperature for 30 to 40 minutes.

TO SERVE: serve with morning coffee or afternoon tea.

Scotch Gingerbread is shown on the left of this photograph, with Pastry Cream Slices and Brownies in the centre and Madeleines on the right.

Victoria Sandwich filled with jam and topped with glacé icing and walnuts is illustrated below. Lightning Cake and Apple Cake can be seen in the centre photograph with Granny's Fruit Cake in the bottom right-hand corner.

Victoria Sandwich

The beauty of freezing a basic cake like a Victoria Sandwich is that it can be used for so many occasions. The fillings, flavourings, icings and toppings can be added to the basic cake once thawed, and in this way you can very quickly make the cake fit the occasion.

Metric/Imperial
225 g/½ lb butter or margarine
225 g/½ lb caster sugar
4 eggs, beaten
225 g/½ lb self-raising flour
Pinch of salt
3–4×15 ml spoons/3–4 tablespoons warm water

American
1 cup butter or margarine
1 cup sugar
4 eggs, beaten
2 cups flour sifted with 2 teaspoons baking powder
Pinch of salt
3–4 tablespoons warm water

Cream the butter or margarine and sugar until light and fluffy. Beat in the eggs a little at a time. Sift the flour and salt together, then beat 1×15 ml spoon/1 tablespoon of the flour into the butter mixture. Fold in the remaining flour. Add enough water to give the mixture a consistency which just drops from the spoon. Grease two 20 cm/8 inch diameter sandwich tins (layer pans) and line with greased greaseproof (parchment) paper. Divide the mixture evenly between the two tins (pans).

Bake just above the centre of a fairly hot oven (190°C/375°F or Gas Mark 5) for 20 to 25 minutes or until well risen and golden. Remove from oven, turn out onto a wire rack and leave to cool.
TO FREEZE: wrap cakes in aluminium foil, overwrap in a freezer bag, seal, label and freeze.
TO THAW: unwrap and leave for 4 to 5 hours at room temperature.
TO SERVE: sandwich cakes together with jam or lemon curd (cheese), whipped double cream or buttercream icing (frosting). Sprinkle the top of the cake with sifted icing (confectioners') sugar, or spread with flavoured buttercream and sprinkle with chopped nuts or grated chocolate. Or dribble glacé icing over the top and decorate with nuts, crystallized fruits or vermicelli (sprinkles). For a festive occasion, pipe the cake with rosettes of whipped cream or buttercream icing.

Lightning Cake

As its name suggests, this cake is quick to make. It is also quick to thaw and, therefore, is an ideal standby to keep in the freezer for unexpected tea or coffee guests or to serve with fruit compote for a quickly made dessert.

Metric/Imperial
125 g/¼ lb butter
125 g/¼ lb caster sugar
2 eggs, lightly beaten
125 g/¼ lb self-raising flour, sifted
Finely grated rind of ½ lemon
50 g/2 oz flaked almonds
25 g/1 oz caster sugar, for topping
1×5 ml spoon/1 teaspoon ground cinnamon

American
½ cup butter
½ cup sugar
2 eggs, lightly beaten
1 cup flour, sifted with 1½ teaspoons baking powder
Finely grated rind of ½ lemon
½ cup slivered almonds
2 tablespoons sugar, for topping
1 teaspoon ground cinnamon

Cream the butter and sugar together until light and fluffy, then beat in the eggs a little at a time. Fold in the flour and lemon rind. Grease two 27×16.5 cm/10½×6½ inch rectangular baking tins (pans). Spread mixture into a ½ cm/¼ inch thickness. Sprinkle over the flaked almonds. Mix the (caster) sugar with the cin-

namon and dredge this mixture evenly over the almonds. Bake in a fairly hot oven (190°C/375°F or Gas Mark 5) for 10 to 15 minutes or until golden brown. Remove from the oven, cut immediately into diamond or rectangular shapes and place on a wire rack and leave to cool.
TO FREEZE: place in a rigid container, box or tin, cover, label and freeze.
TO THAW: leave for 15 to 20 minutes in container at room temperature.
TO SERVE: as suggested above.

Apple Cake

This apple cake can double as a coffee cake or dessert, and keeps beautifully fresh and moist in the freezer.

Metric/Imperial
225 g/½ lb butter or margarine
125 g/¼ lb caster sugar
1 egg, lightly beaten
175 g/6 oz self-raising flour, sifted
1×15 ml spoon/1 tablespoon milk
½ kg/1 lb cooking apples
1×2.5 ml spoon/½ teaspoon ground cinnamon (optional)
300 ml/½ pint fresh whipping cream, softly whipped, to serve (optional)

American
1 cup butter or margarine
½ cup sugar
1 egg, lightly beaten
1½ cups flour, sifted with 2 teaspoons baking powder
1 tablespoon milk

Victoria
Sandwich
Lightning Cake
Apple Cake
Granny's Fruit
Cake

| 1 lb tart or cooking apples |
| ½ teaspoon ground cinnamon (optional) |
| 1¼ cups heavy cream, softly whipped, to serve (optional) |

Cream the butter or margarine and half the sugar together until light and fluffy. Beat in the egg, flour and milk. Grease a 25 cm/10 inch diameter shallow round baking tin (pan) and pour in the mixture — it should be approximately 1.5 cm/½ inch deep. Peel, core and slice the apples thinly, then lay on top of cake mixture, close together in circles, so that their rounded edges are just sticking out. Mix the remaining sugar with the cinnamon (if using) and sprinkle over the apple slices. Bake in a fairly hot oven (200°C/400°F or Gas Mark 6) for 35 to 40 minutes or until the cake is cooked and the top is light brown. Remove from oven and leave to cool for 20 minutes in the tin (pan), then turn out carefully onto a wire rack (apple side up) and leave until cold.

TO FREEZE: open (flash) freeze until solid, then wrap in cling film and overwrap in aluminium foil or a freezer bag. Seal, label and return to freezer.

TO THAW: unwrap and leave for 4 to 5 hours at room temperature.

TO SERVE: cut into slices and serve with whipped cream, if liked.

Granny's Fruit Cake

A rich fruit cake is always a family favourite, so it's a good idea to keep one in the freezer. This one will take approximately 4 hours to thaw.

Metric/Imperial
225 g/½ lb self-raising flour
Pinch of salt
175 g/6 oz butter or margarine, cut into small pieces
175 g/6 oz dark brown sugar
175 g/6 oz seedless raisins
175 g/6 oz sultanas
50 g/2 oz candied peel, chopped
50 g/2 oz glacé cherries, quartered
1×2.5 ml spoon/½ teaspoon ground ginger
1×2.5 ml spoon/½ teaspoon ground cinnamon
3 eggs, beaten
2×15 ml spoons/2 tablespoons black treacle or golden syrup
A little milk, if necessary

American
2 cups flour sifted with 1 tablespoon baking powder
Pinch of salt
¾ cup butter or margarine, cut into small pieces
1 cup dark brown sugar
1 cup seedless raisins
1 cup golden raisins
⅓ cup chopped candied peel
⅓ cup candied cherries, quartered
½ teaspoon ground ginger
½ teaspoon ground cinnamon
3 eggs, beaten
2 tablespoons dark molasses or golden or light corn syrup
A little milk, if necessary

Sift the flour and salt together into a mixing bowl, then rub in the butter or margarine. Stir in the sugar, dried fruit, candied peel and glacé cherries, then the ginger and cinnamon. Beat in the eggs and treacle (molasses) or syrup. If the mixture seems too dry, beat in a little milk, a spoon at a time. The mixture should just drop from the spoon when shaken. Grease a 1 kg/2 lb/8½×4½×2½ inch loaf tin (pan) or 20 cm/8 inch round cake tin (pan) and line with greased greaseproof (parchment) paper. Spoon the mixture into the tin (pan) and bake in a warm oven (160°C/325°F or Gas Mark 3) for approximately 1½ hours or until a skewer inserted in the centre comes out clean. Cover the top of the cake with greaseproof (parchment) paper if it becomes too brown during the cooking. When cooked, remove from the oven, leave to cool in the tin (pan) for 10 minutes, then turn out onto a wire rack, remove lining paper and leave until cold.

TO FREEZE: wrap in aluminium foil, then overwrap in a freezer bag, seal, label and freeze.

TO THAW: unwrap and leave for approximately 4 hours at room temperature or until thawed completely.

The Hunting, Shooting and Fishing Cake

Black Forest Gâteau is shown on the pedestal behind The Hunting, Shooting and Fishing Cake on the left and Coffee Cake on the right.

This cake is so nourishing, that a couple of slices carried in the pocket can see a sportsman through a whole long wet day—hence the name. If that is how you will actually use the cake, it is a good idea to cut it into chunks or slices, and wrap and freeze them individually.

Metric/Imperial

225 g/½ lb butter or margarine

225 g/½ lb dark brown sugar

4 eggs, lightly beaten

275 g/10 oz flour

2×5 ml spoons/2 teaspoons mixed spice

225 g/½ lb seedless raisins

125 g/¼ lb currants

225 g/½ lb sultanas

125 g/¼ lb walnuts or blanched almonds, chopped

8×15 ml spoons/8 tablespoons stout

American

1 cup butter or margarine

1⅓ cups dark brown sugar

4 eggs, lightly beaten

2½ cups flour

1 teaspoon grated nutmeg

1 teaspoon ground allspice and cloves, mixed

1⅓ cups seedless raisins

⅔ cup currants

1⅓ cups golden raisins

⅔ cup chopped walnuts or blanched almonds

½ cup malt liquor

Cream the butter or margarine and sugar together until light and fluffy, then beat in the eggs a little at a time. Sift the flour and spices together and beat all but 1×15 ml spoon/1 tablespoon into the creamed mixture. Sprinkle remaining flour onto dried fruit and nuts and turn well so that the fruit and nuts remain separate and do not stick together. Stir into the cake mixture together with half the stout (liquor). Butter a 20 cm/8 inch round cake tin (pan) and line with buttered greaseproof (waxed) paper. Spoon in cake mixture and bake in a warm oven (160°C/325°F or Gas Mark 3) for 1 hour. Reduce the heat to cool (150°C/300°F or Gas Mark 2) and bake for another 1 to 1½ hours. Remove from the oven, leave to cool in the tin for 1 hour, then turn out onto a wire rack, remove paper and leave to cool completely. Prick the base with a long-pronged fork or skewer and gently spoon over the remaining stout (liquor). Leave overnight.

TO FREEZE: wrap the whole cake in aluminium foil, label and freeze. Or cut into chunks and slices and wrap individually in foil or cling film, then pack in a freezer bag, seal, label and freeze.

TO THAW: leave whole cake in wrappings for 6 hours at room temperature, slices for 1 to 2 hours.

Black Forest Gâteau

Irresistibly dark and rich, this cake from the Black Forest, Germany, combines chocolate, cherries and cream. Serve it with coffee as a grand dessert at a buffet supper. This is a more difficult type of cake to make, so follow the recipe carefully for best results.

Metric/Imperial

200 g/7 oz plain or bitter eating chocolate, broken into pieces

2×15 ml spoons/2 tablespoons milk

200 g/7 oz unsalted butter, cut into cubes

200 g/7 oz caster sugar

75 g/3 oz flour, sifted

Pinch of salt

4 eggs, separated

FOR THE FILLING:
300 ml/½ pint fresh double or whipping cream

225 g/½ lb black or Morello cherry jam, or tinned or frozen cherries, drained

15 g/½ oz plain or bitter eating chocolate, scraped or grated into curls

American

7 squares (7 oz) semisweet chocolate, broken into pieces

2 tablespoons milk

scant 1 cup unsalted butter, cubed

scant 1 cup sugar

¾ cup flour, sifted

Pinch of salt

4 eggs, separated

FOR THE FILLING:
1¼ cups heavy cream

½ lb jar black cherry or Morello cherry jam, or canned or frozen cherries, drained

½ square (½ oz) semisweet chocolate, scraped or grated into curls

Serves 6 to 8

Put the chocolate in a heatproof bowl, add the milk and stand the bowl over a pan of simmering water until the chocolate melts. Remove from the heat. Beat in the butter, then the sugar, and continue to beat for a few minutes until the mixture thickens a little and becomes pale. Beat in the flour and salt, then the egg yolks one at a time.

Beat the egg whites until stiff, then gently fold them into the chocolate mixture. Butter a 20 cm/8 inch springform pan or loose-bottomed cake tin. Spoon in the cake mixture and bake in a fairly hot oven (190°C/375°F or Gas Mark 5) for 55 minutes or until a skewer inserted in centre of cake comes out clean. Remove from the oven, leave to cool for five minutes, then turn out onto a wire rack and leave to cool completely.

Cut the cake into three layers. Whip the cream lightly and spread a third of the cream on the bottom layer. Spread on half the cherry jam or cherries; reserve some cherries for the top. Repeat, then decorate the top with the remaining ingredients and the chocolate. Alternately cut cake in two and divide ingredients accordingly.

TO FREEZE: open (flash) freeze until solid, then wrap loosely in aluminium foil or place in a rigid container, box or tin. Cover, label and return to freezer.

TO THAW: unwrap and leave for 2 to 3 hours at room temperature.

TO SERVE: as suggested above.

Coffee Cake

This cake is frozen ready to serve.

Metric/Imperial

125 g/¼ lb butter

125 g/¼ lb caster sugar

1×15 ml spoon/1 tablespoon powdered instant coffee, dissolved in scant 1×15 ml spoon/1 tablespoon boiling water

75 g/3 oz flour

1×5 ml spoon/1 teaspoon baking powder

Pinch of salt

2 eggs, well beaten

50 g/2 oz ground almonds

FOR THE ICING:
50 g/2 oz unsalted butter

100 g/¼ lb icing sugar, sifted

1×15 ml spoon/1 tablespoon powdered instant coffee, dissolved in scant 1×15 ml spoon/1 tablespoon boiling water

8 walnut halves, to finish (optional)

American

½ cup butter

½ cup sugar

1 tablespoon powdered instant coffee, dissolved in 1 tablespoon boiling water

¾ cup flour

1 teaspoon baking powder

Pinch of salt

2 eggs, well beaten

⅓ cup ground almonds

FOR THE ICING:
¼ cup unsalted butter

⅔ cup sifted confectioners' sugar

1 tablespoon powdered instant coffee, dissolved in 1 tablespoon boiling water

8 walnut halves, to finish (optional)

Cream the butter and sugar together until light and fluffy, then beat in the dissolved coffee. Sift the flour with the baking powder and salt, then beat 2×15 ml spoons/2 tablespoons into the creamed mixture. Beat in the eggs, a little at a time, then fold in the remaining flour and the ground almonds. Butter two 18 cm/7 inch sandwich tins (layer pans) and divide mixture evenly between them. Bake in a fairly hot oven (190°C/375°F or Gas Mark 5) for 20 to 25 minutes until cake has shrunk from the sides of the tins (pans). Remove from the oven, leave to cool for 10 minutes, then turn out onto a wire rack and leave to cool completely.

To make the icing: cream together the butter and icing (confectioners') sugar, then flavour with the dissolved coffee. Sandwich the cakes together with half the icing and spread the remaining icing over the top. Draw a fork through the icing to make a line decoration, and decorate with the walnut halves.

TO FREEZE: open (flash) freeze, then wrap in cling film and overwrap in aluminium foil or a freezer bag, or place in a rigid container, box or tin. Seal or cover, label and return to freezer.

TO THAW: unwrap, transfer to a cake plate or dish and leave for 2½ to 3 hours at room temperature.

TO SERVE: cut into wedges.

The Hunting, Shooting and Fishing Cake
Black Forest Gâteau
Coffee Cake

The delicate cream topping of the Lemon Cream Gâteau complements the deep colour of the Rich Chocolate Cake in the photograph opposite.

Lemon Cream Gâteau

Light, creamy and scrumptious, this delicate confection can be served for a celebration or as a dessert for a special lunch or dinner. Though impressive, it is quite simple to make.

Metric/Imperial

FOR THE CAKE:
6 eggs, separated
175 g/6 oz caster sugar
2×15 ml spoons/2 tablespoons water
Finely grated rind of 1 lemon
Pinch of salt
150 g/5 oz flour
25 g/1 oz cornflour
FOR THE CREAM TOPPING: 1 egg
150 g/5 oz caster sugar
25 g/1 oz cornflour
Juice of 1½ lemons
300 ml/½ pint fresh double cream
50 g/2 oz flaked almonds, toasted

American

FOR THE CAKE:
6 eggs, separated
¾ cup sugar
2 tablespoons water
Finely grated rind of 1 lemon
Pinch of salt
1¼ cups flour
¼ cup cornstarch
FOR THE CREAM TOPPING: 1 egg
⅔ cup sugar
¼ cup cornstarch
Juice of 1½ lemons
1¼ cups heavy cream
⅓ cup browned slivered almonds

Whisk the egg yolks, sugar, water, lemon rind and salt together until thick, white and fluffy. Beat the egg whites until stiff and fold into the mixture. Sift the flour and cornflour (cornstarch) together, then stir lightly into the egg and sugar mixture. Butter and flour three 20 cm/8 inch round cake pans and divide mixture equally among them. Bake in a moderate oven (180°C/350°F or Gas Mark 4) for 20 to 25 minutes or until risen and light golden brown. Remove from the oven, then turn out onto a wire rack and leave to cool completely.

To make the cream topping: put the egg, sugar and cornflour (cornstarch) in a heatproof bowl and beat until light and fluffy. Beat in the lemon juice, then stand the bowl over a pan of simmering water and stir until the mixture becomes clear and begins to thicken. Remove from the heat and leave until quite cold, when it will become thick.

Whip the double (heavy) cream lightly, then fold in the lemon mixture. Sandwich the cake layers together with some of the cream, then cover the top and sides with the remainder. Sprinkle with the almonds.

TO FREEZE: open (flash) freeze until solid, then wrap in cling film and overwrap in aluminium foil or a freezer bag, or place in a rigid container, box or tin. Seal or cover, label and return to freezer.

TO THAW: unwrap, transfer to a cake plate or dish and leave for 3 to 4 hours at room temperature.

Rich Chocolate Cake

This is a really rich and fudgy chocolate cake which can be served for a luscious dessert with icecream, or whipped cream, lightly flavoured with rum or brandy.

Metric/Imperial

125 g/¼ lb butter
125 g/¼ lb caster sugar
125 g/¼ lb self-raising flour, sifted
75 g/3 oz ground almonds
50 g/2 oz unsweetened cocoa powder
25 g/1 oz powdered drinking chocolate
2 eggs, lightly beaten
2×5 ml spoons/2 teaspoons strong black liquid coffee
2×5 ml spoons/2 teaspoons sherry
FOR THE BUTTER ICING: 50 g/2 oz butter
100 g/¼ lb icing sugar, sifted
50 g/2 oz plain or bitter eating chocolate, melted
2×5 ml spoons/2 teaspoons strong black liquid coffee
2×5 ml spoons/2 teaspoons sherry
FOR THE GLACÉ ICING: 100 g/¼ lb plain or bitter eating chocolate
1×15 ml spoon/1 tablespoon strong black liquid coffee
Knob of butter
50 g/2 oz icing sugar, sifted
Chopped walnuts or split blanched almonds, to finish

American

½ cup butter
½ cup sugar
1 cup flour, sifted with 1½ teaspoons baking powder
½ cup ground almonds
½ cup unsweetened cocoa powder
2½ tablespoons powdered drinking chocolate
2 eggs, lightly beaten
2 teaspoons strong black liquid coffee
2 teaspoons sherry
FOR THE BUTTER ICING: ¼ cup butter
1 cup confectioners' sugar, sifted
2 squares (2 oz) semisweet chocolate, melted
2 teaspoons strong black liquid coffee
2 teaspoons sherry
FOR THE GLACÉ ICING: 4 squares (4 oz) semisweet chocolate
1 tablespoon strong black liquid coffee
Knob of butter
½ cup confectioners' sugar, sifted
Chopped walnuts or split blanched almonds, to finish

Cream the butter and sugar together until light and fluffy. Blend together the flour, almonds, cocoa powder and drinking chocolate, and mix a little at a time into the butter and sugar mixture alternately with the eggs. Stir in the coffee and sherry. Butter a 20 cm/8 inch loose-bottomed cake tin or springform pan and spoon in the cake mixture. Bake in a moderate oven (180°C/350°F or Gas Mark 4) for 50 minutes to 1 hour. Remove from the oven, leave to cool for 15 to 20 minutes in the tin (pan), then turn out onto a wire rack and leave to cool completely.

To make the butter icing: beat the butter and icing (confectioners') sugar together until white and fluffy, then beat in the chocolate, coffee and sherry. Slice the cooled cake in half and sandwich together with the butter icing.

To make the glacé icing: melt the chocolate with the coffee and butter over a low heat, then stir in the icing (confectioners') sugar until the mixture is smooth. Increase heat gently and as soon as the mixture begins to bubble, pour over the cake, smoothing over with a palette knife dipped in hot water. Decorate with the nuts and leave to set.

TO FREEZE: open (flash) freeze until solid, then wrap in cling film. Overwrap in aluminium foil or a freezer bag, seal, label and return to freezer.

TO THAW: unwrap, transfer to a cake plate or dish and leave for 3 to 4 hours at room temperature.

TO SERVE: as suggested above.

Savarin is illustrated below, with Orange Marmalade Cake on the left of the photograph opposite and Stolle on the right.

Savarin

A Savarin is a French yeast cake that is soaked in a rum and sugar syrup. The centre is often filled with fruits in season.

Metric/Imperial

225 g/½ lb strong plain flour
Pinch of salt
1×15 ml spoon/1 tablespoon caster sugar
4×15 ml spoons/4 tablespoons lukewarm milk
1½×5 ml spoons/1½ teaspoons dried yeast
4 eggs, beaten
50 g/2 oz butter, softened
FOR THE SYRUP: 350 g/¾ lb sugar
400 ml/¾ pint water
4–6×15 ml spoons/4–6 tablespoons rum
FOR THE GLAZE: 3×15 ml spoons/3 tablespoons apricot jam
1×15 ml spoon/1 tablespoon water
Seasonal fresh fruit, to finish

American

2 cups flour
Pinch of salt
1 tablespoon sugar
4 tablespoons lukewarm milk
1 envelope dried yeast
4 eggs, beaten
¼ cup butter, softened
FOR THE SYRUP: 1½ cups sugar
2 cups water
4–6 tablespoons rum
FOR THE GLAZE: 3 tablespoons apricot jam
1 tablespoon water
Seasonal fresh fruit, to finish

Serves 6

Sift the flour and salt into a warm mixing bowl. Stir the sugar into the warm milk, then sprinkle over the dried yeast. Leave in a warm place for 10 minutes or until frothy. Make a well in the centre of the flour and pour in the yeast mixture with the eggs. Mix together to form a loose, wet dough. Beat the dough with the hands for about 5 minutes, slapping it up and down until smooth. Scrape down the batter and cover the bowl with a damp cloth. Leave to rise in a warm place for 1 hour or until doubled in bulk.

Add the butter to the dough, beating it with the hands again until thoroughly mixed. Thickly butter a 20 cm/8 inch/2½ quart ring mould. Spoon in the dough, distributing it evenly around the ring mould. Leave in a warm place again until the batter has risen to the top of the mould.

Bake in a fairly hot oven (200°C/400°F or Gas Mark 6) for 20 to 25 minutes or until golden brown on top and the savarin has shrunk away from the sides of the tin (pan). Turn out onto a wire rack and leave to cool.

TO FREEZE: wrap savarin carefully in aluminium foil, then overwrap in a freezer bag. Seal, label and freeze.

TO THAW: leave in wrappings for 2 hours at room temperature, then remove freezer bag. Place foil-wrapped savarin on a baking sheet and reheat in a fairly hot oven (200°C/400°F or Gas Mark 6) for 15 to 20 minutes or until heated through. Unwrap and put on a wire rack. To make the syrup: put the sugar and water in a small saucepan and stir to dissolve the sugar over gentle heat. Bring to the boil and boil rapidly for 3 minutes or until a syrup is formed. Remove from the heat and stir in the rum. Pour this hot syrup over the savarin, catching it in a bowl underneath the wire rack. Leave to soak, spooning over the syrup from the bowl, until no syrup is left.

TO SERVE: transfer savarin to a serving platter. To make the glaze: put the apricot jam and water in a small pan and heat gently. Sieve (strain), then brush over the savarin. Fill the centre with seasonal fresh fruit tossed in (caster) sugar and more rum, if you like.

Orange Marmalade Cake

This is best made with a fairly thick, coarse-cut marmalade.

Metric/Imperial

110 g/¼ lb butter or margarine
110 g/¼ lb caster sugar
2 eggs, lightly beaten
3×15 ml spoons/3 tablespoons marmalade
Finely grated rind of 1 orange
Finely grated rind of 1 lemon
225 g/½ lb self-raising flour, sifted
FOR THE ICING: Juice of ½ orange
Juice of ½ lemon
100 g/¼ lb icing sugar, sifted
Crystallized orange and lemon pieces, to finish

American

½ cup butter or margarine
½ cup sugar
2 eggs, lightly beaten
3 tablespoons marmalade
Finely grated rind of 1 orange
Finely grated rind of 1 lemon
2 cups flour, sifted with 1 tablespoon baking powder
FOR THE ICING: Juice of ½ orange
Juice of ½ lemon
⅔ cup sifted confectioners' sugar
Crystallized orange and lemon slices, to finish

Cream the butter or margarine and sugar together until light and fluffy, then beat in the eggs a little at a time, the marmalade and the orange and lemon rinds. Fold in the flour. Butter a 23×13×7.5 cm/9×5×3 inch loaf tin (pan) and pour in the mixture. Bake in a fairly hot oven (190°C/375°F or Gas Mark 5) for 60 to 70 minutes or until a skewer inserted in centre of cake comes out clean. Remove from the oven, leave to cool for 20 minutes in the tin (pan), then turn out onto a wire rack and leave to cool.

To make the icing: stir the orange and lemon juices into the icing (confectioners') sugar and beat well with a wooden spoon. Spread smoothly over the top of the cake, allowing it to run down the sides. Decorate as illustrated. Leave to dry.

TO FREEZE: open (flash) freeze until solid, then wrap in cling film and overwrap in foil or a freezer bag, seal, label and return to freezer.

TO THAW: unwrap, and leave for 4 to 5 hours at room temperature.

Stolle

This traditional German Christmas loaf is much lighter than a Christmas cake, more like a very rich tea bread. It can be eaten plain or buttered, and is especially good for breakfast on Christmas morning. It keeps fresh for months in the freezer.

Metric/Imperial
225 g/½ lb currants
150 g/5 oz sultanas
2×15 ml spoons/2 tablespoons rum
25 g/1 oz fresh (compressed) yeast
125 g/¼ lb sugar
150 ml/¼ pint lukewarm milk
450 g/1 lb flour
Pinch of salt
175 g/6 oz butter, melted
75 g/3 oz mixed candied peel, roughly chopped
50 g/2 oz blanched almonds, roughly chopped
TO FINISH:
15 g/½ oz butter, melted
1×15 ml spoon/1 tablespoon icing sugar, sifted

American
1½ cups currants
1 cup golden raisins
2 tablespoons rum
1 package compressed fresh yeast or 1 envelope dried yeast
½ cup sugar
⅔ cup lukewarm milk
4 cups flour
Pinch of salt
¾ cup butter, melted
½ cup roughly chopped mixed candied peel
⅓ cup blanched almonds, roughly chopped
TO FINISH:
1 tablespoon melted butter
1 tablespoon confectioners' sugar, sifted
Makes 2 loaves

Soak the currants and sultanas (golden raisins) in the rum. Dissolve the yeast and a spoonful of sugar in the warm milk, then leave in a warm place for 10 minutes. Sift the flour and salt into a warmed bowl. Make a well in the centre and pour in the yeast mixture. Sprinkle with a little of the flour, cover with a clean dampened towel and leave to rise in a warm place until risen to at least twice its original quantity. Gradually mix in the remaining flour, sugar and the melted butter. Knead on a floured board until smooth, then cover and leave to rise again for 1 hour. Knock down, add the fruit, peel and almonds and form into a split loaf shape. Place on a buttered baking sheet and leave to rise for another 10 to 20 minutes.

Bake in a moderate oven (180°C/350°F or Gas Mark 4) for 50 to 60 minutes until firm and pale brown. Remove from the oven, transfer to a wire rack and leave to cool.

TO FREEZE: wrap in cling film, then overwrap in aluminium foil or a freezer bag. Seal, label and freeze.

TO THAW: leave in wrappings for 4 to 5 hours at room temperature.

TO SERVE: unwrap, brush with melted butter, sprinkle generously with icing (confectioners') sugar and slice before serving.

**Savarin
Orange
Marmalade Cake
Stolle**

Meringue Chantilly

Meringues are a useful item to store in the freezer. This recipe is for meringues sandwiched together with cream — just take them out of the freezer and within a few hours they are ready to eat. If you like, the meringue shells can be frozen without the filling, packed in the same way, then they can be used in numerous ways: with a filling of your own choice; as a decoration for gâteaux and desserts, or as a quick dessert with cream, hot chocolate sauce and finely chopped hazelnuts.

The photograph below shows Meringue Chantilly. Chocolate Chip Cookies and Christmas Stars are illustrated opposite in front of the diamond-shaped Carolina Cookies.

Metric/Imperial
2 egg whites
100 g/¼ lb caster sugar
FOR THE FILLING: 150 ml/¼ pint fresh double cream
1 egg white
1×15 ml spoon/1 tablespoon vanilla sugar

American
2 egg whites
½ cup sugar
FOR THE FILLING: ⅔ cup heavy cream
1 egg white
1 tablespoon vanilla sugar

Put the egg whites in a large mixing bowl or copper bowl and beat until stiff. Fold in 1×15 ml spoon/1 tablespoon of the sugar, then beat again until the mixture looks smooth and glossy. Fold in the remaining sugar with a large metal spoon. Put the meringue into a piping (pastry) bag fitted with a 1.25 cm/½ inch plain nozzle (tube) and pipe approximately eight mounds onto non-stick silicone paper or aluminium foil placed on a baking sheet. Bake in a very cool oven (120°C/225°F or Gas Mark ¼) for 3 to 4 hours or until the meringues are crisp and dry. The meringues should be off-white; if they seem to be turning brown, open the oven door slightly. Remove from the oven and leave to cool on a wire rack. When completely cold, peel the paper or foil off carefully.

To make the filling: whip the cream until thick. Beat the egg white until stiff and fold in the sugar. Combine cream and egg white and use to sandwich meringue shells together.
TO FREEZE: open (flash) freeze until frozen. Put in a rigid container, separating each meringue with cardboard or foil to prevent breakages. Cover, label and return to freezer.
TO THAW: remove from container, arrange on a serving platter and leave for 1 to 2 hours in a cool place.
TO SERVE: serve within 1 hour as the cream will not hold longer.

Chocolate Chip Cookies

These are so good that unless you hide them in the freezer they are impossible to keep. They will also stay fresh much longer if frozen.

Metric/Imperial
200 g/7 oz flour
1×2.5 ml spoon/½ teaspoon baking powder
Pinch of salt
110 g/¼ lb butter
110 g/¼ lb caster sugar
2×15 ml spoons/2 tablespoons golden syrup
1 egg, lightly beaten
100 g/¼ lb chocolate polka dots, or plain or bitter eating chocolate, cut into small chips

American
1¾ cups flour
½ teaspoon baking powder
Pinch of salt
½ cup butter
½ cup sugar
2 tablespoons golden or light corn syrup
1 egg, lightly beaten
¼ lb chocolate chips or morsels

Sift the flour, baking powder and salt. Cream the butter, sugar and syrup together until light and fluffy, then beat in the egg. Stir in the flour and blend in the chocolate pieces.

Place teaspoonsful of the mixture on well-greased baking sheets, leaving plenty of space between each one to allow for spreading during cooking. Bake in a fairly hot oven (190°C/375°F or Gas Mark 5) for 12 to 15 minutes. Remove from oven, lift cookies carefully off baking sheets with a palette knife and leave to cool on a wire rack.
TO FREEZE: place in a rigid container, box or tin, cover, label and freeze.
TO THAW: leave in container for 10 to 15 minutes at room temperature.
TO SERVE: serve with tea or coffee or with icecream for dessert.

Christmas Stars

These German Christmas biscuits (cookies) are especially good served with nuts and raisins, port or Madeira at the end of Christmas dinner; they also make very pretty Christmas decorations.

Metric/Imperial
1 egg white
175 g/6 oz caster sugar
150 g/5 oz ground almonds
2×5 ml spoons/2 teaspoons ground cinnamon
Pinch of ground cloves
Finely grated rind of ½ lemon
FOR THE ICING: 1 egg white
100 g/¼ lb icing sugar
Squeeze of lemon juice
Coloured sugar strands or hundreds and thousands

American
1 egg white
¾ cup sugar
1 cup ground almonds
2 teaspoons ground cinnamon
Pinch of ground cloves
Finely grated rind of ½ lemon
FOR THE ICING: 1 egg white
⅔ cup confectioners' sugar
Squeeze of lemon juice
Colored sugar or sprinkles

Beat the egg white with all but 2×15 ml spoons/2 tablespoons of the (caster) sugar until thick and white, then beat in the ground almonds, cinnamon, cloves and lemon rind. Chill the mixture for approximately 1 hour in the refrigerator.

Sprinkle half the remaining (caster) sugar onto a pastry board. Flatten the chilled dough mixture onto the board, then sprinkle on the remaining sugar. Roll out very thinly, then cut into stars or other shapes. Place on greased baking sheets and bake in a fairly hot oven (190°C/375°F or Gas Mark 5) for 10 to 15 minutes, or until they have risen slightly and are pale brown. Remove from the oven, lift biscuits (cookies) carefully off baking sheets with a palette knife and leave to cool on a wire rack.

To make the icing: beat the egg white, icing (confectioners') sugar and lemon juice together until very thick. Spread thickly on biscuits (cookies), then dust with sugar strands (colored sugar) or hundreds and thousands (sprinkles).

TO FREEZE: place in a rigid container, box or tin, cover, label and freeze.

TO THAW: leave in container for 20 to 30 minutes at room temperature.

TO SERVE: serve with tea or after dinner, or hang on the Christmas tree.

Carolina Cookies

Serve these light, spicy cookies on their own, or with icecream and fruit desserts.

Metric/Imperial
225 g/½ lb butter or margarine
175 g/6 oz light brown sugar
1 egg white
2×5 ml spoons/2 teaspoons ground cinnamon
1×5 ml spoon/1 teaspoon ground ginger
Pinch of salt
275 g/10 oz flour, sifted

American
1 cup butter or margarine
1 cup light brown sugar
1 egg white
2 teaspoons ground cinnamon
1 teaspoon ground ginger
Pinch of salt
2½ cups flour, sifted

Cream the butter or margarine and sugar together until light and fluffy, then add the egg white, cinnamon, ginger and salt and beat until the mixture is creamy. Beat in the flour. Spread very thinly onto three or four well-greased baking sheets, 30×20 cm/12×8 inch, with a floured palette knife. Bake in a fairly hot oven (190°C/375°F or Gas Mark 5) for about 15 minutes or until they have risen slightly and are pale brown. Remove from the oven, then cut into squares or diamonds and leave to cool for a few minutes. Transfer to a wire rack to cool completely.

TO FREEZE: place in a rigid container, box or tin, cover, label and freeze.

TO THAW: remove from container and leave for 10 to 15 minutes at room temperature.

TO SERVE: as suggested above.

Meringue Chantilly
Chocolate Chip Cookies
Christmas Stars
Carolina Cookies

Jars of Marmalade are standing on the shelf of the dresser opposite with Lemonade and Lemon Curd (Cheese) below. Truffles have been arranged in a silver basket for the photograph on this page.

Truffles

These homemade truffles, which keep beautifully fresh in the freezer, are as good as the best commercially made truffles but can be produced at a fraction of the cost.

Metric/Imperial
125 g / ¼ lb plain or bitter eating chocolate, broken into pieces
1×15 ml spoon/1 tablespoon milk
1×15 ml spoon/1 tablespoon golden syrup
125 g / ¼ lb unsalted butter
125 g / ¼ lb icing sugar, sifted
2×5 ml spoons/2 teaspoons powdered instant coffee
50 g/2 oz unsweetened cocoa powder

American
4 squares (4 oz) semisweet chocolate, broken into pieces
1 tablespoon milk
1 tablespoon golden or light corn syrup
½ cup unsalted butter
⅔ cup confectioners' sugar, sifted
2 teaspoons powdered instant coffee
½ cup unsweetened cocoa powder

Put the chocolate, milk and syrup in a small pan, heat gently until melted, then remove from the heat and leave to cool a little. Beat the butter, icing (confectioners') sugar, coffee powder and half the cocoa powder together until light and fluffy, then slowly beat in the melted chocolate mixture and continue beating until the mixture is pale and fluffy.

224

Leave the mixture to set in the refrigerator for 1 hour, then roll lightly into walnut-sized balls. Roll these in the remaining cocoa powder.
TO FREEZE: place in a rigid container, cover, label and freeze.
TO THAW: leave in container overnight in the refrigerator, or for 1 to 2 hours at room temperature.
TO SERVE: serve with after-dinner coffee.

Lemonade

Homemade lemonade is infinitely nicer than the mass-produced variety, and it is easy to make up a large quantity of the concentrated form when lemons are relatively inexpensive. Keep it in the freezer, in small quantities, ready to take out and dilute with water or soda water as required. Citric and tartaric acids and the salts are available at chemists (pharmacies).

Metric/Imperial
1¼ kg/2½ lb sugar
15 g/½ oz citric acid
25 g/1 oz tartaric acid
15 g/½ oz Epsom salts
Juice of 3 lemons, rinds reserved
Juice of 2 oranges, rinds reserved
¾ litre/1½ pints boiling water
TO FINISH: Ice cubes
Lemon slices

American
5 cups sugar
½ oz citric acid
1 oz tartaric acid
½ oz Epsom salts
Juice of 3 lemons, rinds reserved
Juice of 2 oranges, rinds reserved
3¾ cups boiling water
TO FINISH: Ice cubes
Lemon slices

Put the sugar, citric and tartaric acids and the Epsom salts in a large bowl. Pour over the lemon and orange juices. Put the lemon and orange rinds in the bowl and pour over the boiling water. Stir well until the sugar has dissolved. Cover and leave to cool. Strain, squeezing out as much juice from the rinds as possible, then discard them.
TO FREEZE: pour into small waxed or plastic cups, or cartons, leaving headspace. Cover, label and freeze.
TO THAW: leave in containers for 30 to 40 minutes at room temperature, depending on quantity.

TO SERVE: dilute with water or soda water in the proportions of approximately four to one. Stir well and serve with ice cubes and slices of lemon in the jug (pitcher) or glasses.

Lemon Curd (Cheese)

Because lemon curd (cheese) is made with fresh eggs and butter it has a relatively short life in the store cupboard. However, if stored in the freezer it will keep for up to 3 months.

Metric/Imperial
Finely grated rind and juice of 4 lemons
½ kg/1 lb sugar
4 eggs, beaten
100 g/¼ lb unsalted butter, cut into small pieces

American
Finely grated rind and juice of 4 lemons
2 cups sugar
4 eggs, beaten
½ cup unsalted butter, cut into small pieces
Makes approximately 1 kg/2 lb

Put all the ingredients in a large heatproof bowl over a saucepan of boiling water, or put in the top of a double boiler. Stir until the sugar has dissolved, then leave until the mixture begins to thicken, stirring occasionally. Do not allow to boil. When the mixture is quite thick, remove from the heat and leave until the curd (cheese) is completely cold.
TO FREEZE: pour into small containers — yogurt, cream, sour(ed) cream or cottage cheese pots, or rigid plastic containers. If you like, pour into glass canning jars. Cover, seal, label and freeze.
TO THAW: leave for approximately 3 to 4 hours at room temperature.
TO SERVE: use as for fresh lemon curd (cheese) — spread on bread, scones or toast. Or use as a filling for sandwich-type cakes and sponges.

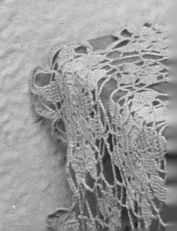

Marmalade

This recipe uses frozen Seville oranges — see Marmalade (page 74) and has a fairly bitter taste. If you prefer a sweeter marmalade, substitute 1 or 2 sweet oranges for the Sevilles, or for a three fruit marmalade, substitute 1 grapefruit and 2 lemons.

Metric/Imperial

½ kg/1 lb frozen Seville oranges

1 litre/2 pints water

1 kg/2 lb sugar

American

1 lb frozen Seville oranges

5 cups water

4 cups sugar

Makes approximately 1½ kg/3 lb marmalade

Put the oranges in a large saucepan with the water and bring slowly to the boil. Cover and simmer for 2 to 2½ hours or until the fruit is quite soft — you should be able to prick the rind easily with a skewer. Take the oranges out of the water one at a time, leave to cool slightly, then cut into quarters or eighths, and then into shreds, cutting across the sections. Set the fruit aside in a basin and return the pips (seeds) to the pan. When all the fruit has been cut up in this way, simmer the water and pips (seeds) for 10 minutes, then strain over the fruit. Return to the pan, simmer for 10 minutes, then add the sugar and heat gently until dissolved, stirring constantly. Bring to the boil, then boil fast until setting point is reached.

Remove from the heat, leave to cool a little, stir well to distribute the fruit evenly, then pour into clean, dry, warmed jam jars. Leave until completely cold, then cover, label and store in a cool, dry place.

Freezer Know-how

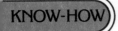

Types of Freezers Available

A food freezer must be capable of storing food at −18°C/0°F, and of lowering that temperature to at least −28°C/−18°F when fresh or cooked food is to be put into the cabinet without affecting the frozen food already being stored. When buying a freezer, particularly if buying one second hand, check that there is this low temperature facility, and that what you are offered is not simply a conservator for storage purposes (see **Conservator**).

In the U.K., all approved freezers are marked with a 4-star marking ✿∗∗∗, which guarantees this facility. In Australia, you should check the guaranteed temperature of the freezer with the manufacturer.

There are three main types of freezer: the chest freezer which has a top-opening lid; the upright, with one or two front-opening doors; and the combination refrigerator/freezer, which is front-opening and which has the refrigerator and freezer linked, either one on top of the other or side by side.

Chest Freezer

Chest freezers are available in sizes ranging from approximately 113–706 l/4–25 cu ft capacity. In Australia, standard sizes are 140–405 l/5–16 cu ft. On the whole, chest freezers tend to be less expensive than uprights of equivalent capacity, and to give more storage space for a given external dimension. However, they are more difficult to organize — you can't see so readily what you have in stock, and if you happen to want to take out a package that is stored at the bottom, you may have to move everything else before you can reach it. One or two plastic-covered baskets are usually supplied with a chest freezer to help with this storage problem, and additional baskets are readily available.

Some chest freezers have a separate 'fast freeze' section with refrigeration all round, while others have refrigeration on three walls only.

Upright Freezer

Uprights tend to be slightly smaller than chest models, with a minimum capacity available of approximately 50–565 l/1.75–20 cu ft. In Australia, sizes of uprights are the same as for chest models (see above). An upright takes up less floor space than a chest model (though more height of course), and gives you much easier access to the food. The smallest (apartment) models are intended to stand on top of a work surface or existing refrigerator; some small upright freezers can stand on the floor of the kitchen and be used as an additional work surface.

It is particularly important when buying an upright freezer to check the nett capacity rather than the gross capacity; the two may be quite different because the system of storage is less efficient in an upright than it is in a chest freezer. More cold air is lost from an upright because of the front-opening door(s), and it will need defrosting more frequently than a chest model — two or three times a year as against once or twice — but it is usually an easier job.

Combination Refrigerator/Freezer

Combination models are popular because they are so convenient to use, particularly if space is limited in the kitchen. The freezer size is usually around 170 l/6 cu ft, although some are smaller with a larger refrigerator, some larger with a smaller refrigerator. As a whole, the unit will be designed to fit neatly into a modern range of kitchen fitments more easily than any other type of freezer. It usually consists of a freezer mounted on top of a refrigerator, although sometimes they stand side by side or the refrigerator is mounted on top of the freezer.

Freezer Size

Consider carefully what size freezer you are likely to need. Nothing is more annoying than a freezer that is too small, but it is very expensive to run one that is permanently half empty. As a rough guide, you can assume that each 28 l/1 cu ft of freezer space will store approximately

Types of freezers
1 *Upright freezer.*
2 *Refrigerator/freezer.*
3 *Small upright freezer designed to stand on top of a work surface or refrigerator.*
4 *Chest freezer.*

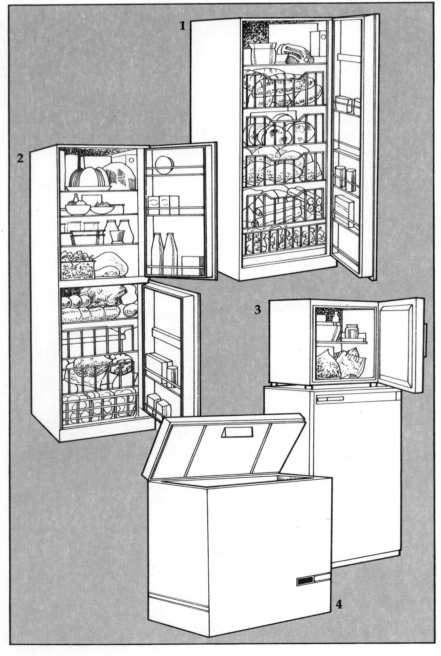

9–11 kg/20–24 lb of food, depending on how it is packed. It is normally considered reasonable to allow 57 1/2 cu ft per person in the family (85 1/3 cu ft per person in the family in Australia). Allow extra if you entertain a lot, grow your own fruit and vegetables, or expect to buy (or produce) large quantities of meat at a time (for example, a whole lamb would take up approximately 57 1/2 cu ft of space; a hind quarter of beef approximately 225 1/8 cu ft).

Position of Freezer

Where you will put the freezer must affect the one you choose. If you want it in the kitchen you will almost certainly want an upright or combination model, taking up the least possible floor space, and you must buy a model designed to run efficiently at high ambient temperatures. It is, of course, convenient to have your frozen food close at hand when you are cooking, but it will almost certainly cost you more to run than one kept in a cooler situation.

If the freezer is to go in an outhouse, storeroom or garage, choose the most sensible shape for the space available.

Wherever you decide to put the freezer, there must be sufficient space for air to circulate freely round it, and it should not be near any direct source of warmth such as hot water pipes. Check also that the floor is strong enough to support the full weight of freezer and food. The electricity supply should preferably be a single socket outlet, close to the freezer, to minimize the possibility of someone switching it off accidentally. As an added protection against this happening, it is a good idea to stick tape securely over the switch and plug for the freezer.

If the freezer is to go in a garage or outhouse, be sure it is dry, or the cabinet will quickly start to rust. In any case, one to two coats of wax polish will help to protect it. Also, be sure the wire (cord) is grounded if stored in an open area.

The ability to lock either the freezer door or the door of the outhouse/storeroom/garage where it is kept, is an advantage. The contents of a freezer can be extremely valuable, both in terms of the cost of the contents, and the time spent in preparing food for the freezer. Although you can insure against theft, it is wise to take precautions to protect yourself. Some freezers are fitted with an integral lock*; if not, then it is possible to fit a padlock* arrangement on most models. Failing that, always lock the door of the room in which the freezer is stored.

There is another possible hazard to guard against when owning a freezer: if it contains goodies like iced lollipops (popsicles) or icecream, it is a great attraction to children, and it is perfectly possible for a small child to open an unlocked freezer, climb in and have the lid close on top. This is unlikely to happen with an upright freezer, but a significant hazard with a chest model. Be safe, fit a lock* and remember to use it at all times.

If your freezer will not fit into any of the places mentioned above, a spare bedroom or hallway may do just as well, but the motor on some models is louder than on others. In this situation you would be well advised to look for a freezer with a quiet-running motor, or the noise may be obtrusive.

*Freezer locks are illegal in Australia.

How Freezing Works

Freezing preserves food by arresting the organic processes that normally cause it to age and deteriorate. Food that goes into the freezer in good condition should come out in exactly the same condition when thawed. Once it has thawed, ageing and deterioration will then continue in the normal way, or slightly faster than normal.

The best results are obtained if food is frozen quickly. If freezing is slow, large ice crystals form in the food and distort the cell structure so that when it is thawed you find the texture of the food has changed. If you freeze it quickly at a very low temperature, the ice crystals that form are tiny and do not disturb the cell structure. While a temperature of −18°F/0°F is right for

the storage of frozen foods, a lower temperature of −28°C/−18°F is necessary for freezing fresh foods; in a domestic freezer this is achieved by the use of the 'fast freeze' control.

Fast Freezing

The basic mechanism in a freezer is the cooling system: when the motor is working the freezer is getting colder all the time. In the normal way, a thermostat cuts in when the freezer reaches the required temperature for storage (−18°C/0°F) and stops the motor; when the temperature starts to rise again the motor comes back into operation.

The 'fast freeze' control is designed to freeze fresh or cooked foods as quickly as possible. It operates by over-riding the freezer thermostat so that the freezer goes on getting colder and colder, the longer the 'fast freeze' switch stays 'on'. The temperature eventually drops to around −28°C/−18°F. (Some freezers go lower than this, but these are generally for commercial purposes.)

'Fast freezing' also ensures that food already frozen stays that way when fresh or cooked food is put into the freezer. Fresh and cooked food is warmer than frozen food and, unless steps are taken to compensate for the introduction of warm air and, therefore, a raising of the temperature, partial thawing can start in stored food. It will not become unsafe to eat, but it can cause it to 'age' prematurely, with a resulting loss in flavour and texture.

When you want to put fresh or cooked food into the freezer, first switch on the 'fast freeze' control to start the temperature dropping. If there is only a small quantity to freeze, perhaps a few cakes, casseroles or some vegetables, 2 to 4 hours on 'fast freeze' should bring the temperature down to a suitable level. (Consult manufacturer's instructions for recommended 'fast freeze' times.) Put the food in the freezer and leave the 'fast freeze' control on until the food is really solid, perhaps another 4 to 5 hours.

Fresh meat needs a much lower temperature if the cold is to penetrate to its centre quickly enough, so the 'fast freeze' control should be on for approximately 6 hours before putting the meat in the freezer and should then stay on for another 24 hours or thereabouts.

For small amounts of food such as a single pie or two loaves of bread there is no need to use the 'fast freeze' control. Just put the food in the

Centre: Tape over the switch and plug for the freezer so it cannot be switched off or disconnected by mistake.

coldest part of the freezer where it cannot touch food that is already frozen; the temperature will be low enough to freeze small amounts satisfactorily.

How much food can be 'fast frozen' in every 24 hours depends greatly on the type of freezer, and it is essential to follow the manufacturer's recommendations. As a general rule, one-tenth of a freezer's total storage capacity can be 'fast frozen' in every 24 hours. Do not try to 'fast freeze' more than the freezer is designed to cope with: if you do, the cold is likely to be distributed unevenly and may not penetrate packages as quickly as it should.

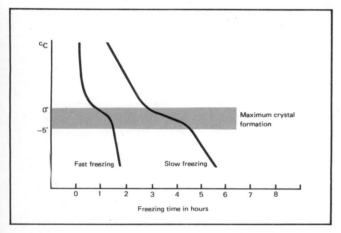

The graph above illustrates how the cell structure of food is damaged by the formation of large ice crystals during slow freezing.

Switch to 'fast freeze' before going out on a bulk buying trip, even if only ready-frozen foods are to be bought. If you go to a freezer centre, say once a month, you will be bringing back quite large quantities of food — perhaps several bulk packages of beefburgers, fish, icecream, frozen meat and vegetables, for example. Although the food is ready-frozen, it will have been out of the freezer long enough on your journey home for the packages to start to become warmer. Therefore, the colder the freezer when they go in, the better it will be for the new stocks and for the food already there.

Fast Freezing Compartment

This is insulated from the rest of the freezer and should be used when putting in fresh or cooked food. When the food is frozen, it can be transferred to the main storage area. If there is no 'fast freeze' compartment in your chest freezer, then food to be frozen should be placed on the floor of the cabinet (moving already frozen packages away first), or against the walls. Upright freezers usually do not have special 'fast freeze' compartments, so try to keep one shelf, or part of a shelf, empty in readiness for fresh foods. Choose a shelf in the coldest part of the freezer:

this will be against the walls if the cooling system runs through the walls, or in the centre of the shelf if the condenser coils are built into the shelves.

Running Costs

Tests and surveys indicate that the average freezer consumes electricity at a rate of roughly 1½ kiloWatt hours per 28 l/1 cu ft per week. How close your consumption will be to the average will depend on many factors. The least amount of electricity is used if you: have a chest model, keep it in a cool room with plenty of space for air to circulate, open it only occasionally and briefly, keep it crammed full of frozen foods, do not use the 'fast freeze' control too often, and never let frost build up to more than 6 mm/¼ inch thick.

In addition to the cost of the electricity, you must allow for the cost of disposable packaging materials. Packaging for the freezer is extremely important, and materials such as aluminium foil, freezer bags and tissue, cling film and polythene (polyethylene) are expensive and have a limited life.

These running costs, added to the purchase price and the cost of insurance and/or repairs, are quite substantial. It is important also to bear in mind that bulk buying requires you to spend large sums of money at a time. If you are used to running a weekly or monthly housekeeping budget, you may find it difficult to cope with the necessary adjustments.

Taking all these factors into account, you can assume that if you actually want your freezer to save you money you will have to bulk-buy and grow your own food on a large scale. Generally, the advantage is convenience rather than economy — fewer shopping trips, fewer cooking sessions, varied food on hand at all times. But you can balance out the cost of the convenience against the cost of the freezer if you shop carefully and use your freezer sensibly.

Insurance

Freezers do not often break down, but if they do the fault is usually in the motor. Replacing a motor is expensive, both in terms of new parts and labour and the cost of any food that may thaw and become uneatable while the freezer is out of action. Insurance is, therefore, worthwhile and can cover not only parts and labour involved in repairs, but also the cost of any food spoiled. Usually

both breakdowns and power cuts are covered, though rarely accidental switching off of the electricity supply.

Some freezer centres run their own insurance schemes, or a broker will help. Specialists in freezer insurance are likely to give the best terms, but also obtain a quotation from whoever handles the rest of your household insurance.

Defrosting and Maintenance

A freezer requires very little basic maintenance: if you keep it clean, it should work happily for you for years. The most important attention it demands is defrosting once or twice a year for a chest freezer, two or three times for an upright. Some freezers have an automatic defrosting device and therefore do not need defrosting manually.

Defrosting will obviously be less of a chore if you can do this job when stocks are fairly low, because taking all the frozen food out and putting it back again is a large part of the operation. Defrost as soon as the ice is more than approximately 6 mm/¼ inch thick, as this coating will begin to impair the efficiency of the cooling system. Initially, heavy frost will not affect the storage of frozen food, but if the build-up is allowed to continue, then the freezer has to work overtime to try and regulate the temperature.

Take everything out, pile all the food together in as cool a place as you can find (some of the food can go in the refrigerator), and cover with thick blankets, rugs or towels to trap the cold air. Switch off the electricity and remove the plug from its socket, or turn the controls to defrost. Pull out the bung in the bottom, if the freezer has one, so that the melted ice can run into a tray. Line the bottom of the freezer with thick layers of newspaper and, if it is an upright model, put some on the floor in front of the freezer. Put a large bowl of hot water in the bottom of the freezer and close the lid or door; this will start loosening the ice. When the ice starts to loosen, begin to scrape it off gently with a wooden or plastic spatula. Never use anything metal or you will damage the surface. Work as quickly as you can, wearing gloves to protect your hands from the cold.

Lift off the ice as it falls onto the newspaper and throw it away before it has time to melt. Always try to work with ice rather than water: if you have a chest freezer it is very difficult to ladle a great puddle out of the bottom; if you have an upright you will find

yourself flooding the floor around and underneath the freezer in no time at all if you let the ice melt. The exception, of course, is a freezer with a built-in drain hole, designed so that you can melt the ice completely and simply open the drain to dispose of the water.

If the ice is really thick, you may need a second bowl of hot water after scraping off the first layer of ice. When all the ice is removed, wipe the inside of the freezer thoroughly with a solution of warm water and bicarbonate of soda (baking soda); do not use dish washing-up liquid as the smell is difficult to remove. Use approximately 2 × 5 ml spoons/2 teaspoons soda to 600 ml/1 pint/2½ cups water. Finally, when all the ice has been removed and the inside of the freezer is thoroughly clean, wipe all the surfaces dry with a clean towel.

If you have a freezer that operates on a condenser system, take this opportunity to clean the dust off the grille, and the fan if there is one. Some grilles unscrew so that the dust can be cleaned off easily.

Close the lid or door of the freezer and reconnect plug and power supply. Switch on to 'fast freeze' or the coldest setting for at least 30 minutes before repacking. While the cabinet cools, clean the outside and wax it lightly if the freezer is in a place where it might get damp. Wash the baskets or shelves in the soda solution, then dry them. When the cabinet is thoroughly cold, replace all the food. Leave freezer on 'fast freeze' or coldest setting for 4 to 6 hours or overnight (until the temperature reaches −18°C/0°F), then return to its normal storage temperature.

Apart from defrosting and cleaning the condenser grille, there is nothing more to be done in the way of maintenance. If you are lucky enough to have a freezer with an automatic defrosting device, then all you will have to do is clean the inside of the freezer once or twice a year, and polish the outside occasionally. It is also a good idea to check the internal temperature of the freezer with a thermometer from time to time, but this is more for reassurance than maintenance.

Service Contracts

Although your freezer does not need regular maintenance by an engineer, it will need repairing quickly if it breaks down. It is therefore important to check what servicing facilities are available when you buy the freezer. Usually either the manufac-

turer or supplier will contract to repair your freezer and there should be an emergency telephone number, manned at weekends as well as weekdays. It should be part of the contract that the service organization will either store your frozen food or loan you a replacement freezer should the repair take more than a few hours. Often this comes as part of an insurance scheme, which gives you extra assurance of service: if they do not either fix your freezer or store your food, the same organization will then have to bear the cost of any food losses. A service contract is as valuable as an insurance scheme — look into both.

Emergency Procedure

Be prepared for breakdowns and power cuts. Make a note of the emergency telephone number given on your service contract, and put it where you know you can find it. It also helps to make a mental note of the various people you know who also own freezers; if you are truly stuck they may be able to help out by storing at least some of your frozen food. Also check to see if your local butcher or nearest freezer centre can help. A conservator, if you have one, is useful in an emergency, and ice-making compartments of refrigerators can be handy as well.

Most freezers are fitted with a set of indicator lights. There is generally a light to indicate that the freezer is working, and a red light that comes on when the internal temperature rises above −18°C/0°F. Make a habit of checking the lights whenever you pass the freezer. If your freezer is kept outside the main part of the house, you may find it worthwhile to fit an audible alarm to sound if the temperature rises.

The most common emergencies are a power failure or a fault in the freezer. In the event of a power failure, first check that the switch has not been turned off accidentally or that a fuse has not gone. The likely duration of a power failure needs immediate checking with the local electricity board. Having established how long it is likely to be, the next priority is to save the contents of the freezer. Providing the cabinet is three-quarters full or more, food should stay frozen hard for a minimum of 12 hours. During this time it is essential that the lid or door is not opened unnecessarily, thus allowing warm air to enter and raise the temperature. If the lid or door is inadvertently opened during this

time, then quickly pack round the food inside with newspapers.

In the event of an extended local power cut, perhaps as a result of storms, when all your neighbours are in the same boat and there is a likelihood of more than a day without power, consider hiring a portable generator; several families could share the cost, using it a few hours at a time on each freezer. If the freezer has actually broken down, a faulty thermostat perhaps, or more seriously the compressor, check your guarantee or service agreement, then get in touch immediately with the maintenance or service department of the freezer supplier/manufacturer. Not all departments operate a 24-hour emergency service, so if repairs are likely to take a long time, seek alternative storage of your contents (see above).

If it seems likely that the freezer will be out of operation for some time, then fill up any space in the freezer with crumpled newspaper — this should be the only time the lid or door is opened until the power returns or repairs are made — and insulate the cabinet with blankets, rugs, sacks or towels.

As soon as the emergency is over, remove insulating materials from both inside and outside, switch on to 'fast freeze' or coldest setting for approximately 4 to 6 hours or overnight (or until temperature reaches −18°C/0°F), and resist the temptation to open the freezer to check the contents until that time has elapsed.

In the event of food starting to thaw long before the discovery of a power failure or breakdown, it is still sometimes possible to salvage some items. However, the golden rule in such circumstances is: if in doubt, throw out. Food packs that are still very frosty inside and unyielding to firm pressure can be transferred immediately to another freezer or, providing there's room, to the ice-making compartment of an ordinary refrigerator. Otherwise, all raw fish, meat, poultry and vegetables must be cooked and then eaten immediately or re-frozen. If anything has a strong, unpleasant odour or looks bloody, get rid of it at once. All cooked dishes must be eaten within 24 hours or thrown away; they should *never* be re-frozen. This rule also applies to desserts and icecream made with fresh cream. Biscuits (cookies), breads, plain cakes, fruit and pastries can be safely re-frozen, although in the case of fruit there is likely to be some loss in colour, flavour, juice and texture.

Packaging Materials

Above: Aluminium foil can be used for wrapping awkwardly shaped foods, for padding protruding bones and for making lids for foil pie dishes. Freezer wrap (freezerproof cling film) is useful for wrapping sausages, tarts and portions of cheese or cake.

Centre top: Aluminium foil freezer trays and pie plates. The casserole is about to be frozen. The lemon meringue pie had its topping added after freezing and before baking, and is now ready to be served.

Centre bottom: Reheat in boiling water, frozen sauces or soups packed in boil-in-the-bags.

Apart from temperature control, the factor that most affects the quality of frozen foods is packaging. Unless food is properly wrapped, it will rapidly dry out and, when thawed, will be completely changed in taste and texture from the original. Everything that is put in the freezer must be wrapped in a material that prevents the moisture vapour from escaping from the food, and as much air as possible should be excluded from the package. Packaging must also protect food from damage during storage or from bad handling, or carriage from one place to another; it must be durable at low temperatures so that it does not split, burst or leak. Keep all freezer packaging in a clean, dry place, and check for broken packages in the freezer from time to time.

Alumin(i)um Foil

Heavy-gauge freezer foil is the best to use, but ordinary kitchen foil can be used double. Use foil to wrap awkwardly shaped foods such as meat joints (cuts), because foil will mould to any shape and, if the edges are carefully folded together, the package will be airtight. Foil is also useful to make lids for foil dishes.

Foil does puncture easily however, and it is as well to overwrap it with a freezer bag for extra protection; ordi-

nary thin-gauge bags will do for this, or cotton stockinette. Re-use foil that has been in the freezer for cooking purposes, but in the freezer it should be used again for short-term storage only.

Alumin(i)um Foil Dishes and Pie Plates

Use these for casseroles and pies that are to go directly from the freezer into the oven. They can be used for all kinds of food, but it is their freezer-to-oven capability that makes them most useful. Foil trays are available in portion sizes, enabling you to freeze food in convenient amounts.

Some foil dishes are provided with cardboard-backed foil lids. If no lid is provided, cover the dish with foil or freezer wrap (not forgetting to remove it before putting the dish in the oven). If you are making your own lid of foil or freezer wrap, overwrap the dish with a freezer bag to protect the lid from damage. Cardboard-backed lids are good and strong and will not need overwrapping if the edges are sealed carefully, but the lid can be used only once.

Foil dishes can be used many times if carefully washed after use, but do check for damage every time.

Boil-in-the-bag*

This is a special polythene (polyethylene) bag in which cooked foods can be frozen and later reheated in boiling water for serving. These bags are available in various sizes and can be sealed with twist-ties, string or by heat. They are a great convenience, especially at times when you are in a hurry, but are not reusable. Some commercially prepared frozen foods are also packed in boil-in-the-bag wrappings for quick serving.

*Available only in commercially prepared packs in Australia.

Cardboard Plates and Boxes

Use cardboard plates to support fragile pie crusts, or piles of floppy pancakes (crêpes). Use cardboard boxes to protect a fancy decorated cake or dessert. Be sure to overwrap in polythene (polyethylene) or foil as well, to make the package airtight.

Freezer Wrap (Freezerproof Cling Film)

It is essential to use the heavy-gauge/high density film (pliofilm) designed for freezer use; general-purpose cling film is not moisture-

and vapour-proof at freezer temperature. Freezer wrap moulds easily, like foil, and fastens by clinging to itself. It cannot be re-used, however.

Glass Containers

Some glass jars and bottles are resistant to freezer temperatures, but it is advisable to test such a container first. Place the empty container in a freezer bag and leave in the freezer for 24 hours. If it shatters, then the bag will keep the pieces of glass together so they can be removed easily. (In the U.S., most popular brands of canning jars are freezer resistant.)

Above: Test glass containers by freezing empty wrapped in polythene bags. Use cardboard plates to support pancakes (crêpes), then wrap in foil or polythene.

Left: Freezer bags and boil-in-the-bags can be sealed by heat using an electric heat sealer or an iron with brown paper underneath.

Top: Waxed cartons are suitable for sauces or open-frozen fruit for the freezer. Polythene containers can be used for many kinds of foods, including cakes. Freezerproof dishes are ideal for freezing foods to be served in their dishes.

Inset: Interleave chops, hamburgers and sandwich cake layers with foil or cling film.

Interleaving Sheets

Buy freezer tissue or cling film, or cut up used freezer bags or alumin(i)um foil to use for interleaving each portion, then pack several portions together in alumin(i)um foil or a freezer bag. This way you can take out slices of cake, portions of pâté, or pieces of fish or steak, for example, one piece at a time, then reseal the package.

Ovenware Dishes

Many ovenware dishes are now tested and approved for use at freezer temperatures, earthenware freezer-to-oven-to-table dishes and ceramic glassware, in particular. Do not use ordinary dishes in the freezer unless on manufacturer's recommendations —the extreme temperature may shatter them. Decorative tableware is expensive and you are unlikely to want to hide it in the freezer for long periods; however, it can be extremely helpful to make a special dish for a party, say a week ahead, and store it already in its serving dish.

Polythene (Polyethylene)

Bags: use heavy-gauge/high density freezer bags for wrapping all kinds of food. Mould the bag as closely to the shape of the food as you can, squeeze out all the air (see **Air**), then fasten tightly with a paper-covered wire tie or a plastic tie, or heat seal it (see **Heat Sealing**). Bags can be re-used if thoroughly washed, sterilized and dried, but make sure that a used bag has not been punctured before it is used again.

Containers: rigid polythene (polyethylene) containers with airtight lids can be used for all kinds of food in the freezer. They are expensive to buy but, unlike their foil counterparts, they will last for years.

If the seal around the lid becomes suspect as the box gets old, seal it with freezer tape (see page 235). For preference, choose square-sided boxes that stack best. For short-term storage, collect containers from products like cottage cheese, cream and yogurt. These are extremely useful for small quantities of food, sauces and stocks, etc.

Waxed Cartons

These are suitable for liquids, and are available for freezer use. They are not re-usable. Never put anything hot into a waxed carton, or the surface will be spoiled and the carton will become porous. Do not use waxed cardboard cartons saved from non-frozen products as they are unlikely to be of an adequate quality to protect your food in the freezer.

Labels and Tape

Frost-covered packs and containers all look alike in a freezer; therefore, they must be clearly labelled if they are to be found quickly and conveniently. You may recall what a certain item looks like a few days after freez-

ing, but you are unlikely to recognize that item after several weeks, even months, have elapsed. Write clearly on the label the contents, weight and date of freezing, together with any special instructions for thawing, heating and serving.

Adhesive labels should be stuck on a dry, grease-free surface, and freezer bags should be filled *after* labelling. Only use adhesive labels with a special adhesive that is durable at low temperatures or they will drop off in the freezer, leaving you with an assortment of 'mystery' packages. Some makes of freezer bag have a

labelling panel incorporated in them, but it is just as easy to slip a label inside a transparent pack before sealing, or tape on a label with special freezer tape, masking or insulating tape — ordinary tape peels off.

Another popular type of labelling is the combined label and tie made either in paper or re-usable coloured plastic.

Always use a waxed pencil or non-water-based felt-tipped pen for writing on labels, as water-based inks will run and lead pencil fades away. Coloured labels used in conjunction with other colour-coded packaging materials are a great help in identifying different foods.

Above: A selection of labels and tape, with pens and a roll of freezer tape.

Left: Liquids can be poured into a freezer bag in a preformer (forming container), open frozen until solid, then removed from the container for storing. Freezer bags can also be used for wrapping many different types of food including poultry and blanched vegetables.

Other Equipment

Apart from packaging materials, there is very little 'special' equipment necessary for freezing. Some of the products available are listed here and, although not all of them are necessary, you may find some of them a help, depending on the type of foods you freeze.

Baskets and Bags

Several strong plastic-coated baskets are needed in chest freezers to divide the cabinet into compartments. In both chest and upright models, it is often convenient to put foods of one type into different-coloured string bags to avoid confusion. Or use coloured freezer bags and matching labels as an identification code.

Blancher/Blanching Basket

This is essential for freezing fresh vegetables because it ensures the maximum penetration of boiling water to individual vegetables. A frying basket can be used instead, otherwise a collapsible wire basket that fits a large pan.

Open (Flash) Freeze Trays

Special plastic-coated wire or moulded plastic trays are available for open (flash) freezing, and these fit neatly into the freezer, stacking one on top of the other. They are particularly useful for soft fruits and free flow vegetable packs, as the stacking arrangement allows large quantities to be frozen at the same time. As an alternative but perhaps a little less convenient, foil-lined baking sheets or wooden trays can be used, with equally good results.

Heat Sealer

For sealing freezer bags. Electrically operated heat sealers make a very quick and neat finish, although bags can also be sealed with an ordinary domestic iron (*see* **Heat Sealing**).

Freezer Thermometer

A thermometer is not a necessity, but it is reassuring to be able to check the temperature of the freezer from time to time, to make sure it is running efficiently. Put the thermometer in a flat tray and cover with water. Freeze until solid, then check temperature.

Freezer Knife

Ordinary kitchen or household knives are likely to break if used frequently to cut frozen blocks of food. Freezer knives are specially strengthened to prevent this from happening, and therefore it is well worth investing in one.

Icecream Scoop

Unless it is the 'soft scoop' kind, icecream straight from the freezer tends to be extra hard, and is likely to bend an ordinary spoon. An icecream scoop will not bend, and gives an attractive portion.

Lollipop (Popsicle) Moulds

Homemade iced lollipops (popsicles) are generally cheaper than the commercially prepared varieties and re-usable moulds and sticks are now widely available for making them in the freezer. These are particularly useful if there are children in the house.

Record Book or Diary

This is an essential aid to good freezer management. It is a book in which all the contents of a freezer are recorded, showing where food is stored, its date of freezing, how much has already been used, size of pack, etc. It will help you to use stocks in rotation so that nothing is forgotten, and foods are not stored longer than the recommended time.

There are record books on sale, but they can easily be made at home from exercise or loose-leaf books. A card-index system or any other system may also be used to tell you at a glance what is in the freezer.

Keep the record book near the freezer and be sure to keep the entries up-to-date.

Freezer Pump

These are becoming increasingly popular and widely available as a means to extract air from soft packages, and are one of the most efficient and hygienic methods of doing so. See **Air**.

Below can be seen a selection of useful freezing equipment: lollipop (popsicle) moulds, a freezer pump, a blanching basket, an electric heat sealer, a freezer thermometer, an icecream scoop, a freezer knife and a record book with a pen.

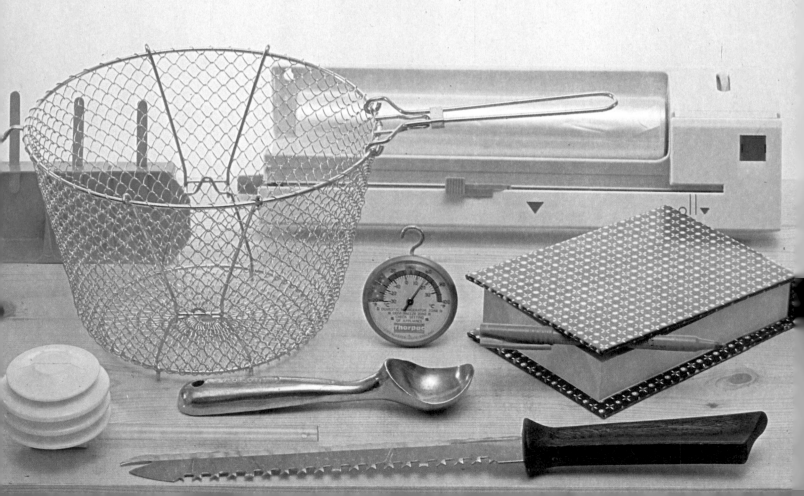

Vegetables

Vegetable	Preparation	Packaging	Thawing	Storage Time
Artichoke, Globe	Discard coarse outer and lower leaves. Trim off spiky tops and remove stem. Wash under cold running water. Blanch with lemon juice 7–10 minutes. Drain, cool in iced water. Drain upside-down. Squeeze dry. Or to freeze artichoke hearts: boil whole artichokes until tender, drain, discard leaves. Scoop out choke. Leave to cool.	Pack whole artichokes in freezer bags. Pack hearts in rigid containers, interleaving layers with foil.	Thaw in wrappings 4 hours at room temperature. Use as for fresh.	6 months.
Artichoke, Jerusalem	Peel, slice or cut into cubes. Steep in water and lemon juice, then drain and blanch 1–2 minutes. Drain, cool in iced water. Drain and pat dry. Or scrub and boil 15 minutes, then rub off skins and sieve or purée.	Pack slices or cubes in freezer bags.	Cook blanched slices or cubes from frozen in boiling salted water approx. 8 minutes. Or thaw in bags at room temperature, then add to salads and stews, or cook 'au gratin'. Thaw puréed artichokes in containers at room temperature, or use from frozen to make soups.	3 months.
Asparagus	Blanch: 1 minute (sprew), 2 minutes (small), 3 minutes (medium), 4 minutes (thick). Drain. Cool in iced water, drain and pat dry.	Pack in rigid containers or freezer bags.	Unwrap and thaw sprew in a strainer or on a tea (dish) towel. Thaw thicker stems until easy to separate, then boil 2–4 minutes.	9 months.
Asparagus Pea	Wash, pat dry. Steam 1 minute. Cool in iced water. Drain and pat dry.	Pack in freezer bags.	Steam from frozen: 1 minute.	6 months.
Aubergine (Eggplant/ Breadfruit)	Leave unpeeled if young. Wash, cut into rounds 2 cm/¾ inch thick. Blanch 4 minutes. Cool in iced water. Drain and pat dry.	Pack in rigid containers, interleaving layers with foil or cling film. Or pack in freezer bags leaving headspace.	Thaw in wrappings in refrigerator or at room temperature. Pat dry before cooking as for fresh aubergine (eggplant).	12 months.
Avocado	Remove skin. Dice or pulp flesh with lemon juice. Work quickly to prevent flesh from discolouring. Or freeze as part of a dish — dip or soup for example.	Pack *immediately* in rigid containers.	Leave in unopened containers 2 hours at room temperature. Use immediately after thawing to prevent discoloration.	2 months.
Bean, Broad (Fava) Tips, Pods and Shelled	Wash. Blanch 2 minutes. Cool in iced water. Squeeze out water from tips. Pat dry pods and shelled beans.	Pack in small quantities in rigid containers or freezer bags.	Boil from frozen: 3–5 minutes, according to size.	12 months.
French (Green)	Top, tail and wash. Blanch whole 1–2 minutes. Drain. Cool in iced water. Drain and pat dry.	Pack in freezer bags.	Boil from frozen: 5–7 minutes, according to size.	12 months.
Runner (Snap)	Top, tail, string if necessary. Wash. Slice or cut into 2.5 cm/1 inch pieces. Blanch as for *French (Green) Bean* above.	Pack in freezer bags.	Boil from frozen: 5–7 minutes, according to size.	12 months.
Waxed	Top, tail and wash. Leave whole or cut into 2.5 cm/1 inch pieces. Blanch whole beans 3 minutes, pieces 2 minutes. Drain. Cool in iced water. Drain and pat dry.	Pack in freezer bags.	Boil from frozen: 5–7 minutes, according to size.	12 months.

Vegetable	Preparation	Packaging	Thawing	Storage Time
Bean Sprout	Blanch 1 minute. Drain. Cool in iced water. Drain and pat dry.	Pack in freezer bags.	Thaw in bags in refrigerator, or unwrap and thaw rapidly at room temperature. Use in cooking — bean sprouts are not crisp enough to use in salads after freezing.	2 months.
Beetroot (Beets)	Wash small beetroot (beets), then boil 10–20 minutes until tender. Drain. Leave to cool. Rub off skin. Leave whole, dice or slice.	Pack dry in rigid containers.	Thaw in containers in refrigerator, or unwrap and thaw rapidly at room temperature.	6 months.
Bindi	see Okra			
Bok Choy	see Cabbage, Chinese			
Breadfruit	see Aubergine (Eggplant)			
Broccoli (Sprouting)	Wash in salted water, then rinse. Blanch: 2 minutes (thin), 3 minutes (medium), 4 minutes (thick). Drain. Cool in iced water. Drain and pat dry.	Pack in rigid containers or freezer bags, alternating heads and stalks.	Boil from frozen: 3–7 minutes, according to size.	12 months.
Brussels Sprouts	Freeze only small sprouts. Trim and discard outer leaves. Wash. Grade into sizes. Blanch: 2 minutes (very small), 3 minutes (small), 4 minutes (medium). Drain. Cool in iced water. Drain and pat dry. Cook large sprouts until tender, then purée.	Pack in freezer bags.	Boil whole sprouts from frozen: 4–8 minutes, according to size.	12 months.
		Pack puréed sprouts in rigid containers.	Use puréed sprouts from frozen in making soups, etc.	
Cabbage, Chinese (Bok Choy)	Shred. Blanch 1 minute. Drain. Cool in iced water. Drain and pat dry.	Pack in freezer bags.	Unwrap and thaw few minutes at room temperature.	12 months.
Green, Red, White	Discard tough, outer leaves. Shred inner leaves. Blanch 1 minute. Drain. Cool in iced water. Drain and pat dry.	Pack in freezer bags.	Boil from frozen: 5–8 minutes, according to size.	6 months.
Capsicum	see Pepper, Sweet			
Cardoon	Cut stems to even lengths. Remove any outer strings. Wash. Blanch 3 minutes. Drain. Cool in iced water. Drain and pat dry.	Pack in rigid containers or freezer bags.	Boil from frozen: 8 minutes. Or thaw in wrappings at room temperature, then fry as for fresh cardoon.	12 months.
Carrot	Leave small, early carrots whole. Cut off tops. Wash and scrape to remove soil (not skin). Blanch 3 minutes. Drain. Cool in iced water. Drain and rub off skin. Cut off tops and peel large, old carrots. Slice, dice, chop or grate. Blanch in salted water 2 minutes. Drain. Cool in iced water. Drain and pat dry.	Pack in rigid containers or freezer bags.	Boil whole carrots from frozen: 4 minutes. Add sliced, diced, chopped or grated carrots frozen to casseroles, soups, etc.	9 months.
Cauliflower	Do not freeze whole. Break into florets, wash and grade into sizes. Blanch with lemon juice 3 minutes. Drain. Cool in iced water. Drain and pat dry.	Pack in freezer bags.	Boil from frozen: 4 minutes.	6 months.
Celeriac (Celery Root)	Peel. Grate and blanch 1 minute, or dice/slice and blanch 2 minutes. Drain, cool in iced water, drain and pat dry. Or boil whole until tender, drain, peel and slice.	Pack in freezer bags or rigid containers.	Thaw in wrappings at room temperature, or cook from frozen.	6 months.
Celery	Trim and remove strings. Scrub and cut into short lengths. Blanch 3 minutes. Drain. Cool in iced water. Drain and pat dry.	Pack in freezer bags.	Boil from frozen: 10 minutes. Or add frozen celery to casseroles and soups, etc.	6 months.
Chard, Swiss (Seakale Beet)	Wash leaves. Blanch 2 minutes. Drain. Cool in iced water, drain and squeeze dry. Cut inner ribs into short lengths. Blanch 3 minutes. Drain and cool as for leaves.	Pack in freezer bags.	Cook leaves from frozen in butter: 7 minutes. Boil ribs from frozen: 7 minutes.	12 months.
Chicory (Aust. & U.S. Endive)	Wipe clean. Blanch 5 minutes. Drain. Cool in iced water. Drain and pat dry.	Pack in freezer bags.	Thaw in bags 2 hours at room temperature. Squeeze out excess moisture before cooking.	6 months.
Collards	see Spring Greens			

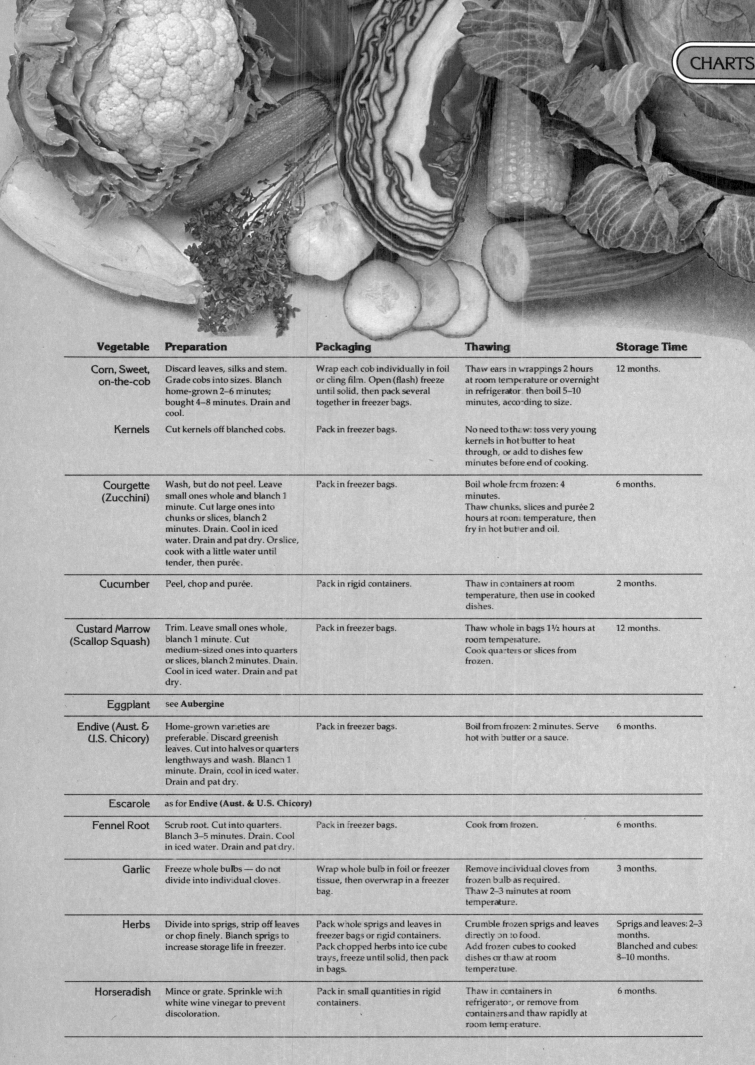

Vegetable	Preparation	Packaging	Thawing	Storage Time
Corn, Sweet, on-the-cob	Discard leaves, silks and stem. Grade cobs into sizes. Blanch home-grown 2–6 minutes; bought 4–8 minutes. Drain and cool.	Wrap each cob individually in foil or cling film. Open (flash) freeze until solid, then pack several together in freezer bags.	Thaw ears in wrappings 2 hours at room temperature or overnight in refrigerator, then boil 5–10 minutes, according to size.	12 months.
Kernels	Cut kernels off blanched cobs.	Pack in freezer bags.	No need to thaw: toss very young kernels in hot butter to heat through, or add to dishes few minutes before end of cooking.	
Courgette (Zucchini)	Wash, but do not peel. Leave small ones whole and blanch 1 minute. Cut large ones into chunks or slices, blanch 2 minutes. Drain. Cool in iced water. Drain and pat dry. Or slice, cook with a little water until tender, then purée.	Pack in freezer bags.	Boil whole from frozen: 4 minutes. Thaw chunks, slices and purée 2 hours at room temperature, then fry in hot butter and oil.	6 months.
Cucumber	Peel, chop and purée.	Pack in rigid containers.	Thaw in containers at room temperature, then use in cooked dishes.	2 months.
Custard Marrow (Scallop Squash)	Trim. Leave small ones whole, blanch 1 minute. Cut medium-sized ones into quarters or slices, blanch 2 minutes. Drain. Cool in iced water. Drain and pat dry.	Pack in freezer bags.	Thaw whole in bags 1½ hours at room temperature. Cook quarters or slices from frozen.	12 months.
Eggplant	see **Aubergine**			
Endive (Aust. & U.S. Chicory)	Home-grown varieties are preferable. Discard greenish leaves. Cut into halves or quarters lengthways and wash. Blanch 1 minute. Drain, cool in iced water. Drain and pat dry.	Pack in freezer bags.	Boil from frozen: 2 minutes. Serve hot with butter or a sauce.	6 months.
Escarole	as for **Endive (Aust. & U.S. Chicory)**			
Fennel Root	Scrub root. Cut into quarters. Blanch 3–5 minutes. Drain. Cool in iced water. Drain and pat dry.	Pack in freezer bags.	Cook from frozen.	6 months.
Garlic	Freeze whole bulbs — do not divide into individual cloves.	Wrap whole bulb in foil or freezer tissue, then overwrap in a freezer bag.	Remove individual cloves from frozen bulb as required. Thaw 2–3 minutes at room temperature.	3 months.
Herbs	Divide into sprigs, strip off leaves or chop finely. Blanch sprigs to increase storage life in freezer.	Pack whole sprigs and leaves in freezer bags or rigid containers. Pack chopped herbs into ice cube trays, freeze until solid, then pack in bags.	Crumble frozen sprigs and leaves directly on to food. Add frozen cubes to cooked dishes or thaw at room temperature.	Sprigs and leaves: 2–3 months. Blanched and cubes: 8–10 months.
Horseradish	Mince or grate. Sprinkle with white wine vinegar to prevent discoloration.	Pack in small quantities in rigid containers.	Thaw in containers in refrigerator, or remove from containers and thaw rapidly at room temperature.	6 months.

Vegetable	Preparation	Packaging	Thawing	Storage Time
Kale	Wash. Blanch 1 minute. Drain. Cool in iced water. Drain and pat dry.	Pack in freezer bags.	Boil from frozen: 8 minutes.	12 months.
Kohlrabi	Cut off tops and trim. Leave young small ones whole, peel and dice or slice older ones. Blanch whole ones 3 minutes, diced 2 minutes. Drain. Cool in iced water. Drain and pat dry.	Pack in freezer bags.	Thaw in bags at room temperature. Boil when still crisp: 10 minutes. Or thaw diced or sliced, pat dry and deep fry.	12 months.
Leek	Discard roots and green tops. Wash thoroughly and stand upside-down in water 30 minutes. Leave small ones whole, slice large ones. Blanch 3 minutes. Drain. Cool in iced water. Drain and pat dry.	Pack in freezer bags.	Boil from frozen: 6–8 minutes.	6 months.
Lettuce	Blanch 2 minutes. Drain. Squeeze out water.	Pack in freezer bags.	Use from frozen in soups.	6 months.
Marrow (Large Summer Squash)	Peel, cut into chunks and remove seeds. Blanch 2 minutes. Drain. Cool in iced water. Drain and pat dry.	Pack in rigid containers, leaving headspace.	Steam, uncovered, from frozen: 1–2 minutes.	6 months.
Mushroom	Wipe, but do not peel. Trim off stems.	Open (flash) freeze whole until solid, then pack in rigid containers or freezer bags. Freeze stems in separate bags.	Cook from frozen: toss in butter or grill (broil). Or thaw in wrappings in refrigerator for use in composite dishes.	3 months.
Okra (Bindi/Gumbo)	Cut off stems without breaking pods. Blanch 3 minutes. Drain. Cool in iced water. Drain and pat dry.	Pack in rigid containers or freezer bags.	Boil from frozen: 6–8 minutes. Or add frozen to soups and stews, etc. Or fry frozen in butter.	12 months.
Onion	Peel small whole onions, blanch 2 minutes, then drain. Cool, drain and pat dry. Peel large onions and chop or slice. Pack raw or blanch 1 minute, drain, cool and dry as for whole onions.	Pack in freezer bags and overwrap.	Add whole and chopped or sliced onions frozen to casseroles, sauces, stews, etc. Thaw raw onions in refrigerator and use slightly frosted in salads.	3 months.
Parsnip	Trim and peel or scrub. Dice or cut into rings or strips. Blanch 2 minutes. Drain. Cool in iced water. Drain and pat dry.	Pack in freezer bags.	Boil from frozen: 10–15 minutes. Or thaw at room temperature and use in cooked dishes.	6 months.
Pea	Shell. Blanch 1 minute. Drain. Cool in iced water and drain.	Open (flash) freeze until solid, then pack in freezer bags.	Boil from frozen: 4 minutes.	12 months.
Mange Tout (Snow/Sugar Pea)	Top and tail pods. Blanch ½–1 minute. Drain. Cool in iced water. Drain and pat dry.	Pack in freezer bags.	Boil from frozen: 3 minutes.	12 months.
Pepper, Sweet (Capsicum), Green and Red	Wash. Remove stems. Cut in half, remove seeds and membranes. Leave in halves or slice. Blanch, if wished: halves 3 minutes, slices 2 minutes. Drain. Cool in iced water. Drain and pat dry.	Open (flash) freeze unblanched and blanched peppers until solid, then pack in freezer bags.	Thaw in bags 1–2 hours at room temperature.	12 months.
Potato, Chipped (French Fried)	Deep fry 2–3 minutes. Drain and cool.	Pack in freezer bags.	Unwrap and thaw at room temperature. Pat dry. Re-fry 3–4 minutes.	3 months.
Croquette or Duchesse	Form mashed potatoes into shapes on baking sheets. Freeze before or after cooking in the usual way, whichever is most convenient.	Open (flash) freeze uncooked or cooked shapes until solid, then pack in rigid containers.	Bake uncooked croquettes from frozen: brush with beaten egg and bake in fairly hot oven 20–30 minutes. Thaw cooked croquettes in containers 2 hours at room temperature, then reheat in moderate oven 20 minutes.	3 months.
Pumpkin	Peel and remove seeds. Cut into pieces. Bake, boil or steam until soft, then drain. Mash, if wished. Leave to cool.	Pack pieces or mashed pumpkin in rigid containers.	Reheat from frozen in double boiler. Or thaw in containers 2 hours at room temperature.	12 months.
Quelite	as for **Spinach**			
Radish	Use winter variety only. Peel and grate. Or peel and dice, then blanch 2 minutes. Drain. Cool in iced water. Drain and pat dry.	Pack in freezer bags.	Thaw grated radish in bags 2 hours at room temperature. Use in salads. Boil diced radish from frozen: 5–10 minutes, according to size. Serve as a hot vegetable.	6 months.

Vegetable	Preparation	Packaging	Thawing	Storage Time
Rutabaga	see **Swede**			
Salsify (Scorzonera/ Oyster Plant/ Vegetable Oyster)	Scrub roots. Do not peel. Blanch 2 minutes. Drain. Cut into short lengths, remove skin, then leave to cool. Or boil until almost tender, peel and leave to cool.	Pack in freezer bags.	Thaw in bags 2 hours at room temperature. Or cook from frozen according to recipe.	12 months.
Scallion	see **Spring Onion**			
Scorzonera	see **Salsify**			
Seakale	**DO NOT FREEZE**			
Seakale Beet	see **Chard, Swiss**			
Shallot	as for small **Onions**			
Snow/Sugar Pea	see **Mange Tout**			
Spinach (Silverbeet)	Wash. Blanch thinnings 30 seconds, thicker leaves and stems 2 minutes. Drain. Cool in iced water, then squeeze out excess moisture with hands.	Pack in freezer bags.	Thaw thinnings in colander or strainer 30 minutes at room temperature, then toss quickly in hot butter. Boil thicker leaves and stems from frozen: 5–7 minutes. Or cook gently in butter from frozen.	12 months.
Spring Green (Collards)	Wash. Peel or discard hard stems. Leave whole or chop. Blanch 2 minutes. Drain. Cool in iced water. Drain and pat dry.	Pack in freezer bags.	Boil from frozen: approximately 5 minutes until tender.	12 months.
Spring Onion (Scallion)	Discard roots and green tops. Wipe and peel off outer skin. Leave whole or chop.	Pack in small quantities in freezer bags and overwrap.	Thaw in wrappings 30 minutes at room temperature. Use slightly chilled in salads.	2 months.
Squash	as for **Custard Marrow** and **Marrow**			
Swede (Rutabaga)	Wash and peel. Boil 15 minutes. Drain and purée. Leave until cold.	Pack in rigid containers.	Reheat from frozen in double boiler.	6 months.
Sweet Potato (Yam)	Peel. Cut into slices or rounds Parboil, drain and leave to cool. Or peel, halve and boil until tender. Drain. Cool in iced water. Drain and pat dry. Purée, if wished.	Pack slices and rounds in freezer bags. Pack purée in rigid containers.	Thaw slices and rounds in bags at room temperature, then pat dry and fry in hot butter, or in hot butter and sugar until caramelized. Or deep fry from frozen. Reheat puréed sweet potatoes from frozen in double boiler.	6 months.
Sweetcorn	see **Corn, Sweet**			
Tomato, Whole	Wipe and remove stalks. Do not skin.	Pack in small quantities in freezer bags.	Thaw in bags 2 hours at room temperature. Use in cooking.	12 months.
Juice	Wipe and remove stalks. Cut into quarters. Simmer until soft, then sieve and season to taste. Leave to cool.	Pack in rigid containers.	Thaw in containers in refrigerator.	12 months.
Purée	Prepare as for *Juice*, return sieved tomatoes to pan and reduce. Leave to cool.	As for *Juice*.	As for *Juice*.	12 months.
Sauce	As for *Purée*, adding onions and seasonings to taste.	As for *Juice*.	As for *Juice*.	12 months.
Truffle	Peel. Sauté until almost cooked, then leave to cool.	Pack in rigid containers or freezer bags.	Thaw 2 hours at room temperature, then reheat.	3 months.
Turnip	Trim off tops and roots. Peel thinly. Leave small ones whole and blanch 1 minute. Or peel, dice and blanch larger ones 2 minutes. Drain. Cool in iced water. Drain and pat dry. Or boil until tender, drain and purée.	Pack whole and diced turnips in freezer bags. Pack puréed turnips in rigid containers.	Boil whole and diced turnips from frozen: 5–10 minutes, according to size. Or thaw in bags 2 hours at room temperature, then heat in butter and sugar to caramelize. Reheat purée from frozen in double boiler.	12 months.
Watercress	Wash and dry. Simmer 10 minutes in butter. Leave to cool.	Pack in rigid containers.	Use from frozen in cooking sauces, soups, etc.	6 months.
Yam	see **Potato, Sweet**			
Zucchini	see **Courgette**			

Fruit

Fruit	Preparation	Packaging	Thawing	Storage Time
Apple, Dessert	Peel and core, then dice or slice into solution of lemon juice and water.	Drain and pack immediately in medium syrup in rigid containers.	Thaw in unopened containers 1 hour at room temperature.	Rings and slices: 8–12 months.
Apple, Cooking (Tart)	Peel and core, then cut into rings or slices. Blanch 1 minute. Drain, cool and dry. Or cook to a purée with or without sugar and with a very little water.	Pack in rigid containers or freezer bags.	As for *Apple, Dessert* or use from frozen to make sauces, or in pies and puddings.	Purées: 8 months.
Apricot	Scald firm fruit 10–15 seconds. Rub off skins, halve and remove stones (pits). Skin and stone (pit) ripe fruit under cold running water. Leave whole or slice, brush with lemon juice.	Pack immediately in medium syrup.	Thaw in unopened containers 3 hours in refrigerator.	12 months.
Avocado	see **Vegetable Chart**			
Banana	Peel and mash with sugar and lemon juice.	Pack immediately in rigid containers.	Thaw in unopened containers 5 hours in refrigerator. Use immediately.	6 months.
Bilberry (Blueberry)	Wash fruit that is only just ripe in very cold water, drain and dry.	Open (flash) freeze, then pack in freezer bags. Or pack dry, or in heavy syrup, in rigid containers.	Thaw in bags or containers 2½ hours at room temperature.	12 months.
Blackberry (Bramble)	As for **Bilberry**.	Open (flash) freeze, then pack in freezer bags. Or pack dry in rigid containers.	As for **Bilberry**.	12 months.
Blackcurrant	see **Currant**			
Boysenberry	as for **Bilberry**			
Bullace (Golden Damson)	Wash in iced water, cut in half, remove stones (pits). Cook to a purée, if wished.	Pack halves in medium syrup in rigid containers. Pack purée in small quantities in freezer bags or rigid containers.	Thaw in containers 2 hours at room temperature. Or cook from frozen if to be served warm.	12 months.
Calamondin	see **Citrus Fruit**			
Cape Gooseberry (Goldenberry)	As for **Bilberry**.	Open (flash) freeze, then pack in freezer bags. Or pack dry in rigid containers.	As for **Bilberry**.	12 months.
Cherry	Remove stalks, wash and halve. Remove stones (pits), if wished.	Pack in medium syrup, or pack dry, in rigid containers.	Thaw in containers 3 hours at room temperature. Use immediately.	12 months.
Chinese Gooseberry (Kiwi Fruit)	Peel off skin.	Pack dry.	Use slightly thawed.	6 months.
Citron	see **Citrus Fruit**			

Fruit	Preparation	Packaging	Thawing	Storage Time
Citrus Fruit (Calamondin, Citron, Clementine, Grapefruit, Kumquat, Lemon, Lime, Mandarin, Orange, Pomelo, Satsuma, Tangelo, Tangerine)	Leave whole or peel, remove pith and divide into segments or slice. Remove any pips (seeds).	Wrap whole fruit individually in foil or cling film. Open (flash) freeze segments and slices, then pack in freezer bags. Or pack segments and slices dry with or without sugar in rigid containers. Or pack segments or slices in syrup in rigid containers — light syrup for calamondin, citron, grapefruit, lemon, lime, pomelo, tangerine; medium syrup for clementine, kumquat, mandarin, orange, tangelo.	Thaw segments and slices in containers 2–2½ hours at room temperature. Thaw whole unwrapped lemons and Seville oranges 1½ hours at room temperature.	12 months.
Clementine	see **Citrus Fruit**			
Crab Apple	Wash small ones thoroughly, pat dry. Treat large crab apples as **Apple, Cooking.**	Pack in freezer bags.	Use from frozen to make crab apple jelly.	8 months.
Cranberry	As for **Bilberry.** Or cook to a sauce with sugar.	Open (flash) freeze, then pack in freezer bags. Pack sauce in small quantities in freezer bags or in rigid containers.	As for **Bilberry.** Or cook from frozen.	12 months.
Currant (Blackcurrant/ Redcurrant/ White Currant)	Remove fruit from stems. Wash and dry. Leave whole. Or crush with sugar. Or cook to a purée with a little water and sugar.	Open (flash) freeze, then pack in freezer bags. Or pack dry with or without sugar, or in heavy syrup in rigid containers. Pack crushed and puréed currants in rigid containers.	Thaw in wrappings 45 minutes at room temperature.	12 months.
Damson	Wash, cut in half and remove stones (pits). Or cook to a purée with sugar.	Pack dry or in medium syrup in rigid containers.	Thaw in containers 2 hours at room temperature.	12 months.
Date	Leave whole or cut in half and remove stones (pits).	Pack whole dates in freezer bags. Pack halved dates in light syrup in rigid containers.	Thaw in wrappings at room temperature.	12 months.
Elderberry	as for **Cranberry**			
Fig	Wipe if necessary (do not wash). Snip off stems.	Open (flash) freeze, then pack in freezer bags. Or pack dry without sugar, or in light syrup, in rigid containers.	Thaw in wrappings 1½ hours at room temperature.	12 months.
Gooseberry	Top, tail and wash. Leave whole. Or cook and purée with sugar.	Open (flash) freeze, then pack in freezer bags. Or pack dry in rigid containers. Pack purée in small quantities in freezer bags or rigid containers.	Thaw in wrappings 2½ hours at room temperature. Or use from frozen in pies, puddings, etc.	12 months.
Grape	Leave seedless grapes in bunches. Peel, halve and seed large grapes.	Open (flash) freeze bunches of grapes, then pack in freezer bags. Pack halved grapes in light syrup in rigid containers.	Thaw in wrappings 2 hours at room temperature.	12 months.
Grapefruit	see **Citrus Fruit**			

Fruit	Preparation	Packaging	Thawing	Storage Time
Greengage	Cut in half. Remove stones (pits). Do not skin. Or cook and purée with sugar.	Open (flash) freeze halved fruit, then pack in freezer bags. Or pack in light syrup in rigid containers. Pack purée in rigid containers.	Thaw in wrappings 2 hours at room temperature.	12 months.
Guava	Wash thoroughly. Remove stem and blossom. Peel, halve and scoop out seeds. Slice or cook, if wished, and purée in light syrup.	Pack halves and slices dry with sugar, or in light syrup, in rigid containers. Pack purée in small quantities in freezer bags or rigid containers.	Cook from frozen.	12 months.
Huckleberry	as for **Bilberry**			
Japonica (Quince)	Peel, core and slice, then cook in syrup until just tender.	Pack in cooled cooking syrup in rigid containers.	Thaw in containers at room temperature. Serve still frosted.	12 months.
Juneberry	Wash, drain and dry.	Open (flash) freeze, then pack in freezer bags. Or pack dry with sugar in rigid containers.	Thaw in wrappings 2½ hours at room temperature.	12 months.
Kiwi Fruit	see **Chinese Gooseberry**			
Kumquat	see **Citrus Fruit**			
Lemon	see **Citrus Fruit**			
Lime	see **Citrus Fruit**			
Loganberry	Wash, drain and dry. Or cook with sugar and purée.	Open (flash) freeze, then pack in freezer bags. Or pack dry in rigid containers. Pack purée in small quantities in freezer bags or rigid containers.	Thaw in wrappings 2½ hours at room temperature. Or use from frozen for poaching, in pies and puddings.	12 months.
Lychee	Shell off jackets.	Pack in heavy syrup in rigid containers.	Thaw in containers in refrigerator. Serve still frosted.	12 months.
Mandarin	see **Citrus Fruit**			
Mango	Peel. Cut out large stone (pit), then slice.	Pack in medium syrup, in rigid containers with 1 × 15 ml spoon/1 tablespoon lemon juice to every 1 litre/2 pints/5 cups.	Thaw in containers 1½ hours at room temperature.	12 months.
Melon	Cut in half. Remove seeds and peel. Cut into cubes or slices.	Pack immediately in light syrup, or pack dry with sugar, in rigid containers.	Thaw in containers in refrigerator. Serve still frosted with lemon juice to prevent discoloration.	12 months.
Mulberry	Wash, drain and dry.	Open (flash) freeze, then pack in freezer bags.	Thaw in bags 2 hours at room temperature. Or use from frozen for poaching, in pies and puddings.	12 months.
Nectarine	Wipe. Skin, if wished; steep in boiling water 20–30 seconds, plunge into cold water 2 minutes, then rub or peel off skins. Cut in half. Remove stones (pits). Slice, if wished.	Pack halves or slices immediately in heavy syrup in rigid containers.	Thaw in unopened containers 3 hours in refrigerator. Use immediately, sprinkled with lemon juice to prevent discoloration.	12 months.
Orange	see **Citrus Fruit**			
Papaya (Pawpaw)	Peel and cut in half. Remove seeds and slice flesh.	As for **Mango.**	As for **Mango.**	12 months.
Passion Fruit	as for **Mango** Freeze as soon as possible after harvesting			
Peach	as for **Apricot**			
Pear, Eating	Peel and core. Cut in halves or quarters. If fruit is soft, poach with lemon juice and flavourings in light syrup 1½ minutes. Drain and cool.	Pack halves and quarters immediately in medium syrup in rigid containers. Pack poached fruit in fresh light syrup in rigid containers.	Thaw in unopened containers 3 hours at room temperature.	12 months.
Pear, Cooking	Peel. Leave whole or cut in halves. Poach in a little water and sugar until just tender. Cool.	Pack in cooking syrup in rigid containers.	Thaw in unopened containers 3 hours at room temperature. Reheat after thawing, if wished.	12 months.
Persimmon	Choose very ripe fruit. Peel. Leave whole or cut into chunks or slices.	Wrap whole fruit individually in foil. Pack chunks and slices in heavy syrup in rigid containers with 2 × 5 ml spoons/2 teaspoons lemon juice to every 1 litre/2 pints/5 cups.	Thaw in wrappings 3 hours at room temperature. Use immediately.	Whole fruit: 2 months. Syrup pack: 12 months.

Fruit	Preparation	Packaging	Thawing	Storage Time
Pineapple	Peel and core. Cut into chunks or slices. Crush leftover pieces with sugar.	Pack dry without sugar in rigid containers, interleaving slices with foil. Or pack dry with sugar, or in light syrup, in rigid containers.	Thaw in containers 3 hours at room temperature.	12 months.
Plantain	Freeze as part of a cooked dish.			
Plum	Wash. Do not remove skin. Halve and remove stones (pits). Pat dry.	Pack in medium syrup in rigid containers.	Thaw in unopened containers 2 hours at room temperature. Use immediately.	12 months.
Pomegranate	Do not freeze whole. Cut in half, scoop out juicy pips (seeds), removing membrane from fruit.	Pack pips (seeds) in heavy syrup in rigid containers.	Thaw in containers 3 hours at room temperature.	12 months.
Pomelo	see **Citrus Fruit**			
Prickly Pear	Peel, halve and remove seeds.	As for **Mango**.	As for **Mango**.	12 months.
Prunelle	as for **Plum**			
Quince	see **Japonica**			
Raspberry	Do not wash unless absolutely necessary. Leave whole. Or purée raw, or cooked with sugar, then sieve.	Open (flash) freeze, then pack in freezer bags. Or pack dry in rigid containers. Pack purée in small quantities in freezer bags or rigid containers.	Thaw in wrappings 2 hours at room temperature. Serve still frosted.	12 months.
Rhubarb	Wash and dry. Cut into 2.5 cm/1 inch lengths. If wished, blanch 1 minute, drain and cool in iced water. Drain.	Pack dry with sugar in rigid containers. Pack blanched pieces in heavy syrup in rigid containers.	Thaw in containers 3 hours at room temperature. Use unblanched fruit from frozen for poaching, in pies and puddings.	12 months.
Rowanberry	Wash and remove stalks. Cook and purée with or without brown sugar.	Pack in small quantities in rigid containers.	Cook from frozen.	12 months.
Sloe	Wash and dry thoroughly.	Pack whole in freezer bags.	Cook from frozen.	12 months.
Strawberry	Do not wash unless absolutely necessary. Leave small firm berries whole. Mash large, soft berries with sugar.	Open (flash) freeze, then pack in freezer bags. Or pack dry in rigid containers. Pack mashed fruit in small quantities in rigid containers.	Thaw in wrappings 1½ hours at room temperature.	12 months.
Tangleberry	as for **Bilberry**			
Tangelo	see **Citrus Fruit**			
Tangerine	see **Citrus Fruit**			
Ugli Fruit	Grate or shred off outer peel. Remove pith and strands. Divide into segments. Remove skin from segments, if wished, and/or slice.	Open (flash) freeze whole segments, then pack in freezer bags. Pack skinned or sliced segments dry with sugar, or in light syrup, in rigid containers.	Thaw in wrappings 2 hours at room temperature.	12 months.

Fish

Fish	Preparation	Packaging	Thawing	Storage Time
Oily Fish **Brisling, Herring, Mackerel, Pilchard, Salmon, Sardine, Shad, Smelt(s), Sprat, Trout (River), Tuna, Whitebait, Whale**	Only freeze very fresh fish. (Mackerel should be frozen within 1 hour of catching.) Clean carefully. Leave very small fish whole, wash and pat dry. Remove head, tail, backbone and as many small bones as possible from herring, mackerel and trout, if wished, then open out; or leave whole, with or without head and tail. Leave salmon whole, gutted or ungutted, or cut into slices.	Pack very small fish in usable quantities in freezer bags. Pack larger fish together in bags, interleaving each one with cling film. Whole salmon can be 'Ice Glazed'.	Thaw very small fish in refrigerator for 1 hour or until they will separate, then cook as for fresh fish. Grill (broil), or fry larger fish and salmon slices. Thaw whole salmon for 6 hours in refrigerator.	3 months.
Shellfish **Abalone, Clam, Cockle, Crab, Crawfish, Crayfish, Lobster, Mussel, Ormer, Oyster, Periwinkle, Prawn, Scallop, Scampi, Shrimp, Snail, Whelk**	Only freeze freshly caught shellfish. Remove shells from clams, cockles, oysters, periwinkles, scallops. Shells can be left on or removed from mussels, prawns and shrimps. Snails are best frozen with garlic butter, ready to serve. Cook freshly caught crab and lobster in boiling water and prepare as usual.	Pack shelled shellfish in juices or cooking liquid in rigid containers. Pack fish with shells in rigid containers or freezer bags. Pack white and brown crab meat in separate rigid containers or repack in crab shell, cover with cling film and overwrap in foil or a freezer bag. Lobsters can be packed whole in freezer bags or foil after cooking, or shell can be split, meat taken out and packed in bags or containers.	Thaw in bags or containers in refrigerator for 2–3 hours (6 hours for lobsters and oysters), then serve raw or cook as for fresh shellfish. Or use frozen shellfish in cooked dishes and cook for minimum length of time.	Abalone, Clam, Cockle: 3 months; Crab, Lobster, Mussel, Ormer, Oyster, Periwinkle, Prawn, Scallop, Scampi, Shrimp, Snail, Whelk: 1 month.
Smoked and Cured Fish **Bloater, Buckling, Finnan Haddie, Haddock, Kipper, Mackerel, Salmon, Trout**	Only freeze freshly smoked fish in peak condition. Check that bought fish has not been previously frozen and thawed, because it must NOT be re-frozen.	Wrap individual fish or pieces of fish in cling film, then overwrap in a freezer bag.	Thaw in wrappings in refrigerator for 3 hours, then serve cold or cook as for fresh smoked fish.	3 months.
White Sea and Freshwater Fish*	Only freeze very fresh fish — within 12 hours of catching. Prepare as quickly as possible. Clean and remove scales, remove head and skin if wished. Cut large fish into thick steaks or fillets, leave small fish whole.	Pack several steaks or fillets together in one freezer bag, interleaving each piece of fish with cling film. Or wrap each fillet or steak individually before packing several together in a bag. Wrap whole fish in cling film or foil, then overwrap in a freezer bag.	Cook steaks and fillets from frozen as for fresh fish, allowing extra cooking time. Whole fish can be cooked from frozen, but if to be baked and stuffed thaw for 4 hours in refrigerator, then proceed as for fresh whole fish.	3 months.

*Barracouta, Barracuda, Bass, Bluefish, Bream, Brill, Butterfish, Carp, Catfish, Char, Chub, Cod, Conger Eel, Dab, Eel, Flathead, Flounder, Garfish, Grayling, Grilse, Gudgeon, Gurnet, Haddock, Hake, Halibut, Inkfish, John Dory, Lamprey, Ling, Mullet, Octopus, Perch, Pickerel, Pike, Plaice, Pollack, Pompano, Red Snapper, Roach, Rock Salmon, Salmon Trout, Scrod, Shark, Skate, Sole, Squid, Sturgeon, Swordfish, Turbot, Whitefish, Whiting

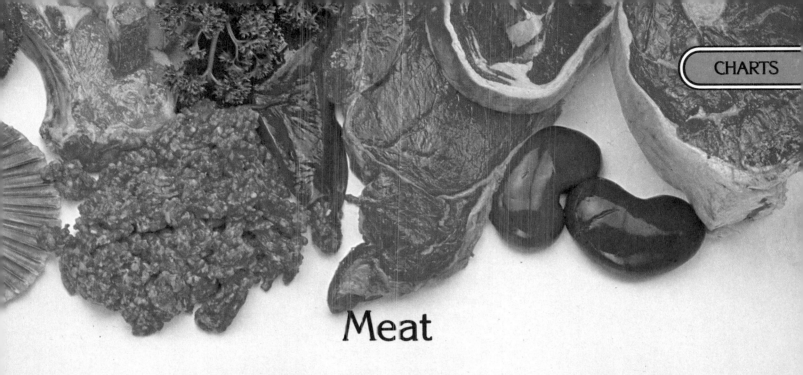

Meat

Meat	Preparation	Packaging	Thawing	Storage Time
Beef Large Joints (Cuts)	Cut or have butchered into usable sizes. Bone if possible to economize on freezer space. Boned joints may be rolled for freezing but not stuffed. Remove any surplus fat.	Wrap in aluminium foil or cling film and pad any protruding bones with foil or film. Overwrap in foil or a freezer bag.	Cook from frozen if on the bone and under 1.5 kg/3 lb. Roast in a moderate oven for 45 minutes to the ½ kg/1 lb for medium, 50 minutes for well done. Thaw large and boned and rolled joints overnight in the refrigerator, then roast as for fresh.	8 months.
Steaks	Cut into individual steaks approx. 2.5 cm/1 inch thick and trim away surplus fat and skin.	Wrap individually in cling film, then pack several steaks together in a freezer bag.	Grill (broil) or fry from frozen: brush with oil or butter and cook gently, allowing half as long again as when cooking thawed meat. Or thaw overnight in the refrigerator then cook as for fresh.	8 months.
Braising and Stewing Beef	Trim away surplus fat and cut into usable-sized portions or 2.5 cm/1 inch cubes.	Weigh straight into freezer bags in convenient-sized amounts — ½ kg/1 lb is a useful quantity. Expel as much air as possible from bag.	Thaw overnight in the refrigerator, then cook as for fresh meat. Or thaw cubed beef until pieces can be separated, then coat in flour and cook in the usual way, allowing extra cooking time.	8 months.
Minced (Ground) Beef	Only freeze lean meat.	As for braising and stewing above. Can also be shaped into patties and wrapped individually in foil.	Thaw overnight in the refrigerator or cook gently from partially frozen, stirring constantly to prevent sticking.	3 months.
Lamb Joints (Cuts)	As for **Beef** above.	As for **Beef** above.	Cook from frozen if on the bone and under 1.5 kg/3 lb: roast whole legs in a warm oven, half legs and shoulders in a moderate oven. Allow 45 minutes to the ½ kg/1 lb, or thaw as for **Beef**.	6 months.
Chops	As for **Beef**, *Steaks* above.	As for **Beef**, *Steaks* above.	As for **Beef**, *Steaks* above.	6 months.
Stewing Lamb	Cut into suitable-sized pieces for casseroles, etc., and leave 'on the bone' if necessary.	Wrap in foil if lamb contains many bones, then pack in freezer bags.	As for *Stewing Beef* above.	6 months.
Veal Joints (Cuts), Chops, Cubed and Minced (Ground)	As for **Beef** above.	As for **Beef** above.	As for **Beef** above. Roast joints (cuts) from frozen in a moderate oven for 50 minutes to the ½ kg/1 lb.	Joints and chops: 6 months; Cubed and minced (ground): 3 months.
Offal/Variety Meat/Fancy Meat	Clean and remove any fat. Wash under cold running water and pat dry.	Wrap individual items in cling film or foil, then pack several together in a freezer bag.	Thaw or cook from frozen, whichever is most convenient.	3 months.
Pork Joints (Cuts)	As for **Beef** above.	As for **Beef** above.	Cook from frozen if on the bone and under 1.5 kg/3 lb in weight: roast in a moderate oven for 60 minutes to the ½ kg/1 lb for thick joints (cuts), 55 minutes for thin. Meat thermometer should read 87°C/190°F. Or thaw as for **Beef**.	6 months.

Meat	Preparation	Packaging	Thawing	Storage Time
Chops, Fillet End of Leg, Streaky Slices, etc.	As for **Beef**, *Steaks* above.	As for **Beef**, *Steaks* above.	As for **Beef**, *Steaks* above. Streaky slices should be slow roasted.	6 months.
Cubed and Minced (Ground) Pork	As for **Beef** above.	As for **Beef** above.	As for **Beef** above. Use in casseroles, pies, stuffings, etc.	3 months.
Sausages/ Sausagemeat	Only freeze very fresh sausages or sausagemeat that are not too highly seasoned.	Pack in usable quantities in freezer bags or rigid containers.	Partially thaw until sausages can be separated, then fry or grill (broil) gently. Or thaw overnight in refrigerator and cook as for fresh sausages. Thaw sausagemeat overnight before using in recipes.	1 month.
Bacon and Cured Pork	Freeze only very fresh, mildly cured bacon, with as little fat as possible. Vacuum-packed bacon is ideal for freezing.	Wrap joints (cuts) tightly in foil, then overwrap in freezer bag. Divide rashers (strips) into convenient-sized amounts, wrap in foil and overwrap in freezer bag. Pack chops or steaks in bags, interleaving each one with cling film. Vacuum-packed bacon can go straight in the freezer.	Thaw small joints (cuts) 24 hours in refrigerator or 8–12 hours at room temperature. Thaw small packs of rashers (strips) 6 hours in refrigerator, 2–3 hours at room temperature. Cook as soon as possible after thawing.	Smoked joints (cuts) and rashers (strips): 2 months. Unsmoked joints (cuts): 5 weeks. Unsmoked rashers (strips), chops and steaks: 2–3 weeks. Vacuum-packed bacon: 4–5 months.

Poultry and Game

Poultry and Game	Preparation	Packaging	Thawing	Storage Time
Poultry and Game Birds **Capon, Chicken, Duck, Duckling, Goose, Gosling, Guinea Fowl, Poussin, Turkey, Dove, Grouse, Hazel Hen, Ortolan, Partridge, Pheasant, Pigeon, Plover, Ptarmigan, Quail, Snipe, Squab, Wigeon, Wild Duck, Woodcock**	Pluck, hang and truss if necessary, then wash thoroughly inside and out. Pat dry with absorbent kitchen paper. Leave whole, halve (split) or joint (cut up).	Whole birds: wrap several thicknesses of foil or cling film around extremities of bird, then wrap whole bird in large piece of foil and overwrap in freezer bag. Check wrappings in freezer in case of puncturing by legs, wing tips, etc. Halved (split), jointed (cut up): wrap individual pieces in foil or cling film then pack several pieces together in freezer bag.	Whole birds MUST be thawed completely before cooking. Thaw in wrappings in refrigerator: 24–36 hours for poultry under 3.5 kg/8 lb; 36–48 hours for 3.5–6.25 kg/8–14 lb; 48–60 hours for 6.25–9 kg/14–20 lb; 72 hours for over 9 kg/over 20 lb; etc. Thaw halved (split), jointed (cut up) for 12–15 hours in refrigerator, although these can be cooked from frozen or partially frozen if time is not available. Always cook game immediately after thawing to prevent maturing process recommencing.	Chicken: 10–12 months; Duck: 4–6 months; Goose: 4–6 months; Turkey: 10–12 months. Store game birds for 6 months, or up to 12 months if a stronger flavour is liked (after 6 months in freezer, the 'ageing' process begins as it would if it were being hung, although at a slower rate).
Giblets	Split and clean gizzard and discard sac. Separate liver from rest of giblets. Leave raw or cook in usual way and leave to cool.	Pack raw or cold cooked giblets in freezer bag. Pack liver in separate bag.	Leave in wrappings in refrigerator for approximately 12 hours. Use as for fresh giblets.	2–3 months.
Game Animals **Bear, Beaver, Boar, Hare, Kid, Leveret, Moose, Muskrat, Rabbit, Raccoon, Reindeer, Squirrel, Venison (Deer), Woodchuck**	Freeze only young animals. Skin if necessary and remove all fat. (Remove glands in back and forelegs of beaver, squirrel and woodchuck). Hang if necessary, then have large animals butchered into usable-sized joints (cuts), steaks and stewing meat. Leave small animals whole, or joint (cut up).	Pack joints (cuts), steaks and stewing meat of large animals in freezer bags as for **Beef**. Pack small animals (whole and jointed/cut up) as for **Poultry and Game Birds** above.	Thaw cuts of large animals as for corresponding **Beef** cuts. If possible, thaw in a marinade or marinate before cooking to tenderize. Thaw small animals as for **Poultry** above.	Bear, Beaver, Boar, Hare, Kid, Leveret, Muskrat, Rabbit: 8 months; Raccoon, Squirrel, Woodchuck: 6 months; Moose, Reindeer, Venison (Deer): 12 months.

Dairy Produce

Dairy Produce and Eggs	Preparation	Packaging	Thawing	Storage Time
Butter	Only freeze very fresh butter, as soon as possible after purchase. Freeze in 225 g/½ lb packs.	Leave in original wrappings and overwrap in foil or a freezer bag.	Remove overwrapping. Thaw 4 hours in refrigerator, 2 hours at room temperature. Use quickly.	Salted: 3 months. Unsalted: 6 months.
Buttermilk	Freeze only very fresh buttermilk in usable quantities.	Leave in waxed cartons or decant into small rigid containers.	Thaw in cartons or containers 8 hours in refrigerator. Whisk before use.	6 weeks.
Cheese				
Blue	Freezing only advisable if for cooking.			
Cottage	Does not freeze successfully, unless as part of a cooked dish.			3–6 months, according to condition and freshness at time of freezing.
Cream	Only freeze cream cheese that contains at least 40% butterfat. Or freeze as part of a dip, etc.	Pack in cartons or rigid containers.	Thaw in cartons or containers overnight in refrigerator. Whisk before use.	
Curd	as for *Cottage Cheese*			
Grated	Grate in the usual way.	Pack in freezer bags.	Use from frozen: grated cheese remains free flowing in bag.	
Hard (Cheddar, Cheshire, Edam, etc.)	Cut into 225 g/½ lb blocks.	Wrap in foil or cling film, then overwrap in a freezer bag.	Thaw in wrappings overnight in refrigerator. Use quickly.	
Soft (Brie, Camembert, Mozzarella, etc.)	Cut into usable-sized portions. Freeze only mature cheeses.	As for hard cheese.	Thaw 24 hours in refrigerator, then 24 hours at room temperature.	
Cream	Only freeze very fresh cream that contains at least 40% butterfat. Chill, then whip lightly. Add a little sugar if to be used for sweet dishes, as this will help its keeping qualities.	Pack in usable quantities in cartons or rigid containers, leaving headspace.	Thaw in cartons or containers 8 hours in refrigerator. Whip again before use.	3 months.
Egg(s)	Only freeze very fresh eggs. Do not freeze in shells. Do not freeze hard-boiled eggs.			
Whole Eggs	Whisk lightly. Add 1 × 2.5 ml spoon/½ teaspoon salt to every 3 eggs for savoury dishes; 1 × 5 ml spoon/1 teaspoon sugar for sweet.	Pour into waxed cartons or rigid containers.	Transfer to bowl and thaw at least 1 hour at room temperature. Use as soon as possible.	6 months.
Egg Yolks	Add 1 × 1.25 ml spoon/¼ teaspoon salt to every 3 yolks for savoury dishes; 1 × 2.5 ml spoon/½ teaspoon sugar for sweet.	As for *Whole Eggs*.	As for *Whole Eggs*.	6 months.
	Or freeze egg yolks individually in ice-cube trays or egg cartons.	Open (flash) freeze until solid, then pack in freezer bags.	As for *Whole Eggs*.	6 months.
Egg Whites	Freeze in usable quantities or individually as for egg yolks.	Pour into small rigid containers, or open (flash) freeze cubes until solid, then pack in freezer bags.	As for *Whole Eggs*.	6 months.

Dairy Produce and Eggs	Preparation	Packaging	Thawing	Storage time
Icecream	Freeze homemade and commercially prepared icecream.	Pack homemade icecream in usable quantities in rigid containers. Decant catering-size commercial packs into usable-sized cartons or containers.	Do not allow to thaw. Icecream should not be re-frozen once thawed. Homemade icecream should be 'softened' for approx. 1 hour in refrigerator before eating. It is best not to return uneaten home-made icecream to the freezer. Return cartons of commercial icecream to freezer immediately after use, do not allow to soften.	Homemade icecream: 3 months. Commercially frozen icecream: 4–6 weeks.
Milk	Only freeze homogenized milk. Do not freeze in bottles.	Pour usable quantities into rigid containers, leaving headspace.	Thaw in containers overnight in refrigerator. If milk separates on thawing, bring to a boil in a saucepan, then leave to cool. Use quickly after thawing.	1 month.
Yogurt	Do not freeze homemade yogurt. Commercially prepared fruit yogurts and some plain can be frozen successfully.	Freeze commercially prepared yogurts in original cartons.	Thaw slowly in refrigerator. Whisk briskly if yogurt has separated on thawing.	6 weeks (fruit yogurts only), 2 weeks (plain).

Baked Goods

Baked Goods	Preparation	Packaging	Thawing	Storage Time
Biscuits (Cookies) Baked	Freeze baked biscuits (cookies) with a high fat content for best results.	Pack cooled biscuits (cookies) in rigid containers, separating each with foil or freezer tissue.	Thaw in containers 30 minutes at room temperature. If necessary, refresh 5 minutes in fairly hot oven.	6 months.
Unbaked Dough	Roll into cylindrical shape.	Wrap in foil.	Soften 30–45 minutes in refrigerator, then slice off and bake according to recipe used.	
	Or pipe or shape onto baking sheets.	Open (flash) freeze until solid, then pack in rigid containers.	Bake from frozen, allowing extra baking time.	
Bread Dough	Make dough and knead. Do not allow to rise.	Put in a large greased freezer bag, seal tightly, label and freeze.	Remove from freezer. Re-seal bag at top and leave to rise: 5 hours at room temperature or overnight in refrigerator. Remove from bag and proceed with original recipe.	Unrisen plain dough: 1 month. Unrisen enriched dough: 3 months.
	Or make the dough, put in a large greased freezer bag and seal at top to allow room for rising. When risen, remove from bag, knock out air and knead.	Pack in greased freezer bag, seal tightly, label and freeze.	Thaw and proceed with original recipe as above.	Risen dough: 2 weeks.
Loaves	All homemade and commercially baked loaves should be as fresh as possible and completely cold before freezing.	Wrap in freezer bags or foil.	Thaw in bags at least 3 hours at room temperature. Or reheat from frozen in foil wrapping: approx. 45 minutes in fairly hot oven.	White and brown plain bread: 6 months. Enriched: 3 months. French/Italian: 1 week. Viennas: 3 days.
Partially Baked Loaves	Freeze homemade or bought.	Wrap in freezer bags.	Unwrap and bake from frozen: approx. 30 minutes in hot oven.	Homemade partially baked: 4 months. Commercial partially baked: 2 months.
Sliced Loaves	Only freeze very fresh.	Leave in original wrappings and overwrap in a freezer bag.	Toast individual slices from frozen. Or thaw whole loaves 3 hours at room temperature.	6 months.
Rolls, Baps, etc.	Freeze homemade or bought.	Pack in a single layer in freezer bags or rigid containers.	Thaw approx. 1½ hours at room temperature. Or unwrap and bake from frozen: approx. 15 minutes in fairly hot oven.	As for *Loaves* above.
Partially Baked Rolls	Freeze homemade or bought.	Pack in a single layer in freezer bags or rigid containers.	Unwrap and bake from frozen: approx. 15 minutes in a hot oven.	As for *Partially Baked Loaves* above.

Baked Goods	Preparation	Packaging	Thawing	Storage Time
Cakes Large and Small	Make cakes in usual way, using freshest possible ingredients. Avoid synthetic essences, jam fillings, and glacé, royal, boiled and fondant icings. Large cakes can be cut into slices before freezing, so that individual slices can be taken out of freezer as required.	Wrap undecorated large cakes in foil, then overwrap in a freezer bag. Open (flash) freeze decorated and iced cakes until solid, then wrap in foil or a freezer bag. Open (flash) freeze small cakes until solid, then pack in rigid containers, separating each cake with greaseproof (waxed) paper. Pack slices of cake in a freezer bag, interleaving each slice with foil or greaseproof (waxed) paper.	Thaw all cakes at room temperature, except those containing fresh cream, which should be thawed overnight in refrigerator. Thaw large cakes in wrappings up to 4 hours. Unwrap decorated and iced cakes before thawing, or the wrapping will spoil the decoration. Unwrap small cakes and slices of cake and thaw approx. 1 hour.	Plain, fruit, sandwich-type, sponges made with fat: 4 months. Fat-free sponges: 10 months. Decorated and iced cakes and gingerbread: 2 months.
Pastry and Pastry-based Dishes Unbaked Dough	Make in the usual way. Divide into 225 g/½ lb blocks.	Wrap individual blocks in foil, then pack several together in a freezer bag.	Thaw in wrappings 2–3 hours at room temperature or overnight in refrigerator. Use as for fresh pastry.	3 months.
Unbaked 'Shells' and Pie 'Lids'	Make in usual way, roll out and use to line pie or flan dishes, and to fit dishes as 'lids'.	Open (flash) freeze shell in the dish, then remove from dish and wrap in foil or a freezer bag.	Return frozen 'shell' to original dish and bake from frozen with fresh or frozen filling.	3 months.
		Pack 'lids' in freezer bags interleaving each lid with foil.	Thaw 'lids' at room temperature until manageable, then use as for fresh 'lids'.	3 months.
Unbaked Double Crust Pies and Filled Tarts, etc.	Freeze unbaked pies with uncooked fillings for best results. Make in usual way, in foil containers if possible.	Open (flash) freeze until solid, then remove from containers and wrap in foil or a freezer bag.	Unwrap and return to original container. Bake from frozen, allowing extra cooking time.	3 months.
Unbaked Flaky and Puff Pastry	Prepare up to last rolling. Roll dough into oblong shape.	Wrap in foil and overwrap in a freezer bag.	Thaw in wrappings overnight in refrigerator, or 3–4 hours at room temperature.	3 months.
Unbaked Vol-au-vents	Make in usual way. Shape on freezer trays.	Open (flash) freeze until solid, then pack in freezer bags.	Unwrap and bake from frozen, with or without filling.	3 months.
Baked Pastry	Not as successful as unbaked pastry dough. Make and bake in usual way, using foil dishes if possible. Brush inside pastry base with egg white if sweet or fruit filling to be used, with melted butter if savoury filling. Cool completely before freezing.	Wrap pastry and dish in foil or freezer bags Or open (flash) freeze until solid, remove pastry or pie from dish, then wrap in foil or bags.	Thaw in wrappings approx. 3 hours at room temperature. Handle with care: frozen baked pastry is very fragile. Refresh in oven if to be served hot.	6 months (3 months if containing meat fillings).

Index

Acknowledgments

Photography by:

ARS 210; Rex Bamber 132, 190, 206, 207, 214, 222; Michael Crockett 126 below, 31 above, 61, 176, 188; Fruit Producers Council 194; Melvin Grey 4–5, 11, 12 left and right, 13, 21, 22, 24, 25, 28–29, 31 below, 32–33, 34 left and below, 35, 36, 37, 39 and 6, 41 above right, 42 above, 43, 45, 46, 47, 49, 51, 52, 53 right and left, 54, 55, 59, 60, 63, 66 above left and above right, 69, 72–73, 75, 76 left and right, 77 left and right, 82, 83, 84 above and below, 85, 86, 87 above and below, 88, 88–89, 89, 90–91, 92, 93 above, 95, 105 above and centre, 106, 108–109, 110, 111, 112, 113, 114 above and below, 115 below left and below right, 116, 118 above, 121, 122, 122–123, 123, 135, 136–137, 138–139, 140, 141, 142–143, 153, 156–157, 160–161, 162–163, 165, 168–169, 171 above and below, 173, 174–175, 182 below left, 187, 191, 192–193, 195, 200–201, 202, 209 and 6, 211, 212–213, 216–217, 218–219, 220 below, 223, 232, 233, 234, 235, 236; Paul Kemp 1, 2–3, 8–9, 10, 15, 16, 17, and 6, 20, 23, 26, 27 above and below, 29, 30, 38, 41 left, 42 below, 44–45, 48 and 6, 50 left and below right, 64–65, 66 below, 67, 68, 71 right, 72, 73, 74, 79 and 6, 80, 81 above and below, 81 above and below, 86–87, 91, 93 below, 94 above and below, 97 above and below, 98–99, 101, 103, 104, 105 below, 107, 117 above and below, 118 below left and below right, 119, 124–125, 127, 128–129, 130–131 and 6, 132–133, 144, 148–149, 154–155, 158–159, 166, 172, 177, 178–179, 184–185, 189, 196–197, 199, 203, 204–205, 214–215, 221, 224 inset, 224–225, 226–227, 237, 238, 239, 242, 243, 244, 245, 246, 247, 248, 249, 250, 251; Lawrey's Food Inc. 146; Michael Leale 151; National Magazine Co. 133, 142; New Idea Magazine 147; Norman Nicholls 186, 198; PAF International 126, 180, 183, 215; Roger Phillips 134, 170; RHM Foods Ltd. 182 above right; Syndication International Ltd. 164, 167, 181.

The publishers would like to thank Alcan Foil for the photographs on 232 (foil, and freezer trays and pie plates), 233 (freezer wrap), 234 (interleaving), 235 (freezer bags), and the following companies for the loan of accessories for the photography in this book:
Alcan Foil; Bejam Group Ltd; Craftsmen Potters' Association; Cross Tableware; Cucina; David Mellor; Divertimenti; Elizabeth David; Gered, Regent Street; Harrods; Heal's; Jacksons of Piccadilly and Sloane Street; Jaeggi and Sons Ltd; Lakeland Plastics; Merchant Chandler; Paxton and Whitfield Ltd; Royal Doulton Tableware Ltd; Tupperware.

Jacket photography by Paul Kemp.

Notes

All recipes serve 4 people unless otherwise stated.

Plain/all purpose flour and granulated sugar are used unless otherwise stated.

All spoon measures are level.

Ovens should be preheated to the specified temperature.

Follow only one column of measures. They are not interchangeable.

Australian Users

All measures in this book are given in metric, imperial and American. Australian users should remember that as their tablespoon has been converted to 20 ml, and is therefore larger than the tablespoon used in all columns in this book, they should use 3×5 ml spoons where instructed to use 1×15 ml spoon or 1 tablespoon. If Australian users do not follow the metric column they should also remember that the imperial and Australian pint is 20 fl oz, whereas the American pint is 16 fl oz.

PDO 82-0459